"Deep knowledge about terrorists combined with common sense about nuclear weapons equals a book that is sobering and educational. Help yourself and learn!"
    —George P. Shultz, former secretary of state, and currently
        distinguished fellow, Hoover Institution, Stanford University

"Brian Michael Jenkins is one of the world's most renowned experts on terrorism. With an instructive, provocative book that reads like a novel, Jenkins combines cool analysis with common sense to describe the threat of nuclear terrorism. He also shows that we must guard against nuclear terror—corrosive fear that prevents sensible action and weakens our democracy. Jenkins makes a powerful case that we must take strong steps against both to make each less likely."
    —Sam Nunn, United States senator, co-chairman and CEO
        of the Nuclear Threat Initiative

"A clear-eyed and elegantly written analysis that builds to a gripping finale that thrusts the reader into the Oval Office at a moment when no one would envy the president. Jenkins's book is at once informative, entertaining, disturbing, yet reassuring."
    —Lt. Gen. Brent Scowcroft, USAF (Ret.), former national security adviser
        to former presidents George H. W. Bush and Gerald Ford

"In *Will Terrorists Go Nuclear?* Brian Michael Jenkins brings a lifetime of experience and expertise to today's most pressing national security question. With skill and clarity he separates fact from fiction, laying the groundwork for a thoughtful approach to confronting the nexus of nuclear weapons and terrorism. This is an important book on an urgent threat confronting the American people."
    —Lee H. Hamilton, vice chairman of the 9/11 Commission,
        and president and director of the
        Woodrow Wilson International Center for Scholars

"There are things that rightly terrify us in this world, and Jenkins names them carefully. But fear is also used to control us. Beyond manipulation, this saps our strength and our spirit, leaving us immobilized, not fully human at all. Learning to distinguish the two is the gift of this book."
    —Carolyn Tanner Irish, Episcopal bishop of Utah

"Finally, a rational intellectual tonic for America's hysterical nuclear terror mania. To be taken before considering any new, additional policies."
  —Henry Sokolski, executive director of the
    Nonproliferation Policy Education Center, appointed by Congress
    to the Commission on Preventing WMD Proliferation and Terrorism

"This is the book to read if you want an expert and sensible guide to lead you past the mind-numbing hype of nuclear terror—purveyed by self-serving officialdom and sensationalist media—to the facts of nuclear terrorism, which are grim enough."
  —Dr. Victor Gilinsky, former commissioner,
    Nuclear Regulatory Commission, and nuclear physicist

"Anyone interested in a careful evaluation of the dangers of nuclear terrorism should read this timely and well-written book by one of America's leading experts. Brian Jenkins not only provides careful assessments of the risks posed by al Qaeda and others but warns that a good deal of the damage from nuclear terror comes from our own inappropriate reactions."
  —Joseph S. Nye, University Distinguished Service Professor at
    Harvard University and author of *The Powers to Lead*

"Jenkins provides an invaluable corrective to a topic that has generated much heat but little light. His expertise, attention to detail, and common sense shine through on every page."
  —Daniel Byman, director, Center for Peace and Security Studies,
    Georgetown University, and senior fellow,
    Saban Center for Middle East Policy at the Brookings Institution

"Superb! Insight and thoughtful analysis are too frequently early casualties in the battle against terrorism. Brian Jenkins provides a unique, penetrating analysis of our psychological vulnerability to the threat of nuclear terrorism—an analysis we cannot afford to ignore."
  —James N. Breckenridge, PhD, professor of psychology, PGSP/Stanford,
    associate director, Center for Interdisciplinary Policy,
    Education and Research on Terrorism

"The dean of America's scholars on terrorism, Brian Jenkins shows how vulnerable we Americans are to nuclear terror. He begins with the main ingredients of terror—the nuclear weapons and the terrorists themselves. But then we see that the terror enterprise extends well beyond them to our society and government—the media, political leaders, literature, 'experts' on terrorism, and, yes, even think tanks. The entire enterprise magnifies and even goes beyond the facts to scare us into either immobility or rash action. The book ends with the ultimate challenge: how can we put our fears in perspective after the worst imaginable has happened—a nuclear explosion on our own soil."
　　—James A. Thomson, president and CEO of the RAND Corporation

"Perhaps only Brian Jenkins could have written this critically important book. He has the credibility borne of more than three decades not just of studying terrorism but being on the front lines of the fight. By focusing on the terrorists, not on our own vulnerabilities, he hardly dismisses the threat of nuclear terrorism but does provide a welcome antidote to the overheated commentary of the new experts pontificating on the subject. In the end he returns to the central theme of his previous book, *Unconquerable Nation*: nuclear terrorism may occur, but until then we need not inflict nuclear terror on ourselves. The choice is ours."
　　—Gregory F. Treverton, director, Center for Global Risk and Security,
　　　RAND Corporation; former vice chair of the
　　　National Intelligence Council, CIA; and author of the forthcoming
　　　Intelligence for an Era of Terror

"Jenkins's ambitious goal seems to be not to downplay the nuclear threat posed by terrorists but to get Americans to address it logically and dispassionately; his thoroughly documented and carefully reasoned study is an important step in that direction."
　　—*Publishers Weekly*

"In this important new book, Brian Jenkins makes a critical distinction between 'nuclear terrorism'—the possibility that terrorists may get their hands on and use nuclear weapons, and 'nuclear terror'—paralyzing anxiety and apprehension. Ensuring our national security, and the peace of the world, requires sensible measures to deal with both. A provocative and essential read."
　　—Bob Graham, United States senator, chairman of the
　　　Commission on Prevention of WMD Proliferation and Terrorism

WILL TERRORISTS

GO NUCLEAR?

WILL TERRORISTS
GO NUCLEAR?

BRIAN MICHAEL
JENKINS

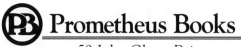 **Prometheus Books**

59 John Glenn Drive
Amherst, New York 14228–2119

Published 2008 by Prometheus Books

Inquiries should be addressed to
Prometheus Books
59 John Glenn Drive
Amherst, New York 14228–2119
VOICE: 716–691–0133, ext. 210
FAX: 716–691–0137
WWW.PROMETHEUSBOOKS.COM

12 11 10 09 08   5 4 3 2 1

Library of Congress Cataloging-in-Publication Data

Jenkins, Brian Michael.
 Will terrorists go nuclear? / Brian Michael Jenkins.
  p. cm.
 Includes bibliographical references and index.
 ISBN 978–1–59102–656–3 (hardcover : alk. paper)
 1. Nuclear terrorism—United States. 2. Terrorism—Prevention. I. Title.

HV6433.86.J46 2008
363.325'5—dc22

                                                                      2008020485

Printed in the United States of America on acid-free paper

CONTENTS

CONTENTS

PREFACE

In 1982 I wrote in *International Security*, "Sometime in the 1980s an organization that is not a national government may acquire a few nuclear weapons. If not in the 1980s then in the 1990s."

It's now 2008 and it hasn't happened. Why not? And if not the 1990s, the 2000s? Or the 2010s? Brian Michael Jenkins has been the most persistent student of this issue that I know, and his new book, like his earlier one, *Unconquerable Nation,* is not only an authoritative analysis of likelihoods but, beyond likelihoods, the terrorist effects of the *possibility*, not just the likelihood.

As Jenkins shows in this exhaustive review, there is the phenomenon of self-terrorism, of stimulated terror. "Government officials concerned about national security, analysts worried about terrorists acquiring nuclear weapons, journalists hunting for stories, networks look for ratings, talking heads seek attention, writers search for plot lines, attention-deficit audiences look for jolts, believers seeking confirmation of imminent doom–all collaborate in creating a fission of fear." "Collaborate" is a powerful diagnosis. He says, "Our enemies are not stupid, and they realize that a campaign of terror might even yield what an act of terrorism could not."

Jenkins asks a question I have often asked myself: "Terrorists have always had the capacity to kill more people than they have killed, without resorting to exotic weapons, but for some reason they have chosen not to. Why?" I like his reasoning.

Much of the terror is propagated via electronic media. "On 9/11 there was only a handful of jihadist sites on the Internet. Today, there are thousands–a true network where there is inspiration from the center but deliberately no central control. . . . The purpose of the media jihad is both to recruit new members–indoctrinating them and instructing them in the means of violence–and to keep the enemy in a perpetual state of alarm."

Actually, this book is more about *terror* than about *terrorists.* In retrospect Jenkins says, "The primary attraction of going nuclear for terrorists, I thought, was not that it would enable them to cause mass casualties, but rather that almost any action in the nuclear domain would automatically generate fear in the minds of the public. It would create nuclear terror."

One of Jenkins's most powerful arguments is that our national government, wittingly or not, contributes to the promotion of terror. "While President Franklin D. Roosevelt told the American people that 'the only thing we have to fear is fear itself,' President George W. Bush and much of his administration warned incessantly that we must be afraid, very afraid."

There have been a few excellent books on how nonstate organizations might acquire nuclear weapons or the materials to make them, on the requirements of expertise and secrecy, on the difficulties of dealing in black markets without exposure, and on how a weapon might be delivered to a target or be proven to exist. Jenkins does the finest job I have seen.

The book has a fascinating climax: you are the president, a nuclear explosion has just occurred in Manhattan. You and your advisers explore all the possibilities you can think of–that Brian Jenkins can think of. This is the one part of the book that I wish to be available to the president and his cabinet and advisers if such an event ever occurs—preferably before it occurs. As on 9/11, there will be decisions to be made in a hurry, and no time to explore all the angles and possibilities. I doubt the president, whoever he or she is, will have devoted study in advance; I hope a copy of Jenkins's book will be in the office of every senior official with a bookmark at the appropriate chapter.

The final chapter, following the president's (the reader's) detailed exploration of options in a nuclear emergency, is a thoughtful reflection on the whole subject, and I find it on the whole not just reasonable but somewhat hopeful. Fear itself, in the words of Franklin Roosevelt, may not be the only thing we have to fear, but unless tempered with analytical vision, it can be a burden and a distortion and an obstacle to urgently needed clarity and understanding.

–Thomas C. Schelling, Nobel laureate

FOREWORD

At the height of the cold war during the mid-1970s, when the US national security community had its collective eye on the Soviet Union and its perceived threats, Brian Michael Jenkins was thinking and writing about terrorism. Since that time, a quarter century before September 11, 2001, his voice and pen have been consistently prophetic.

While US policy makers and planners were preoccupied with the cold war, Jenkins was peering into the twenty-first century and into the mind of a kind of warrior not seen since the eleventh century.

Yet, in contrast to more latter-day terrorism "experts," of whom there are now battalions, Mr. Jenkins has remained both more advanced and more realistic, while also being more thoughtful, knowledgeable, and, as his latest book reveals, even more literate. His specialty throughout has been, if you will, the psychology of terrorists and terrorism. He was an early proponent of getting inside the mind of both the perpetrator of terrorist action and its victims, the terrorized.

I know of no one else working the terrorism precincts who

could write of our hopeless but obsessive amateur plotting to get one step ahead of the wily killers that "there is a tiny armchair terrorist in all of us." And there is most certainly no other explorer of these murky depths who could characterize this trait as "a Dionysian talent."

It is a great credit to the author that he manages to be both frightening and reassuring, that is to say, realistic, all at once. In the process he has created the definitive handbook, everything that needs to be known about the age of nuclear terrorism and its principal by-product, nuclear terror.

In 1999, the US Commission on National Security for the 21st Century concluded that "America will be attacked by terrorists using weapons of mass destruction, and Americans will die on American soil, possibly in large numbers." At least one member of that commission, myself, was moved to that conclusion in part by familiarity with the writings of Mr. Jenkins.

The title of this book is taken from a seminal paper Jenkins wrote in 1975 in which, as he writes, he "chose to explore [the terrorists'] possible motives" for pursuing the highly dramatic, and destructive, nuclear form of terrorism. He believes that death on whatever scale is not the principle objective. "Terrorism," he writes, "is a calculated campaign of violence intended to create an atmosphere of fear and alarm, which in turn causes people to exaggerate the strength of the terrorists. Terrorists purposefully target innocent civilians, not just because they are easy targets, but in order to draw attention to the terrorists' existence, demonstrate capability, inspire constituencies, create a sense of insecurity, drain resolve, scare off investment, polarize opinion, and provoke overreaction that will alienate the public."

Beginning with a "shiver of terror," Mr. Jenkins then constructs a journey through the terrorist briar patch that is part history, part physics, part political science, part mass psychology, part cultural analysis, part strategy, and all highly informative.

This journey begins at the dawn of the nuclear age, when even its explorers feared the unintended consequences of the magic of their physics. From virtually the first day when formulas for fission were sketched on a laboratory blackboard, physicists were concerned with "What if . . . ?" Images of mass destruction, vividly come to life in Hiroshima and Nagasaki, were thereafter permanently implanted in the collective cerebellum.

The motives of especially the jihadist brand of terrorism are examined. Do they want us scared out of our wits, out of the world of Islam, or simply dead? Mr. Jenkins then enters the mordant world of black market arms and, inter alia, inspects the mysterious weapon called "red mercury," which may, or may not, exist and which may, or may not, constitute the ultimate neutron bomb, the so-called capitalist bomb that kills people but leaves property intact. Along the way we are led on a search for the equally elusive "suitcase nukes."

Mr. Jenkins examines the American psyche and seeks to understand whether we are especially vulnerable to the terror produced by the very idea of terrorism. In this regard, he is particularly effective at distinguishing between the two. He further shows how al Qaeda has become the first terrorist nuclear power even if it does not (or does it?) possess nuclear materials or weapons. In this, he finds that the media's "addiction to sensationalism" plays a very large role.

Knowing virtually everything that needs to be known about nuclear terrorism at this point, the reader is then placed in the president's chair in the Oval Office and faced with an incident of nuclear terrorism. Faced with confusing advice, muddled information, mixed messages, and totally unpalatable choices, you, the reader, must decide what to do. But first, as the author notes, "You will have to think."

Were you, the reader, ever to find yourself in that situation, you would be far in advance of the game having read this book.

Indeed, if you are asked by the next president what he or she should know about terrorism generally and nuclear terrorism particularly, you should introduce the president to the master of the psychology of terrorism, Brian Michael Jenkins, but then say, "First read this book."

−Gary Hart, United States senator (Ret.);
co-chair, United States Commission on
National Security for the 21st Century

ACKNOWLEDGMENTS

While authors must remain solely responsible for errors and omissions, a book, as every author knows, is a group effort. Many people assisted in this project.

I wish to first thank Senator Gary Hart, former governor James Gilmore, and Nobel laureate Thomas Schelling for their encouraging comments and their thoughtful introductory essays, which put my arguments in the context of today's national security challenges. I also wish to thank Victor Gilinsky and Henry Sokolski, both of whom have extensive government experience in dealing with nuclear proliferation, for their thorough reviews, numerous communications, and suggested corrections. Among my many colleagues at RAND, I want to especially thank Paul Davis, with whom I co-authored *Deterrence and Influence in Counterterrorism: A Component in the War on al Qaeda*, for his helpful comments in this work.

I am indebted to Gail Bass-Golod, Peter DeLeon, William Fowler, Bruce Hoffman, Joseph Krofcheck, Geraldine Petty, Robert Reinstedt, David Ronfeldt, Ralph Strauch, Karen Treverton, and Peter Tripodes, members of that splendid, eccentric company of RAND analysts whose decades of work on nuclear terrorism I describe in this volume. All merit credit for their contribution to understanding the motives and attributes of potential nuclear terrorists.

Konrad Kellen passed away while the manuscript was still being written, but I greatly benefited from three decades of challenging discussions and helpful guidance from him. He was a mentor, a tough critic, and a dear friend.

I am grateful for the assistance of RAND's entire team of reference librarians, with a very special thanks to Barbara Neff, Ellen Kimmel, Kristin Lang, and Roberta Shanman. Arthur Alexander, my lifelong running buddy and math tutor, assisted me in interpreting the survey results.

I would like to thank Linda Regan, my editor at Prometheus Books, for her encouragement and support of the project, and for her patient but persistent reminders of chapters yet to be written and deadlines to be met.

For their always brilliant assistance in organizing and editing the text, helping me to distill and communicate my ideas, and demanding clear and precise prose, I am deeply indebted to John Godges and Janet DeLand. More than editors, they became comrades in thought. David Egner lent his newsman's instincts and considerable editorial skills in an additional read. And my thanks also to Julia DeGraf for hunting down the elusive errors and renegade typos that multiple readings missed, although I am certain that among the hundred thousand words and near four hundred footnotes in this book, there still lurks at least one that got away. Those who think we can devise a perfect system to account for all of the nuclear material in the world take note. I finally want to thank Nicole Lecht for her arresting cover design.

I still write by hand—I don't compose on the computer or type on a machine. I print, actually, in large and tiny multicolored, primitive script, which must be translated and transformed into legible text. My very special thanks to Terry, who performs this unenviable task as no one else can. With endless patience and good nature, she helps me decipher what I might possibly have had in mind when scribbling in the middle of the night, listens to endless readings aloud, asks questions, and demands easily understandable explanations. And she alone can tell me when to go away and do something else.

PART I
INTRODUCTION

INTRODUCTION

Will terrorists go nuclear? It is a question that haunts government policy and decision makers. What must be done to prevent terrorists from acquiring and using nuclear weapons? How will the nation respond if they do? How likely are they to succeed?

These are difficult questions that involve assessments of terrorists' intentions, estimates of terrorists' capabilities, their access to scientific know-how, the availability of nuclear material, the existence of nuclear black markets, and the effectiveness of security and intelligence services. As Brian Michael Jenkins points out in this volume, experts' estimates of the probability that terrorists will somehow acquire and detonate a nuclear bomb range from virtually impossible to inevitable and imminent. There is no obvious consensus, and, of course, no one knows for sure. The uncertainty only increases our anxiety.

As chairman of the Advisory Panel to Assess Domestic Response Capabilities for Terrorism Involving Weapons of Mass Destruction, I was privileged to lead a distinguished group of Americans in examining how we as a nation, dedicated to liberty and justice for all, could effectively respond to almost unthinkable terrorist threats while retaining our fundamental freedoms.

Jenkins was one of the first analysts to recognize this challenge. More than thirty years ago, he warned that "power, defined crudely as the capacity to kill, destroy, disrupt, alarm, compel society to devote vast resources to security, was descending into the hands of smaller and smaller groups. The capacity for violence once possessed only by powerful armies was coming into the hands of gangs whose grievances, real or imaginary, it will not always be possible to satisfy. . . . How we as a democracy will deal with this and remain a democracy," Jenkins observed, "is one of the major challenges of our era."

For five years, our advisory panel wrestled with this issue. Our labor began when the panel was created in 1999, more than two years before the terrorist attacks of 9/11. Our fifth and final report was delivered in December 2003–twenty-seven months after our nation was so viciously attacked. In the five volumes delivered during this period, we examined the escalating terrorist threat; the necessity of good intelligence and sober, not fear-mongering, threat assessments; the need for and components of a successful national strategy; the kinds of structures we would need to ensure preparedness at the local, state, and federal levels; and most important, the need to sustain the principles set forth by our Founding Fathers.

There is no doubt that the idea of nuclear weapons may appeal to terrorists. It is the responsibility of our leaders to ensure that we have good intelligence and the ability to assess the capability of terrorists to acquire nuclear weapons. Likewise, decisive action should be taken to recognize, prevent, and intercept efforts by terrorists to acquire such weapons. Nuclear nonproliferation must be a top priority of all nations seeking to maintain a free and tolerant civilization. Yet, the obstacles to the acquisition or fabrication of nuclear weapons by terrorists remain formidable. Policy makers tend to focus their attention on the remote high-consequence event–a terrorist nuclear bomb–believing that if government can handle this worst-case scenario, everything of lesser consequence will be covered. That may not always be the case. The safety of the nation requires that we not ignore the higher-probability, lower-consequence events. This was a conclusion of the advisory panel. As Jenkins shows, terrorists are extremely effective at exploiting our fears to leverage their psychological power, creating nuclear terror even without a commensurate nuclear capability. It only proves that terrorism succeeds in creating terror.

Succumbing to nuclear terror can promote dangerous passivity. Asked what plans had been drawn up for responding to a terrorist nuclear explosion in an urban area, one state homeland security official admitted that nothing had been done–everyone simply assumed the city would be gone. In fact, the destruction of a city would require a nuclear explosion of a magnitude far beyond anything terrorists conceivably could achieve.

Nuclear terror can also have another insidious effect, one that imperils our very democracy. Terrorism does pose a terrible danger, but our fear of real and imagined threats must not persuade us to diminish our freedoms or our core values. There is no trade-off between security and liberty. One does not exist without the other.

Ancient cartographers used to populate the edge of their known worlds with dragons and other mythical monsters. We tend to do the same at the edge of our knowledge. But we must be careful not to let dangerous fantasies become the perceived reality that dictates our course of action. That is exactly what this book is about.

As in his last book on terrorism, *Unconquerable Nation: Knowing Our Enemy, Strengthening Ourselves,* Jenkins is always analytical, thoughtful, and provocative. An independent thinker, he doesn't care whether you agree or disagree with every one of his arguments; rather, he compels you to think. Nowhere is that more effectively done than in his harrowing chapter 17 of this volume, where the reader is thrust into the role of the president—an unenviable position given the scenario Jenkins unfolds. It is a lip-biting read that forces one to reflect upon what he or she holds dear.

Jenkins does not leave us wringing our hands in despair. He concludes with a set of sensible steps, many of which coincide with the recommendations of the advisory commission. But at the end, he points out—correctly, in my view—that while preventing nuclear terrorism is government's responsibility, defeating nuclear terror is the task of every citizen. Rejection of unfounded fear together with decisive steps to secure the nation from real threats ensures the survival of our country and all it stands for, most important, our dedication to liberty for all time.

–James S. Gilmore III, former governor of Virginia
and chairman of the Advisory Panel to Assess
Domestic Response Capabilities for
Terrorism Involving Weapons of Mass Destruction

Chapter 1
A SHIVER OF TERROR

Suicide bomber strikes near nuclear site in Israel.

"Suitcase nukes" missing in Russia.

The threat of nuclear weapons falling into terrorist hands is "very real."

Al Qaeda nuclear weapons expert was the real target of the recent CIA air strike in Pakistan.

Al Qaeda operatives are planning a large-scale attack "on par with Hiroshima and Nagasaki."

Do these terrifying headlines foreshadow a "nuclear 9/11"? An "American Hiroshima"? Might America's cities ever be the target of a terrorist atomic bomb? Will London? Moscow? Or Mumbai? Many think so. In fact, two out of five Americans believe that terrorists will detonate a nuclear bomb somewhere in the United States in the next five years. Imagine that. It is a national nightmare.

This book is about nuclear terror. Nuclear terrorism and nuclear terror are different phenomena. Nuclear terrorism is about events. Nuclear terror is about imagination, about what might be. Alfred Hitchcock understood this perfectly. "The terror is not in the bang, only in the anticipation of it." It is appropriate that we should quote a master director of suspense films, for nuclear terror is shaped largely by popular culture—novels, films, tabloid journalism. Nuclear terror is also shaped by myth and by religious belief.

If terrorists detonated a nuclear bomb, that would, of course, create nuclear terror, but nuclear terror can be created without nuclear terrorism. One of the most remarkable developments in terrorism during the last decade has been the terrorists' ability to create terror virtually. No longer old-fashioned bomb throwers, terrorists have exploited modern communications to become increasingly skillful illusionists. Media savvy, they excite our fears not only through actual attacks but with words and conjured images that create a vivid sense of reality.

During the cold war, Americans feared a massive nuclear strike from the Soviet Union. We learned to live with that threat, increasingly confident that Soviets would not be crazy enough to start a nuclear war. But today, the coexistence of the cold war has been replaced by widespread fear of nuclear terrorism—a calamity not sufficient to destroy the nation but surely powerful enough to dwarf the September 11, 2001, attacks.

Nuclear terrorism, upon close examination, turns out to be a world of truly worrisome particles of truth. Yet it is also a world of fantasies, nightmares, urban legends, fakes, hoaxes, scams, stings, mysterious substances, terrorist boasts, sensational claims, descriptions of vast conspiracies, allegations of cover-ups, lurid headlines, layers of misinformation and disinformation. It is hard to separate truth from myth. Much is inconclusive or contradictory. Only the terror is real.

What is true, and what is not?

We have evidence of al Qaeda leader Osama bin Laden's long-term interest in acquiring nuclear weapons, but his quest has been described as naive, poorly informed, and vulnerable to con artists. Khalid Sheikh Mohammed, al Qaeda's key planner and the man who directed the September 11, 2001, terrorist attacks, reportedly told his interrogators that al Qaeda's investigation of nuclear weapons never got beyond the Internet. But there are documents and other interrogations indicating that it went further than that.

Nuclear terrorism is not a new concern. The first nuclear explosion ignited the disturbing thought that malevolent actors, outside of any government, might secretly build a nuclear weapon and use it to threaten destruction and world domination. But that itself was not a new idea. What physicists wrought, novelists had anticipated in science fiction and suspense thrillers, such as H. G. Wells's *The World Set Free* and Saxe Rohmer's Fu Manchu series—where mad scientists and criminal masterminds commanded armies of fanatically loyal followers and sought to rule the world with weapons of unimaginable destructive power.

Nuclear weapons continue to fuel terrorism plots. More than forty years ago, Ian Fleming's James Bond tracked down nuclear-armed terrorists in *Thunderball.* Today, Jack Bauer chases nuclear terrorists on the Fox TV show *24.*

Concern about nuclear terrorism, however, also fired the imagination of a relative handful of maverick scientists, terrorism analysts, and a few government officials who in the late 1960s began to debate the issue.

Yet four decades of discussion have produced little consensus. There are those who argue that if terrorists got their hands on the requisite nuclear material, they would be able to fabricate at least a crude nuclear device. Perhaps it would not be in the ten-kiloton range (the atomic bomb dropped on Hiroshima yielded an explosion equivalent to thirteen thousand tons of high explosive), but it is believed that such a device would at least reach the one-kiloton or tenths of a kiloton range—the equivalent of one hundred tons or more of TNT. But other experts equally knowledgeable say that the fabrication of even a crude nuclear device is a difficult and complex project that remains far beyond the reach of terrorists, even that of the al Qaeda that existed in Afghanistan before 9/11.

The public discourse betrays few doubts. We are bombarded with news stories. Scary and incessant, they fill the headlines and infest the Internet. National commissions and top government officials warn us repeatedly that nuclear terrorism is the number one threat to national security. A nonprofit organization ran television ads during the 2008 primary election campaign urging voters to ask how candidates would secure loose nuclear materials around the world to prevent a nuclear 9/11.[1]

Skip to the bibliography of this book and scan the hundreds of books and articles devoted to nuclear terrorism. The titles alone tell the story of probable, inevitable, and imminent nuclear doom.

But public fear would be even greater if Americans were to see every raw intelligence report, every terrorist boast, every scenario conjured up by the government's "red cells" that try to anticipate terrorist planning. To the reader unaccustomed to the genres of intelligence, terrorist-speak, or war games, this blizzard of threats would indeed be terrifying.

Will terrorists go nuclear? It would seem that they already have. At least, that is the impression.

And that impression appears to be confirmed by the scale and complexity of America's efforts to counter nuclear terrorism. These include intelligence programs, heightened security around nuclear facilities, and diplomatic initiatives aimed at nuclear proliferation and nuclear trafficking. There are American-funded efforts to enhance nuclear security in Russia and to dispose safely of its vast stockpile of weapons-grade nuclear material, as well as preemptive American purchases of fissile material from the republics of the former Soviet Union.

There are police stings to apprehend nuclear smugglers, and

radiation detectors at US ports, border crossings, and around critical facilities. Nuclear Emergency Search Teams remain at the ready to assess nuclear threats and track down terrorist nuclear devices. And the Department of Homeland Security practices how to deal with the consequences of terrorist nuclear attack. Efforts to improve America's ability to trace the origins of any material that might be used in a terrorist nuclear attack continue. If the defenses are a measure, the nuclear terrorist threat is significant.

However, the history of nuclear terrorism can be quickly summarized. There hasn't been any–that is, if by "nuclear terrorism" we mean the successful sabotage of an operating nuclear reactor, the deliberate release of any significant amount of radioactive material, or the detonation by terrorists of a nuclear bomb. Many people would hasten to add "yet," since they believe that while none of these events has happened, they inevitably will. It is not a matter of "if" but "when." The anticipation of nuclear terrorism, not its history, drives the defense.

What we have seen is illustrated by the headlines cited earlier. Terrorists have, in fact, carried out low-level actions with nuclear backdrops to guarantee them dramatic headlines. The suicide bombing at Dimona, Israel, tragically killed an Israeli woman but had no connection with the nearby nuclear reactor, other than being in the same town.[2]

According to some accounts, the terrorist operative killed in Pakistan by a CIA missile, as noted in the above headlines, was al Qaeda's point man for a "dirty bomb."[3] Terrorists, including al Qaeda planners, have indicated interest in dirty bombs–bombs that use ordinary explosives to disperse radioactive material. Chechen rebels planted one such device in Moscow but decided not to detonate it.

Government concerns about nuclear weapons falling into terrorists' hands are very real and entirely sensible. Still, the above headlines about nuclear weapons falling into the hands of terrorists come from the remarks of India's minister of external affairs, and they may reflect just another, seldom missed opportunity by the Indian government to criticize a nuclear-armed Pakistan.[4]

Authorities believe the reference to Hiroshima and Nagasaki in the overheard terrorist plans for a large-scale attack was metaphorical, not literal.[5] And in any case, nothing happened. Nonetheless, terrorists are fascinated by the idea of a nuclear 9/11. References to an American Hiroshima regularly turn up in their fantasies.

In this much broader sense, nuclear terrorism comprises a spectrum of actions, from the hoaxes of lunatics to a terrorist Hiroshima.

This brings us to the core concept of terrorism: dramatic violence choreographed to create an atmosphere of fear and alarm, which causes people to exaggerate the threat. And it often works. Terrorists do not have to reach the highest registers of violence to create widespread alarm. Indeed, our media-saturated society inadvertently provides terrorists with the remarkable ability to leverage their pretensions and threats into real anxiety.

Such is the power of language that the mere proximity of the words *nuclear* and *terrorism* elicits a shiver of terror, which is what this book is about. But rather than simply succumb to the fear of terrorists, we will take a closer look to separate what we fear from what we might reasonably expect.

A dirty bomb technically would be within terrorists' reach today. The effects of such a device would depend on the properties and quantities of the radioactive material it contained. However, considerable debate has been waged about what terrorists could obtain, in what quantity, and whether they could handle it without first being killed by the radiation themselves.

There is also considerable difference of opinion about whether terrorists might be constrained by their own political or strategic calculations. Escalation in terrorist violence over the years, the

9/11 attacks, and subsequent terrorist assertions of their right to kill millions suggest that whatever self-imposed constraints might once have applied no longer exist today. Terrorists seem bent upon mass murder. But on close examination we see evidence of debate among terrorists that suggests more complex calculations.

Some argue that the acquisition of nuclear weapons by rogue states like North Korea and Iran will inevitably lead to the transfer of those weapons to terrorist surrogates. Others believe that no government would be crazy enough to risk retaliation by turning over any of its tiny nuclear arsenal to terrorists.

Some view the lesser acts of nuclear terrorism—the hoaxes, the threats—as harbingers of more serious attacks. Others argue that the nuclear hoaxes are for the most part the products of disturbed minds, while the terrorist threats reflect aspirations, fantasies, or efforts to frighten us, not the actual capabilities of the terrorists. There is no inexorable progression to a nuclear 9/11 or a terrorist Hiroshima.

Experts argue about how to interpret the lack of serious nuclear terrorism. Certainly, the fact that something has not occurred does not guarantee that it could not or will not occur. But if a nuclear terrorist attack is easy, why hasn't someone carried one out already?

This volume will not resolve these debates. It will not argue whether terrorists can fabricate a nuclear bomb or how destructive such a bomb might be. It offers no final judgment on the probability of a terrorist nuclear bomb, although it offers the judgments of experts and explores these estimates as a reflection of perceptions. Whether we dangerously underestimate the capabilities of terrorists while dangerously overestimating their rationality, or endow them with super technical powers and pit bull brains, the actuality remains elusive, a matter of basic belief, not of historical fact or scientific evidence.

Accounts of nuclear terrorism follow a well-worn path

involving the same ensemble cast: corrupt Russian officials, the Chechen Mafia, international arms traffickers, Pakistani scientists, Japanese cultists, and, of course, al Qaeda terrorists. We will meet them all. We also will look at the artifacts: Aum Shinrikyo's attempts to recruit Russian scientists and buy an atomic weapon; the Chechens' dirty bomb; reported incidents of smuggling of nuclear material; and Russia's missing suitcase nukes. We'll also examine A. Q. Khan's private nuclear black market; bin Laden's nuclear acquisition efforts and his discussions with Pakistani physicists; documents found at al Qaeda's training camps in Afghanistan; and fatwas justifying the murder of millions.

Cited again and again, the incidents and anecdotes recounted in this book comprise the core exhibits of the case for the inevitability of nuclear terrorism. They have acquired the patina of authenticity that comes with repetition. They make an impressive argument.

It is only when the individual bits of evidence are separated, taken out of their combined display, and examined individually that we begin to note their fragility. Examined closely within the context of surrounding events, we see that the dots some connect to "prove" that nuclear terrorism is headed our way do not form a solid line after all.

Mighty America, triumphant after victory in the cold war and the fall of the Soviet Union and Eastern European communism, was not supposed to be a terrorized nation. Americans were supposed to be the masters of shock and awe, supposedly able to strike terror in the hearts of our foes. Full of hubris, high and mighty officials in Washington boasted that our power was so great that we transcended the world of facts to rewrite reality. In the long hunt for al Qaeda, in Afghanistan and in Iraq, we rediscovered hard earthbound reality. Meanwhile, it is our terrorist foes who, lacking great arsenals, are nonetheless forcing us to spend trillions of dollars on national defense and homeland security. And despite our expenditure of resources, we remain apprehensive.

Still, we should not overly credit terrorist sophistication and planning. Terrorists have been the unintended beneficiaries of technological developments in communications–the Internet, twenty-four-hour news channels, and the generational shift from reading to watching. In creating terror, our terrorist foes had a more visceral understanding of virtual terrain, something we only dimly understood and, given our superior military strength, refused to recognize.

We contribute to nuclear terror ourselves through our own deep-rooted anxieties. We see ourselves as the most likely target of a terrorist nuclear attack. We understandably fear faceless enemies wielding the power of annihilation. We are addicted to public discussion of every imaginable vulnerability. We focus exclusively on worst-case scenarios. Our politicians mobilize public support through dire warnings; they assault our sensibilities with relentless messages of fear. No wonder terror works.

Will Terrorists Go Nuclear? takes us on a journey from the first imaginings of the possibility of nuclear terrorism to visions of mass destruction that dominate our perceptions today. We explore terrorist motives and consider whether even those we label terrorists face self-imposed constraints. And we speculate whether terrorists might employ nuclear weapons to coerce concessions or to simply inflict mass destruction on their enemies. We also examine the threat of black markets as well as the mysterious weapon known as "red mercury." We further search for the notorious lost suitcase nukes.

We then trace how terrorism escalated, propelling us into an age of alarms. We explore why the American psyche seems especially vulnerable to nuclear terror. And we show how al Qaeda, without (insofar as we know) possessing any nuclear weapons, has become the world's first terrorist nuclear power.

We face our greatest fear in the last section of this book, which begins by making you the president of the United States. An incident of nuclear terrorism has just occurred. As president, you will receive updates on the situation as more is learned about this terrible event. You will hear the arguments of your most trusted advisers. They will speak bluntly about what must be done. Stripped of the jargon that comes with government, these arguments will cut to the essence of the difficult decisions you will have to make in the first hours after a nuclear explosion.

Your advisers will disagree on almost every major issue. You are the decider. You will decide what must be done to help those directly affected by the event, to maintain control in a desperate situation, to reassure a nation in shock, to ensure the continuity of government, to protect the country against further attack, to determine how this thing happened, to learn who is responsible, and to respond to this unprecedented attack upon the United States. No experience in government, no expertise in terrorism or nuclear weapons can prepare you. You will have to think.

PART II
GROWING CONCERN

Chapter 2
THE FIRST IMAGININGS

Initial concerns about nuclear theft, nuclear black markets, and nuclear terrorism were prompted not by any specific criminal or terrorist events but rather by an imagined future—part foresight, part invention, by intellectuals fascinated with weapons, including some of the same people who designed nuclear weapons for America's arsenal.

In the 1960s, nuclear proliferation was a big concern, as it is now. China detonated a nuclear bomb in 1964, bringing the total number of nuclear weapons states to five. Two years later, China successfully tested a thermonuclear device. This was the shortest interval to date between the testing of an ordinary fission bomb and the testing of a fusion bomb, and it suggested that the supposedly closely guarded secrets for making nuclear weapons had leaked, making the task easier for each subsequent nuclear aspirant.

Israel was known to also be developing nuclear weapons at the time. This was a secret project in which several Western nations, especially France, were complicit, just as the Soviet Union initially had assisted China's nuclear weapons program. While France provided Israel with the necessary technology, the United States, although worried about a nuclear arms race in the Middle East, publicly looked the other way. These projects involved the clandestine transfer of nuclear know-how and material. And while arming allies may have been understandable from the respective foreign policy perspectives, it was setting some worrisome precedents.

Of particular concern was the possibility that an American firm may have illegally diverted two hundred pounds of highly enriched uranium to Israel. The case was investigated by several government agencies, but despite circumstantial evidence and widespread suspicion in official circles that the missing material went to Israel, the allegation was never proved.[1]

Of even greater concern to some, however, was the projected expansion of civilian nuclear energy and the development of the nuclear fuel cycle to support it. Most people thought it was a great idea, but to those worried about nuclear safeguards and security, it meant that the technology and knowledge of enrichment and separation—the essential techniques for making nuclear bombs—would spread even further. Every new reactor would be producing plutonium as a by-product. And at the time, the plutonium was expected to be used for a new generation of plutonium-fueled breeder reactors that would produce even more plutonium—much of it of high enough quality to be used in weapons. Within a decade or so, thirty nations would be making tons of it! It meant also that the capacity for creating plutonium would be in civilian hands, beyond the security clearances and tight controls of military weapons programs. To those who were accustomed to strict security regimes, that was a radical and disturbing idea.

How would these civilian facilities be protected? Would nuclear reactors be targets of sabotage or bombardment in wartime? Could safeguards—the control of fissile material, the essential ingredient of bombs—be maintained in a global plutonium economy? How would adequate security be guaranteed?

But the adversaries about whom the analysts were worried

didn't exist yet. There were no reports of criminal entrepreneurs who were diversifying into the trafficking of nuclear material, and contemporary international terrorism did not emerge until the late 1960s. And even then, the first generation of terrorists was hardly the model for potential nuclear terrorists. The early terrorists set off little bombs and kidnapped government officials. Most were barely competent–dynamite was a challenge for them. To imagine a nuclear terrorist was a breathtaking extrapolation from what hardly was to what might be. However, the idea attracted researchers and agitated Congress.

Writing in 1967, just before the dramatic development of international terrorist activity, members of the Advisory Panel on Safeguarding Special Nuclear Material, known as the "Lumb Panel," said that "safeguards programs should also be designed in recognition of the problem of terrorist or criminal groups clandestinely acquiring nuclear weapons or materials useful therein. Although such illegal groups are more likely to steal finished components or weapons than divert materials from peaceful programs, criminal organizations may be attracted to divert such materials if a black market develops, as it is likely to."[2]

In 1974, when I was writing my own first essay on the possibility of nuclear terrorism, I asked Ralph Lumb, the panel's chairman, what the members had in mind when they wrote this. Who were the terrorist groups in 1966, when the panel was convened? He responded that they had no particular terrorists in mind. "We just took a shot," he said. He went on to explain that one of the panel members had some experience with cases involving commodity diversions. If the world was moving toward widespread, large-scale production of plutonium, as seemed likely in the mid-1960s, why would nuclear material not also be vulnerable to criminal diversions?[3]

Worried that too much discussion of nuclear safeguards would frighten the public, the nascent nuclear-energy industry downplayed these concerns. Who would want to steal nuclear material? And if someone did, what could they do with it anyway? They couldn't build a bomb. Building a nuclear bomb would require another Manhattan Project. Wouldn't it?

Perhaps not. In 1960, three young researchers, without any access to secret documents, used "unclassified literature and their own calculations to create . . . a crude paper design for bombs."[4] Officials at Lawrence Livermore Laboratory conducted a more elaborate controlled experiment in 1964. They picked a couple of young postdoctoral physicists "out of the sky" to design a nuclear weapon. The physicists would have no access to classified information. Twenty-eight months later, they submitted their final design. Computer simulations and a murder board of experienced weapons designers concluded that it would work.[5]

The question also fascinated Theodore Taylor, a talented designer of nuclear weapons working at Los Alamos National Laboratory. A thoughtful man, Taylor said that he had had a change of heart about nuclear weapons. In 1966, after designing nuclear weapons for years while working in the Pentagon, he did an "about face" in his "perception of nuclear weaponry" and pressed for nuclear disarmament for the rest of his life.

Years later, he recalled that his "rejection of nuclear power, because of its connection with nuclear weapons, took longer and was not complete until about 1980."[6] By the late 1960s, however, he was raising serious concerns about the implications of a rapidly expanding nuclear power industry. In 1968, Taylor wrote a paper titled "Reactor Safety Considerations Related to Sabotage and Wartime Bombardment of Nuclear Power Plants."[7] In 1969, he wrote "International Safeguards of Nonmilitary Nuclear Technology 1: The Rapid Growth of Nuclear Technology: Implications for Nuclear Safeguards."[8] Neither essay had the kind of title destined to attract widespread readership, but in a series of brilliant articles appearing in the *New Yorker* magazine in 1973, John

McPhee profiled Ted Taylor and explained his arguments in simple terms that everyone could understand. The articles were subsequently published in McPhee's book *The Curve of Binding Energy*.[9] It made Taylor an international figure and lifted his concerns out of the arcane world of nuclear weapons design and into the public domain.

Sabotage and safeguards were important issues, but what really challenged Taylor was the question of whether a terrorist making a nuclear bomb was a possibility. Taylor had designed Hamlet, the most efficient bomb ever made in the kiloton-yield range. He had designed big bombs, including the largest-yield fission bomb ever exploded. It delivered a yield in the megaton range—equivalent to millions of tons of TNT—destructive power usually achieved only by hydrogen bombs. And he had also designed the smallest fission bomb ever made. These were elegant, sophisticated designs, but Taylor also became interested in primitive devices. Would it really require another massive Manhattan Project with hundreds of scientists and engineers and thousands of technicians and workers to make a crude nuclear bomb? Would it even require classified knowledge? Taylor thought not.

The same inquisitive inventiveness that had propelled Taylor's weapons designs moved him and others to speculate about how a group outside of secret laboratories in secret cities might make a nuclear weapon. Some in the nuclear field viewed this as an eccentric pursuit. As one physicist observed, "All these weapons people were a little wacky." Taylor's objective was not to create the most powerful bomb or the most efficient bomb. "Try to see what is the simpleminded way to make something that could knock over the World Trade Center," he said in 1973. "Try to see how sloppy you can get."[10] Taylor mentally designed a variety of simple nuclear bombs, enough to satisfy himself that it would be possible to make one without using classified information and without anything approaching a Manhattan Project.

In 1974, Taylor teamed up with Mason Willrich to write *Nuclear Theft: Risks and Safeguards.* The two authors worried about the possibility of both terrorist nuclear bombs and "plutonium dispersal devices," what today we would call "dirty bombs."[11] They contended that "a few persons, possibly even one person working alone, who possessed about ten kilograms of plutonium oxide and a substantial amount of chemical high explosive, could within several weeks, design and build a crude fission bomb."[12] It would yield something in the tenth- or tenths-of-a-kiloton range—each tenth of a kiloton being the equivalent of one hundred tons of TNT. They also thought that someone could build such a bomb with the right quantities of highly enriched uranium or uranium-233.

This was worrisome. The usual material of nuclear bombs was metallic plutonium-239, produced for the purpose in special government reactors, not plutonium oxide. Plutonium oxide could be found in commercial channels, if, as envisioned, the plutonium was separated from the spent reactor fuel by reprocessing and used for new fuel. What was the likelihood that terrorists would get their hands on this material? Taylor and Willrich proposed that in an environment of increasing terrorism, the "scope of risk of theft by terrorist groups would seem to depend on how widespread terrorist behavior becomes in the future." They concluded that "*if present trends continue, it seems only a question of time.*"[13] There it is—a presumption as far back as 1974 that nuclear terrorism was inevitable.

John McPhee used Ted Taylor as a paradigm to chronicle the debate about nuclear energy and nuclear weapons. For those who weren't there, it leaves the erroneous impression that Taylor was the only one concerned that commercial reactor plutonium could be used to make a bomb. There were others. In 1970, J. Carson Mark warned against the "old notion" that "reactor-grade plutonium is incapable of producing nuclear explosions."[14] Mark's paper had great influence. This was no big deal to the United States or the Soviet Union, which had ample supplies of weapons-grade plutonium, but it could be significant to a country that had no nuclear weapons at all or to a group that aspired to have them. David Hall, another Los Alamos manager, said in 1972 that a bomb built with commercial plutonium might be "unpredictable, but not impossible."[15] Others said predictability was a function of design. A crudely designed weapon might be unpredictable. A more sophisticated design would offer predictability. Departing from Taylor's view somewhat, Hall thought that the degree of sophistication required to build a successful device with this material was greater—Taylor thought a primitive design would work—but Hall went on to say that one should not assume that such sophistication does not exist in the world of criminals and fanatics.[16]

This was a narrow debate within a small universe with an underlying theme. As one inside observer noted, the "one thing that drove all of those guys is emphasizing the importance of nuclear weapons—their life's work—even if it meant projecting their use by terrorists."[17]

By 1972, Victor Gilinsky, then head of the physics department at the RAND Corporation, initially skeptical, agreed that commercial plutonium posed a weapons threat. Serving later as a commissioner on the Nuclear Regulatory Commission, Gilinsky became a forceful advocate for better security at licensed US facilities. He took me along on surprise inspections of facilities in Tennessee and West Virginia, where remarkable quantities of weapons-suitable uranium and plutonium were held—quantities sufficient for many nuclear bombs. I recall a manager at one site where security, in my view, was less than formidable, remarking, "If this were gold, I suppose you'd guard the hell out of it."

In 1976, Robert W. Seldon, one of the young physicists who participated in the 1964 experiment and now a seasoned nuclear weapons developer at Lawrence Livermore Laboratory, warned that commercial plutonium could produce yields in the kiloton range, even with low technology.[18] A test was later conducted, detonating a bomb made from what would have been reactor-grade plutonium and proving Seldon's claim. Still, many in the United States and abroad remained unconvinced. In 1977, Gilinsky persuaded the government to allow Seldon to put together an unclassified briefing for an international audience. Up to that time, even the International Atomic Energy Agency didn't believe anyone could make nuclear bombs out of commercial plutonium. Seldon told them different. Gilinsky was present at the briefing with the IAEA director general, "and saw his jaw drop—literally."[19]

Many thought that terrorists would prefer to use uranium instead of plutonium because the design requirements were much simpler. The young postdocs in the Livermore experiment chose to design a plutonium device because "designing a mere gun bomb would have been 'a pretty crummy showing'" while designing a plutonium implosion bomb would have been a "career-enhancing move."[20] The bomb dropped on Hiroshima was a uranium device using a simple gun design in which a plug of uranium was propelled by a conventional explosion into a hollow cylinder of uranium. Simply smashing two subcritical hemispheres of uranium could produce a nuclear explosion. The challenge for terrorists would be to get a sufficient quantity of highly enriched uranium.

The quantity and purity of the uranium that terrorists could use to build a crude bomb continued to be a matter of debate. Uranium found in the ground contains only a fraction of a percent of U-235, the isotope most suitable for nuclear weapons. It has to be distilled or enriched to make it suitable for fission. Commercial reactors use uranium enriched to between 3 and 6 percent. Research reactors use almost pure U-235, that is, containing at least 90 percent U-235. Anything beyond 20 percent is considered highly enriched uranium. "Weapons-grade" uranium is enriched to 90 percent or better.

That doesn't mean, however, that terrorists could use only weapons-grade uranium. For a crude weapon, less-enriched uranium will still work. In theory, even 6 percent uranium can be made into a bomb.[21] The trade-off is between purity and quantity– the lower the percentage of U-235, the more uranium needed.

So, for example, the so-called whiskey barrel bomb, consisting of a few kilograms of uranium enriched only to 20 percent packed in a whiskey barrel filled with explosives, is simply not realistic. The minimum quantity for a sphere of uranium enriched to 90 percent is about 50 kilograms–110 pounds. But the minimum quantity for a critical mass of uranium enriched to only 20 percent is around 400 kilograms, or nearly half a ton.[22] Add to this the quantity of explosives necessary to move or squeeze this amount, plus the metal case to initially contain the explosion, and you have a huge device. The bomb dropped on Hiroshima weighed four and a half tons, of which only 132 pounds were uranium.[23] Accumulating a half ton of uranium would pose a challenge. Nuclear research laboratories and other facilities where 20 percent uranium was likely to be found represented a vulnerability, but in a nuclear-powered economy, plutonium was likely to be much more abundant.

Pursuing the issue of nuclear theft, Ivan Waddoups at Sandia Laboratories wrote his famous, and still classified, paper, "Malevolent Use of Less Than Strategic Quantities of Plutonium"–the dirty-bomb threat–in 1974.[24] I jumped into the discussion in 1975 with my own work, *Will Terrorists Go Nuclear?*[25] According to a Sandia Laboratories veteran of the era, that was pretty much the corpus of literature on nuclear terrorism in the mid-1970s. But that situation rapidly changed. Growing international terrorism impelled nuclear scientists and terrorism analysts to take on the topic. Their concern was paralleled in the realm of popular culture, where the idea of nuclear terrorism excited people's imagination. Fictional offerings on the topic also increased in number.

The mere possibility of nuclear terrorism was seized upon by individuals with causes–nuclear disarmament, opposition to nuclear energy, world peace. "Ban the Bomb" people had been around for a long time, but the 1970s saw a growing antinuclear movement opposing the expansion of nuclear energy. Many of the protesters found their way to that movement via the anti–Vietnam War protests. American withdrawal from Vietnam removed the reason for the latter, but not the organizational and social momentum behind them.

As in all protest movements, fervency ranged from peaceful demonstration to provocative confrontation to violent assault. For existing terrorist groups, the antinuclear movement represented another potential constituency. The scattered acts of low-level sabotage that occurred were directed mainly against reactors under construction. Antinuclear extremists and terrorists were responsible for a few of these incidents, but many small acts of sabotage were also carried out by workers trying to prolong the projects and their paychecks.

The antinuclear movement sought to capitalize on fears that terrorists might steal nuclear material and build a bomb, but their primary focus was on the possibility that terrorists might seize and sabotage a nuclear reactor, thereby causing the release of radioactive material. A terrorist nuclear bomb was too abstract. The threat it posed was difficult to localize. And anyway, people had lived with the terror of nuclear war for decades. Reactors were visible physical objects, and in the event of a core meltdown and radioactive release, a sort of giant dirty bomb, the surrounding population would have to evacuate. That could be more easily imagined.

Robert Jungk, a liberal Austrian historian who had written several books about the development of nuclear weapons, including an excellent account of the Manhattan Project called *Brighter Than a Thousand Suns*, foresaw a different kind of nuclear terror. In his 1979 book, Jungk argued that the necessary protection of nuclear secrets, nuclear material, and nuclear facilities against theft or sabotage would inevitably require the creation of a police state to ensure security. Nuclear power was a Faustian bargain that exchanged civil liberty for convenient energy. Preventing nuclear terrorism would produce state terror.[26]

As a Jewish student who lived in Berlin when Hitler came to power, Jungk had firsthand experience with totalitarian social control. He had been arrested by the Nazis, was released, and fled to Paris, but he later returned to Germany to work in an underground press service. After the war, Jungk turned his attention to the development of nuclear weapons and, subsequently, to the expansion of nuclear power and its consequences for society. He became a vocal opponent of nuclear energy.

Jungk called his book *Der Atom-Staat*–the nuclear state. The literal translation of its title, however, lost the impact that was obvious to any German reader. *Der Atom-Staat* was a direct allusion to Der Polizeistaat, the police state of Nazi Germany. The book was published in English as *The New Tyranny: How Nuclear Power Enslaves Us.*[27]

Jungk credits Ted Taylor, who by then had acquired the zeal of a missionary, with having initially persuaded him of the dangers of nuclear power. It was Taylor who, while serving at the UN's International Atomic Energy Agency in Vienna, approached Jungk, not the other way around. Jungk at first thought Taylor to be "something of a crackpot," but he soon became convinced by Taylor's harrowing hypothetical scenarios and his claims of just how easy it was to obtain fissile material and fabricate a crude nuclear device.[28]

In one of Taylor's scenarios, a band of concerned nuclear scientists enlists the help of organized crime to acquire a vast quantity of nuclear material, which they use to secretly fabricate an array of nuclear weapons that are clandestinely deployed throughout the world. No ordinary terrorists, these noble physicists use their weapons, gradually escalating from demonstration attacks in remote areas to explosions in population centers, to force nuclear disarmament and bring all nuclear facilities under international control.[29] It is an elaborate and revealing fantasy.

Jungk interviewed me for his book. Among other things, we talked about the proliferation of inner perimeters, the rings of security that were the first geographic clues of a shift from national defense to homeland security.[30] Jungk's personal experience left him with a view that was far more ominous than the simple provision of homeland security. The "legitimate terror of nuclear annihilation," in his view, would lead to a technology-driven totalitarian state, in which government would continually inflate the threat in order to create a permanent state of siege. Driven by fear, it would be a tightly controlled society, marked by the widespread use of background checks, undercover agents, informers, wiretaps, constant searches, preventive detention, possibly even torture in interrogations–a "new inquisition," all of which would be acquiesced to by a frightened population.[31] And if an actual incident of nuclear terrorism ever occurred, whatever vestiges of democracy remained would be swept away in the response.

Jungk's arguments were embraced by the American antinuclear movement, which already regarded corporate America and government authority with deep suspicion. His book confirmed their fear that an evil nuclear industry would, as one prominent antiwar and antinuclear protester put it, "eventually rob us of our freedoms, if not of our lives."[32]

To the ultras in the antinuclear movement, nuclear terrorism was a sideshow, a mere consequence of the terror produced by existing nuclear arsenals, which threatened world survival. In their view, the only way to prevent nuclear terrorism was to reverse "original sin"–the splitting of the atom. Since this evil knowledge could not be taken back, the solution to the threat of nuclear terrorism was not better security but the universal renunciation of nuclear weapons and nuclear energy.[33] The descendants of Adam and Eve would forever banish apples from their table.

Fears of a terrorist nuclear bomb free-floated toward the popular culture, where the uncertainties and caveats of the scientific debate were washed away. Journalists put nuclear terrorism within the grasp of any bright lunatic. The only thing needed was a coffee can of plutonium wrapped with explosives.

All this provoked some reaction from the nuclear power industry and from government. Creating anxiety about the consequences of nuclear energy did not suit an industry dedicated to expanding its use, or the US government, which had made the promotion of nuclear energy official policy. Indeed, the industry insisted for many years that reactor-grade plutonium could not be used for bombs. Ted Taylor was cautioned not to discuss classified details of nuclear weapons design in public. Taylor countered by pointing out that everything he had said could be found in a public library.

Some criticism also came from inside the nuclear weapons establishment, where skeptics noted that Taylor was a "conceptual designer." He worked with a calculator but had never actually built a nuclear weapon, which those who had done so said was a lot more difficult. Actually, Taylor had always argued for creating a team to build a crude device with reactor-grade material, employing tools that would be readily available and using only unclassified information, then testing it to see if it worked. If it did, that would end the debate.

Those arguing that it would be possible to build a crude nuclear device were not offering a threat assessment. The "who" was still hazy. The terrorists imagined by the weapons designers simply did not yet exist. It is essential to keep in mind that these early discussions were about what terrorists theoretically *could* do, not what terrorists *would* do. Participants in the debate came primarily from science backgrounds. They possessed little knowledge about terrorism.

Nor was anyone in the late 1960s or even the early 1970s suggesting that terrorism would ascend to its current levels. In fact, had anyone at the time presented a briefing anticipating the actual headline terrorist events of the following thirty years—OPEC's oil ministers held hostage in Vienna; jumbo jets bombed out of the sky; huge truck bombs in the heart of London and Oklahoma; nerve gas in Tokyo's subways; planes crashing into and bringing down the World Trade Center—he would have been dismissed as the author of entertaining science fiction and shown the door.

Those who had serious reservations about the dissemination of nuclear know-how and material, who wanted safeguards and security measures improved, used the passive voice to describe the mischief that could be done. They did not describe who or why beyond the vaguest references. The threat was theoretical. As one old hand at Sandia Laboratories reflected many years later, "Thank God, some real terrorists came along to support our case for better security."[34]

Some of the ongoing debate about nuclear terrorism was reflected in *Studies in Nuclear Terrorism*, edited by Augustus Norton and Martin Greenberg and published in 1979.[35] They made an interesting pair. Norton was a Middle East expert who had spent extensive time with Hezbollah and other militant groups in Lebanon, while Greenberg was described as a "speculative fiction anthologist" who had compiled and reviewed numerous works of science fiction. Their volume was the most comprehensive anthology of analyses of nuclear terrorism at the time.

A chapter on the clandestine fabrication of a nuclear bomb was written by the Nuclear Energy Policy Study Group, which had been created by the Ford Foundation. Its purpose was to examine the future of nuclear power amid the increasingly bitter debate between its proponents and its opponents. In an earlier study, the group had concluded that "nuclear energy would and should be a major source of electric power in the future," but that plutonium separation, or spent-fuel reprocessing to obtain plutonium, was both economically unnecessary and, given the risks of proliferation, extremely dangerous. In 1977, the group persuaded President Carter to defer indefinitely the commercial reprocessing and recycling of plutonium.[36]

In the Norton-Greenberg book, the group carved a line between Ted Taylor and those who dismissed the idea of a terrorist nuclear bomb. The group concluded that the clandestine fabrication of a crude nuclear bomb was feasible, but its "difficulty should not be underestimated." Even if terrorists managed to assemble such a device, there was a "good chance that the weapon would not work." That would depend on who was doing it and how sophisticated they were.[37]

Both Taylor and Waddoups had earlier addressed the issue of plutonium dispersal. Even a terrorist nuclear bomb that fizzled could make a dangerous, radioactive mess. In the Norton-Greenberg volume, scenarios of radiological dispersal (dirty bombs) were broadened to include other radioactive isotopes, including cobalt, cesium, iodine, and strontium, that are used commercially and therefore are more vulnerable to theft.[38]

The authors in the Norton-Greenberg volume also concluded that terrorists could conceivably attempt to create a radiation incident by seizing a nuclear reactor and threatening to take actions that would lead to a meltdown and breach of the containment structure, thereby releasing radioactive material into the atmosphere. However, even if the security of reactors were judged to be inadequate, such an operation is not easy. The terrorists would have to know a lot about nuclear-reactor operations. Moreover, they said, the terrorists, *few of whom show suicidal tendencies*, probably would be killed in the event.[39] This was written in 1979, before the first suicide terrorists shocked the world. However, an accidental fire broke out in the nuclear power reactor at Three Mile Island that same year. Although the fire was quickly extinguished and resulted in only a small release of radioactive material, the authorities handled the public communications badly, causing considerable alarm and underscoring the danger.

Drawing heavily on research at the RAND Corporation, a chapter by the US Congress Office of Technology Assessment noted that although some terrorist groups conceivably might attempt to go nuclear, there was no evidence to indicate that any group was doing so. That was not necessarily reassuring, since intelligence efforts may fail to pick up any indicators or provide any warning. We simply might not know in advance. As for nuclear terrorism being only a matter of time, the Office of Technology Assessment foresaw no inexorable progression from current terrorist actions to nuclear terrorism. And the nuclear-threat hoaxes that had become a feature of the late 1970s provided no indication of terrorist intent.[40]

The Norton-Greenberg volume added much to the analysis but left the reader and the policy maker with the classic dilemma: the probability of nuclear terrorism seemed extremely low, but the consequences, if the terrorists succeeded, were potentially disastrous.

With international terrorism escalating, another attempt to summarize views was made in 1986, when the Nuclear Control Institute teamed up with the State University of New York to assemble an international task force on the prevention of nuclear terrorism. The Nuclear Control Institute is a research and advocacy center dedicated to preventing nuclear proliferation and nuclear terrorism, and the State University of New York hosted a research center on terrorism.

The task force comprised an impressive roster of scientists, terrorism analysts, government officials, and representatives of private industry. It included Ted Taylor and Mason Willrich, who had become a senior vice president at Pacific Gas and Electric, along with Harold Agnew, the former director of Los Alamos National Laboratory; Victor Gilinsky, physicist and former commissioner of the Nuclear Regulatory Commission; and Stansfield Turner, the former director of the CIA.

In addition to its own deliberations, the task force commissioned a series of papers, including another review of the question that had fascinated Ted Taylor more than fifteen years earlier: Can terrorists build nuclear weapons? Five scientists, all of whom had worked on nuclear weapons at Los Alamos Laboratory and one of whom had participated in the Manhattan Project, tackled the issue.

The five veterans concluded that terrorists could build a crude nuclear device using either weapons-grade material (highly enriched uranium or plutonium-239) or material used in research or commercial reactors (including highly enriched uranium or plutonium). But it would by no means be easy either to acquire the greater quantities of material needed or to fabricate the weapon. The "coffee can" and "kitchen table" atom bombs that were so popular in the media were not realistic. Neither was the "one bright lunatic" scenario judged to be credible. Building a nuclear bomb would require at the very least a team of specialists with knowledge of physics, the properties of nuclear material, metallurgy, and explosives. And the team would need some special equipment. The undertaking would be dangerous. The outcome would be uncertain. The actual yield of a crude device was likely to be in the tenths-of-a-kiloton range. (Some thought that it would be easier to design and build an improvised nuclear bomb if the terrorists could get their hands on a sufficient quantity of highly enriched uranium, but highly enriched uranium was viewed as harder to come by, and most projected terrorist scenarios focused on plutonium.)[41]

These results were communicated in the final report of the task force and later published in *Preventing Nuclear Terrorism*, along with the other conclusions reached by the participants. The volume was edited by Paul Leventhal, the director of the Nuclear Control

Institute, and Yonah Alexander, an Israeli professor and authority on terrorism.[42]

Like the authors in the Norton-Greenberg volume, the Nuclear Control Institute/SUNY task force accepted nuclear terrorism as "technically, politically, and psychologically plausible," although it noted that "as yet there are no public signs that any terrorists have the essential combination of capability and will to engage in an act of nuclear violence."[43] Nevertheless, the task force judged the probability of nuclear terrorism to be increasing. Terrorists were becoming more sophisticated and more lethal, and some groups could count on the support of national governments. Nuclear weapons were deployed in areas of terrorist activity, which in the mid-1980s meant western Europe. The number of terrorist targets in civil nuclear programs was increasing. And there was a potential for nuclear black markets. All this made nuclear terrorism possible, "but not necessarily imminent or inevitable."[44]

The task force pointed out that the obstacles were not negligible. Security had improved. The push to use plutonium fuel in power programs had not proceeded as quickly as had been projected only a few years before. And weapons-usable forms of uranium were being phased out of civilian research reactors. (This has been a slow process that continues more than twenty years later. There are still quantities—albeit small quantities—of weapons-grade uranium in lightly guarded or unguarded research reactors.)

The task force also eliminated two more popular attack scenarios. One was the idea that terrorists would seize and reprocess spent fuel. This, the task force judged, was "more difficult and dangerous than popularly supposed." As for the second scenario, standoff attacks or sabotage, the task force noted that nuclear power plants were designed to resist rocket attacks and would automatically shut down if power lines to or from a plant were cut. Whether a nuclear power plant could withstand a direct hit by a large commercial jet without releasing radioactive material remains to this day a topic of debate.[45] The reactor containment structure itself might or might not survive the crash. If, however, the plane were to hit the spent fuel ponds, it could result in a significant radioactive release.

The 1987 task force report pretty much remained the equivalent of a national threat assessment until the collapse of the Soviet Union raised new concerns about nuclear security and the possibility that terrorists might acquire nuclear weapons through Russian mafias in league with corrupt Russian officials. As in the case of the initial concerns about nuclear terrorism, the fears of a Russian-fueled nuclear black market anticipated rather than trailed developments. Apart from numerous scams, there were only a handful of confirmed incidents in which very small quantities of weapons-grade material were offered for sale. And just as early concerns, even if imaginary and often exaggerated, led to improvements in nuclear safeguards and security, concerns about Russia's nuclear weapons led to an imaginative preventive initiative championed by Senators Sam Nunn and Richard Lugar. The United States would pay to improve security at Russian nuclear facilities, assist the Russians in rendering safe their huge stockpiles of fissile material, and ensure continued employment for Russian weapons scientists.[46]

Insofar as we know, it worked. Whether Russian security was always better than Americans thought—despite the political chaos, the Russian army still functioned (and even unpaid soldiers shoot back)—or whether American funds prevented the wholesale looting of Russia's nuclear arsenal, we can't say, but it turned out well. There have been, insofar as we know, no thefts of nuclear weapons or of more than minute quantities of weapons-grade material.

The terrorist attacks on 9/11, not surprisingly, renewed all of the old debates—whether terrorists could get their hands on nuclear weapons or fissile material, whether terrorists could fabricate nuclear weapons, and if they did, what the consequences might be. One major difference between the discussion of nuclear terrorism in the early twenty-first century and the discussions in the 1970s is that different people were doing the talking. In the 1970s, the discussion of nuclear terrorism was initiated and dominated by scientists and a handful of terrorism analysts. Having settled the science with a rough consensus on the plausibility of terrorists clandestinely fabricating a crude nuclear bomb, the Los Alamos generation gradually faded from the scene. From the 1990s on, and especially since 9/11, the discussion of nuclear terrorism has been taken over by policy makers, most of whom possess little knowledge of technical matters. They are backed up by a press that tends to be somewhat ignorant of science and by what one critic has called the "terrorism industry."[47] That label may be a bit cynical, but the tone of the current debate is decidedly more alarming and alarmist.

It is difficult to determine exactly when, why, or how the estimated yield of a clandestinely fabricated, crude terrorist nuclear device rose from a tenth or a few tenths of a kiloton to today's "standard" assumption of ten kilotons—a fiftyfold to hundredfold increase. Both are mere estimates, to be sure. Neither the analysts nor the terrorists themselves know what yield they might achieve. And a yield of a tenth of a kiloton—roughly ten times the size of the largest truck bomb that we have seen—is capable of bringing down a skyscraper. Ted Taylor reckoned that a half-kiloton device could topple one of the World Trade Center towers. A tenth of a kiloton might do it.[48] But there is a difference. A ten-kiloton device is roughly the size of the atomic bomb dropped on Hiroshima. It would obliterate several city blocks of high-rise buildings.

The nuclear bomb tested by the North Koreans in 2006 had a yield of about a half-kiloton. By modern weapons standards, it was close to a dud. The nuclear bombs tested by India and Pakistan in

1999, in contrast, were in the six- to twelve-kiloton range. One has to wonder how terrorists, working under difficult circumstances, would manage to build a nuclear bomb ten to twenty times more powerful than the North Korean bomb. The issue here is not the accuracy of the estimated yield, but the tendency over time to inflate estimates of terrorist capabilities and, thereby, the potential consequences of a terrorist nuclear attack.

The same thing happens when we talk about dirty bombs or radioactive dispersal devices. A single Americium battery and a stick of dynamite technically qualifies as a dirty bomb, but current discussions of the consequences of a dirty-bomb attack almost invariably assume the widespread dispersal of significant quantities of radioactive material.

The escalation comes not from the science but in the transition from the realm of analysis to the realm of policy. Policy makers are not necessarily doomsayers, but they operate from a different perspective. If the scientists from Los Alamos say that terrorists could build a crude nuclear bomb, then something has to be done about it. That means getting public attention and mobilizing political will, which is hard to do in a noisy democracy. This is the realm of polemics where people push the limits to make a point. Once scientists established that terrorists theoretically could make a nuclear bomb, its yield became a dramatic device. One way to get people to listen is to scare them to death—make them feel the heat of the blast, count the dead, worry about their own lives.

Chapter 3
MOTIVES

I n 1975, I was invited to Los Alamos, New Mexico, to present a paper on nuclear terrorism. The primary focus of the meeting was nuclear proliferation–assessing which countries might develop nuclear weapons and how US policies might try to dissuade them from doing so–topics I knew very little about. Terrorism was an add-on to the agenda.

On technical matters, I had little to offer these distinguished scientists–people who had actually designed and built nuclear weapons, arms control experts, and cold war strategists who spoke easily of megatons and mega deaths. I took a different tack. Instead of debating whether terrorists could successfully obtain the requisite fissile material and fabricate a working nuclear device, I chose to explore their possible motives. This became an ongoing inquiry.

Most studies of the possibility of nuclear terrorism in the early 1970s left motives out of the equation. Written for the most part by scientists and engineers who knew physics but who were not especially knowledgeable about terrorists or other criminal adversaries, these highly technical studies generally struck me as cold and mechanical. One approach was to assess the vulnerabilities in the security systems at nuclear facilities and project hypothetical scenarios to exploit them. This method of analysis was similar to that used in studying the potential and consequences of nuclear accidents and in assessing the vulnerabilities of the United States to various scenarios of nuclear attacks launched by the Soviet Union. Another approach assigned certain physical and technical capabilities to a hypothetical adversary and then evaluated the ability of the existing security systems to respond to an attack.

Both approaches were useful in designing and testing the viability of security systems, and as a result, security at nuclear facilities was improved during the 1970s and 1980s. Neither approach, however, told us much about why any adversaries would carry out a particular nuclear action or what they would hope to achieve by doing so. And both approaches assumed the perspective of the defender. The adversaries were hypotheses, not human beings, their actions an assumption. My interest focused on the motives of the terrorists, their objectives, and their possible modes of action. Looking at it from their point of view, I asked, Why would terrorists go nuclear?[1]

Since, by definition, terrorism is violence carried out to create terror, and nuclear weapons are the ultimate weapons of terror, it is natural to assume that all terrorists would want them. With nuclear weapons, terrorists could inflict mass destruction on their enemies or terrorize them with the prospect. Yet that did not seem to be the case. In fact, none of the terrorist organizations operating at the time—the IRA in Northern Ireland, Spain's ETA, Italy's Red Brigades, Germany's Red Army Faction, and the urban guerrilla groups in Latin America—had sought to acquire nuclear weapons, or at least we had no evidence of their doing so. Nor did we have any evidence that they even discussed the use of nuclear weapons.

A possible exception was the Palestinian terrorist organizations. Observers familiar with the Palestinian groups that had carried out airline hijackings, assassinations, and armed assaults, as well as dramatic hostage seizures like that at the Munich Olympics in 1972, suggested that these same organizations were at least aware of the possibility of stealing a nuclear weapon or building one after obtaining fissile material on the black market. Interestingly, however, the Palestinians raised the issue in the context of discussions concerning whether or not Israel had developed nuclear weapons—at the time, a topic of much speculation. They asserted that if Israel developed nuclear weapons, the Palestinians would be able to get their own nuclear weapons, but this seems to have been an abstract discussion; there is no evidence that any of the Palestinian groups ever tried to do so.[2]

Things must look different from the other side, however. My idea, therefore, was to approach the question not from the perspective of government policy makers or those charged with nuclear safeguards and security, but from the viewpoint of the adversary—"the terrorists." This meant more than mere role-playing. It was closer to method acting, internalizing the terrorists' mind-set and worldview, making them one's own. It probably helped to be an outsider, even a bit subversive.

It was also analytical wing walking, for in 1975 there was very little to go on. We had no history of nuclear terrorist attacks from which we could examine motives, nor did we have any public declarations or internal memoranda written by terrorists discussing why or how they might employ nuclear weapons. Our information, of course, may have been incomplete. The thought of going nuclear may have crossed the minds of terrorists and fueled their fantasies, but the absence of discussion suggests that nuclear weapons may not have been quite as appealing to terrorists as many imagined. Either terrorists regarded nuclear weapons as having little utility in the context of their specific struggles, or they figured that acquiring a nuclear capability was simply too far beyond their reach to be worthy of serious consideration. That put our analysis in the domain of hunches, educated guesses, and inferential leaps. The resultant predictions were, as I pointed out at the time, highly conjectural, tentative, and quite possibly dead wrong.

This analytical approach was risky in another sense. Attempting to understand terrorism from inside the terrorist's mind can be viewed as the analytical equivalent of "consorting with the enemy." To most people, terrorists are villains—depraved, crazy fanatics, evil to the core. To address their motives beyond mental disorder or Satan's command, to even listen to their words, can be seen as legitimizing their deeds. It implies at least a temporary suspension of moral condemnation, not just empathy, but sympathy, giving them voice.

That, of course, was never my intent. In the movie *Patton*, the actor George C. Scott, upon defeating a German armor column in North Africa, shouts triumphantly, "Rommel, you magnificent bastard, I read your book." Of course, we would read the books written by German generals. It informs us how they fight. It does not change our minds about the necessity to do so. Would reading *Mein Kampf* to understand Hitler's mind-set make one an apologist for the Third Reich? Would reading *Das Kapital* to understand the theory of Marxism make one a communist sympathizer? When I was a young army officer in Special Forces, I pored over the works of Mao Tse-tung and Che Guevara to understand the revolutionary mind-set. Several generations of Kremlinologists diligently studied how Soviet leaders viewed the world, how they thought about war, formulated strategy. America's cold war strategy was informed by this research. Why should we not also try to get inside the minds of our terrorist foes?

The problem is that terrorism is a "hot" war, not a cold war. Terrorism provokes extraordinary fear. It is a source of periodic alarm and continuing anxiety. Our leaders may have referred to the Soviet Union as an "evil empire," but terrorists provoke far more emotion. I have on occasion been asked to edit the speeches of government policy makers. In vain, I have tried to remove displays of affect, eliminating words like "barbaric," "heinous," "savage," "cowardly," "inhuman," "insane," to deliberately craft a more phlegmatic response that would deprive terrorists of any notion that they had moved us. But the politicos inevitably put the podium-pounding rhetoric back in–they knew what their audience wanted to hear, which was not the cool response I wanted to signal to the enemy.

In 1975, I was able to identify only a small number of incidents of sabotage or armed attack on nuclear facilities or threats involving nuclear material. The evidence showed that the greatest threats were far more mundane, pedestrian, and downright human than we had imagined.

In January 1961, a worker at a US Army reactor in Idaho Falls pulled out a control rod, exposing himself and two coworkers to lethal doses of radiation. It was a murder-suicide resulting from a lovers' triangle.

In October 1970, the Orlando Police Department received a note threatening the city of Orlando, Florida, with destruction by a "hydrogen bomb." The note was accompanied by a crude diagram of the alleged bomb. The author demanded $1 million in cash and a guarantee of safe passage out of the country. The city was given twenty-four hours to comply–or risk annihilation. Authorities judged the threat to be a hoax–the first of many–and police later apprehended a tenth-grade student who admitted responsibility. There was no nuclear device.

In November 1971, a fire set by arsonists caused $10 million of damage at Consolidated Edison's nuclear generating plant in New York. In a letter to the *New York Times,* a group calling itself Project: Achilles Heel claimed that "Indian Point Guerrillas" carried out the attack out of concern for the environment. Project: Achilles Heel and the Indian Point Guerrillas turned out to be one former Con Edison employee who was undergoing psychiatric treatment at the time. Later that same year, two bombs exploded near the experimental linear accelerator at Stanford University in California. No suspects were ever arrested.

In March 1973, a nuclear power plant under construction near Buenos Aires was briefly occupied by fifteen members of the People's Revolutionary Army, a Trotskyist urban guerrilla group in Argentina. The guerrillas painted slogans on the walls, raised their own flag over the facility, and stole weapons, but they made no attempt to enter the reactor area.

In February 1974, a saboteur toppled a four-hundred-foot meteorological instrument tower at a proposed nuclear power plant site in Massachusetts. An individual later turned himself in to the police and confessed he was motivated by the danger that construction of a nuclear facility at the site would pose to the local community.

In April 1974, a man claiming to be a member of the Justice Guerrillas warned that train coaches on the Vienna-Rome Express had been deliberately contaminated with radioactive material. Investigators found strong but not lethal traces of radioactive iodine-131, normally used in medical diagnosis, under the seat of one compartment of the train. The "Justice Guerrilla," who was later arrested, turned out to be an individual with a history of insanity. He said that his action was meant as a protest against the treatment of the mentally disturbed in Austria.

In October 1974, Italian officials announced that they had uncovered a plot by right-wing terrorists to poison Italy's aqueducts with radioactive material stolen from a nuclear research center in northern Italy. The alleged threat was associated with revelations of a planned assassination and coup by right-wing elements in Italy. An engineer was arrested, but the allegations were never substantiated, and the case became tangled in legal difficulties. (This incident coincided with a number of neofascist terrorist plots in Italy. Twenty years later, one of those investigated in the case would turn up in France as a broker for red mercury, a mysterious chemical compound, which would, it was advertised, enable terrorists to construct miniature nuclear bombs.)

In May 1975, two bombs exploded at a nuclear power station under construction in France. The reactor itself did not yet contain fissionable material. Shortly before the bombs exploded, a caller identifying himself as a member of the Meinhof-Puig Antich Group warned everyone at the site to evacuate the area. The Meinhof-Puig Antich Group had never been heard of before. Ulrike Meinhof was one of the leaders of the Baader-Meinhof Gang in Germany, awaiting trial at the time; Puig Antich was an anarchist who had recently been executed by the Spanish government.

These events gave us a small, but varied sample of villains: a jealous lover, a disturbed adolescent, an environmental extremist, two mental patients, some Trotskyists and anarchists, and one neofascist—hardly the imagined group portrait of nuclear terrorists today. It told us that there was not likely to be a single, typical nuclear terrorist.

Terrorism is a term that is used promiscuously. Among those we call terrorists, we find common criminals, political crusaders, and authentic lunatics. The categories are not always mutually exclusive. Purely criminal organizations may carry out acts of terrorism, as the Mafia has done in Italy and drug lords have done in Colombia. Terrorist organizations may include individuals with mental disorders.

The range of actions can be equally broad. Anyone who attempts to steal nuclear material, seize or sabotage a nuclear facility, build a nuclear device, disperse or threaten to disperse radioactive material, or threaten nuclear destruction is likely to be labeled as a terrorist. The Unabomber, who was responsible for a seventeen-year bombing campaign, was mentally deranged but nonetheless was referred to as a terrorist. An Egyptian limousine driver who in 2002 opened fire on passengers waiting at the El Al counter of Los Angeles International Airport had no history of political involvement and left no message indicating a cause, but an angry public insisted that he be called a terrorist. The person who in 2001 sent media figures and public officials letters containing anthrax was never identified, and his motives can only be surmised. Nonetheless, it was considered an act of terrorism.

Even within a tighter definition of *terrorist*, there is no generic mind-set. Terrorists share tactics, not politics. They certainly do not all think the same way about their struggles. Nor would all terrorists necessarily think about nuclear weapons or nuclear sabotage the same way.

In my 1975 paper, I laid out a spectrum of possible actions:

- *A nuclear hoax:* Terrorists could threaten to detonate a nuclear device or disperse radioactive material in a populated area to make demands or simply create panic. To bolster their credibility, they could enclose convincing diagrams of weapons or perhaps even a tiny amount of nuclear material.
- *A bogus nuclear device:* Terrorists could detonate conventional explosives or a pyrotechnic device that would simulate the signature mushroom cloud of a nuclear bomb. The device could even be laced with a limited amount of radioactive material to create alarm. I had in mind something less than what would be described today as a "dirty bomb."
- *Low-level sabotage of a nuclear facility:* Terrorists could set off explosives or damage facilities at a nuclear reactor—in today's tactics, probably a truck bomb—causing no radioactive release but attracting widespread publicity. Attention has subsequently focused on serious sabotage that results in a radioactive release.
- *Takeover of a nuclear facility:* Terrorists could seize hostages at a nuclear site and threaten to set off explosives to damage

the facility. The actual nuclear threat might be low, but the publicity and alarm would be considerable.

- *Overt theft of a nuclear weapon:* If thieves got away with a nuclear weapon, this could be very dangerous. But even if they only approached nabbing a nuclear weapon, the incident would still attract enormous attention and cause alarm.
- *Deliberate radioactive contamination of a symbolic target:* The term *dirty bomb* had not yet gained currency. This was my early, light version. Terrorists could disperse small amounts of radioactive waste material or radioactive material stolen from a hospital or other facility, by means of conventional explosives, contaminating some symbolic target. (I mentioned the New York Stock Exchange as a possibility. "Their intent," I wrote in 1975, "might not be to produce any casualties at all, but simply to draw attention to themselves. Conceivably, however, they could prevent the use of the building for a period of time.")
- *Deliberate dispersal of plutonium or other radioactive material:* This is the dirty-bomb scenario we think of today. I thought of it then as the dispersal of small quantities of radioactive material in a busy contained area such as a subway station. The intent would be to cause some casualties and mass panic.
- *Detonation of a stolen or homemade nuclear bomb in a populated area:* This would be the most devastating form of attack.

In reading that essay decades after it was written, I was discomforted to discover that I had made two references to New York's World Trade Center as a potential target of large-scale terrorism. It was, I wrote, "a favorite scenario of those who warned of the potential consequences of nuclear terrorism," which ten pages later was expanded to "In an extreme scenario, the detonation of a nuclear bomb at the base of the World Trade Center in

New York City would cause tremendous casualties and potentially widespread contamination." This was eighteen years before the 1993 World Trade Center bombing, where terrorists tried to bring down the towers with fifteen hundred pounds of explosives, and twenty-six years before the 9/11 attacks, which destroyed the towers.

There was another possible scenario we were aware of at the time. In 1972, three criminals on the run hijacked a commercial jet flying from Birmingham, Alabama. This began the longest hijacking in American history. The plane flew from Birmingham to Jackson, Mississippi, to Lexington, Kentucky, to Key West, Florida, to Cleveland, Ohio, to Toronto, Canada, to Havana, Cuba, ultimately landing in Orlando, Florida, where FBI agents shot out the tires of the aircraft to halt the saga. On one of its laps, the hijackers threatened to crash the hijacked jet into the nuclear facilities at Oak Ridge, Tennessee. The reactor there was promptly shut down. This hijacking led to the imposition of a rule that all airline passengers would be screened for weapons, which was implemented in 1973. It also foreshadowed later threats that hijacked aircraft might be used as missiles. This was a growing concern right up to 9/11: the possibility that terrorists might crash a hijacked airliner into a nuclear facility, breaching the containment structure that houses the reactor and causing a radioactive release or a scattering of radioactive waste material stored on site. We know that terrorists later contemplated such attacks.[3]

I laid out these possible terrorist scenarios in order of ascending consequences (also of ascending difficulty), from hoax to detonation of a nuclear device. The consequences were indicated by a sharply ascending concave curve from zero direct casualties in a hoax to tens of thousands or even hundreds of thousands of casualties from detonation of a nuclear bomb. I drew a convex curve that ascends more rapidly, to indicate the fear and alarm that such actions might produce:

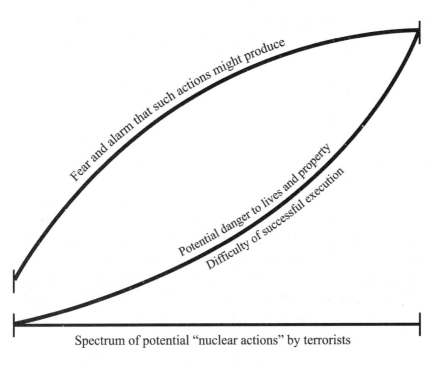

Spectrum of potential "nuclear actions" by terrorists

Figure 1

My intention in introducing a range of actions was twofold: I wanted to emphasize first that in focusing on the higher end of the spectrum—a nuclear explosion—we should not ignore the possibility of lesser actions, and second, because the mere mention of the words *nuclear* and *terrorism* in close proximity were likely to produce great alarm, terrorists could achieve their traditional tactical goals of publicity, fear, and possibly tactical leverage without having the resources or running the risks of building a nuclear bomb, and therefore, lesser acts were more likely.

Indeed, the primary attraction of going nuclear for terrorists, I thought, was not that it would enable them to cause mass casualties, but rather that almost any action in the nuclear domain would automatically generate fear in the minds of the public. It would create nuclear terror. Drawing attention to themselves and their causes and creating alarm—which had been typical objectives of terrorists—could be achieved by undertaking less-sophisticated actions at the lower end of the spectrum. This is exactly what terrorists had been doing. They carried out dramatic, but for the most part limited, acts of violence in order to create an atmosphere of fear and alarm. Terrorists were effective manipulators of apprehension.

In the decades that followed, terrorist violence would escalate, but the principle remains. Today, we talk about terrorists employing *weapons of mass destruction*—scenarios involving thousands or tens of thousands of casualties—and *weapons of mass effect*, such as dirty bombs that might kill few people but nonetheless could easily provoke public panic.

The decades since 1975 have provided more information. Although mentions of nuclear weapons appear in the literature of only a few groups, they are instructive. The fictional destruction of US cities that are attacked with nuclear weapons appears in William Pierce's *The Turner Diaries*, a violent racist novel about a future war of resistance against a Zionist-run US government, widely read by right-wing extremists in the United States.[4] This 1978 novel may have been a possible source of inspiration for the 1995 bombing of the Alfred P. Murrah Federal Building in Oklahoma City. In the novel, a white resistance movement uses its captured nuclear weapons to set off a nuclear war between the United States and the Soviet Union. This ignites an even wider world war, which destroys the old order, allowing the white race to ultimately establish control. It ends with the protagonist preparing for a suicide mission to fly a plane loaded with a nuclear bomb into the Pentagon.[5] Pierce, an activist in white supremacist movements, founded his own religion called Cosmotheism, which incorporated his racist ideology.

There was a report in 1991 of a letter faxed to one of Russia's nuclear research centers, purportedly from Islamic Jihad, offering to buy a nuclear weapon. The likelihood of any terrorist group openly faxing an inquiry to purchase a nuclear bomb raises questions about its authenticity.

In the midst of the war in Bosnia, the leader of Bosnia's Serbs threatened to use atomic weapons, a threat that was taken seriously, at least by Croatian scientists, who claimed that Yugoslavia had been working on developing its own nuclear weapons since the 1950s. In fact, Bosnian Serbs reportedly went to Moscow to try to purchase a "special nuclear device" on the black market. They returned with what they thought was a device, but instead of plutonium, it was a dud that contained only a nonradioactive substance.[6] These are all words, not deeds, but they suggested that thoughts of nuclear weapons would arise in the context of racial, ethnic, or religious conflict.

Three case studies demonstrate the range of motives that have driven the most virulent and threatening terrorist nuclear efforts around the world. The perpetrators have been the Aum Shinrikyo religious cultists in Japan, the Chechen rebels in Russia, and the al Qaeda jihadists led by Osama bin Laden.

SHOKO ASAHARA'S DARK VISION

Not until the emergence of Aum Shinrikyo, the strange cult in Japan that was responsible for releasing nerve gas on Tokyo's subways in 1995, did we find evidence of an effort to acquire nuclear weapons. The motives for the attempt seem to have arisen in the fevered mind of one man.

Shoko Asahara, the cult's supreme leader, started out as an acupuncturist and yoga instructor; he later became a religious instructor and, ultimately, the guru, founder, and supreme leader of his own religious sect. A charismatic con man, a megalomaniac, a paranoid and vindictive tyrant who ordered the murder of errant followers, increasingly psychotic but not unintelligent, he preached the end of the world—Armageddon—as a consequence of an inevitable nuclear war between the United States and Japan. In his scheme, Japan was doomed to be destroyed by nuclear weapons. But not just Japan. According to Asahara's predictions, in the ensuing global conflict, Russia, China, and the United States would also collapse. Civilization would end. According to his calculations, the end would begin in 1996. Salvation, however, was possible.[7]

"From the rubble of this post-apocalyptic world will arise a race of 'super-humans'"—these would be Asahara's devoted followers. They would survive. "All-out nuclear warfare," the guru explained, "is not a big problem for one who has attained enlightenment." Survival was to be assured through deep concrete bomb shelters to which cult members would retreat, and spiritual practice, which would enable sect members to voluntarily stop breathing, thereby suspending their oxygen consumption and enabling their bodies to survive radiation.[8]

This master race of enlightened sect members, led by scientists who would be recruited to the cult, would build a new civilization. As David Kaplan and Andrew Marshall point out in their brilliant book *The Cult at the End of the World*, Asahara seems to have lifted much of this scenario of total destruction and reconstruction of civilization under the direction of scientist-priests from a series of science fiction novels by Isaac Asimov.[9] The idea of a nuclear holocaust as the prelude to the rebirth of civilization led by more-enlightened leaders appears in an even earlier source than Asimov's Foundation Trilogy. In 1914, H. G. Wells wrote his prophetic novel *The World Set Free*, which envisions the destruction of the world by "atomic bombs"—Wells coined the term—followed by the emergence of a new world order.[10]

Aum Shinrikyo's whole belief system was a hodgepodge of mystic religion, science fiction, and new age notions. Asahara himself was fascinated with survival after nuclear war, in particular, with the 1959 movie *On the Beach*, which portrays the last days of a handful of doomed survivors of a nuclear war that has wiped out most of civilization.

The idea of inevitable confrontation with America, fears of a nuclear holocaust, imminent doom, salvation through enlightenment and weird science, as preached by Asahara, resonated with the angst and anomie that seems to be inherent in postwar Japanese society. Mutant monsters, visions of violence and destruction, and survivors navigating futuristic postwar wastelands are all common themes in postwar Japanese films, novels, and comic books. The cult soon attracted thousands of followers in Japan, and in the early 1990s, Aum Shinrikyo successfully expanded the cult to Russia, a society then in the throes of uncertainty following the collapse of the Soviet Union, where it also attracted thousands of followers.

It is not clear how much of Asahara's dark vision derives from his own lack of sight. As an infant, he had suffered from congenital glaucoma, which left him blind in one eye and partially blind in the other. His brother was completely blind. Congenital glaucoma is a birth defect. Theoretically, it could have been connected with his parents' exposure to radiation—Asahara was born and grew up in Kumamoto Prefecture on the island of Kyushu, fewer than fifty miles from Nagasaki, where on August 7, 1945, the United States had dropped its second atomic bomb.

Although Asahara was ferociously anti-American, we have no evidence that he blamed the United States for his affliction; as His Holiness, the master did not dwell on his own disability. He did, however, have an obsession with the nuclear attacks on Japan, referring frequently to the suffering of the Japanese in World War II. He personalized the experience. In relating one of his dream-like visions in which he returns to a post–nuclear war Japan, Asahara says, "I had a vision of being hit by radiation. . . . From outside, my body appeared to be unchanged, but I had apparently been exposed to radiation."[11]

American psychiatrist Robert Jay Lifton sees Asahara's dream as an admission of fear of his own vulnerability to delayed radiation effects.[12] This was not unusual in Japan. The invisible long-term effects of radiation, perhaps extending over generations through broken chromosomes and birth defects, were a source of terror for all Hiroshima and Nagasaki survivors, and to some extent, their children. It is perhaps also noteworthy that some of Asahara's weapons schemes involved blinding his opponents. Asahara later did claim that the Americans had unleashed chemical weapons on him and his followers.

But Asahara's focus on weapons of mass destruction was not exclusively that of a victim. Lifton, who interviewed members of the cult, points out that Asahara's "early sense of nuclear weapons became a touchstone for all his actions and imaginings."[13] He viewed nuclear weapons as "near deities, possessing a capacity not only for unlimited destruction but also for godlike creation." Lifton calls this exaltation "nuclearism." (In the 1968 movie *Planet of the Apes*, another science fiction piece set in a post–nuclear war future, the surviving humans worship the idol of a nuclear bomb.)

Driven by its leader's apocalyptic view of the world, the Aum sect set about attempting to acquire weapons of mass destruction. We know that Aum actively recruited scientists from Japan's top universities to support its quest. Concurrent with its efforts to develop chemical and biological weapons, the sect pursued parallel paths to acquire nuclear weapons: by attempting to purchase one from Russia or by attempts to fabricate its own device. Although more than thirteen years have passed since the Tokyo sarin attack and the arrest of Aum's leaders, we still have only the sketchiest outline of this effort.

We do know that beginning in 1992, Aum's leaders contacted senior officials in Russia, where the cult was successfully recruiting members. The objective of these emissaries was to gain access to advanced weapons technologies. Russian officials, who at first denied contacts with the cult's leaders, later admitted to meetings and explained that they saw the wealthy Japanese, who seemed to have large sums to spend, as possible sources of philanthropic funding for their own needy research programs. The Russians were right about the wealth of the Japanese—Aum had an annual income of more than a billion dollars, a sum greater than many national defense budgets. At the same time, Russian officials were understandably wary of these well-heeled but strange Japanese, although it is also possible that Russian intelligence saw the sect as a potential source of classified information about Japan's research programs. In any case, we are not sure what the terms of the exchange were, but Aum, according to one account, got the recipe it later used to fabricate nerve gas, and Russian researchers received some money.[14]

With regard to Aum's specific interest in nuclear weapons, we have only the cryptic notes of one of its senior representatives, referring to the purchase of a nuclear weapon for $15 million. We do not know if this reflected his budget, an offer he had made, or a negotiated price. (According to another account, the note simply read, "Nuclear warhead. How much?") No nuclear weapon was ever delivered, and further acquisition efforts were not pursued.

The cult, however, did manage to recruit at least two Russian nuclear scientists, one from Moscow University, the other from the Kurchatov Institute in Moscow, which operated a number of research reactors and reportedly possessed hundreds of kilograms of highly enriched uranium. It is not clear, however, that the scientists ever actually did anything for the cult.[15]

Meanwhile, Aum pursued other possible paths to nuclear weapons. One step was the purchase of land in Australia where it could mine uranium. Another was the use of its extensive business empire to set up front companies in the United States to buy equipment that could be used in the construction of nuclear weapons. These moves suggest that Aum's leaders were thinking about fabricating their own nuclear device, a more ambitious and long-range task than obtaining a weapon from the Russians.[16]

The nuclear efforts failed, but the group had some success in the chemical domain. This led to the sarin attack on the Tokyo subway, unprecedented in the annals of terrorism. It brought about the cult's downfall.

In 1995, Asahara ordered his lieutenants to disperse sarin–nerve gas–on the subway lines that converged on government offices, specifically the headquarters of the police, who he believed were planning an imminent assault on the sect. Owing to the poor quality of the nerve gas and the primitive method of its dispersal, only twelve persons died, although more than five thousand became ill. Had the sarin been of higher quality and the dispersal less crude, hundreds–possibly thousands–conceivably might have died, which, we have to believe, was the intended consequence of the attack. Clearly, in Asahara's eyes, killing hundreds or thousands of Japanese was not a constraint.

The shocking attack provoked an immediate nationwide crackdown by Japanese authorities. Aum's facilities were raided, and within days, most of its top leaders had been arrested. Its links with Russian officials and Australian property were soon revealed. While cult leaders were put on trial and were ultimately convicted of murder, the cult itself was allowed to continue operating under a new name and management. And despite increased police scrutiny, its interest in nuclear facilities apparently continued. Subsequent investigations found that cult members had hacked into computers to obtain classified information about nuclear facilities in Russia, Ukraine, China, South Korea, and Taiwan. Moreover, through software companies owned by the sect–commercial fronts established by the original Aum—members had collected information about Japan's own nuclear facilities and nuclear research programs, including the names of participating scientists.[17] Shoko Asahara himself awaits execution.

THE CHECHENS' DIRTY BOMB

Russia's Chechen separatists get credit for thus far being the only group that has actually fabricated a dirty bomb. Brutalized by their bloody conflict with Russia, increasingly radicalized by Islamic extremism, and assisted by their reported connections with Chechen criminal networks, Chechen fighters have carried out some of the most ambitious and ruthless terrorist attacks, killing hundreds; bombing apartment buildings, airplanes, and subways; and taking thousands of persons, including children, hostage. Nuclear threats were one small part of the Chechen fighters' repertoire.

The war in Chechnya grew out of the collapse of the Soviet Union. With the Socialist Republics that made up the Soviet Union suddenly independent, the issue of contention became whether the government in Moscow would hold onto the numerous semiautonomous ethnic enclaves within the new federation of Russia. In general, the Russian government succeeded in holding the country together by guaranteeing the non-Russian entities a measure of political autonomy and offering more favorable arrangements for revenue sharing. By 1994, eighty-seven of these entities had negotiated their deals and formally joined the federation. Chechnya was the lone holdout.

Its intransigence reflected a long and bitter history of incessant conflict between ethnic Russians and the fiercely independent Chechens. Chechnya had been conquered and annexed by Russia in 1870, but after annexation, it continued to fight for independence. With the Soviet Union flying apart, Chechnya again proclaimed its independence in 1991. This prompted an exodus of ethnic Russians who had been deliberately settled there by Stalin. From 1991 to 1994, the situation in Chechnya remained chaotic, while relations between Russia and Chechnya deteriorated. In October 1994, Russian aircraft began bombing Chechnya's capital, Grozny. Russian troops launched a ground attack on Chechnya in December. The First Chechen War had begun.

There is no question that the war in Chechnya was a horrific conflict. The Russian army's mission was to crush the Chechen revolt by any means, not to win hearts and minds. Its one advantage over the lightly armed Chechen guerrillas was its massive firepower—air strikes and heavy artillery, which it used with little constraint. Russia, moreover, did not recognize the Chechens as legitimate combatants. There were no rules of war. Nor did the Chechens, some of whom were little more than bandit thugs, give quarter. Guerrilla wars always blur the distinction between fighters and civilians, and neither side in Chechnya tried hard to make one. Frightened Russian conscripts, who were often treated miserably by their own commanders, inflicted their pain on the Chechens. Villages and towns were leveled, populations scattered, rape and looting were common. After months of bombardment, Grozny lay in ruins. Its surviving occupants were sullen and defiant, while guerrilla warfare continued in the mountains. It is against this bloody background that the Chechen nuclear threats must be examined.

In 1992, Dzhokhar Dudayev, the Chechen rebels' president, threatened to attack nuclear plants in Russia, and in 1995, he publicly boasted that Chechen operatives had smuggled five packages into Moscow, at least two of them containing dirty bombs.

Dudayev's most ambitious plot was not revealed until 2002 when Russian authorities discovered his personal archive. According to the accounts given to reporters by the commander of the Russian forces in Chechnya, Dudayev planned in 1995 to send a team of Russian-looking fighters to a Russian naval base where they would hijack a Russian submarine. A later report on Russian television said that the Chechens planned to remove one of the nuclear warheads from the submarine and return with it to Chechnya. With the nuclear weapon in hand, the Chechen rebels would force Moscow to withdraw its troops from Chechnya and recognize the republic as an independent state.[18] It was not explained exactly how the Chechens would take over the vessel and remove the warhead, or why the Russian government would permit the Chechens, even if they held hostages, to board a plane with a nuclear weapon and return to Chechnya. It seems an ambitious fantasy of the kind often found in terrorist hideouts.

In November 1995, a Chechen team under the command of Shamil Besayev planted a device in Ismailovsky Park in Moscow. The device itself has been variously described as "a parcel of cesium-137," "a cache of radiological materials," "a lead container with radioactive cesium-137," "a shielded cancer treatment device, packaged up with dynamite," "a crude bomb containing a mixture of cesium-137 and dynamite," and a "bomb . . . made of seventy pounds of cesium-137."[19] Since the entire package, including its lead shielding, weighed about seventy pounds, its payload could not have been anywhere near seventy pounds. In fact, the amount of cesium was estimated to be 10 to 50 millicuries, a very small amount. We do not know how many people would have been killed by the explosion itself or how many, if any, would have been harmed by exposure to the radioactive material. One source says that in a best-case scenario, hundreds would have died soon after exposure, with thousands more exposed to cancer-causing radiation that would show up years later.[20] In a 1987 incident, however, two hundred and fifty persons, including children, were accidentally exposed, both internally and externally, to radiation from cesium. A number of them suffered symptoms of radiation poisoning, and four died, but the radiation in that case was tens of thousands of times greater.[21]

Significantly, the Chechens made no attempt to detonate the device. Instead, they notified a television station of its location and contented themselves with demonstrating their capability and with creating alarm. They increased this alarm by claiming, apparently falsely, that three more explosive devices had been planted at other locations in Moscow. The one at Ismailovsky Park was found where the terrorists said it would be, and the parcel was removed without any casualties.

Since this may be the only confirmed case of terrorists having a dirty bomb, it makes sense to inquire deeper into the motives of the Chechens in planting the device and then not detonating it. By July 1995, the Russian army had occupied Grozny, installed an obedient government, and pushed the remaining separatist fighters into the mountains. A cease-fire was in place, although it was frequently violated, while Moscow and the Chechen rebels engaged in peace talks aimed at ending the struggle.

Initially, the talks went well, but they fell apart when a Russian commander was critically wounded in a car-bomb attack, presumably by Chechen assassins. By late November 1995, sabotage, guerrilla warfare, and terrorist attacks were again increasing. The Russians again responded with artillery and air strikes. It was in this climate of stalled negotiations, renewed violence, and Chechen desperation that Besayev, the leader of the Chechen hard-liners, decided to demonstrate that the Chechens could carry out terrorism in Moscow if they wanted to.

Five months before, Besayev had saved the Chechen struggle with a stupendous terrorist attack inside Russia. In June 1995, at the head of a force of Chechen fighters, he bribed his way through checkpoints to reach the Russian town of Budyonnovsk, where he and his men attacked the police station and town hall. The Chechens then rounded up several hundred military and civilian hostages, barricaded themselves in the town's hospital, and threatened to kill all the hostages if Russia did not agree to withdraw its army from Chechnya. After two failed attempts by Russian commandos to storm the hospital, Moscow agreed to a cease-fire, the renewal of negotiations to end the war, and safe passage for Besayev and his men back to Chechnya, where he returned to a hero's welcome.

It was an act of terrorism, to be sure, but Besayev, who often spoke with foreign journalists, dismissed the label. "You talk about terrorism forfeiting our moral superiority before world public opinion. Who cares about our moral position? Who from abroad has helped us, while Russia has brutally ignored every moral rule? If they can use such weapons and tactics, then so can we."[22]

Besayev himself had reason to hate. In June 1995, shortly before the Budyonnovsk raid, a Russian bomb had struck his home, killing eleven members of his family, including his wife and children. (Besayev himself was killed by a bomb in 2006.) It is not difficult, therefore, to understand the Chechens' motivation to terrorize Russians, especially Muscovites, who, far from the wild Caucasus, felt safe in their own homes.

Why, then, did they not detonate the device in Ismailovsky Park? Perhaps because Besayev knew the device would not work or that it would have little actual effect—it was far more useful as an instrument of terror. It is also possible that the Chechens worried about provoking Russian reprisals that would fall on the civilian population of Chechnya.

History gave them reason to fear. In 1944, in response to reports that some Chechens had collaborated with German military units that were then occupying the Northern Caucasus, Stalin ordered that the entire populations of Chechnya and neighboring Ingushetia, about 1.5 million people in all, be deported to Siberia. It was reported that four hundred and twenty-five thousand of them were rounded up in a single day. Between one-fourth and half of them died along the way. Their houses, land, and livestock were turned over to Russian settlers. It was not until 1957 that Premier Khrushchev allowed the exiled Chechens to return. This historic event was still a living memory fifty years later. In 1995, it remained a source of concern. The First Chechen War had already resulted in two hundred and fifty thousand Chechen civilian casualties and two hundred thousand deportees. Would a nuclear attack in the heart of Moscow give the Russian government an excuse to again depopulate Chechnya?

The primary reason for not going through with the attack, however, may have been a strategic calculation. Besayev's earlier raid at Budyonnovsk was primarily intended to force the Russians into negotiations, thereby buying time for the Chechen rebel forces, which, by June 1995, were in a desperate situation. And it worked. With armed clashes increasing in the autumn of 1995, Besayev may again have been playing for time by trying to frighten an already war-weary Russian public into supporting continued negotiations, rather than provoking them with nuclear terrorism.

Significantly, none of this background appears in subsequent discussions of nuclear terrorism, in which Besayev's device is seen solely as an incident of nuclear terrorism, confirmation of a trend, and a portent of worse things to come. The explanation here, of course, does not remove the label of terrorism from the incident, nor does it minimize the threat of nuclear terrorism. It does, however, take the terrorists in this particular case out of the realm of mindless fanatics and suggest that even terrorists make political calculations.

Chechen fascination with things nuclear seems to have continued during the ongoing Second Chechen War, although the evidence, as always, remains murky. In 1999, Russian security authorities in the Caucasus reported that they had discovered a container filled with radioactive material attached to an explosive mine hidden near a railway line. Chechen rebels operating in the area were the obvious suspects. In 2000, rebels reportedly stole radioactive material from the Grozny nuclear waste plant. And in 2002, the press reported that Chechen rebels had stolen radioactive materials from the Vogodonskaya nuclear power station, a claim the authorities denied.

In 2002, a team of forty Chechen rebels armed with explosives seized control of the Dubrovka Theater in Moscow during a performance and took more than eight hundred and fifty hostages. It was a spectacular coup. The Chechens threatened to kill the hostages unless Russia withdrew its forces from Chechnya. The standoff lasted for three days until, in desperation, Russian authorities pumped into the theater an aerosolized anesthetic that incapacitated the terrorists and their hostages. The authorities then sent in commandos. All but a few of the terrorists were killed, but 129 hostages also died from exposure to the gas. Of particular interest to us here is the fact that it was later learned that before settling on the theater as their target, the Chechens had reconnoitered the Kurchatov Nuclear Research Center. This was the same institute from which Aum Shinrikyo sought to recruit scientists for its nuclear efforts. Seizing control of Kurchatov would have provided a dramatic venue and a dangerous event, but the Chechens reportedly judged the security there to be too tight and chose the theater instead.

Notions of hijacking nuclear missiles, threats involving the dispersal of radioactive material, and the reconnaissance of nuclear facilities in Moscow by Chechen rebels are all viewed as confirmation of terrorist interest in acquiring nuclear weapons—which they are, to a degree. But the Chechen story also allows another conclusion, that is, that Russia's so-called loose nukes may not be all that loose.

Chechen rebels would appear to be the terrorist group best positioned to obtain a Russian nuclear warhead or fissile material. Along with the Russian mafia, they are frequently mentioned as likely intermediaries in al Qaeda's attempts to obtain nuclear weapons. And they have motives themselves. The Chechens see their rebellion as an existential struggle. They have been brutalized by two bloody wars. They are willing to kill in quantity, as they have demonstrated in a number of large-scale terrorist attacks. They would also seem to have capability. They live in Russia. They speak the language. The leaders have money. Reportedly, they have connections with organized crime. Some have served in the Soviet and Russian armed forces. They are well armed. They have a sophisticated knowledge of explosives. They have demonstrated their ability to move large, well-armed commando units through Russian lines, into the heart of Moscow itself. They are obviously willing to accept extreme risks, even willing to carry out suicide attacks. They easily exceed the designated threat used by the US Department of Energy to design security at US nuclear facilities. Indeed, the Chechens possess the rare combination of attributes seen in the wartime commando raids, terrorist assaults, and high-value heists that we will discuss later. In sum, they theoretically possess the psychological and physical wherewithal to execute a nuclear attack.

And yet, despite this, insofar as we know, the Chechens have not succeeded in acquiring a nuclear weapon or fissile material. They have made no overt assaults on Russian nuclear weapons storage sites that we know of. They have made no overt threats involving nuclear weapons, apart from dispersal devices. And they did not detonate the one dispersal device they had. Either the Chechens have decided that in the context of their conflict, going nuclear makes no sense, or getting nuclear bombs in Russia is not as easy as it looks.

BIN LADEN AND THE BOMB

Aum Shinrikyo's nuclear program lasted three years, from the cult's first contacts with Russian officials in 1992 to the arrest of its leaders in 1995. Al Qaeda's efforts to acquire nuclear weapons spanned nearly a decade even before 9/11, and they appear to have been more determined. Beginning in the early 1990s, Osama bin Laden began to look for ways to buy a nuclear weapon or acquire fissile material and the necessary expertise to build one. As usual, our information is incomplete.

Al Qaeda's nuclear efforts differ from those of Aum Shinrikyo and the Chechens in several respects. The Ismailovsky Park incident received very little news media coverage outside of Russia, and Aum's nuclear forays, not considered by most analysts to be very serious anyway, were overshadowed by its nerve-gas attack on Tokyo's subways. In contrast, al Qaeda's possible possession of nuclear weapons was the subject of widespread public speculation even before 9/11, and even more speculation in the wake of the attacks. The headlines appear increasingly certain that al Qaeda has nuclear weapons and are increasingly certain about their use. The titles alone tell the story: "Atomic device: Bin Laden is looking for a nuclear weapon. How close has he come?" "How close has bin Laden come to acquiring N-bomb?" "Can Osama bin Laden go nuclear?" "Bin Laden's nuclear connection." "Bin Laden and the bomb." "Al Qaeda has nuclear weapons." "Bush, Blair, warned of bin Laden nukes." "Bin Laden and Hiroshima." "American Hiroshima: al Qaeda plotting nuclear attack with weapons already in the U.S." "Al Qaeda: We will destroy New York in 35 days." "Al Qaeda threatens to nuke New York on February 2."

This public speculation makes it difficult to separate what we actually know through captured documents and the testimony of captured terrorists from surmise and speculation; from often sensational but unreliable media reports citing vaguely identified intelligence sources or experts; from even more sensational but dubious claims that al Qaeda already has nuclear weapons; and from al Qaeda's own communications, which are calculated to fuel the fear of nuclear attack.

Al Qaeda's communications are especially interesting because they lay out its rationale for the acquisition and use of nuclear weapons. That brings us to another difference: al Qaeda talks. No other guerrilla group or terrorist organization has devoted as much effort to public communications as al Qaeda has. To be sure, many terrorist organizations communicate. Germany's Red Army Faction wrote lengthy letters to the news media. The Symbionese Liberation Army, a tiny terrorist group that briefly plagued California in the 1970s, produced a number of bizarre, rambling screeds. Italy's Red Brigades issued lengthy strategic directives filled with impenetrable, mind-numbing prose, proving that even without guns and bombs, terrorists might still bore you to death. But al Qaeda is different. No idle chatter, al Qaeda's communications reflect its primary goal, which is to create an army of believers, spread its ideology, galvanize its constituents, radicalize its followers, recruit them to its cause, and incite them to action. Its activities and words are all dedicated to that goal. This is, of course, the classic theory of late nineteenth- and early twentieth-century terrorism: proselytization plus propaganda of the deed to explain, inspire, and instruct.

What we know about al Qaeda's nuclear efforts can be quickly summarized. Beginning in 1992, while still in Sudan, bin Laden transferred funds to Sudan's National Islamic Front (NIF), which controlled the state-owned Military Industrial Corporation. In return, the NIF provided "laboratory assistance," which analysts believed meant assisting bin Laden in acquiring advanced weapons.[23]

Then in 1993, bin Laden specifically appointed Mamdouh Mahmud Salim as his "point man" on nuclear weapons. Salim had little success. We know that in 1993, he tried to purchase enriched uranium. Con artists sold him low-grade reactor fuel instead.[24] Another al Qaeda operative, Jamal Ahmad al-Fadl, who was arrested for participation in the bombings of the American embassies in East Africa, turned witness for the prosecution and testified that in 1993, al Qaeda had a budget of $1.5 million for acquiring uranium. He said that he had been sent to meet a man outside Khartoum, a South African who was selling uranium, but that he did not know if any deal ever took place.[25] Al Qaeda's untrained buyers appear to have been the naive victims of repeated scams, buying radiological waste and even the mysterious "red mercury," the elusive compound found in the files of all seeking to clandestinely develop nuclear weapons.

A captured internal al Qaeda document, probably written in 1994, refers to Russia as a possible source, remarking that "jihadists can look forward to Russian gangs selling nuclear weapons and ultimately providing nuclear arms for the jihad."[26]

Al Qaeda's quest for nuclear weapons continued after bin Laden moved in 1996 to Afghanistan, where the organization had a safe sanctuary and was able to use the Taliban-run government to mask its weapons-development programs. According to one report, the Taliban tried to recruit a former Soviet nuclear weapons expert, but Russian authorities disrupted the scheme.[27]

Al Qaeda had greater success in recruiting technical assistance from Pakistan. Two Pakistani nuclear scientists have admitted that in August 2001 they met with Osama bin Laden, Ayman al-Zawahiri, and other al Qaeda officials and had long discussions about nuclear, chemical, and biological weapons. Both men were "long beards"–Pakistani scientists but also dedicated Islamic fundamentalists who were unhappy with Pakistan's secular political course. Bin Laden told the two that he was "intensely interested" in nuclear, chemical, and biological weapons and that he had or could get his hands on radiological material that had been somehow acquired by the Islamic Movement of Uzbekistan. Both scientists told bin Laden that it would not be possible to manufacture a nuclear weapon with this material.

The sympathies of the two men were well established. One of

the two men, Sultan Bashir-Ud-din Mahmood, had been pressured to resign from Pakistan's nuclear agency in 1999 because of his pro-Taliban and al Qaeda sympathies. He and Chaudiri Abdul Majeed were cofounders of Ummah Tameer-e-Nau (Reconstruction of the Muslim Community), an organization set up in 2000 to conduct relief work in Afghanistan but suspected of being a front for weapons acquisition. Both men saw Taliban-ruled Afghanistan as a model for Islamic government.

Mahmood also had a fascination with Koranic visions of doomsday and wrote a lengthy treatise about how the world would end. In another book on human destiny, Mahmood foresaw the deaths of millions from "mass destruction weapons, hunger, disease, street violence, terrorist attacks, and suicide."[28]

It is not clear how much advice or technical assistance the two scientists provided. Under interrogation by Pakistani authorities, both claimed that their discussions were purely academic, but others who know the case claim that they gave away secrets, including what one Pakistani official described as a "road map" for building a nuclear weapon that identified key technology and suppliers. The two men may also have facilitated al Qaeda's access to other disgruntled and potentially sympathetic scientists in Pakistan's nuclear program.[29]

The meetings with the Pakistani scientists took place just one month before 9/11. By November 2001, al Qaeda's leadership was on the run, leaving behind in Afghanistan a rich trove of documents—manuals, target folders, schematics, diagrams, records of meetings—which have provided further insights into the organization's nuclear efforts. The documents confirm al Qaeda's ambitions to acquire nuclear weapons but offer no evidence that al Qaeda had any success in its quest.

Some of the papers left in Afghanistan contained crude diagrams that describe the basic components of nuclear weapons. One hand-drawn diagram showed a design for a dirty bomb. A twenty-five-page handwritten document with the ominous title "Super-bomb" contained a general discussion of "various types of nuclear weapons, the physics of nuclear explosions, the properties of nuclear materials needed to make them, and the effects of nuclear weapons." It appears to have been not a blueprint but an instructor's lesson plan, perhaps the last class in a training course on explosives. According to a knowledgeable physicist who was asked to examine the document, it does not indicate the knowledge necessary to make a nuclear bomb. Although its author apparently understood general theory and even some shortcuts for making a crude nuclear device, critical steps are missing, and the diagrams in the document are simply not credible weapons designs—a bomb based upon them would merely have dispersed nuclear material, not produced a nuclear explosion.[30] Nor was there any other evidence that al Qaeda had fissile nuclear material or the essential technologies, or even that it knew all of the critical steps in manufacturing a nuclear weapon. Still, other documents indicate a curious mixture of technical knowledge and naive fantasy that is characteristic of al Qaeda thinking.

There also are persistent media reports that al Qaeda was able to obtain nuclear weapons from Russia. These rumors, which began in 1998, variously claim that through contacts with Chechen and Russian mafiosi or other Central Asian middlemen, al Qaeda was able to purchase nuclear warheads and "suitcase nukes."[31] These are small atomic demolition munitions that could be used to destroy bridges or other tactical targets. The reports describe al Qaeda purchases of from two to forty-eight suitcase nukes and more than twenty nuclear warheads, a nuclear arsenal larger than that of Pakistan or North Korea. There is no evidence to confirm these assertions—no subsequent finds and nothing reported from the interrogations of key al Qaeda officials captured since 9/11 (other than an exploratory effort to make a dirty bomb). However, those who believe that al Qaeda has nuclear weapons point out that despite numerous media warnings, Osama bin Laden's own boasts, and intensive intelligence efforts, al Qaeda's nuclear weapons quest remained largely unknown until the invasion of Afghanistan.

What the evidence found in Afghanistan confirms is ambition, not capability. Al Qaeda wanted a nuclear bomb and it was actively pursuing various paths to acquiring one. But there is no evidence that it has a nuclear bomb, has the material for a nuclear bomb, or knows how to make a nuclear bomb.

An American physicist who reviewed all of the evidence concluded, however, that before it was chased out of Afghanistan, al Qaeda was intensifying its nuclear weapon acquisition efforts and "would have likely succeeded, if it had remained powerful in Afghanistan for several more years."[32] Others have challenged this conclusion.

There is, of course, the possibility that the captured documents do not tell the whole story, that they were left behind to deliberately misinform those who would find them, indeed that al Qaeda had a secret effort, unknown to the authors of the documents that were discovered.

It is also possible that al Qaeda, as it fled the American-led assault, got away with most of the documents that, if captured, would have revealed evidence of its real nuclear capabilities. According to this theory, the documents found in Afghanistan were nothing more than the crude drawings and lesson plans of al Qaeda underlings who knew nothing about what would have been a compartmentalized project known only to a few. Or perhaps the documents left behind contained the information al Qaeda's leaders wanted us to find—enough to create fear, not enough to gauge actual progress.

Some would go further and assert that the US government, in fact, knows that al Qaeda has nuclear weapons but is concealing this knowledge to avoid creating public panic. That the government might conceal knowledge of a nuclear threat is not an unreasonable surmise. It has done so on a number of occasions.

In October 2001, a CIA agent code-named Dragonfire reported that al Qaeda had managed to acquire a ten-kiloton nuclear bomb that had been stolen from the Russians. This weapon, the agent said, had already been smuggled into New York City. The CIA had no independent confirmation of Dragonfire's information, and there were some doubts from the beginning, but the government decided to treat it as plausible. Certainly it could not be dismissed, especially just one month after 9/11. Nuclear search teams were deployed to secretly scour the city for traces of radiation, as they had been many times in response to previous nuclear threats. Those cases had not been publicized, and neither was this one. Not even city officials were informed. No bomb was found, and Dragonfire's report was later judged to be inaccurate.[33]

But the government's handling of the incident encourages speculation. Secrecy allows a handful of authors, despite the lack of evidence, to claim that al Qaeda not only has nuclear weapons but that it has already smuggled them into the United States. This raises the further question, If determined reporters can find out about al Qaeda's nuclear weapons, why can't the government? Is the government that hopelessly incompetent, or is it concealing what it knows? This takes us into the realm of conspiracy theories.

Our purpose here, however, is not to debate whether or not al Qaeda has nuclear weapons but to look at al Qaeda's motives in seeking them. Al Qaeda is especially interesting in this regard because it is the only organization that has publicly talked about its determination to obtain nuclear weapons and how they fit into its view of warfighting–al Qaeda has a nuclear policy.

Since bin Laden's early efforts to acquire material for nuclear weapons precede al Qaeda's public commentary, and since bin Laden's buyers were not privy to his thoughts about how the weapons might be used, we can only surmise his initial motives. What was Osama bin Laden thinking about in 1993 when he appointed a point man to pursue nuclear weapons? He was not then the leader of a global terrorist enterprise. The jihad in Afghanistan was over. The Soviets had withdrawn from the country. Those Arab volunteers who could return home had already dispersed. Bin Laden remained a dedicated warrior, but one without a war, or a country. Saudi Arabia had rejected his offer to lead an army of volunteers against Saddam Hussein after Iraq's invasion of Kuwait. With the Soviets no longer in Afghanistan, the ever-bellicose bin Laden had become an embarrassment to Saudi officials. He was given a one-way passport out of the country. Bin Laden briefly returned to Pakistan to organize a new group of volunteers to participate in the continuing fighting in Afghanistan, but he found that most of his followers there had transferred their loyalties to one or another of Afghanistan's local warlords. His former comrades bluntly told him that he was no longer a leader. His day was over. Pakistan was also eager to see these troublesome Arabs leave. Frustrated—and one suspects, crestfallen—bin Laden packed up and headed to Sudan, one of the few countries offering sanctuary to those Arab Afghan veterans who couldn't go home.

In Sudan, bin Laden was a businessman—a tycoon by local standards, whose business savvy and wealthy connections were welcomed by the government. But he never abandoned his ambition to lead a global jihad. While pursuing his business projects, he gathered around him a cadre of jihadist exiles and began rebuilding a global network of operatives. In his mind, Islam was in great peril. Part of Yemen, the home of bin Laden's own family, was then still ruled by infidel communists. Muslims were under assault in the Caucasus and the Balkans. Saudi rulers, whom bin Laden regarded as thoroughly corrupt, had committed the heresy of allowing the United States to station its forces in Saudi Arabia—

infidel troops soiling the holy land! As if that were not enough, in 1992, American troops began to arrive in Somalia. In bin Laden's view, they were sent not to ensure the delivery of humanitarian aid but to expand American control. Besieged Muslim fighters everywhere required assistance. Bin Laden would again build a base—al Qaeda. It would be the treasury, recruiting depot, and arsenal for jihad.

The Sudan sojourn from 1992 to 1996 was a period of organizational growth. Bin Laden collected money from sympathetic supporters. He gathered recruits, providing them with salaries and stipends. He launched a string of business projects, which could provide revenue for jihadist activities and cover for weapons acquisition. His quest for weapons of mass destruction began.

Bin Laden's instincts may have been solely entrepreneurial. He was making long-term investments in acquiring new weapons technologies, chemical, biological, and nuclear, without necessarily knowing which one might pay off or, if one proved successful, exactly how it might be used. This would be consistent with what we know about bin Laden's behavior. His strategic visions often have a grandiose quality. If an army of outgunned guerrillas drove the Soviet Union out of Afghanistan, what might a nuclear-armed jihad achieve?

Self-aggrandizement may also have been a factor. The mere possession of one nuclear weapon would make bin Laden's little army of exiles a force to be reckoned with. What power and prestige might flow from al Qaeda's possession of a Muslim nuclear bomb? After all, this was five years before Pakistan tested its own nuclear bomb. Possession alone would guarantee bin Laden's status as the leader of a global jihad—not some has-been political refugee who could be dismissed, exiled, and ignored.

As we have seen, this nuclear effort was unsuccessful. And bin Laden had not yet acquired the status he desired. Instead of becoming a powerful player in the Muslim world, bin Laden was forced to move again. Under pressure from Saudi Arabia, Egypt, and the United States, the Sudanese told bin Laden he had to leave the country. Furious, he had no choice. He and a handful of followers were allowed to return to Afghanistan in 1996, where he continued his campaign to incite a global jihad. In Afghanistan, bin Laden declared a holy war on the United States. His efforts to obtain nuclear weapons gained new urgency, while his subsequent public comments give us a window into how his thinking about nuclear weapons was evolving.

When India, a Hindu nation—an infidel nation in bin Laden's eyes—tested its nuclear bomb in May 1998, bin Laden used the occasion to rally the Muslim world. "We call upon the Muslim community in general, and Pakistan and its army in particular, to prepare for the jihad imposed by Allah and terrorize the enemy by preparing the force necessary for it. This should include a nuclear force to raise fears among all enemies led by the Zionist Christian alliance to overthrow the Islamic world, and the Hindu enemy of Muslim Kashmir."[34] Here, bin Laden endorses the notion of "the Muslim bomb." It was an argument advanced earlier by Pakistan's religious mullahs and by Pakistan's own government in order to elicit from Arab countries financial support for its nuclear weapons program: Pakistan's nuclear ambitions would serve not just Pakistan, but all of Islam. *Bin Laden saw the Muslim bomb as a weapon of terror. Possession, not necessarily use, would create fear among the enemies of Islam.*

Abu Walid al Misri, the editor of the Arabic-language magazine of the Taliban, provides further insights into al Qaeda's thinking about nuclear weapons. As quoted in Peter Bergen's *The Osama bin Laden I Know*, an informative collection of commentary by people who knew bin Laden personally, al Misri indicates that views among the jihadists differed. What he described as a hardline wing saw the necessity of obtaining weapons of mass destruction, including nuclear weapons, and prepositioning them in the

United States "to be used in a fast and direct response to any American aggression against Afghanistan." Then if the United States used weapons of mass destruction, it would "not escape a deadly destruction." But according to al Misri, others in the jihadist camp reckoned that any such weapons possessed by al Qaeda were likely to be primitive and limited in their destructive capability, tactical rather than strategic. Nonetheless, this group agreed to continue to call them "weapons of mass destruction" to create fear. These weapons "will give the mujahideen credibility, prestige, and psychological influence."[35]

Bin Laden's later public statements on the topic emphasize acquisition as a right and a religious duty and seem to indicate possession as a deterrent. In a 1998 interview, he said, "To seek to possess the weapons that could counter those of the infidels is a religious duty. . . . It would be a sin for Muslims not to try to possess the weapons that would prevent the infidels from inflicting harm on Muslims."[36] When asked in another interview shortly thereafter whether he was trying to acquire unconventional weapons, bin Laden repeated the Muslim-bomb argument: "Israel is stockpiling hundreds of nuclear warheads and atomic bombs. The Christian West controls a vast number of such weapons. Hence, we do not regard this as an accusation, but rather as our right."[37]

Except for incessant speculation in the news media, we heard little about al Qaeda's nuclear ambitions again until after 9/11. By that time, al Qaeda's bases in Afghanistan had been dispersed, its leadership was on the run, and its key operational planners were being picked off one by one. These circumstances would make it more difficult for al Qaeda to pursue a nuclear program, unless it could be done at some secret location, known to but isolated from al Qaeda's top commanders, where a small team of nuclear scientists, jihadist sympathizers, or handsomely compensated scientists-of-fortune could be working on bin Laden's bomb. Increased difficulties in acquisition, however, have not deterred al Qaeda from pursuing a communications campaign aimed at creating the impression that it has nuclear weapons.

MOTIVES SECULAR AND DIVINE

The case studies portray three leaders who differed in many respects but who also shared certain characteristics: Shoko Asahara—a paranoid psychopath pretending to be a god, obsessed with the end of the world; Shamil Besayev—a man whose family was wiped out in a brutal war, facing the possible annihilation of his entire tribe; Osama bin Laden—convinced that God is on his side, determined to punish the infidels for their aggression. All three, willing to contemplate violence on a grand scale, convinced of the absolute righteousness of their cause, desperate men, looking at the extinction of their cult, their community, their followers, their faith. All three, highly intelligent, cunning, calculating but at the same time capable of reckless behavior. All three, self-selected saviors, charismatic, skilled motivators of men, able to inspire extraordinary loyalty. Shoko Asahara is awaiting execution; Shamil Besayev was killed by a bomb; Osama bin Laden is a hunted man.

Adding what we know about Aum Shinrikyo, the Chechens, and al Qaeda to the earlier incidents of "nuclear terrorism" suggests a complex array of motives, which appear to fall into two broad categories: the secular and the divine. The difference between the two is whether one's perspective is the here and now or the hereafter.

Secular motives are characteristic of groups that have concrete political goals serving definable and geographically discrete constituencies and affecting territory that they occupy now or would like to control in the future. Nuclear weapons are seen by these groups as legitimate and legitimizing. They are in the arsenals of the world's most powerful nations, which have threatened to use them if compelled; they are deterrents and a means of retaliation. Conceivably, nuclear weapons also could be used as instruments of coercion to gain specific concessions or to force policy changes.

Nuclear weapons are sources of prestige. They are equalizers. In the 1970s, Palestinian groups argued that if Israel has an atomic bomb, Palestinians also must have one. A similar argument was advanced in support of Pakistan's nuclear weapons program. If Christians, godless communists, Jews, and Hindus have nuclear weapons, so must Muslims.

Nuclear weapons are seen as guarantees against extinction. The argument that no state (or group) possessing nuclear weapons will ever be wiped off the map has even been used by some national governments. In sum, secular terrorists see nuclear weapons in much the same way national governments do: possession is useful; use is to be avoided.

The flip side of avoiding extinction is instigating extermination—or genocide. Those who are motivated by racial hatred, even if it is expressed in secular ideologies, sometimes invoke Providence and apocalyptic images to justify mass murder. They speak of nuclear weapons in terms of use, not possession.

Divine—that is, nonsecular—motives characterize groups like Aum Shinrikyo. These are paranoid cults, God-fired fanatics. Al Qaeda's thinking, as we shall see, has evolved from secular motives—prestige, power, deterrence—to divine motives. "Divinists" see nuclear weapons as instruments of ultimate destructive power, of divine revenge and retribution, a trigger for Armageddon, the showdown between good and evil, a final reckoning, a prerequisite to renewal. For the divinists, acquisition means use, not possession. The objective is mass murder. Mass murder, however, as we shall see, provokes debate even among terrorists.

Chapter 4
SELF-IMPOSED CONSTRAINTS

Seemingly ordinary people appear to have an amazing capacity for imagining black deeds–and an even more amazing desire to share the dark creations of their fertile imagination. Almost every time I have spoken to an audience about terrorism, someone has approached me afterward to tell me what he would do if he were a terrorist. Schoolteachers, retired executives, college professors, librarians–all, one presumes, peaceful, law-abiding members of the community–become rivals of the likes of Abu Nidal and Khalid Sheikh Mohammed in their machinations. Sometimes, the ideas they present are spontaneous thoughts provoked by the topic of discussion, but often they are plans to which their authors obviously have given some thought. Their ostensible purpose is often stated to be to enable me to warn the authorities of (unthought-of or unrealized) vulnerabilities, but I doubt that this is really the case. If I ask these individuals a question or two, they seem to derive great pleasure from describing in delectable detail how they would put the operation together, pull it off. Psychologists are aware of this fascination with transgression, violence, violations of moral codes, the frisson that comes with playing at evil. There is a tiny armchair terrorist in all of us.

It is a Dionysian talent that seems to develop with maturity and literacy. Young people, having narrower experience, produce dull, brutal scenarios; fortunately, most terrorists are young. In many cases, the schemes proffered would not work for purely technical reasons or because they are simply too complicated—their success would depend on assembling a perfect team of equally determined, highly intelligent terrorists. In some cases, these ambitious schemes would not work because in the length of time it would take to put them together, at least one or two of our thinking terrorists would likely have second thoughts, flinch at the horror of the endeavor, and wittingly or subconsciously sabotage the enterprise. Mad scientists—murderous fanatics with high technical skills—are precious talent. They rarely come in groups.

Determined efforts by government-sponsored teams to mimic terrorist thinking and planning usually produce the same result: lots of plausible attack scenarios, few feasible ones. Referred to variously as "red cells" or "black hats," or in one more imaginative case, the "Evil Genius Workshop," these teams bring together terrorism analysts, scientists, military planners, science fiction writers, and other novelists—all imaginative thinkers to think as terrorists might to plan terrorist operations. They thereby give observers possible insights into terrorist planning processes and possible vulnerabilities in our defenses that might have been missed. In nondescript locations in Virginia, amid sandwiches and soda cans, they plot scenarios of the nation's destruction. Often the participants are organizational mavericks who find personal satisfaction in making their more conformist superiors sweat.

Often the results of such exercises are classified at a level above what I have access to—officially, I am not cleared to see what I thought. But the team participants are invariably more creative, more diabolical than real-life terrorists, most of whom by comparison are unimaginative dullards. Some of the operational plans proposed reflect the extraordinary technical knowledge of the participants. Some, in my view, are highly creative but underestimate the complexities of implementation. But some schemes are simple, truly frightening, and doable. So why haven't terrorists done these things?

In my 1975 essay, I noted that even those we have labeled terrorists did not do everything they were capable of doing. Technological limitations and operational difficulties aside, terrorists have operated within self-imposed constraints. What I wrote in 1975 was, "Terrorism is theater, terrorists want a lot of people watching, not a lot of people dead."[1] Very little that I have written since has been so often quoted in or out of context.

I sometimes try to capture the essence of an idea in a single phrase. These epigrams may begin or finish a complex train of thought. With repetition, the capsule phrases acquire an axiomatic quality, which they do not deserve. The original thought was longer and more tentative.

There is a great deal of popular mythology about terrorists. They are frequently described as mindless killers, almost in the same category as mass murderers who run amok in a homicidal rage, but in 1975, that did not describe most terrorist groups. Terrorists do kill, and frequently they deliberately kill those who in other forms of combat would be regarded as innocent bystanders. Such violence is indiscriminate, seemingly wanton, but not mindless. In 1975, incidents of terrorist mass murder were rare.

Simply killing a lot of people is not the primary objective of terrorism. The killing of few or many must have purpose. Terrorism is a calculated campaign of violence intended to create an atmosphere of fear and alarm, which in turn causes people to exaggerate the strength of the terrorists. Terrorists purposefully target innocent civilians, not just because they are easy targets but in order to draw attention to the terrorists' existence, demonstrate capability, inspire constituents, create a sense of insecurity, drain resolve, scare off investment, polarize opinion, and provoke over-reactions that will alienate the public.

Since most groups employing terrorist violence are inferior to their foes by conventional measures of power, the violence they carry out must be all the more shocking. Terrorism is violence for effect. The real targets are not the victims but the audience.

The *notion of self-imposed constraints* even on the part of those we label terrorists has provoked an intense debate, one that continues years after 9/11. The debate therefore merits further elaboration.

Terrorists have always had the capacity to kill more people than they have killed, without resorting to exotic weapons, but for some reason they have chosen not to. Why? Terrorists don't always agree on where the red lines are, but there are red lines. Over time, we have learned what these are.

For some terrorists, it is a matter of morality. They see killing innocents, women and children, for example, as wrong. But innocence can be an elastic term. Terrorists debate what constitutes innocence. If Israel or Cuba is the enemy, are countries or companies that trade with these nations legitimate targets? Are tourists who visit these countries, thereby implicitly recognizing their existence or their governments, contributing to their economies with their tourist dollars, guilty of support, and therefore legitimate targets? If the policies of a particular country are the source of the terrorist grievance, do the voters who elect the country's government—the authors of its policies—share culpability? What about voters who vote in the minority?

In the end, terrorists tend to conclude that there are few or no innocents. That doesn't mean that everyone is guilty and should be targeted. It means that those who happen to become victims are guilty principally because they have become victims. A cynical assertion, to be sure, but the very fact that terrorists feel obliged to legitimize their violence indicates concern about morality, or at least about their image.

Contemporary jihadist terrorists deal with this issue by seeking a fatwa, or authorization from a religious figure. Fatwas are usually general rulings, but jihadist terrorist cells may seek religious approval for specific operations.

Self-image is another factor. Wanton murder could tarnish a group's image. Terrorist groups pretending to be armies must try to behave like armies, not like savages. In the early 1970s, some groups avoided kidnapping for ransom, as opposed to kidnapping to make political demands, because they worried that ransom kidnapping would make them appear as ordinary criminals. Some groups would not kidnap at all. Some groups adopted formulas. For example, it was okay to kidnap the ambassador or a corporate executive, but not to kidnap an embassy secretary or a CEO's grandmother. Can fellow workers, coreligionists, members of one's own constituency be killed if necessary to achieve the terrorists' strategic goals? Even within extremist circles, attacks aimed at slaughtering civilians–the 2005 London subway bombing, for example–have been criticized as unmanly.

Terrorists worry about group cohesion. Decision making in terrorist groups is often done by committee, and not all of the members might have the same appetite for carnage. Going too far risks betrayal.

Not alienating perceived constituents is another major consideration. Terrorists imagine themselves to have legions of supporters. They also see themselves as the vanguard of violence, which not all of their perceived supporters might understand or approve of. Slaughter risks losing support–sympathy, contributions, potential recruits. The IRA had to calibrate its bombing campaign against how its American sympathizers might perceive it. Too much carnage could cause contributions to decline.

Terrorists also worry about provoking a reaction that might

enable their government foes to launch massive crackdowns with popular support, or to take retaliatory measures that would endanger the terrorists' own constituency. Terrorists seeking independence or autonomy—future control of a piece of territory—may not be interested in permanently destroying the economy of that territory, contaminating its environment, or generating a cause for permanent vendetta. In sum, most terrorists seek some kind of victory, not the apocalypse.

Operational considerations always govern terrorist violence. Terrorists want every operation to succeed. In a curious way, they are risk-averse, not with others' lives and not always with their own lives, but operationally they are conservative. Failure diminishes their reputation, perceptions of their prowess as warriors, their virtue. More concretely, failure, as any politician can tell you, erodes support. Therefore, terrorists tend to avoid uncertainty and stick to proven tactics, which tend to be less grandiose.

Even those who are motivated by religious fervency, convinced that they have God's mandate to kill, willing to sacrifice their own lives, worry about success. Unconstrained by morality, they nonetheless seek God's approval. In a belief system where God intervenes in battle to reward the faithful, success of an operation confirms God's approbation. Failure of an operation, likewise, suggests God's disapproval. Terrorists want to make sure that things will go right. Suicide bombers get only one try—tactical success is imperative even when survival is not.

It seemed to me in 1975 that larger organizations with national political aims and identifiable constituencies were the most likely to make political calculations, and inherent in these are political constraints. These large organizations were also most likely to have the capacity to carry out complex and sophisticated operations, including building and delivering a nuclear bomb.

The same constraints might not apply to small bands of extremists with nihilistic ideologies, unconstrained by fears of alienating world opinion. It is conceivable that a small band of conspirators might, in the name of some vague objective–the creation of a new world on the ashes of the old, the ignition of a race war, the creation of a master race of survivors–entertain the notion of carrying out an extreme act of violence based upon the possession of nuclear weapons.

An essential component of such a group's philosophy would permit the negation of human values, allowing widespread and indiscriminate murder. The group might claim divine inspiration (or at least tacit approval by God to destroy the wicked or the weak) or adherence to a racist ideology that would permit genocide.

Those most willing to undertake acts that cause widespread death and destruction–the occupants of mental institutions–might be the least able to do so, although one must be careful here. In 1974, the Alphabet Bomber carried out a bombing campaign in California on behalf of "Aliens of America," an imaginary group of which he was a member. His purpose, he indicated, was to protest America's treatment of foreigners–he was an immigrant– and the sexual taboos in Southern California. Since nobody could think of any sexual taboos among consenting adults in California, this was the first clue that he had mental problems. In fact, he had been arrested for sexual misconduct at taxi-dance halls. He was later diagnosed as paranoid schizophrenic.

He planned to spell out Aliens of America in bombs–hence the nickname Alphabet Bomber–beginning with a bomb at Los Angeles International Airport that killed four persons. With "A" standing for airport, his second device was placed in the lobby of a bus terminal–"L" for lobby. Although he was clearly insane, when he was apprehended, police found in his laboratory the formula and ingredients for a nerve gas and plans for attacking the state capitol building in Sacramento. If he had been successful in dispersing nerve gas, he could have killed scores, possibly hundreds, making the point that insanity does not always mean lack

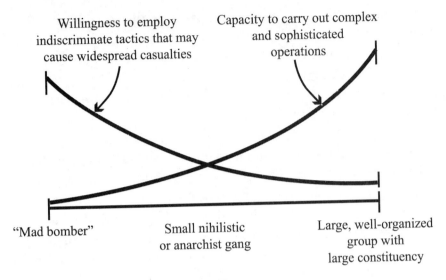

Figure 2

of capability. Nor does it necessarily preclude a madman from becoming the head of a powerful sect or even a head of state.

Still, I felt that there was a rough inverse correlation between a group's capability and its willingness to engage in the murder of thousands. I thought smaller groups with nihilistic aims and little popular support might be willing to use weapons of mass destruction to take the lives of thousands but probably would lack the resources to do so. Larger terrorist groups that were more likely to have the resources to undertake more serious nuclear actions were also more likely to be more cautious.

In 1975, I tried to express this in another set of freehand curves.

The curves do not remain stationary over time. Nuclear weapons could become more accessible. In the 1970s, the world looked ahead to a dramatic expansion of nuclear energy, which could create a significant trade in nuclear material—in fact, fissile material—if nuclear energy moved in the direction of breeder reactors and fuel containing plutonium, as many had anticipated. Increased commercial traffic in fissile material could have led to diversion and the nuclear black market that so many feared.

Or nuclear weapons might become more accessible as a consequence of nuclear proliferation. In the late 1970s, analysts worried that the world of the 1990s might include twelve or twenty nuclear weapons states. More states with nuclear weapons would also have increased the possibility of theft by terrorists or the diversion of a weapon to terrorists.[2]

In both cases, the assumptions were wrong. Nuclear power did not expand exponentially as forecast, and the number of nuclear weapons states did not rapidly multiply as feared. Instead, the Soviet Union collapsed, leading to worries about the security of its vast nuclear arsenal and fears that terrorists could steal a nuclear weapon or buy one from corrupt officials.

Nuclear weapons could also become more accessible through some kind of design breakthrough that would make them easier to build or would reduce the amount of fissile material required to build one. One such material, the mysterious red mercury, was advertised as something that could make any tin-pot dictator or well-heeled terrorist group a nuclear power. But did it even exist?

Any of these developments would push the "X"–the crossover point where intentions and capability met–toward the "mad bomber." It would raise the capability line–more actors could become nuclear terrorists.

Or something could happen that would increase motivation and reduce self-imposed constraints. This might be a worldwide resurgence of ethnic conflict in which genocidal strategies would become more common or (as I indicated in the 1975 paper) the emergence of large groups claiming divine inspiration.[3] These developments would raise the intention line. More actors, including large organizations, might be willing to commit nuclear terrorism. This is exactly what happened.

CONSTRAINTS ARE NOT IMMUTABLE

The self-imposed constraints of terrorists were not universal or immutable. Different groups adopted different codes of behavior. Some groups bombed only symbolic targets—embassy walls, corporate headquarters at midnight—deliberately avoiding casualties. IRA terrorists sometimes, but not always, gave warnings when their bombs were likely to cause casualties. When casualties resulted, they blamed authorities for not heeding the warnings, indicating sensitivity to being blamed for deaths. Other groups were less fastidious, more bloodthirsty.

Within groups, members often debate about how far to go. Tensions exist between the fanatic ideologues who see the use of terrorist tactics strictly in terms of utility, the "soldiers" who derive personal status and self-esteem from participation in acts of violence and who therefore are committed to their continuation, and the thugs who find personal satisfaction and therefore strategic argument in ever-escalating slaughter.

Leaders who counsel caution for strategic reasons find themselves in a traitor's trap, outflanked by more-ruthless challengers who equate conviction with bloodshed. Because it is difficult to be seen as moderate in any organization of extremists, the leadership is often obliged to go along with the thugs or risk losing control. Any evidence of constraint prompts the ruthless wing to hive off and go its own bloody way. Over time, the harder men prevail, and the constraints erode.

Chapter 5
NUCLEAR COERCION: JUST HOAXES?

"**A**nyone who has something like . . . [a nuclear weapon] has enough power to make the Chancellor dance on a table in front of a T.V. camera. And a few other statesmen along with him. That is an I.O.U. of ultimate power." The quote comes from a clandestine 1978 interview with Michael "Bommi" Baumann, a member of Germany's anarchist Red Army Faction.[1] It was an adolescent boast, of course, but Baumann's remark reveals how terrorists—and most analysts in the 1970s—thought terrorists might employ nuclear weapons if they managed to obtain them.

At the time, the majority of terrorist attacks were bombings, and most of these were symbolic acts of violence with few or no casualties. However, one out of every five international terrorist events was a hostage incident—a kidnapping, airline hijacking, or barricade-and-hostage episode, like the 1972 Munich incident in which Palestinian terrorists seized members of the Israeli Olympic team, or the 1975 takeover of the German embassy in Stockholm by members of the Red Army Faction. Hostage incidents caused visible crises for governments, which were forced to make life-

and-death decisions to either yield to the terrorists' ultimatums or risk the murder of the hostages.

When the first terrorist hijackings and kidnappings occurred in the late 1960s, most governments were inclined to meet the terrorists' demands in order to save lives. In 1968, for example, Israel released prisoners it held in exchange for the release of passengers aboard a hijacked El Al airliner. (This was the first airline hijacking with political demands.) The urban guerrillas who kidnapped the American ambassador to Brazil in 1969 demanded that Brazil release fifteen of their imprisoned comrades. The US government urged Brazil to do whatever was necessary to protect the US diplomat, which the Brazilian government planned to do anyway to blunt international criticism that it was a harsh military dictatorship. The exchange was made, and the ambassador was released. This pattern would be repeated three more times in Brazil, with kidnapped diplomats from Japan, Germany, and Switzerland.

As the terrorist tactic of hostage taking spread, however, governments began to harden their positions, although not without consternation and debate. The kidnappers of the British ambassador to Uruguay in 1970 were unable to budge either the Uruguayan government or the British government, which stood firmly behind its refusal to meet the kidnappers' demands. Eventually, some of the prisoners whose release was demanded escaped. The British ambassador was released after nine months of captivity.

In 1973, Black September terrorists took over the Saudi Arabian embassy in Khartoum during a reception and threatened to kill the American ambassador and his deputy, along with the Belgian chargé d'affaires, unless Israel released prisoners and the United States released Sirhan Sirhan, the convicted assassin of Robert F. Kennedy. Such an exchange was unthinkable, and at a press conference President Nixon announced publicly that the

United States would not yield to terrorist blackmail demands.[2] The three hostages were murdered, thereby sealing American policy in blood. By the mid-1970s, most governments had adopted hard-line no-negotiations, no-concessions policies.

Dealing with these hostage situations gave authorities experience in bargaining tactics. The tactics were aimed at buying time and wearing down the resolve of the hostage takers. Hostage episodes grew longer, and hostage takers tried to improve their positions by taking larger numbers of hostages, whom they threatened to kill one by one if their demands were not met.

No government could stand idly by while bodies were being tossed out of windows. If governments would not yield and terrorists would not give up, at some point, action was necessary to end the episodes with force, despite the obvious risks to the hostages. The attempt to rescue the Israeli athletes held hostage at the 1972 Munich Olympics proved disastrous. In a bloody shoot-out at the Munich airport, all of the hostages and most of the terrorists were killed. This tragedy prompted the German government and others to train highly specialized commando units to rescue hostages. The Israelis were the first to successfully rescue hostages, when in 1976 they carried out a daring rescue of passengers aboard a hijacked Air France airliner held in Uganda. It could easily have gone wrong, with slaughter as the result, but it was a smashing success. The following year, German commandos rescued passengers held aboard a hijacked Lufthansa airliner in Somalia. In 1980, British commandos rescued hostages held by terrorists at the Iranian embassy in London. Unfortunately, the American attempt to mount an ambitious military operation to rescue fifty-two hostages held at the American embassy in Tehran failed.

Nonetheless, as a result of improved security and growing refusals by governments to let hijacked airliners land on their territory or give safe passage or sanctuary to terrorist hostage takers, along with tougher negotiating postures and an increased willingness to send in commandos, hostage seizures were becoming more difficult and more dangerous for the terrorists. *To maintain their coercive power, they would have to look for ways to escalate.*

One way of escalating was to take more hostages and prepare for a long siege. The 1990s witnessed some huge hostage situations. In 1996, terrorists in Peru took over the residence of the Japanese ambassador during a party, seizing hundreds of hostages and holding them for 126 days until they were successfully rescued in an armed assault. As noted earlier, Chechen terrorists seized nearly two thousand hostages at a hospital in Budyonnovsk, Russia, twelve hundred children and teachers at a school in Beslan, and more than eight hundred hostages at a theater in Moscow. The Russian government negotiated a resolution of the Budyonnovsk incident, but in Beslan and Moscow, hundreds died in botched rescue attempts.

Armed rescue was an option when the authorities knew where the terrorists were, had them surrounded, and would accept the risk of casualties among the hostages. But what if terrorists were able to hold an entire city hostage with a nuclear bomb? That would escalate terrorism into a new domain.

For most government policy makers and analysts in the 1970s and early 1980s, though, terrorism was still a sideshow. The cold war, nuclear strategy, and proliferation dominated national security concerns. Terrorists were a nuisance, not a major concern. Dealing with them was left to a small cadre of specialists, the same sort that, despite America's withdrawal from Vietnam, continued to muck about in insurgencies and other forms of low-intensity conflict. It was a swamp with no name located somewhere between law enforcement and proper war.

But the thought of nuclear terrorism, of terrorists holding cities hostage, did attract the attention of a handful of cold war warriors, who may have considered ordinary terrorists well beneath their job description but found the idea of terrorists armed with nuclear weapons well worth their attention. Unlike most analysts of terrorism who came from liberal arts or behavioral science backgrounds, these were very methodical scientists and mathematicians. They easily assumed the role of a terrorist adversary bent upon bringing down the country and foresaw a future generation of high-tech terrorists who would engage in sophisticated sabotage of America's vulnerable infrastructure, who would use chemical and biological weapons, who would hold cities hostage with nuclear weapons. They were the apocalypticians. With malicious glee, these armchair extortionists ran their own Manhattan Project of mayhem filled with ingeniously crafted scenarios designed not merely to destroy the economy but to create exquisite pain for those in charge of government, or, as Robert Kupperman, the chief scientist at the Arms Control and Disarmament Agency from 1973 to 1979, once put it, scenarios to make the White House fibrillate.

One occasionally sensed personal motives at play here. Although individuals of achievement, and in some cases, high office, these wizards of vicarious doom patently enjoyed using their wits and imagination to make the cocky, backslapping, sports-minded, brachycephalic politicos they worked for sweat in their tailored suits. It was the revenge of the nerds.

Bob Kupperman was one of these masters of invented malevolence. I had no doubt he, with his doleful countenance, basset eyes, and deep baritone voice, would deliver the keynote address at the banquet preceding Armageddon. After listening to him speak of sarin, ricin, anthrax, and the Marburg virus, teaspoons of which could kill half the population of a large city, audiences would be reluctant to touch their food. It was in the nuclear domain, however, that his intellect glowed.

Although he was sometimes labeled an alarmist, the country is indebted to him. He was ahead of his time. His warnings had purpose. He compelled a reluctant government, albeit sometimes with exaggeration, to pay more serious attention to terrorism, shunting what small funds were available to him to terrorism research. He identified vulnerabilities that the Department of Homeland Security is grappling with today. Long before 9/11, or letters filled with anthrax, or worries about hijacked supertankers or vessels carrying liquefied natural gas, Kupperman had considered all of these, had described them in detail, and had gamed them against skeptical colleagues.[3]

I didn't always agree with his almost-exclusive focus on the uppermost registers of terrorist violence, a focus that became almost advocacy. I often pointed out that most terrorists were a dull lot, not brilliant mad scientists. If Kupperman had become a terrorist, then we would have been in real trouble; fortunately, he was on our side. But he undoubtedly elevated the debate, and he and I remained good friends.

Nuclear blackmail became a new domain of inquiry for Kupperman and others. Strictly speaking, it was not "blackmail," which involves extortion based upon the threat to expose some wrongdoing by the target of the demands. It was nuclear extortion—demands based upon a nuclear threat. Nuclear blackmail simply had a nice ring to it.

By then, terrorists understood the potential. Baumann's 1978 interview took place after several unsuccessful attempts by German terrorists holding hostages to exact concessions from the German government. Baumann realized that the terrorists "have to do something that will work for sure, and what else can that be except the ultimate thing [exploding a nuclear device]. But [he added], an attack on a [nuclear weapons] storage depot is more likely."[4] In other words, possessing nuclear weapons would enable terrorists to crack the resolve of the government. With nuclear weapons, terrorists could make an offer that no government could refuse.

Terrorists with a nuclear weapon would seem to have all the advantages. National authorities could not sacrifice a city. Nor could the government threaten retaliation if terrorists were to detonate a nuclear device. Terrorists held no territory. They had no populations to protect. Seemingly, they had no vulnerabilities. Nuclear coercion was the ultimate nightmare scenario.

It became the scenario of numerous government-sponsored simulations—war games in which government officials were pitted against terrorists armed with nuclear weapons. I helped put together some of the scenarios. On one occasion, I played the role of the president. More often, I was on the terrorist team.

The games revealed that nuclear coercion was more difficult to carry out than it looked. Even assuming that the terrorists had already overcome all of the operational and technical obstacles to stealing or fabricating a nuclear weapon and clandestinely delivering it to its intended target, they still faced the difficult task of establishing their credibility. They had to persuade skeptical authorities that they did have a bomb and that they would use it. Providing diagrams and photographs of nuclear devices alone might not suffice. A well-informed graduate student might get the design right, but that didn't prove the terrorists actually knew how to build a working device or that they had the necessary fissile material.

An accurate diagram and a detailed plan of construction might indicate that the terrorists had the know-how, but it was harder to prove that they had a working device. Even if the terrorists provided a small sample of their precious fissile material, authorities might believe that the sample was all the material they had, not the fifty kilograms of highly enriched uranium most weapons designers consider the minimum for a primitive but workable homemade device.

Proven possession of a stolen nuclear weapon would establish credibility of possession, but not proof that terrorists could bypass "the permissive action links"—technology that would destroy the device without a nuclear explosion if it were tampered with.

Smaller atomic demolition munitions might have less or no such protection, which is why so much attention has been devoted to the so-called suitcase bombs.

Determined to get past all of this and to the main issue of bargaining against nuclear blackmail, architects of the games adjusted the scenarios to provide the terrorists in the game with a credible nuclear capability. This could most easily be demonstrated by directing the authorities to an intact bomb or exploding a nuclear device in a remote area, then threatening to detonate a second one in a populated area. That, of course, would oblige the terrorists to have at least two nuclear devices, a still more daunting accomplishment, while it allowed stubborn holdouts on the government team to argue that the demonstration device would be the terrorists' only weapon and the second was a bluff. But eventually they were obliged to concede that terrorists might have the capability that they claimed. How then would the two sides negotiate?

Fascinating debates arose among the pretend terrorist players about whether the terrorists' coercive communications should be clandestine or public. Publicly communicating a nuclear threat would cause national alarm in the threatened country and could lead to public panic, perhaps spontaneous evacuation, which itself could become a major source of casualties. But while it might increase pressure on the government to yield to the terrorists' demands, it might, at the same time, make it more difficult for the government to publicly surrender, especially with things already going bad. Therefore, some of the pretend terrorists reasoned, they would have a better chance of having their demands met if they communicated their threat and demands privately. Then government could find a way to signal compliance—coded public messages—and quietly meet the demands. Exactly how the terrorists would ensure that their communication would reach only top decision makers, establish their credibility, and make their demands without the story leaking was never clear.

The next big problem for the terrorists was what to demand. Making presidents or prime ministers dance atop tables on national television might be fun, but it would accomplish nothing. Springing some imprisoned comrades hardly seemed worth a nuclear weapon. A huge ransom—the plot of a James Bond novel—raised issues of how the terrorists would take delivery. A change in national policy seemed more commensurate with a nuclear threat, but policy changes were hard to enforce. What if the government yielded under intense pressure but then reversed itself once the threat was removed?

That turned out to be the most difficult problem of all. Terrorists not only had to convince the government that they could and would detonate their nuclear weapon if their demands were not met, they had to persuade the government that they would remove the threat if the demands were met. Simply promising not to detonate it was not enough. Trust didn't work here. If the government could not absolutely verify disarmament, it had no incentive to yield to the demands. Why should the government give in only to find itself faced with new demands from terrorists who would still be holding a city hostage? What began as coercive bargaining became a matter of governance. Either the government would run the country or the terrorists would.

It was equally difficult for the terrorists in the scenarios to give up their nuclear weapon, which was their only means of enforcement and their only protection. Even if they were willing to do so, it would be difficult to convince the government of their sincerity. In matters of mutual distrust, a third-party guarantor can sometimes play a role, but what country or entity would be willing to take possession of a terrorist nuclear weapon and continue to enforce the terrorists' demands?

The games had different endings. Sometimes the government yielded. Sometimes the terrorists kept their promise. Often the negotiations broke down, and the terrorists ended up detonating their device. Nuclear coercion was not effective. In national strategy, the possession of nuclear weapons was useful as a deterrent. As instruments of coercion, nuclear weapons were far less effective.

If there were any lessons to be learned from these exercises, it was that nuclear coercion didn't work very well. Whatever their original intention, terrorists armed with a nuclear weapon were likely to use it. That put increased emphasis on prevention through better security, but also on preemptive action to prevent terrorists from acquiring nuclear weapons in the first place.

Of course, we have no knowledge of terrorists running their own exercises to work out the dilemmas of nuclear coercion, despite Baumann's dark fantasies. We do know that no terrorist organization of his era attempted to coerce governments on the basis of claimed possession of weapons of mass destruction. There were no bluffs. Terrorist coercive strategy was inherently just that: The terrorist campaign would continue with conventional weapons until the terrorists achieved their objectives. But it was never refined beyond that—at least through the 1960s.

Beginning in the 1970s, however, a number of nuclear threats emanated from other quarters. They apparently began with the 1970 hoax in Orlando, Florida, although it is difficult to believe that there had been no such threats in the quarter century since the bombing of Nagasaki.

Let us ponder the possibilities. It is possible that until the use of nuclear energy began to expand in the late 1960s, there was little public discussion of nuclear issues, at least at the local level. But public debate could then have prompted threats. It is true that some of the threats received had an antinuclear theme. It is also possible that growing terrorism in the 1970s excited those on the edge of mental stability to take action, or at least to take up their pens. Or it is possible that the increase in nuclear-threat messages reflected growing public discussion of the threat of nuclear terrorism itself. In tracking mentions of nuclear terrorism in the media at the time, I was initially intrigued to find articles in the Middle East press, only to subsequently discover that these were no more than discussions of Ted Taylor's own warnings. As noted earlier, Taylor was one of the first to call public attention to the possibility of nuclear terrorism. Our concerns had created a public discourse; we were listening to ourselves.

Or it may simply be that those who were the most precariously balanced mentally were the most sensitive to the new anxieties about nuclear terrorism, and they expressed themselves in communications that were consistent with their own disorders. In addition to the threats and hoaxes, we also began to see an increase in scams involving nuclear material and stories about the mysterious red mercury. *The crazies and the criminal fringes of a society are the weathervanes of its worries and vulnerabilities.*

All of these explanations assume that no (or few) nuclear-threat letters were received prior to 1970, and that the increase reflected a change in the environment. But there might be an additional explanation.

It is possible that many threats were received prior to 1970 but were simply dismissed by local authorities as crackpot letters not worthy of reporting or recording. Only when growing terrorism and mounting concern about nuclear security issues brought such threats to the attention of the FBI did the federal government set up special procedures to deal with them. In other words, the apparent increase, which began in the 1970s, after the Orlando incident, may merely reflect better reporting. It is not that an increase in nuclear threats produced increased concern, but rather that increased concern produced an ostensible increase in communicated threats.

The Orlando threat was easily dismissed as an obvious hoax. But the possibility of nuclear material becoming more available as a consequence of expanding nuclear power programs and knowledge of nuclear weapons design no longer being confined to a handful of men caused authorities to worry about the day when they might receive a threat that could not be readily dismissed.

As a precaution against this type of threat, a nuclear emergency search team (NEST) was formed in 1975 to conduct secret searches for hidden nuclear weapons and to investigate any devices that were found. To assist authorities in assessing the credibility of threats where no devices could be found, in guiding negotiations, or in rendering devices safe, a separate credibility assessment team was created later. It comprised six separate teams. Four teams assessed the technical and operational aspects of the threat: technical jargon, diagrams, any samples of material sent by the author of the threat. Two teams separately assessed the behavioral aspects of the threat, attempting to profile the author demographically (origin, level of education, professional training) and psychologically (mind-set, intent, mental stability). Members of all six teams were on call twenty-four hours a day, summoned when needed to make a rapid assessment of any threat received. The teams worked independently and could not see the initial assessments of the other teams until they had submitted their own assessments. Usually, a consensus was achieved easily, but in some cases there were sharp differences.

In the early years, one behavioral team was established at the RAND Corporation in Santa Monica, California, under the direction of Dr. Joseph Krofcheck, a psychiatrist with long experience in criminal investigations and the behavioral aspects of intelligence operations. A second behavioral team operated out of Syracuse University in New York under the direction of Dr. Murray Myron, who had developed psycholinguistics, a technique of profiling based on the use of language. Later, the Syracuse team was disbanded and the Santa Monica team relocated to Virginia, remaining under Krofcheck's direction.

Criminal profiling was still in its infancy at the time, and the kind of behavioral profiling done by the teams in Santa Monica and Syracuse was new territory. The team members were creative and eccentric. The Santa Monica team, on which I served, was particularly eclectic. Unlike the Syracuse team, which worked using an established method, the Santa Monica team was charged with the dual mission of researching analytical approaches to behavioral assessment and providing assessments when cases arose. We dismissed no angle.

Krofcheck developed a method of "interviewing" an unknown author as he might interview a patient. His assessment was based upon observed behavior—appearance, dress, comportment—except that in this case, the communicated word was all we had to go on. Konrad Kellen, another of the RAND team members, was an expert in psychological operations and propaganda analysis. Another member, Peter Tripodes, developed a system called psycho-logic, which he used to match characteristics of speech with personality traits. Others brought knowledge of criminal behavior and terrorist operations. We looked at paper, postmarks, presentation, placement of words on the page, peculiarities of foreign-born speech or regional idioms, even handwriting, for what it might tell us about the author. We monitored the press for articles that might inspire communications and we compared patterns of communication in threat letters with patterns of communication in known hoax messages.

I read every nuclear terrorist novel, first to see how novelists might solve some of the problems inherent in nuclear coercion. How did their villains establish credibility? What did their villains demand? How did they take delivery or enforce continued compliance? These were all problems that, as we have seen, real-life nuclear terrorists would face. We also reckoned that the novels themselves might inspire similar threats, so we tracked fictional plots and the technical information they provided. Piles of dog-eared, highlighted paperbacks filled my office. It paid off. One threat was lifted directly from a recently published novel.

Some of the assessment techniques remain classified, as do the assessments themselves, but the results were often extraordinary. Even when they are concealing their identity, people communicate a great deal about themselves in the way they communicate. At the same time, the analysis comprised as much art as it did science. The process depended not only on techniques but also on the breadth and variety of experiences of the team members themselves, their remarkable empathy, their gut instincts.

In attempting to flesh out the profile of one actual threat author, Krofcheck opined that he was "fortyish." This was too much for me—I worried that we would destroy our credibility by this sort of extravagant guess. Krofcheck patiently explained to me why the man—the author was definitely a male—could be neither much older nor much younger, based solely on what could be distilled from his communication. I reluctantly agreed that the estimate of age could be included in our assessment, but only if it was labeled as a long shot. The author was later apprehended, in large measure based on information provided by the behavioral analysis. He was thirty-nine.

Of the nearly one hundred nuclear threats received in the decades following the Orlando incident, all but two were apparent hoaxes, apparent in the sense that no perpetrators were ever arrested or nuclear devices ever found. We cannot say with absolute certainty that their authors did not have the capability they claimed, but they were, in fact, fairly obvious hoaxes. Someone who demands that a briefcase be filled with a billion dollars in tens and twenties probably lacks the mental faculties to construct a nuclear bomb.

The two incidents that were not hoaxes were also not difficult calls, because neither involved fissile material. In one case, the author had stolen low-enriched uranium; it posed little hazard to public safety, and the perpetrator was arrested. In the other case, the author of the threat did not claim to have a nuclear device, but he claimed to have built an extraordinary conventional explosive device–a doomsday machine that could not be deactivated but could, for a multimillion dollar ransom, be rendered safe enough to move to a remote location to detonate. The device itself had been secretly delivered to a casino in Stateline, Nevada. While bomb specialists attempted to defuse the device, real-life behavioral teams were given the letter that had been left with it. It was an utterly convincing communication. The analysts had no doubt that the device was the huge bomb its author claimed. The attempt to defuse it remotely failed, and the resulting explosion destroyed a large portion of the casino and the hotel, which had been evacuated. Nobody was harmed. The perpetrators were arrested years later.

The hoax threats of the 1970s and 1980s fell into three broad categories according to their motives. Many of the nuclear threats we examined were merely *expressive*. The authors wanted to make a statement on some issue of national or international concern: nuclear disarmament, opposition to nuclear power, opposition to the war in Vietnam, and so on. Concerned, angry, frustrated, determined to be heard, these authors chose to wrap their grievance in a nuclear threat, thereby at least guaranteeing an audience.

Some of the hoaxes were *disruptive*, intended to create trouble. These were examples of the common bomb scare escalated to the nuclear level. The authors had no expectation that their demands would be met, but they derived some satisfaction from knowing that they might have frightened some people and that they at least imposed a cost on their foes.

Many of the hoaxes were *coercive*. The authors believed that by threatening nuclear destruction they could terrify the recipients into meeting their demands, many of which consisted of the delivery of a cash ransom. Not the clearest of thinkers, the authors often had trouble with the amounts they wanted. Their demands were either far too low, far less than it would cost to build a nuclear bomb, or far too high to be realistic. Again, asking for a billion dollars to be placed in a briefcase does not win points for credibility.

Many of the hoaxes evidenced obvious mental disorders: disorganized, illogical, grandiose, paranoid ramblings of individuals overwhelmed by events around them, threatening to level cities while making impossible demands, deriving satisfaction from the sense of power gained by associating themselves with nuclear destruction. Few of the authors were ever identified. Half of those who were identified were mental patients.

These were one-time messages. The authors seldom included in their messages any means of further communication, even if the target of the demands happened to be willing to comply.

Their devices were "A-bombs," "H-bombs," "Plutonium bombs," without further details, although in one case, the author described a trigger for nuclear fission, using words taken verbatim from a recent novel.

Many of the authors of the hoaxes claimed to be members of actual terrorist organizations or of groups (that clearly existed only in their heads). Claiming membership in a group was a ploy to increase credibility and power, or in some cases, it was entirely imaginary and reflected mental disorder. None of the authors was believed to be actually associated with a real terrorist group.

This raises the question of whether real terrorists ever bluff. In some cases, they do. During the IRA's bombing campaign, the organization would sometimes increase the disruptive effects of its attacks by planting a few actual devices and simultaneously calling in numerous threats. With credibility established by the real bombs, none of the threats could be ignored. The tactic snarled transportation systems and exhausted responders. Too many hoaxes, however, would have risked loss of credibility, which the IRA wanted to maintain. Overuse would also increase the risk that authorities might ignore an actual warning, leading to heavy civilian casualties, another outcome the IRA often wanted to avoid. The Chechens who planted the dirty bomb in Moscow and then notified the news media were also more interested in creating fear than causing casualties. What we can say for sure, though, is that terrorist incidents invariably inspire hoaxes by *others*: wannabes, copycats, malicious pranksters, individuals who for various motives want to incite disruption, share the "glory," or exploit the moment to pursue some personal agenda.

Bombs still do most of the talking, but terrorism has become more sophisticated than it was during the IRA's campaign. The jihadist enterprise spawned by al Qaeda is a global operation. It speaks in many tongues through many media, although most of its communication is on the Internet. In addition to the official announcements from al Qaeda Central's top hierarchy, its affiliates provide a vast second tier of broadcasts, bulletin boards, shared files and Web sites, and chat rooms that are fueled by and elaborate upon the messages from the top. Within this cacophony of exhortation, strategic debate, threats, boasts, and warnings, there are clandestine communications that deliver actual instructions to and among jihadist operatives. Add to the sum of these communications intelligence reports from thousands of sources and you have the chatter that is continuously monitored by intelligence services and private counterterrorist Web sites for clues to future terrorist operations.

With so many communicators, so many outlets, and so many middlemen, all with their own agendas, it is difficult to distinguish boasting that is intended to make al Qaeda's leaders appear powerful and their followers feel good from intelligence deliberately passed through informants and public communications aimed at rattling nerves, creating alarm, and diverting intelligence resources down false paths. Some of the communications may also be deliberate disinformation introduced by actors other than al Qaeda.

But because the 9/11 terrorist attacks so firmly established al Qaeda's credibility, which has been maintained by the continuing jihadist terrorist campaign, it is difficult to dismiss any of its threats.

The effects of the jihadist communications can readily be seen in the public responses to them: government warnings, visible increases in security, the proliferation of talking heads on television to instantly assess the latest threat. Al Qaeda has become increasingly effective in waging this war of nerves. Its leaders have learned the power of communications. They have increased the frequency and improved the production quality of their messages. They know that whatever they say will be elaborated upon and reinforced by thousands of jihadists. They can set a story running virtually assured of its coverage and they use this capability to keep their potential targets on edge.

As one intelligence analyst noted, "al Qaeda Central uses its propaganda to incite terrorist attacks by any 'homegrown' radicals . . . it creates a 'feeding frenzy' that migrates to the al Qaeda affiliates and supporters who are being electronically monitored" by intelligence services.[5] Through leaks and official comments, concerns raised by the elevated chatter work their way into the news media, where they generate further speculation and alarm. Seeing this inspires even more chatter. The result is terror unconnected to any specific operational planning.

A wave of threats in the summer of 2007 provides a perfect example. A US National Intelligence Estimate released in July indicated that al Qaeda had regained much of its operational capacity and remained determined to pursue its terrorist campaign against American targets abroad and in the United States.[6] This conclusion was underscored in an assessment prepared by the National Counterterrorism Center. The terrorist threat to the US homeland remained serious. Tension increased with new tapes from Ayman al-Zawahiri and Osama bin Laden, who had not been seen in a videotape for more than a year.

Reacting to the increased volume of threats, Secretary of Homeland Security Michael Chertoff said in an interview with editors at the *Chicago Tribune* that he had a "gut feeling" that something was up.[7] The secretary's "gut feeling" provoked a wave of questions: What was behind it? What did it mean? Nearly six years after the 9/11 terrorist attacks, was the secretary's gut feeling the best intelligence we had? Although I was not aware of what specifically had agitated Secretary Chertoff, I found myself defending his gut feeling on principle. The opposite of a gut feeling, I pointed out, was "credible and specific intelligence," which was rarely available. And when authorities did have specific intelligence, they could take specific actions to thwart the terrorist attack. Experienced intelligence analysts often reached beyond the bits and pieces of intelligence on display to fathom when something might be up. They did so on the basis of their knowledge and experience, but also on the basis of instincts and gut feelings. Physicians and street cops often do the same.

Richard Clarke, the national security adviser for terrorism in 2001, said that the intelligence community did not know that nineteen terrorists had moved in to hijack four airplanes and planned to crash them into the World Trade Center, the Pentagon, and the White House, but he and CIA director George Tenet became increasingly convinced in the summer of 2001 that something was up, so much so that Clarke said Tenet "had his hair on fire."[8] Decision makers should have paid more attention to Mr. Tenet's hair. Gut feelings are no substitute for good intelligence, but they have a legitimate role in its analysis.

On August 1, 2007, an al Qaeda Web site jangled American nerves with the promise of a "big surprise" that would occur.[9] The threat did not specify the nature of the surprise, but the accompanying visual showed a montage of President Bush with then-visiting Afghan president Hamid Karzai and Pakistani president Pervez Musharraf against the backdrop of a White House in flames.

Jural Aviv, a self-proclaimed former agent of Israel's Mossad, added to the country's worries by announcing on Fox television that jihadist terrorists would attack the United States within ninety days.[10]

This was followed on August 5 by a lengthy video broadside from Adam Gaddahn, the American-born spokesman for al Qaeda, warning that American embassies would be attacked. Gaddahn did not say where, but a separate voice on the tape spoke about Russia, India, and Israel.[11] Threats of terrorist attacks against American embassies were nothing new, and Gaddahn, although an intriguing figure, was no bin Laden. His diatribe quickly became old news.

This, in turn, provoked a remonstrance from an al Qaeda Web site, warning against the "error of failing to take seriously the videotape . . . of American al Qaeda spokesman Adam Gaddahn." Said the message, "They will soon realize their mistake when American cities experience quality operations."[12] Other jihadists joined the chorus, but although one mentioned the Gaddahn message, there was no connection or coordination between them and the center. They merely expressed irritation that Gaddahn's message had not received the attention it merited.

Another message then followed, saying that the Gaddahn attacks would be carried out "by means of trucks loaded with *radioactive* material against America's biggest city and financial nerve center."[13] That meant New York, but a third message broadened the field, mentioning New York, Los Angeles, and Miami as targets. "The attack, with Allah's help, will cause an economic meltdown and a financial crisis on a scale that compels the United States to pull its forces out of many parts of the world, including Iraq, for lack of any other way of cutting down costs."[14]

Taken as a whole, this parcel of communications reveals a great deal about how al Qaeda works and the role that nuclear terror plays in its communications strategy. Gaddahn's videotape threatened no specific action. Rather, it identified targets that should be attacked: American embassies in three countries. It was an incitement to others.

The jihadists look for a response to their missives. They don't want to be ignored. They want to see us sweat. Therefore, they reinforce the communications from al Qaeda's leadership with their own threats. These are more explicit, but diverse. Each author adds his own scenario–burning down the White House, promising a quality operation, contamination of America's financial center with radioactive material, attacking three cities–all consistent with established al Qaeda themes, but all different from the leaders' exhortation and from each other. Each would be categorized as an expressive message–a determination to be heard, an opportunity to express anger in a favorite violent scenario, the mere description of which provides the author with some measure of satisfaction. This is virtual jihad, unconnected with capability or operational planning. The overall effect is intended to be disruptive, to provide visible evidence of fear and alarm.

The warning that Gaddahn must be taken seriously, the promise of a "quality operation," and the introduction of radioactive material into the discourse are intended reinforcements that, in fact, achieve the opposite effect. They are the characteristics of hoaxes. The description of the dire consequences that will result– the White House in flames, an economic meltdown–are further indications of an empty threat. A man holding a gun does not need to tell his victim the effects of a bullet on human flesh. And whether the economic meltdown caused by a catastrophic terrorist attack would provoke Americans to attack jihadists with greater ruthlessness or persuade them to withdraw from the Middle East in order to avoid further attack cannot easily be forecast, but withdrawal from Iraq and Afghanistan to cut costs betrays naive thinking.

Al Qaeda's leaders are calling for action. The authors of the threat messages are responding with verbal volleys that lack credibility. However, that does not mean the terrorist threat can be dismissed. The high volume of chatter, which certainly existed in the summer of 2007, is an indicator of the level of agitation within the jihadist hive that can result in attacks by local terrorist cells. We cannot doubt the intentions or the capabilities of al Qaeda adherents to carry out some kind of attack. And, these messages apart, within the buzz there may be communications among suspected conspirators that provide clues to imminent attacks. Moreover, the continuing flow of videos and messages, resulting in heightened concern, official warnings, and media speculation, keeps the country on edge. Even with a high proportion of dismissed threats, the overall campaign of terror works.

Chapter 6
DESIGNING THE THREAT

In the late 1970s, the newly created US Department of Energy asked the RAND Corporation to conduct research on the attributes of individuals who might carry out criminal attacks on nuclear programs–that is, of energy and weaponry. "Criminal attacks" covered a broad range of actions–sabotage of nuclear facilities, theft of nuclear material or nuclear weapons, illicit sale or purchase of nuclear material, threats involving improvised nuclear bombs or nuclear dispersal devices, even nuclear hoaxes. What capabilities were these criminal adversaries likely to have? What sorts of resources would they be able to mobilize? How would they carry out their operations? Would they come over the walls, guns blazing in an open assault, or would they attempt to recruit insiders with money or threats?

The results of RAND's research were delivered to Sandia Laboratories in Albuquerque, New Mexico, which was charged with developing the procedures and technology to thwart nuclear attacks. Essentially, RAND would design the threat, and Sandia would figure out how to defeat it.

A small multidisciplinary team was assembled at RAND to

conduct the research. The project attracted researchers from throughout the organization—the "free radicals" who were not deeply ensconced in other ongoing research programs. Although most of them came from backgrounds in history and the behavioral sciences, the team included area specialists with knowledge of the Middle East and Latin America, mathematicians, game theorists, engineers, strategic analysts, economists, and computer jockeys, most of whom had been involved in RAND's research on terrorism. It was an eclectic group—RAND prefers the term *multidisciplinary.* If there was one shared attribute, it was eccentricity. The team included former soldiers, an artist, a poet, a psychiatrist, and a devotee of new-wave self-enlightenment techniques. It was creative, innovative, and inherently subversive. In addition to producing a set of reports that the Department of Energy acknowledged had determined the characteristics of its designated threat, the team also won permission to print the first-ever RAND report with an illustration on its cover—an astonishing bureaucratic achievement. The cover depicted a compartmentalized head, of the type once typically displayed by phrenologists to depict which parts of the brain contained criminal tendencies, but in this case, the brain was segmented into various nuclear icons. It was about motives.

The team also forced, to the great consternation of the corporate management committee, the inclusion, for the very first time in a RAND publication, of the word *fucking,* quoting one terrorist bomber who in an interview about why he had chosen to blow up a particular bank, answered that the building "was so fucking ugly, it had to go." RAND discreetly adopted the newspaper formula, printing it as "f——." While the members of the team thought it important to accurately convey the capriciousness of the terrorists' target selection, this was at the same time the kind of confrontation with the front office that team members relished. The "victory" was much celebrated.

But the eccentricities of its RAND researchers did not diminish the value of the work or the import of its conclusions. How does one profile the capabilities of an adversary that has not existed in real life? Had there been a history of nuclear crime, we could have done case studies. Fortunately for society, we still had little real history of nuclear terrorism. To the best of our knowledge at that time, no nuclear installations in the United States had been attacked, seized, or seriously sabotaged. No nuclear weapons had been stolen or illegally detonated. No nuclear materials had been taken by force and used for blackmail or made into bombs. No radioactive material had been maliciously released. A few low-level incidents had taken place abroad, but it was not much upon which to build a profile of the adversary.

So we began by collecting and examining several hundred incidents of criminal, terrorist, and paramilitary actions that in some way could be seen as analogous to nuclear incidents. The analogues included high-value heists—the spectacular burglaries and armed robberies that provide scenarios for exciting movies like *The Thomas Crown Affair, The Great Train Robbery,* or the *Ocean's 11* series. In real life, these types of crimes demonstrate good intelligence, thorough reconnaissance, often inside assistance, sometimes years of planning, high technical competence, and precise execution. At the same time, the perpetrators show little inclination to accept a high risk of capture or death. These attributes mirrored many of the terrorist operations of the day. That was to change.

We also looked at terrorist assaults on other nonnuclear targets in which highly dedicated individuals were willing to accept great personal risks. Unlike the criminal elite, terrorists were quick to brandish weapons and explosives and were ready to kill, but they rarely assaulted well-defended facilities where the probability was high that they would be defeated before even reaching their objective.

We looked at small-scale military commando raids as well. This was the only category of incidents in which well-armed, specially trained, highly dedicated task forces attacked defended targets, usually with the intent of destroying them. When used as national efforts in wartime, the commando raids were generally informed by the best intelligence available, and the participants trained for weeks–or months. They had the element of surprise and they succeeded close to 80 percent of the time.

We also looked at industrial sabotage, which, because it was carried out by hostile employees or former employees, utilized insiders' access and knowledge. We looked at symbolic bombings, incidents of arson, and campaigns of violence waged by mad bombers. And we examined whatever nuclear incidents were available.[1]

Using this information, we built a database of attributes, and from this, we constructed both a typical composite profile and a high-level composite profile. The typical composite was something defenders had to be prepared to handle. We had observed this combination of capabilities in action. The high-level composite was a combination that we hadn't seen in real life: a well-trained, highly disciplined, heavily armed squad of suicidal engineers and physicists. The objective of security became to force potential adversaries into the realm of unprecedented combinations–and to prepare for them in advance.

The attributes likely to be possessed by high-level adversaries suggested that physical barriers might delay an attack, but by themselves they were not enough to defeat one. Well-armed guards, ready to shoot, had to be a component of the defenses. Guards had some deterrent value, but a response that depended too heavily on external reinforcements to prevent adversaries from reaching their targets or that relied on containment after attackers were already inside would not deter the most-determined attackers. They had to be stopped before they reached their targets.

Predictable security routines and responses were dangerous.

Skillful attackers would observe and identify these and determine how to obviate or defeat them. Attackers invariably exploited predictability. Other research confirmed that predictable security had little value.

Conversely, uncertainty caused the biggest problem for attackers. It was hard to overcome guard forces whose immediate strengths and routines could never be confidently ascertained, technologies whose function and capabilities could not be fathomed, as well as built-in mysteries.

This principle of unpredictability extends beyond security systems and may help to explain why we haven't seen terrorists using more exotic weapons despite the apparently obvious attraction they have for them. The effects, results, and reactions of such weapons are not as predictable as tried-and-true tactics, and therefore the exotic options increase the odds of operational failure or unforeseen consequences. Terrorist organizations tend not to have a high tolerance for failure.

The study of operational attributes tells us nothing about motives. Who was likely to go after nuclear targets or utilize nuclear material? Was nuclear crime likely to attract organized crime? What would nuclear terrorists try to achieve? Was there a relationship between the adversary's motives and his capabilities?

To get a better understanding of motives, we again had to reach for analogous events. We looked at ideologically motivated villains (terrorists); we looked at economically motivated villains (ordinary criminals and organized crime); we looked at psychotics (mad bombers); we looked at hostile employees; and we looked at individuals who were opposed to nuclear energy or weapons.[2]

Antinuclear extremists were of particular interest because in the two years between the report on attributes and the report on motives, the debate about the growth of nuclear energy programs had intensified. This was in the wake of the 1979 accident at the Three Mile Island nuclear power plant in Pennsylvania, along with the debate about new nuclear weapons being deployed in Europe. The numbers of antinuclear protests, incidents of low-level sabotage, and nuclear-threat hoaxes had all increased. This demonstrated that the threat was affected by the current social and political environment.

To some, the accident at the Three Mile Island reactor must have seemed similar to the 1979 movie *The China Syndrome*, which had a strong antinuclear theme (although, in fact, the incidents were not similar). In the movie, an employee at a nuclear power plant desperately tried to warn the public that the reactor was unsafe and could go critical, resulting in a meltdown of the core, which would burn through the center of the earth–the "China syndrome." The real-life accident at the Three Mile Island power plant resulted in a small release of radioactive steam. The release posed no significant danger to the public, but poor communications by authorities fanned media speculation and allowed people to infer that they were in peril. In fact, when the reactor itself was opened up several years later, it was discovered that half the core had melted. Had the situation gone on unchecked for as little as a half hour, hundreds of tons of melted uranium could have breached the pressure vessel leading to a powerful steam explosion and major radioactive release. The Three Mile Island episode became a lesson in how not to manage a crisis. It seemed to confirm the premise of the movie, thus also confirming its credibility. To many critics of nuclear energy, that, in turn, lent credence to the movie's portrayal of nuclear industry officials as being willing to resort even to murder to conceal the shortcomings of the industry and its danger to society.

Suspicion that industry and government officials might not be telling the public what they knew further fanned anxieties about possible adverse effects on the health of those living anywhere near Three Mile Island, as well as the dangers to those living near any nuclear power plant. Conspiracy theorists were quick to allege a cover-up. Halting nuclear power became even more urgent. With lives at stake, extreme measures were felt to be justified.

Some went further, alleging that the Three Mile Island incident was not an accident but an act of sabotage. Under the headline "Sabotage by Bizarre Cult Suspected in Three Mile Island Crisis," the *National Enquirer* ran a story alleging that the sabotage had been carried out by "the maniacal leader of a bizarre cult and his zombie-like followers." (There was no evidence to support the allegation, but ironically, the story anticipated by sixteen years the revelation of the Aum Shinrikyo cult's efforts to obtain nuclear material and its nerve-gas attack on Tokyo's subways.)

We foresaw terrorists moving in two possible directions. First, and more likely, terrorist actions might be intended to appeal to opponents of civilian or military programs, whom the terrorists might regard as a potential constituency. Such actions could include sabotage of nuclear facilities under construction to delay their becoming operational, attempted takeovers of nuclear sites to demonstrate danger and inadequate security, and actions against executives or security officials at nuclear facilities. Left-wing extremists in Germany and separatists in Spain and France provided examples. The Basque ETA terrorist organization waged a campaign of sabotage and terrorism against a nuclear power plant under construction in Iberduero. When access to the facility itself became more dangerous, owing to the deployment of Spanish Civil Guard units to protect it, the ETA terrorists switched their sights to the facility's engineers and executives, warning that they would kill any company men who set foot on the site. After a year of staying off the premises, an engineer went to the site and was promptly murdered. Ultimately, the construction project was abandoned.

Attacks by terrorists aimed at appealing to the antinuclear crowd had significance beyond what they achieved tactically. They proved that terrorists were sensitive to the social and political environment. Terrorists with broader political agendas discerned that the growing public debate about nuclear energy had awakened deep anxieties about things nuclear, which terrorists could exploit to gain attention for themselves. Moreover, they could inspire greater terror by operating in the nuclear domain. *It wasn't necessary to acquire a nuclear capability; it sufficed to have a nuclear backdrop.*

Concerns about nuclear energy had provoked strong opposition. Many in the antinuclear movement were too young to have participated in the antiwar movement during the Vietnam War and saw the nuclear issue as a cause into which they could channel their idealism and energy. The movement also included many veterans of previous "Ban the Bomb" marches of the 1950s and 1960s and the anti–Vietnam War movement of the 1960s and 1970s–determined peace "warriors" willing to confront authority and, in some cases, go further. Terrorists adjusted their targeting and rhetoric to appeal to this new constituency. But the constituency also limited terrorists' actions. Antinuclear activists might applaud sabotage of a nuclear facility, but they might be turned off by an attack that caused widespread casualties.

The 1980 RAND report on motives speculated that while some political terrorists might court antinuclear constituencies, others might view nuclear terrorism as a means of increasing their coercive power. We believed in 1980 that the moral and political constraints that dissuaded most terrorists from mass murder still applied, but we recognized that the conventional terrorist tactics– bombings, assassinations, kidnappings, hijackings, and other hostage seizures–seemed to be losing their effectiveness. That could have persuaded terrorists of the need to escalate their violence, although going nuclear would represent an immense leap and was likely to appeal only to the individual crazies, who had no capability, or to the most fanatical groups, those with more-millennial aims as opposed to a concrete political program. That trend would become manifest in the subsequent decade.

Chapter 7
BLACK MARKETS

The nuclear black market is a world of shadows where bomb-seeking fanatics hook up with Chechen gangsters, the Russian mafia, and rogue scientists; where terminally cynical Dutch, German, British, and South African businessmen pretend not to know that the strategic components they sell to distant unknown buyers through discreet middlemen are intended for the construction of nuclear weapons. It is a network that stretches from once secret Russian cities through Vienna, Sofia, Prague, Kiev, Munich, Johannesburg, and Dubai, on to Karachi, Tehran, Tripoli, and Pyongyang.

It is a global supply chain that runs from Russia and South Africa through Europe, Central Asia, and Middle Eastern entrepôts to secret locations in Pakistan, India, Iran, North Korea, and perhaps Afghanistan. This is the popular perception of the nuclear black market and the one that authorities fear will someday provide terrorists with a nuclear bomb. Nuclear black markets are a key component of most scenarios about nuclear terrorism, providing the principal route of access by which terrorists are believed to have acquired, attempted to have acquired, or may attempt to acquire nuclear weapons or material.[1]

Theoretically, terrorists could acquire a nuclear bomb in several ways. They could steal a weapon from the arsenal of an existing nuclear power themselves. A sympathetic government that has nuclear weapons or a sympathetic rogue element within a government could provide them with one. They could buy one on the black market. Or they could build their own. Each of these options presents its own difficulties.

Overt theft is a popular scenario with novelists and screenwriters. The 1994 movie *True Lies* featured Arnold Schwarzenegger chasing nuclear warheads that were stolen in Kazakhstan. The problem with overt theft is that nuclear weapons are usually well protected. It is true that there were concerns, especially during the chaotic decade that followed the breakup of the Soviet Union, that corrupt officials, impoverished employees at weapons plants, and unpaid soldiers had seriously eroded the level of security and made outright theft an easier proposition. Given the widespread economic desperation and cynical greed, facilitated by a collapse of belief in communist ideology, in government, and in the Soviet Union itself, the theft might be organized by high-ranking insiders, as it had been in the majority of sophisticated burglaries and high-value heists postulated by the RAND Corporation.

Insiders, however, would still run very big risks, far greater than pilfering tiny amounts of fissile material. Helping terrorists steal a nuclear bomb is no petty crime. Even in a corrupt country, the penalty would be severe. And once terrorists had the weapon, they would have every incentive to cover their trail, beginning with eliminating their confederates.

Another problem with overt theft is the likelihood that it will trigger an alarm. Authorities will know a weapon has been stolen and will make every attempt to recover it. In fact, the United States in the 1970s and 1980s, fearing theft of a nuclear weapon by terrorists, worked out procedures and protocols for hot pursuit even across international borders, and the two superpowers, before the Soviet collapse, had begun to explore how they might cooperate in case of a lost nuclear weapon. An intense international search would also impede subsequent delivery of the stolen weapon to its intended target.[2]

Again, in post–Soviet Russia, there was concern that corrupt officials might exploit the absence of strict controls to deliberately disguise the loss of a nuclear weapon. Then, outside of the conspirators themselves, no one would know.

Yet another problem with stealing nuclear weapons is that many have additional protection in the form of devices to prevent their being used by unauthorized persons. Initially, these devices were crude, little more than combination locks, but over time they became more sophisticated. Permissive action links were built into nuclear weapons to prevent their being activated for use. Any attempt to tamper with the weapon or extract its nuclear core would trigger its self-destruction in a nonnuclear explosion.

Here again, however, vulnerabilities persisted. It was by no means certain that all nuclear weapons—especially all of those in the Soviet arsenal—had this protection. Reportedly, small atomic demolition munitions, so-called backpack or suitcase bombs, may not have had the same protection. It was also possible that terrorists might go after weapons that were under construction, being serviced, or decommissioned and therefore without their protective devices. And it is not clear what kind of built-in protection, if any, nuclear weapons had in other known or suspected nuclear powers. Finally, it is possible that with inside knowledge and sufficient time, terrorists could "pick the locks"—that is, bypass the permissive action links and render the bombs usable.

That's theory. What do we know? Although reports arose that Chechen rebels reconnoitered Russian nuclear facilities and weapons shipments, to our knowledge, there have been no armed assaults to acquire nuclear weapons in Russia or elsewhere. "To our knowledge" is the operative phrase.

Terrorists could also try to steal–Bonnie and Clyde style–plutonium or highly enriched uranium from a nuclear facility. As with the case of nuclear weapons, facilities holding quantities of fissile material sufficient for a weapon are likely to be well guarded, although again there have been major concerns about the adequacy of security in Russia. There are also numerous research facilities around the world, which hold smaller quantities of highly enriched uranium. Their security in many countries is inadequate. Not all would have sufficient material for a bomb, in which case, several thefts would be required. To reduce this route of acquisition, a program to recover this material is currently in place.

Terrorists could also try to hijack a shipment of plutonium or uranium in transit. This scenario appears in several novels and is given some credibility by one publicized case in which the German freighter *Scheersberg*, carrying two hundred tons of uranium oxide, was taken over allegedly by Israeli commandos and its cargo diverted to Israel. The incident suggests that the anticipated expansion of nuclear energy and resulting traffic in mixed oxide (plutonium and uranium fuels) could increase the opportunities for theft in transit.

Terrorists could also be given sufficient amounts of highly enriched uranium or plutonium by a state patron or by rogue elements within a state. This, however, seems less likely than a state arming terrorists with a nuclear weapon. As outlined below, the potentially grave consequences for the donor state would be the same as providing terrorists with a nuclear weapon, but with less certainty that terrorists receiving the material would be able to fabricate a weapon.

The widespread notion that a sympathetic government might turn over a nuclear weapon to terrorists also merits closer examination. It would require a government to take enormous risks. During the cold war, both superpowers waged war through proxies in what was then called the Third World, materially assisting their proxy avatars. But despite mutual accusations of supporting terrorism, the idea that either superpower would turn over a nuclear weapon to guerrillas or terrorists was absurd. The cold war was a tightly managed contest, with calibrated escalations, not a reckless adventure.

The greater fear was that new nuclear weapons states or suspected aspirants like North Korea, Iraq, Libya, or Iran, all of whom were already identified as state sponsors of terrorism, would sell or give a nuclear weapon to terrorists for them to use as a mode of surrogate warfare. The record of state sponsorship of terrorists lends little support to this thesis. It does not fit the pattern of what we have seen. Apart from bumping off troublesome exiles, or each others' diplomats during war, even state sponsors of terrorism have become more cautious when engaging in larger-scale, higher-risk operations.

North Korea relied on its own well-trained, highly disciplined agents, not terrorists, when it attempted to blow up the president of South Korea and his entire cabinet during a visit to Burma in 1983, and again when it planted a bomb that brought down a South Korean airliner in 1987. Iran sent its own agents to assassinate the former prime minister of Iran in Paris. And it still appears that Libyan agents—government officials, not terrorist surrogates—placed the bomb that brought down Pan Am 103.

Equipping terrorist surrogates with a nuclear weapon means turning it over to an organization not entirely under state control and whose reliability is not certain. The terrorist group may be infiltrated by foreign intelligence. The terrorists may not be competent. Giving them a nuclear weapon almost certainly means use, exposing the state sponsor to retaliation. Providing rockets and tactical missiles is one thing—providing nuclear weapons seems quite another.

If Iran, for example, assuming it eventually acquired a nuclear weapons capability, were willing to risk retaliation, possibly nuclear retaliation, why would it entrust a nuclear mission to unguided terrorists? Even if it were confident the device could not be traced directly back to Tehran, it would still run the unavoidable risk that if a nuclear device went off in Tel Aviv or Tampa, Iran might be attacked anyway.

More realistic and therefore more worrisome is the possibility that rogue elements in a government might turn over a nuclear weapon to terrorists or use it themselves to coerce their own government or provoke a nuclear confrontation. This is the plot line of a number of novels and screenplays where crackpot missile commanders or mad generals, outraged by détente, are determined to set off World War III. The possibility, however, was taken seriously enough on the US side. Fred Iklé led a pioneering effort at RAND to persuade the US government to develop protective measures to prevent an accidental or unauthorized nuclear detonation of nuclear weapons.[3] This eventually led to the implementation of fail-safe procedures that prevent the use of nuclear weapons without presidential authorization. The Soviets had similar measures in place.

There are some interesting cases, probably apocryphal, where there arose concern about who might gain control over nuclear weapons. According to one report, the French government in 1961, threatened by mutinous generals in Algeria, hastened the test of a nuclear weapon at its Algerian test site in order to preclude them from grabbing the weapon.[4] The rumor survived for decades, and I myself was guilty of repeating it until further inquiries with French officials, who had knowledge of these events, put the story in the category of "never happened."[5] It is another nuclear terrorist mirage that runs into the sand.

It was also a major concern of the West and leaders in Moscow during the chaotic period of Soviet disintegration that rogue elements in the military might seize nuclear weapons to overthrow the government. It is believed that one of the reasons the white

South African government willingly gave up its nuclear weapons before relinquishing political power was to preclude them from coming under the control of its hated adversary, the African National Congress, although there are unconfirmed reports that it secretly stashed a few weapons for some future contingency.

With Iraq and Libya currently out of the picture as nuclear weapons aspirants, current concerns focus on North Korea, Pakistan, and Iran, which is still in the suspected-aspirant camp. If there were an economic meltdown and political implosion in North Korea, the big worry is who would control its nuclear weapons and to whom they would report. The world might not be as fortunate in North Korea's transition as it was during that of Russia.

But perhaps the greatest concerns focus on Pakistan, a politically turbulent nuclear weapons state, which always seems perilously close to the edge of sectarian anarchy, and where even in government circles, sympathies for Islamic extremists like the Taliban and al Qaeda run high. Pakistani generals assure worried Westerners that the country's nuclear weapons will remain under tight control whatever Pakistan's tumultuous course may be, but the black market operations that continued undiscovered or unchecked for years under the direction of A. Q. Khan in Pakistan's own nuclear weapons program are hardly reassuring. In a chaotic situation, insiders, outsiders, or a combination of the two might try to grab a nuclear weapon.

Even now, questions remain about who controls certain activities in Iran. Is Iran's supply of increasingly sophisticated know-how and weapons to Hezbollah and Iraq's insurgents approved by its top leaders, or is the country's Revolutionary Guard, a military and commercial empire in its own right, running an independent operation?

Rogue elements, therefore, must be considered a potential threat, especially where governments are in chaos or where loss of control appears imminent. This leads some analysts to conclude that in a political upheaval, external intervention to secure or eliminate nuclear arsenals may be necessary and justified. Yet the fear of external intervention may persuade authorities in those same countries, during moments of internal crisis, to move their arsenals to locations where they will be secure against both internal challengers and outsiders. Such a move, however, may itself easily be misinterpreted as evidence of a loss of control or as a takeover by rogue elements, heightening external concern.

In *Annihilation from Within*, Fred Iklé outlines a scenario in which some future ambitious tyrant might annihilate the nation from within by smuggling a few nuclear bombs into the country to decapitate its leadership and spread nationwide panic. "He would be well prepared to exploit this chaos by seizing complete control of the nation's government and imposing his dictatorship." Seizing power through a nuclear power grab would, of course, be extremely difficult in a large democracy like the United States, but Iklé argues that our government is woefully ill prepared to deal with a sneak nuclear attack.[6]

That brings us to the third terrorist acquisition option: acquiring a nuclear weapon through the black market. We assume here that corrupt officials or organized crime, most likely with inside assistance, have already successfully handled the problems of acquisition and are now offering nuclear weapons for sale or that terrorists have commissioned corrupt officials or gangsters to acquire a nuclear weapon on their behalf. Many analysts consider a black market transaction to be the most likely route of terrorist acquisition, and it certainly is the most popular one in writings about nuclear terrorism.

The first assumption of "theft on spec" requires that the sellers advertise the weapon for sale, albeit clandestinely, or that they know where and how to directly reach their potential terrorist buyer. Advertising is dangerous, creating a requirement for discreet middlemen connected to and trusted by both sides. Otherwise, approaching a potential terrorist buyer is difficult. Intelligence services may be running a sting. Moreover, terrorist leaders are usually the subjects of intense manhunts. They are not easy to reach and they are likely to regard any attempts at contact with suspicion, even with offers of a nuclear weapon on the calling card. This underscores the need to maintain the current hunt for al Qaeda's leaders, not because their capture or death would end the jihadist enterprise–probably it would not–but because the manhunt makes it difficult for anyone else to reach al Qaeda's leaders. The target is not just their heads, but the manhunt also aims to make it difficult for them to procure weapons. It also suggests a strategy of stings, subjecting the jihadist enterprise to frequent offers, fakes, and traps, calculated to keep its leaders wary of all approaches and to spoil the market for would-be suppliers.

Nonetheless, terrorists could try to buy fissile material on the black market, which, it appears, is what al Qaeda has attempted, albeit presumably without success. Very small quantities of plutonium and enriched uranium have been offered for sale to undercover police agents posing as buyers. Given the quantities needed for a nuclear weapon, terrorist buyers would have to accumulate a bomb's worth through numerous black market purchases, unless the seller truly had access to large quantities. It also appears that black market buyers, including al Qaeda and Iraq, have been the victims of scams, buying low-enriched uranium or other material that was radioactive but useless in bomb making.

Finally, terrorists could try to make their own material, primarily by enriching uranium to bomb-grade. This was one of the paths chosen by the Aum sect in Japan. Uranium enrichment, however, is a complex process requiring sophisticated equipment, so Aum scientists abandoned the idea.

A nuclear black market figures prominently in the most nightmarish fears of nuclear terrorism. Many analysts worry that such a market would grow as a problem if the world turned to nuclear energy and if mixed-oxide fuels became more available, like any other commodity.

But does the nuclear black market exist? The answer is yes, although not in the form we imagine. Actually, the term *nuclear black market* refers to two different structures, one high-end and one low-end. The first one trades in raw material, know-how, and the highly complex equipment required for the enrichment and the fabrication of nuclear weapons. Its buyers are recent and aspiring nuclear weapons states. The original nuclear powers have their own capabilities and facilities, and they manufacture or procure their supplies openly. The high-end nuclear black market deals in stolen blueprints, precisely manufactured parts, and specialized equipment, much of which has uses other than making nuclear bombs, providing its suppliers with a fig leaf of deniability.

This nuclear black market is exemplified by the A. Q. Khan network, named after the head of Pakistan's nuclear weapons program who turned his secret procurement network into a personal profit center by offering nuclear know-how and buyers' guides to other aspirants.[7] If the International Atomic Energy Agency, charged with preventing the spread of nuclear weapons, ever took up the practice of issuing fatwas against those who had committed proliferation, A. Q. Khan would be its first candidate. Instead, he remains a national hero punished only with house arrest. Before we criticize Pakistan for leniency, it should be noted that most of Khan's procurers and suppliers remain free men, while others have received only light sentences for their roles in recklessly endangering the planet—hardly a deterrent in the world's dirtiest business.

The very late discovery of the Khan network, which had been operating without interference for more than two decades, caused understandable alarm. It heightened concerns that the black market in nuclear weapons and fissile material for those seeking a shortcut to the bomb was far more developed than we thought.

The breakup of the Khan network disrupted the proliferation black market, which may be less organized now. But it did not eliminate the greed that fueled it. The same people who sold to Khan's agents, one suspects, would, if they thought they could get away with it, sell to the agents of Iran, Syria, or any other buyer with money. It is all a matter of risk and profit.

A. Q. Khan, insofar as we know, did not sell directly to any terrorist organization, but he did sell to countries like Libya and Iran that people worry would pass nuclear weapons or know-how on to terrorist protégés and proxies. And we know that some scientists in Pakistan's weapons program had direct contacts with Osama bin Laden, raising the possibility of a rogue operation within a rogue operation.

This possibility aside, the Khan-style proliferation network is not the one where terrorist acquisition is most likely to occur. Khan's enterprise was organized and managed by a single man as a clandestine global supply chain, initially to support Pakistan's weapons program, later to transfer his acquired knowledge to others. It was not a bazaar open to all buyers, and it was a black market only in that its ultimate purpose was concealed.

The United States, during the cold war, worried about the possibility that the Soviet Union itself might attempt to clandestinely deliver nuclear weapons—using covert agents and special forces to pre-deploy them near selected targets—in order to spring a surprise attack or degrade the capability of the United States to respond to a Soviet first strike. Nonetheless, the clandestine delivery scenario was not considered likely. Given the size and dispersal of the US nuclear arsenal, the pre-deployment of a few weapons would not significantly affect the outcome of an all-out nuclear exchange. And if any of the teams were caught or any pre-deployed weapons discovered, it could trigger a nuclear strike before the Soviets were ready. Moreover, nuclear weapons require maintenance, without which they eventually become useless. Clandestine pre-deployment would require moving weapons in and out or continuing shipments of replacements, further risking discovery.

Our primary interest centers on the second, or low-end, black market where terrorists conceivably might acquire nuclear weapons or the nuclear material for making primitive nuclear devices or dirty bombs. Our knowledge of this market is limited. The very few confirmed events we know about give us only a partial glimpse and may not reflect the total reality. Piled on top of what can be confirmed are layers of unverified information, conjecture, rumors, and sensational but unsubstantiated claims, all reported breathlessly in the news media and repeated by public officials, making it difficult to separate fact from fiction.

What we do know about the second black market suggests that it is far less organized and sophisticated than the proliferation supply network.[8] It appears to be a sort of nuclear swap meet. It trades in pilfered reactor fuel, yellowcake and depleted uranium pretending to be highly enriched stuff, radioactive waste and scrap, and red mercury. Amid this jumble of discs, rods, powder, pellets, and liquids in flasks and canisters are very small amounts of fissile material. As at most swap meets, a lot of what is traded can be called junk. Fakes are abundant, but there may be an occasional "find."

Forty years go, the Lumb Panel, mentioned earlier, worried about the possibility of organized crime trafficking in nuclear material, but that was predicated on the anticipated expansion of nuclear energy and a large-scale commercial traffic in nuclear material. It would presumably become a commodity like any other. With a high commercial value and a large potential market, diversions would be profitable.

That, however, is not the case with fissile material, which, although valuable, has no ready commercial market. There is little commercial incentive. Successful sales would be one-time affairs, not a continuing source of profit like trafficking in drugs, smuggling humans, or selling other illegal commodities. Exposure would be extremely dangerous to the participants and could cause the annihilation of the organization. Terrorist fanatics may be willing to carry out perpetual suicide attacks or spend the rest of their lives in Waziristan. But that is hardly the lifestyle of mafia dons.

The low-end market has been described as "supply driven"—that is, there is no large market demand such as there is for illegal narcotics. Most transactions involve smuggling or offers for sale. The thefts appear to be carried out as a local initiative, rather than being commissioned. There is no evidence of prearranged sales or established underworld commercial outlets.[9] Therefore, the thieves are easy targets for stings.

Those arrested are low-level types, not hard-core or high-powered criminals, although some of the thefts in Russia are reportedly conspiracies between employees at nuclear facilities and corrupt officials in the state security services. But each theft or offer for sale is a one-time event. The lack of continuing activity argues against the involvement of organized crime. Even though analysts worried about the potential participation of organized crime, according to a Russian observer writing in the late 1990s, no evidence exists of any systematic traffic in Russia or of an organized mafia specializing in nuclear traffic. Analysts inside and outside Russia have likewise seen no evidence of organized crime involvement on the international level.

Buyers are few. Instead of terrorists, the buyers in the cases we know about are undercover police, intelligence operatives, and journalists looking for stories. These, of course, are likely to be the cases we learn about. Other end-buyers have not been identified. Some reports indicate buyers in the Middle East, but these are unconfirmed.

The events we know about suggest that the low-end nuclear black market generally follows two paths, both originating in

Russia. One is to the West, as indicated by reports of smuggling and arrests in Ukraine, Bulgaria, Hungary, Poland, the Czech Republic, Austria, Italy, Germany, and Switzerland. Scattered incidents and the lack of a clearly established route suggest the lack of organization. Rather, sellers simply reckon they will be able to sell their wares in the West. The second route seems to flow from Russia through Central Asia, with incidents reported in Georgia, Uzbekistan, and Kazakhstan.

Reports of nuclear smuggling increased sharply after the fall of the Soviet Union. Most of the incidents, however, turned out to be hoaxes and scams. Concern increased in the early 1990s with the first confirmed incident involving tiny quantities of plutonium. This concern persuaded German authorities to initiate a number of sting operations in which German undercover police, pretending to be buyers, apprehended several traffickers offering tiny amounts of fissile material. Publicity surrounding the cases led to the criticism that the Germans were creating a market that didn't exist. Russian officials worried that this would only encourage more thefts in Russia, thereby increasing their problems.

The problem continued, although most of the incidents continued to be hoaxes and scams or involved nuclear junk. It was in the early 1990s that bin Laden's buyers reportedly also got burned by con artists.

The records indicate that 1994 turned out to be the peak year for this market. After that, the number of incidents declined. The decline may have been due to improved security in Russia and the lack of buyers in the West. The improvement in security in Russia could be credited, at least in part, to the far-sighted Nunn-Lugar initiative, which quickly made US funding available to Russia to improve physical security and to safeguard procedures at Russian nuclear facilities and assist those involved in Russia's weapons programs to find gainful employment in other areas. It is noteworthy that there is no documented case of any rogue

Russian scientist working for terrorists or proliferators. In fact, there is no evidence in any of the reported transactions or attempted transactions of complicity by proliferating states. This was not their market.

There was a slight increase in reported incidents of nuclear smuggling in 2001 and two cases of fissile material offered for sale (to undercover police) in the Republic of Georgia in 2006 and 2007, but nothing to suggest an ongoing black market and no evidence of acquisition of fissile material by terrorists. What did increase significantly after 9/11 was the number of stories in the media, often speculative and sensational, about terrorists acquiring nuclear weapons or nuclear material on the black market.

Assuming that terrorists somehow acquired fissile material, they could theoretically attempt to build their own bomb. The debate about whether terrorists have or could acquire the necessary know-how and equipment necessary to fabricate a nuclear device continues. There is no evidence that they have this knowledge now, and what little we know about their capabilities suggests that they do not. José Padilla's reported unsolicited proposal to build a nuclear bomb for al Qaeda based upon plans downloaded from the Internet is ridiculous. It is hard to imagine Padilla as point man for al Qaeda's Manhattan Project; al Qaeda's senior planners thought so too, instead suggesting a plot involving a simpler dirty bomb or even simpler gas explosions in apartment buildings. Even this task seems a stretch for a street hoodlum who, before joining al Qaeda, seemed to be challenged by pulling off a convenience store stickup.

At the same time, many analysts argue that if a well-financed terrorist group had the requisite fissile material, it could assemble a team that, with time, could construct a crude nuclear bomb. Its detonation would be uncertain. It might fizzle, and even if it worked, its yield would likely be low—far less than the Hiroshima bomb or the ten-kiloton blast that is often posited in terrorist nuclear scenarios. But still, it might work. Others, those who have actually built nuclear weapons, are far more skeptical and generally estimate the probability of a successful terrorist nuclear explosion to be much lower than the probabilities estimated for those without this technical background.

Our purpose here is not to resolve this debate but merely to underscore the complexity of its key assumption: Terrorists must have the requisite fissile material–the stuff of nuclear bombs–which means a sufficient quantity of highly enriched uranium or plutonium, plus some other nonfissile strategic materials. Theoretically, there are several ways for terrorists to obtain these items. Theoretically, just about anything is possible.

Chapter 8
A SMALL CUP OF ITALIAN COFFEE

Alan Kidger, forty-nine, sales director of British-owned Thor Chemicals, told his wife that he would be back shortly. Days later, his body was found in the trunk of his luxury car in a black township outside Johannesburg. His arms and legs had been severed, and his torso was smeared with a black oily substance (found to contain mercury). Authorities suspected that Kidger was murdered by foreign agents over a consignment of the mysterious red mercury. Suspicion later fell upon the Mossad, the Israeli spy agency, which reportedly found out that Kidger had been assisting the Arabs in developing weapons of mass destruction.[1]

Two years later, two other South Africans, also believed to have been involved in the sale of red mercury, were killed.[2] Additional details about Kidger's commercial connections later emerged during South Africa's Truth and Reconciliation hearings following the end of apartheid and in subsequent criminal trials of business associates who were involved in illegal drug manufacturing. But the red mercury murders have not been solved. Additional murders connected with red mercury trafficking occurred in Europe. None were ever solved.

In the black market, the names "Vin Rouge," "Beaujolais," "Bourgogne," "Blood," and "Cherry Red" are used. These are not French wines or boosted caffeine sodas. These terms refer to something far more mysterious—red mercury. Stories about red mercury smuggling trickled into the news media in the 1980s, but with the collapse of the Soviet Union, the trickle became a deluge.

"Authorities in Italy and Switzerland have seized . . . 2–4 grams of plutonium at Coreo on 15 October (1991) . . . 29.5 kg of low-grade uranium at Zurich on 11 November; and between 2 and 5 kg of Red mercury in Milan on 8 January. . . . Two intermediaries have died in suspicious car crashes," reported the *Independent* on April 13, 1992.

"Bulgarian police have seized beer-bottle size flasks of Red mercury bearing Soviet military symbols. . . . Ukrainian police announced they had arrested thieves near the border trying to smuggle out 180 kg of Red mercury officially described as a 'strategic material used to build nuclear weapons.' In Poland, 8 kg of Red mercury were found in a Lada car belonging to four Russians," according to the *Times of London*, October 1992.

"I don't know what Red mercury is. It could be for a missile, it could be for anything. They are selling everything on the black markets now, maybe only to get food. But you get three people together who know how [weapons development] *is done, and you can have a big problem,"* said Yanko Yanev, head of Bulgaria's Atomic Energy Committee.

"We are not talking about a real 'weapon' but about a mystification," observed a former Bulgarian intelligence official.[3]

"According to a report prepared by the KGB . . . Red mercury serves as both an easily-shaped detonator and rich source of neutrons thus allowing a simpler nuclear bomb that requires a smaller quantity of plutonium—no more than the volume of a small cup of Italian coffee. To test its efficiency, such a bomb was detonated at an underground test site. Satisfied with the results, the Kremlin ordered the construction of plants to produce Red mercury. The most important of these was at Yekaterinburg in the Ural Mountains, a thousand miles east of Moscow," reported *Panorama*, October 3, 1993.

"According to experts in Russia, Red mercury is the crucial ingredient of a new type of atomic bomb. To those who believe in it, it is one of the most sinister and dangerous materials ever developed, a substance that could transform the regimes of Saddam Hussein, or Qadaffi into nuclear powers overnight," reported the *Sunday Times,* October 18, 1992.

"If all that is true, such a substance . . . could enable construction of bombs using smaller quantities of fissionable material. . . . And it could result in smaller warheads, which would appeal to terrorists."[4]

"The black market in Red mercury for nuclear weapons is a threat to all countries and Russia cannot stop it alone. The West needs to get organized," said Oleg Sadykov, president of Promekologiya, Yekaterinburg, Russia, in October 1992.

"Some brilliant minds have come up with a new element in the Mendeleyev table . . . they're sending abroad this substance, which does not exist in nature, this so-called Red mercury. What is this substance that is being sold in such volumes and at astronomical prices? Where is the money going?" asked Russian vice president Alesander Rutskoi, speaking before the Seventh Congress of People's Deputies in 1992.[5]

"The president of the Russian chemical firm Promekologiya will sue the Russian Vice President Alesander Rutskoi for the loss of a contract to sell Red mercury to an Armenian company. In the Russian Parliament, Rutskoi had accused high-ranking government officials of illegally exporting strategic materials including Red mercury. . . . Rutskoi, according to the head of the Russian chemical firm, released highly confidential information which imperiled the company's sale of 84 tons of Red mercury. 'We have already received confirmation of the payment of $24.2 billion to the Bank of America,'" reported *Moscow Interfax,* April 1993.

"The number of Red mercury cases had increased significantly compared to prior years. Red mercury is claimed to be an essential ingredient in both nuclear weapons and missile guidance systems; the material as described is nonexistent!" declared a US government report in February 1993.

"According to the Russian Federation of Security, 'We have recorded

numerous instances of interest in 'Red mercury,' frequently from abroad.' However, Russian security officials have yet to find any actual traces of Red mercury. And no wonder . . . intelligence services not only in Russia but also in Western countries are fascinated by this mystery . . . their searches only confirm the belief that Red mercury will probably never be found at all, since it does not, from all indications, exist. . . . High level officials assert that Red mercury is a fiction, a myth. And yet people are offering tremendous sums of money. For what?" asked the *Current Digest of the Soviet Press* in 1993.

"The brouhaha around the mysterious chemical substance does not subside. There is even a version that such mercury does not and cannot exist," said a Russian press report in June 1993.

"It is impossible not to feel a deep chill at reports that 'red mercury,' the ultimate terrorists' weapon might really exist," reported the *New Scientist* in April 1995.

"Although there is talk that 'Red mercury' does not actually exist. What is it then?" asked Major General Gurov, director, Russian Security Ministry.

"We have seen the reports, we have not seen any hard evidence to sub-stantiate the reports, but we take all of the reports seriously," said CIA director Robert M. Gates, testifying before Congress in 1992.

"When it comes to fiendish devices like this [a red mercury ultra-low-yield pure-fission bomb] , . . . [the government] *can become very evasive and even lie in its teeth,"* said Sam Cohen, in 2000.[6]

"Red mercury? I wasted a large portion of my professional life on it," a former CIA station chief complained.

"Red mercury? I once asked a colleague of mine—he also was KGB—about Red mercury. He told me, 'Oleg, don't get involved in this. It is dangerous,'" said a former major general in the KGB.[7]

A mysterious substance that may not even exist but that buyers will pay billions of dollars to get? A compound that could turn tin-pot dictators and terrorists into instant nuclear powers? Murky deals! Unsolved murders! Hoaxes, con artists, Russian mafia! Red mercury was an irresistible tale. For a handful of investigators, it became a continuing obsession. Following red mercury stories took one into a labyrinth of tantalizing theories, rumors, and misinformation. It was like chasing the Cheshire cat. Initially reported "facts" faded fast. Everything was half-lit. Every report dissolved into unsolved, uncertain, unknown. Each inquiry provoked only more questions.

By the late 1980s, I had already accumulated a thick file filled with farragoes about red mercury, good for movie scripts but not analysis. Leaving the RAND Corporation to join the private sector did not put an end to my quest. Red mercury crossed the desks of Kroll Associates, the global private investigation firm where I worked from 1989 to 1998. There were unsolicited offers of sale or opportunities to act as go-betweens; potential buyers of red mercury, asking for due-diligence investigations of the sellers; buyers who had been bilked by red mercury scams looking to recover their money—I marveled at the gullibility of otherwise savvy businessmen. What could they have been thinking? Why did they want red mercury to begin with?

Red mercury is of interest to us here not only because it is part of the story of nuclear terrorism, but because, with its mysteries, reports of secret deals, presumed connections between organized crime and political fanatics, multiple agendas, worrisome possibilities, obvious fabrications, and allegations of government cover-ups, *red mercury reflects the nature of nuclear terrorism itself.* Whether red mercury exists or not we can leave to the physicists. Our focus here is on how it has contributed to nuclear terror.

What exactly is red mercury? "According to my research, red mercury was a highly refined form of mercury oxide," said one scientist in Pretoria, South Africa, "but after the murder, I quickly lost interest in it."

According to one description, red mercury is a mercury antimony oxide with a unique molecular structure that makes it a source of immense explosive energy, enough to initiate a chain reaction. According to a Russian informant who spoke with British nuclear physicist Frank Barnaby, who has done a great deal of research on the topic, red mercury is produced by dissolving mercury antimony oxide in mercury, mixing it with some other chemicals, then irradiating the amalgam in a nuclear reactor for twenty days, then evaporating off the excess mercury, leaving behind a cherry-red polymer "having a honey-like or gel consistency."[8] According to this source, there are several different kinds of red mercury–RM 20/20, RM 16/24, RM 20/22. An Italian trafficker based in Paris described RM 20/23 as "top-of-the-range red mercury with a stick of uranium down the middle."[9] This same dealer, years before, had been investigated in Italy for involvement in neofascist terrorist plots. According to this man, his biggest customer was a member of the Saudi ruling family, a claim supported by other sources but never explained.[10]

Red mercury had several theoretical applications in the design and fabrication of nuclear weapons. By lacing the conventional explosives that surround a plutonium core, red mercury would act as an effective reflector of neutrons, bouncing them back into the core, accelerating the fission, making a more efficient fission device. Red mercury would also increase the number of neutrons for a given explosive yield; in other words, it would enhance the radiation effect, creating a neutron bomb with less physical destruction but more lethal radiation. Neutron bombs were developed in the West to penetrate armor and kill crews in tanks and other protected places. Critics charged that neutron bombs were inherently a capitalist weapon that killed people but did not destroy property. One American physicist sarcastically said it was "the perfect weapon if you had cornered Hitler in the Taj Mahal."

Sam Cohen, the man whom some called the father of the neutron bomb (a title others dispute), would nod in agreement. It would be the perfect terrorist weapon. Cohen argued that red mercury itself could produce such a powerful explosion: it would permit the construction of a massively powerful thermonuclear device—a pure fusion bomb. Pure fusion technology could produce a one-kiloton bomb with a simpler design requiring no fissile material—a grapefruit-sized device capable of destroying a skyscraper. Cohen believes that even a baseball-sized nuclear bomb is feasible.[11]

Other scientists have challenged Cohen's assertion that any compound of mercury can duplicate the explosive power of the fission needed to initiate fusion, but if the assertion is true, wrote Barnaby, this would be "calamitous for preventing the spread of nuclear weapons. Because such weapons would be fairly cheap to produce, they raise the spectre of countries producing large numbers of low-yield neutron bombs."[12]

Barnaby goes on to say, "The prospect that terrorists may, at some stage in the future, acquire pure fusion weapons, is an awesome one. Because such weapons would be of very small size and light weight, they would be very attractive to nuclear terrorists." Others have pointed to so-called suitcase nukes, small atomic-demolition munitions that are low-yield fission weapons, as ideal for terrorists.

Nuclear weapons designers and sentinels of nuclear terrorism are fascinated with the idea of tiny atomic bombs—true mini-nukes the size of a suitcase, a briefcase, a grapefruit, a baseball—something that would fit in a sandwich bag. An atomic "Saturday night special"!

However, there is reason to doubt the presumption that terrorists need little nuclear bombs—the ultimate suicide bomber would have a nuclear weapon strapped to his chest. While portability is an attractive operational feature in any type of clandestine delivery, terrorists may be less interested in small devices than they are in simple, easy-to-make devices, perhaps with less-elegant designs but more within the range of their capabilities.

Although red mercury would be valuable to terrorists in that it would permit them to make a nuclear device with less fissile material, this advantage would likely be offset by the increased complexity of manufacture. Moreover, terrorists don't need a nuclear-armed suicide bomber to get close to their target. A one-kiloton device will do just as much damage on the street outside the target. None of the theoretical designs involving red mercury, even if red mercury did exist, sound simple. Most weapons designers anticipate that a terrorist-made nuclear device will be large, inefficient, and low-yield, if not a dud.

However, a pure fusion bomb made with red mercury, according to Cohen, would produce a very small blast, "a pop, not a bang," equivalent to that produced by about a ton of TNT. It would kill primarily by radiation, releasing a flood of neutrons lethal up to one-third of a mile, not so much a dirty bomb as an all-direction ray gun.[13] How might terrorists use such a "mini-neutron" bomb? At a 1995 convention of physicians concerned with disaster preparedness, Cohen offered a scenario involving the president's annual State of the Union address in the Capitol Building.[14]

Nuclear weapons were not the only purported application for red mercury. Some people asserted that it also had utility in missile guidance systems, as well as in coating the surfaces of stealth weapons. Others said it was useful in the manufacture of certain medicines. Still others advertised red mercury as an aphrodisiac.

The variants of red mercury appearing on the black market are nothing as elaborate as that described by Barnaby's Russian informant. They are usually reddish-colored powders that turn out to be ordinary mercuric oxide or mercuric iodide—or in some cases, mildly radioactive waste material that is tinted red with artificial coloring. One shipment was colored with red nail polish.

But the question remains, Does red mercury exist? That is, does a compound that has these capabilities in connection with nuclear weapons exist? The consensus is no, but the debate has never been settled. Frank Barnaby himself was initially skeptical, but his Russian informants provided such detailed information about its manufacture that in later years Barnaby considered it a possibility that should not be ignored.

While there is no doubt that many offers of red mercury on the black market are bogus, it should not be assumed that all are. It is not clear why the authorities are so dismissive of red mercury as an ingredient in nuclear weapons. Perhaps they do not want to admit that the Russians have stolen a march on the West by developing a revolutionary new type of weapon. . . . It is also possible that red mercury is already taken seriously by many governments and that public pronouncements of the substance as a hoax serve merely to divert attention. But given the serious consequences of a flourishing trade in red mercury, the West should face the facts about it and grapple with the issues raised by them.[15]

Where did red mercury come from—not its chemical origins, but its headwaters in history? That, to me, is the most compelling mystery. We may never know who invented this tale or why, but from conversations from New Mexico to Moscow, I was able to piece together a hypothesis based upon bits of information, hints, and hunches. The reader has been warned.

In the 1960s, with the cold war at its height and nuclear arsenals in full production, Soviet weapons designers were searching for ways to make nuclear weapons smaller, more powerful, more efficient, *more elegant*—a weapons designer's term meaning simpler weapons that are easier and cheaper to build. They explored many different designs and numerous materials, including compounds of mercury, which fascinated weapons designers in the West as well. Red mercury was one project among many. We don't know if it was named for the color of mercury compounds, some of which range from dull reddish browns to deep purples, or the cherry-red honey-like gel that Barnaby's informant described, or if instead, the name found inspiration in ideology—a substance that would give the Soviet Union a strategic edge. Sources recall the first mentions of red mercury in 1968.

The story goes that Soviet research on red mercury initially appeared promising—the name alone facilitated funding from Moscow. Red mercury had cachet; money flowed and the research continued but without yielding results. No one, however, could easily admit the failure of red mercury, certainly not the pampered scientists working on the project nor the heads of the research program who had argued for its support. The research had to continue to be promising. Each additional allocation of funds made admission of failure more perilous.

Eventually, some in the Soviet government began to grow skeptical, but by then, red mercury had attracted the attention of Western spies. Whatever its utility in weapons design, it gained utility as a weapon of deception in the intelligence war—a way to make the Americans think that Soviet designers really had made a breakthrough that would enable them to mass-produce cheap, tiny, powerful nukes. At the very least, red mercury provided a useful diversion for American intelligence and for American weapons designers, a honey pot to attract and observe spies. If Moscow admitted, even internally, that the project had failed, the Americans would find out and drop their inquiry. Red mercury became a ruse.

In the secret, highly compartmentalized world of nuclear weapons design and counterespionage, especially in the atmosphere of mutual suspicion that prevailed in the Soviet Union, it is difficult to determine who knew what. Not even high-ranking Soviet officials knew everything that was going on. And who knew what to believe, or what they were supposed to believe? Scientists pursued their research, wanting to believe it would eventually produce results. Others pretended to believe in order to protect their lifestyles, their political position, their heads. Still others encouraged pretense to fool the other side.

The collapse of the Soviet Union gave red mercury new life. Potentates, as well as terrorists eager to build their own nuclear weapons, came looking for know-how and material–strategic metals, uranium, plutonium they knew they needed, and the red mercury they had heard about. If foreigners were determined to buy red mercury, corrupt Russian officials, organized crime, and entrepreneurial con men were prepared to sell it to them. Gold, platinum, cobalt, nickel, and scrap metal poured out of the former Soviet Union. And so did red mercury in hundreds of scams. The red mercury market soared.

According to a former East European intelligence official, the "new capitalists" of Eastern Europe were often talking about red mercury deals. Offers to sell red mercury usually came from Russia and were made to Arab and African buyers. They even promised "certificates" of authenticity. The advertised profits were between ten and a hundred times the investment. There was talk of the former Yugoslavia, then in the midst of its ethnic civil wars, being a potential market in 1993 and again in 1999. There were also reports of red mercury coming through Eastern Europe or the Balkans. These were jointly investigated by British, American, and local intelligence services, but no sales were ever recorded and no deals were ever completed. In one or two cases, a down payment of 10 percent was made, but no goods were ever delivered.[16]

All of the red mercury transactions were peculiar. Apart from Promekologiya's public declaration of its $24 billion deal, there were no identified sellers. And for clandestine reasons, there were no openly identified buyers, only middlemen. That situation is, to a degree, true of all black markets, but in drug trafficking, there are well-known sources and, most important, there are commodities—cocaine, opium, heroin, ecstasy. Indeed, by the early 1990s, red mercury was a well-advertised scam that should have fooled no one. Yet reportedly large sums of money continued to move.

Commodities transactions without commodities raise suspicions. As General Aleksandr Gurov, director of the Scientific Research Institute of Security, observed, "One can only assume that since the substance does not exist, but the documents do, since there are no customers . . . but there are middlemen, and since there are documented bank payments and money is changing hands, it means that what we have here is the laundering of enormous sums of money."[17] This was the view of the FSB, Russia's new external intelligence service, which believed that "'red mercury' deals were used as a cover for large-scale international financial machinations when 'deliveries' from the CIS were used for 'laundering' criminally amassed capital both by Western dealers (narco mafia) and Russian criminal structures."[18]

According to one description of the scheme, a company in Russia would sign a contract to sell red mercury to a buyer in the West. The contract would contain a clause requiring the seller to pay a penalty if the goods were not delivered. Of course, the red mercury would not be delivered, obliging the Russian company to pay the penalty, which, in turn, would allow it to exchange rubles for Western currency at a favorable rate. Later, buyer and seller would split the cash. This could be done with any commodity.

Russian intelligence officials also believed that red mercury was being used as a cover for smuggling actual strategic metals such as gold, platinum, and cobalt out of Russia. But some authorities worried about the more sinister possibility that red mercury was being used as a cover for smuggling weapons-grade nuclear material. So tiresome had red mercury stories become that investigators would veer off once they ran into what appeared to be another red mercury scam. As one Western nonproliferation expert said, "Sometimes we follow a lead and then, half-way through, we hit red mercury. We then assume we are on a false trail." This is a variation of the use of a legitimate front company to disguise a criminal enterprise. In this case, the front is an obvious criminal scam to disguise a more nefarious activity. "We also do not rule out the possibility that criminal groups are using operations involving that substance to camouflage the export of uranium or plutonium."[19]

Western intelligence services saw red mercury as a lure as well as a cover. Knowing that buyers of red mercury were also likely to be buyers of other nuclear material, intelligence services could track red mercury sales to learn more about the acquisition efforts of dangerous end users—clandestine nuclear weapons programs, potentially with terrorist buyers. "We don't think red mercury is a very useful thing," said one government official. "Smugglers are selling a product that won't do what they say it will do. But it's useful to us, because as this trafficking continues, it's possible to glean other useful information, such as the extent of smuggling networks and of various potential buyers' nuclear intentions."[20]

Russian authorities also were aware that Western intelligence services were probing leaks of nuclear material in Russia itself. "The searches [for red mercury] may be initiated by foreign organizations and special services in order to identify channels through which nuclear materials could leak," observed a Russian security official.[21]

In fact, arms inspectors in Iraq found documents indicating that Saddam Hussein's agents had been taken in by red mercury scams. Reportedly, al Qaeda's men had also been fooled by the phony substance. The fact that some of the people who trafficked in red mercury ended up dead in the back alleys of Central Europe or stuffed in the trunks of cars led to the further suspicion among dealers that intelligence agents were not only tracking red mercury sales, they were eliminating the traffickers in lethal stings, as a warning to others who might contemplate arranging deals involving any nuclear material, real or not.

The hunt for red mercury created a secondary market in information. In the intelligence and investigative worlds, advertised interest in a topic invites sellers who possess, may be able to obtain, or simply are willing to fabricate information–for a price or sometimes to serve personal or political agendas, but seldom for a noble cause. The resulting quarry fills files with low-yield ore–many rocks, few nuggets, complicating analysis, worthless but giving the impression of vast activity. The hundreds of official reports and published press articles created further street interest in the substance itself. What is this mysterious stuff? If the KGB, CIA, and Mossad are chasing it, it must be really powerful. Rumor generated interest. Inquiry bred credibility, which bred further inquiry.

Red mercury stories also heightened concerns about nuclear terrorism. Sam Cohen begins reassuringly, "I don't want to sound melodramatic. . . . But red mercury is real and it is terrifying. I think it is part of a terrorist weapon that potentially spells the end of organized society."[22] What, one wonders, would he say if he had wanted to sound melodramatic? "The material means a neutron bomb can be built the size of a baseball, but able to kill everyone within several square blocks," Cohen said in an interview.[23] "The public isn't being warned about this development because the politicians have little desire to combat the menace or to confront nations like Iraq, Iran, and Libya that likely would use such weapons."[24]

In his book *Shame: Confessions of the Father of the Neutron Bomb*, Cohen admitted that Edward Teller, the designer of the original hydrogen bomb, disagreed with his assessment (as did a number of Cohen's former colleagues). "Red mercury is nonsense," said Teller. "I could not find any physical evidence anywhere, classified or unclassified, that is other than pure imagination. I believe, however, that there is not a particle of evidence that there is here a basic new discovery. That this could be at present something for the terrorist, I think, is nonsense."[25] Cohen countered in his book that "Teller did know of red mercury, but said the opposite because he was afraid of what the US government would do to him if he told the truth."[26] This is the impregnable response of the believer. Disagreement by knowledgeable people means they must be part of a conspiracy against the truth.

Terrorists walking around with "suitcase nukes" or nuclear baseballs in their pockets are indeed a terrifying prospect. Yet more than four decades after its reported discovery in the Soviet Union, almost two decades since stories of red mercury sales surged through Russia and the West, more than a decade since Frank Barnaby's analysis, we are still doubtful whether red mercury, with the properties described, actually exists as anything more than a scientist's theory, a con man's scam, and a scary story–impossible to confirm, impossible to kill.

Chapter 9
LEBED'S LOST LUGGAGE

Nothing better illustrates nuclear terror than the persistent urban legend of the missing suitcase nukes. This story combines concerns about the inadequacies of nuclear security in post–Soviet Russia, suspicions that Chechen middlemen are arming terrorists with nuclear weapons, worries that al Qaeda will get (or already has) nuclear weapons, and the perennial American fear of clandestine delivery. And though suitcase nukes are not as tiny as the mythical coffee can atomic bombs or the mini-nukes the size of baseballs suggested by Sam Cohen, the idea that nukes small enough to fit into a briefcase could be powerful enough to level a large part of a city is terrifying. How do we protect ourselves if any ordinary-looking office worker might be packing enough destructive power to blow away Main Street, Wall Street, or Pennsylvania Avenue?

Suitcase nukes have come up in intelligence reports, appear in congressional hearings, and are cited in official FEMA guides posted on the White House Web site. Inevitably, horror stories about such small but enormously powerful weapons have spread to fiction. But are suitcase nukes more fiction than fact? Like nuclear terror itself—indeed, like most rumors, the story of the suit-case nukes has a lapidary quality. Each retelling adds a layer. A decade of repetition has created a durability that defies the thin-ness of the original story.

The story begins with an alarming assertion by former Russian national security adviser General Aleksandr Lebed. In May 1997 Lebed told a delegation of US congressmen visiting Russia that eighty-four one-kiloton nuclear bombs were unaccounted for.[1] He repeated this assertion in an interview broadcast on the CBS News program *60 Minutes,* in which he increased his estimate to say that Russia had lost track of more than one hundred suitcase-sized nuclear bombs. "I'm saying that more than a hundred weapons out of the supposed number of 250 are not under the control of the armed forces of Russia," Lebed said. "I don't know their location. I don't know whether they have been destroyed or whether they are stored or whether they have been sold or stolen."[2]

Lebed said that the missing nuclear bombs were designed to look like suitcases and could be carried to the target and deto-nated by one person within half an hour. According to Lebed, the bombs were developed for special Soviet military intelligence units. They measured only eight inches by sixteen inches by twenty-four inches and weighed fifty pounds, Lebed said, and each had a yield of one to ten kilotons.[3]

Lebed's allegations were promptly dismissed by both Russian and American officials. A US State Department spokesman noted that Lebed's allegations carried "not a lot of credibility."[4] A spokes-man for Russia's atomic energy ministry said, "We don't know what General Lebed is talking about. No such weapons exist."[5]

The Russian denial, however, was disingenuous. In the 1950s, the United States had developed man-portable atomic munitions called SADMs (for Special Atomic Demolition Munition) to be used in case of a Soviet invasion of Europe. These devices, which could be carried in a large backpack, had a low yield and could be detonated to destroy key bridges, tunnels, and other infra-structure in order to channel and delay a Soviet advance.[6] American intelligence began to receive reports in the 1960s and 1970s that the Soviets were developing similar devices. Subsequent reports describe these as weighing about sixty-six pounds and having a yield of between one-half and two kilotons. They were reportedly kept at secret storage facilities in Russia and never released to Soviet troops.[7] In 1991, President Mikhail Gorbachev promised to destroy all of the nuclear backpacks, but as of 2004, this still had not been done. Although they were clearly tactical devices, it was not entirely apparent how the Soviets intended to use them. This renewed concerns about clandestine delivery of nuclear weapons to the United States.

This interpretation was later reinforced by Stanislav Lunev, a Russian military intelligence officer who had defected to the United States in 1992. Lunev claimed in 1998 that small man-portable nuclear weapons "that could be disguised to took like any suitcase" would be used to decapitate the US government and destroy key communications and military facilities. Lunev went further to assert that Soviet doctrine called for prepositioning nuclear weapons during peacetime, before a "crisis or war makes penetration of the U.S. more difficult."[8] Lunev testified that he did not know whether these weapons had, in fact, ever been deployed.

But there it was–J. Robert Oppenheimer's chilling prophecy! Testifying before the Senate a half century before, Oppenheimer, the man who led the Manhattan Project to build the first atomic bomb, warned that to find a nuclear weapon smuggled into an American city, we would have to open "every crate or suitcase."[9] The only useful technology, he said, would be a screwdriver.

Oppenheimer's worrisome observation led to a secret project code-named Cyclops. Since 9/11, some have cited this project as evidence of official concern about nuclear terrorism as early as the 1950s, but Cyclops, as the code name suggests, was about detection, not terrorism. In Homer's epic poem the *Odyssey*, the Cyclops was the one-eyed giant who imprisoned Odysseus and his men in a cave where he proceeded to eat several of them. Odysseus and the others survived by getting the giant drunk and poking his eye out. They then escaped by tying themselves to the undersides of the giant's sheep. Unable to see, the giant felt the tops of his sheep to make sure no one was riding on them when he let them out to graze. The question put to the Cyclops team of physicists was whether a blind giant could detect smuggled nuclear weapons. But Soviet agents, not terrorists, were the presumed foe at the time. The conclusions of the study were delivered in the Screwdriver Report, named after Oppenheimer's quip. It remains top secret.[10] Radiation detection turned out to be extremely difficult, and it remains so. Nonetheless, radiation detection has continued to be the holy grail of homeland security, and radiation detectors are increasingly deployed at ports, border crossings, and around other sensitive facilities.

While no one doubted that the Soviets had some kind of backpack nukes in their arsenal and that security in the former Soviet Union was inadequate, most nuclear experts and intelligence analysts remained skeptical of the prepositioning claims. Such weapons have a very short shelf life as their nuclear cores develop cracks and rapidly decay. They would remain ready to use for no more than six months.[11] Replacement or maintenance would require nuclear expertise, not screwdrivers. To ensure that the bombs would work, the Soviet Union would not only have to clandestinely deliver and preposition a number of weapons but also infiltrate an equipped team of maintenance specialists to ensure that the bombs would work, thereby increasing risks of discovery. Or alternatively, the Soviets could infiltrate the weapons if tensions between the superpowers began to rise—just weeks or days in advance of a possible war. In either case, it would be a provocative high-risk strategy, since the United States could easily regard any attempt to secretly plant a nuclear weapon on US territory, especially if tensions were high, as an act of war itself.

Moreover, US officials found no mention of suitcase or backpack nuclear bombs in Soviet war plans, nor did detailed studies of the Soviet Union's tactical nuclear weapons make any mention of these weapons.[12] That does not eliminate the possibility that Soviet military intelligence, the GRU, had its own covert plans and clandestine capabilities to be offered to Soviet leaders as an option in an imminent war. Other analysis, however, suggests that the Soviet backpack nukes would be used as tactical weapons or sabotage devices in case of a war in Europe.

It is not entirely clear what General Lebed's motives were in making his alarming claim. A respected and popular military commander, he had resigned from the army to run for president of Russia in 1996, but he finished third in the first round of voting, putting him out of the race. He then threw his support to Boris Yeltsin, who won in the second round. Yeltsin returned the favor, naming Lebed to be his national security adviser, but the two men clashed, and Lebed was soon fired.

While still serving as national security adviser, Lebed ordered that the inventory of nuclear weapons be taken. This was in part propelled by fears that Chechen rebels at war with Russia had managed to get their hands on one. It was this inquiry, however, that led to Lebed's discovery that some were missing. But by this time, Lebed also had a score to settle with Yeltsin and a political agenda of his own as he looked ahead to the 2000 elections. By accusing the Russian leadership of losing control of the country's nuclear arsenal, Lebed could embarrass the Yeltsin administration and burnish his own image as a man on horseback–the general who could restore order to the country and protect nervous Russians from nuclear-armed Chechen fanatics. Lebed may simply have wanted the Americans to know about the missing nukes or, given Washington's concerns about the security of Russia's nuclear arsenal, signal that he was the leader Americans could rely on.

Lebed's claims were undoubtedly newsworthy, but some suspected that they were being hyped for other reasons as well. Andrew and Leslie Cockburn, the producers of the *60 Minutes* segment that aired Lebed's revelations, were at the same time promoting their book *One Point Safe*. The book is a highly critical account of what the authors saw as the Clinton administration's limp response to the nuclear threat arising from chaos and incompetence in Russia.[13] And at the same time, the Cockburns were also coproducers of *Peacemaker*, a Hollywood thriller that just happened to be about a stolen suitcase nuke.

This obvious confluence of news reporting, book promotion, and moviemaking was no secret, and it does not detract from the essential facts of the story. The Russians did have portable nuclear weapons in their arsenal. General Lebed did report that some of them were unaccounted for. And the United States was concerned about the security of Russia's weapons. The details provided in the book, although challenged by some, were mostly accurate, and the book received good reviews. What the episode does illustrate, however, is the blurry boundaries between reality and fiction. One observer described the Cockburns' "creative process as art imitating life imitating art."[14] "But," one of the book's favorable reviewers added, "It's not even that simple."[15]

In 1998, Stanislav Lunev, the defector who had supported Lebed on the existence of the suitcase nukes, was promoting his own autobiography, *Through the Eyes of the Enemy*.[16] In the book Lunev warned that in the collective mind of his former Soviet colleagues, the end of the cold war had changed nothing. Russia's post–cold war leaders still regarded the United States as the enemy.

All this made Lunev an ideal candidate to testify in August 1998, and he was invited to testify again at a 2000 congressional hearing on Russian espionage.[17] It was at the latter hearing that

Congressman Curt Weldon, chairman of the Military Research and Development Subcommittee, displayed what appeared to be an actual suitcase nuke. It was, he hastily assured the audience, only a mock-up, which in fact had been assembled by a congressional staffer. But the prop got national attention, and the photo of Pennsylvania Republican Congressman Weldon holding up a suitcase nuke has become an icon of nuclear terror–"proof" that suitcase nukes exist.[18] Weldon hoped the display would persuade President Clinton to pay more attention to his program to deploy nuclear detection devices.

Lunev continued to warn of terrorist nuclear attacks and Russian perfidy. Two weeks after the 9/11 attacks, he wrote: "The planning, network and resources involved in the operation of Sept. 11 suggest to me that one or more countries were behind this, and also that Russian intelligence agencies were likely aware of the possibility of these attacks."[19] Forecasting another terrorist attack worse than 9/11, possibly even a terrorist nuclear attack, Lunev urged President Bush to "warn rogue states, i.e., Iraq, Iran, Syria and Libya, that if these [terrorist] groups use a weapon of mass destruction on an American city, the U.S. military will not do any investigations, there will be no delay–the U.S. will use similar weapons on their population centers and military targets."[20] Lunev saw this as a deterrent strategy.

Meanwhile, the story of Lebed's missing suitcase nukes had migrated from Russia to the Middle East. In October 1998, *al-Hayah*, an Arabic-language newspaper in London, published an article claiming that Osama bin Laden had purchased tactical weapons from one of the former Soviet Muslim republics in Asia.[21] This was followed a month later by an article in *Al-Watan Al-ʿArabi*, a Lebanese magazine, which claimed that al Qaeda was attempting to buy a Soviet nuclear weapon from Chechen rebels.[22] Subsequent accounts conflated the suitcase nukes and the al Qaeda stories. According to *Debka-Net-Weekly*, an often sensational Israeli source, al Qaeda had acquired eight to ten Russian atomic demolition munitions, or "suitcase nukes."[23]

This story was repeated by Yossef Bodansky, who claimed that the Chechens helped al Qaeda "acquire a number of nuclear 'suitcase bombs.'" In his 2007 book *Chechen Jihad*, Bodansky asserts that "by the fall of 1998, there was little doubt in the intelligence community that bin Laden had succeeded in his quest for nuclear suitcase bombs." In return for the suitcase nukes, according to Bodansky, bin Laden's agents paid the Chechens $30 million in cash and two tons of Afghan heroin, worth about $70 million. This was precisely the amount that the earlier Lebanese newspaper account said bin Laden had paid for nuclear warheads. But rather than corroborating the report, the coincidence raises the suspicion that the two stories simply have been blended in a third version.

So what can we conclude? It is highly likely that the Soviets did develop some sort of portable nuclear weapon similar to the American atomic demolition munition, though it was probably much bulkier than Congressman Weldon's pretend briefcase bomb. General Lebed's commission may not have been able to locate the entire inventory of these devices–the commission was disbanded before its work was complete. And we cannot confirm subsequent Soviet reports that all have been accounted for.

It seems highly doubtful, however, that Chechen rebels were able to get their hands on any nuclear weapons. Claims that the Chechen mafia was able to acquire two suitcase nuclear weapons as early as 1994 are undermined by the fact that in 1995, when the Chechens desperately wanted to terrorize the Russians into negotiations, they could manage only to come up with a crude radioactive device. And it seems even more unlikely that during the two bloody wars, the Chechens, if they had a nuclear weapon, would not have found some way to use it. That the Chechens would acquire nuclear weapons solely for the purpose of reselling them to al Qaeda, without keeping any nuclear capability for themselves, stretches credulity even further.

Finally, there is no evidence to support the claims that al Qaeda has suitcase nukes or any other kind of nuclear device. While the absence of use is not proof of absence, possession without use for more than a decade seems highly unlikely, especially given al Qaeda's continued determination to carry out a large-scale attack. Moreover, we can with confidence conclude that any suitcase nukes stashed away for more than decade, without expert maintenance, would no longer be reliable or even usable. Still, we can never be 100 percent certain. And that quantum of uncertainty, no matter how small, keeps the suitcase nuke story alive.

But there is also another phenomenon at work here—a purely psychological one. We fear cancer more than cavalry—tiny unseen threats more than large visible threats, the enemy within rather than the enemy beyond. What makes suitcase nukes so frightening, and nuclear bombs the size of coffee cans or baseballs even more so, is their tiny size compared to their large destructive power. True, there are operational advantages. Miniaturization makes secret nuclear weapons easier to conceal and deliver, but the idea of small unseen devices, the spores of annihilation, being tended to and carried by ordinary-looking individuals, perhaps already in our midst, is the stuff of true terror.

PART III
VISIONS OF MASS DESTRUCTION

Chapter 10
THE "NEW TERRORISM"

I n the early 1980s, we debated whether terrorists in the future would acquire the material and know-how to create and use weapons of mass destruction; would become technically and strategically more sophisticated and go after vital and vulnerable infrastructure; would evolve into a sort of "white-collar terrorism" aimed at disruption rather than death; or would simply become a more brutal version of the terrorists we already saw. I thought the latter, bloodthirsty-thug scenario was the most likely. But none of us foresaw the most profound shift that would occur.

Terrorism evolved slowly in response to new circumstances. The basic terrorist repertoire changed only gradually over the years. Improved security and increased international cooperation reduced the number of airline hijackings but did not entirely eliminate the tactic. Outside of Colombia, where ransom kidnapping persisted, kidnappings gradually declined, mainly because the terrorist organizations responsible for most of the political kidnappings in South America and Europe were suppressed. Hostage seizures in which terrorists barricaded themselves with their captives, like the one in Munich in 1972, proliferated in the 1970s, with terrorists storming embassies and consulates around the world. The tactic then declined in the following decade as security improved and governments became more resistant to meeting terrorists' demands and more willing to use force to end hostage episodes.

But bombings remained the principal terrorist tactic, and the bombings became deadlier. Numbers tell the story.

The first decade of contemporary international terrorism had produced very few incidents of large-scale violence—none with a hundred or more deaths. Then in 1978, terrorists in Beirut detonated a truck filled with explosives, killing more than two hundred people. In 1980 terrorists in Italy set off a bomb at the train station in Bologna, killing seventy-five people. In 1983 a truck bomb with a suicide driver crashed into the American embassy in Beirut, killing sixty-four. In a coordinated attack later that year, two truck bombs killed two hundred and forty-one US marines and fifty-five French paratroopers, also in Lebanon.

While airline hijackings declined, incidents of airline sabotage became more deadly. In 1974 a bomb brought down a TWA flight over the Mediterranean, killing eighty-eight. Two years later, a sabotaged Cuban passenger plane went down with seventy-six on board. Terrorist sabotage of an Air India flight in 1985 killed 329. In 1987 a terrorist bomb brought down a Korean airliner, killing 115; a year later, 270 people were killed in the sabotage of a Pan Am flight over Scotland; and in the year after that, the sabotage of a UTA airliner left 171 dead.

The escalation continued into the 1990s. In 1992 IRA terrorists detonated a massive truck bomb at the Baltic Exchange in the heart of London's financial district. A warning enabled casualties to be prevented, but the bomb caused massive damage. In 1993 Islamist extremists attempted to bring down the towers of New York's World Trade Center by detonating an explosives-filled van in the underground parking structure beneath the towers. The bomb caused extensive damage, but the towers stood; six people died, more than one thousand were injured. That same year, terrorists in Bombay set off a series of bombs that killed 273 people and left more than 700 injured. In 1994 Muslim extremists in Buenos Aires bombed a Jewish Community Center, killing eighty-five and wounding more than two hundred. IRA terrorists struck again in London, detonating a huge truck bomb that caused more than a billion dollars in damage. As before, a warning kept casualties low: one person was killed and forty were injured.

As noted earlier, terrorists in Tokyo attempted a mass poisoning in 1995 by dispersing nerve gas in the city's subways, killing twelve and sending more than fifty-five hundred others to hospitals. That same year, a tiny group of antigovernment fanatics bombed the federal building in Oklahoma City, killing 168.

The following year, a suicide terrorist drove a truck bomb into a US military housing compound in Saudi Arabia. The bomber failed to get close enough to level the building, but nineteen people died and three hundred were injured. In 1998 Algerian Islamists attacked a cinema and a mosque, killing between one hundred and twenty and four hundred. Al Qaeda operatives drove truck bombs into the American embassies in Kenya and Tanzania, killing 224 and injuring more than 4,500. In 1999 terrorists set off a bomb at an apartment building in Moscow, killing 121.

The worst terrorist incidents in the early 1970s were measured in tens of fatalities. The worst incidents from 1978 through the 1980s and 1990s were measured in the hundreds of fatalities. On September 11, 2001, this ascended to the thousands—an order-of-magnitude increase about every fifteen years.

In just ten attacks prior to 9/11, terrorists had killed more than two thousand people and injured more than ten thousand. Terrorist incidents on this scale had been extremely rare in the past. If self-imposed constraints had previously curbed terrorist violence, they now seemed to be eroding as the incidents of large-scale, indiscriminate violence increased.

These totals were comparable to the numbers seen in America's worst explosions and fires, which were themselves rare events. In the twentieth century, there were only seventeen explosions or fires in which one hundred or more people died (not counting a number of mine explosions at the beginning of the century). Fifteen of these tragedies occurred in the first half of the century. Death on this scale rarely occurred anymore in the United States or abroad. Outside of the Johnstown flood in 1889, in which more than twenty-two hundred people died, there was no event in the history of the United States remotely comparable to the 9/11 attack.

Mass murder had replaced disaster. In the 1960s, there were three accidental explosions or fires with one hundred or more fatalities, but no terrorist incidents of that magnitude. In the 1970s, five accidental explosions or fires and three terrorist incidents reached that level. The trend reversed in the 1980s, when only two accidental explosions or fires but six terrorist incidents caused one hundred or more fatalities. And in the 1990s, there were no accidental fires or explosions with one hundred or more fatalities, but five terrorist incidents reached that level.

In the first eight years of the twenty-first century, only one accidental fire caused one hundred or more fatalities, but five terrorist attacks (counting 9/11 as a single attack) killed one hundred or more people.

It wasn't simply that the worst incidents were getting worse. Statistics showed a significant change in terrorist intentions. In the late 1980s, one could say that 57 percent of all terrorist attacks were purely symbolic, that is, meant to gain publicity, not to kill. These attacks involved small bombs that went off away from crowds in the middle of the night. By the mid-1990s, the proportion had dropped to 32 percent. At the same time, the proportion of attacks in which terrorists clearly intended to kill increased from 27 percent to 36 percent. Between the late 1960s, when contemporary terrorism emerged, and the beginning of the twenty-first century, the "lethality rate" of terrorism—that is, the total number of dead divided by the total number of incidents—increased fourfold, and that statistic does not include the September 11, 2001, attack.

The jihadists hit their high-water mark on 9/11. Since then, they have not been able to come close to the scale of that attack. The thirty-three successful jihadist terrorist attacks between 9/11 and the end of 2006 (not counting any attacks in Iraq, Afghanistan, or Russia) killed 1,341 people. Four of these attacks exceeded the one hundred-fatality mark: the 2002 bombing of a nightclub in Bali, the 2003 bombing of a ferry in the Philippines, the Madrid train bombings in 2004, and the bombings of Mumbai's commuter train in 2006. The average number of fatalities per incident was forty; the median was eighteen.

In addition to the mounting death toll since the 1990s, these bombings—especially those in Beirut, London, Nairobi, Oklahoma City, Moscow, and Mumbai—produced images of devastation not seen since World War II.

Beyond the terrorist attacks that succeeded, the number of failed or foiled attacks—where terrorists had intended to cause mass casualties—was also increasing. Several sabotage attempts on passenger airliners were foiled. The bombers of the World Trade Center in 1993 had hoped to topple the towers and kill thousands. A 1995 plot in the Philippines to plant bombs aboard a dozen US airliners was an attempt to kill thousands. Those who dispersed nerve gas in Tokyo's subways in 1995 were bent upon mass murder.

Watching these trends, analysts began to write about the "new terrorism." This new terrorism, as envisaged by the analysts, did not mean simply nastier thugs with bigger truck bombs. It meant even more-fanatic assailants—driven by visions of God—armed with weapons of mass destruction, unconstrained by political calculations, bent upon destruction for its own sake. The emerging terrorism was seen as catastrophic, apocalyptic in its consequences. Terrorism, not the cold war, would deliver Armageddon.

In 1990 Paul Wilkinson, a veteran analyst, wrote *Terrorist Targets and Tactics: New Risks to World Order*.[1] Bruce Hoffman, then director of RAND's research program on terrorism, followed with *Holy Terror: The Implications of Terrorism Motivated by a Religious Imperative* (1993).[2] Aum Shinrikyo's nerve-gas attack in Tokyo underscored the trend and prompted three volumes: *The Cult at the End of the World*, by David Kaplan and Andrew Marshall (1996); *Holy Terror: Armageddon in Tokyo*, by D. W. Brackett (1996); and *Destroying the World to Save It: Aum Shinrikyo, Apocalyptic Violence, and the New Global Terrorism*, by Robert Jay Lifton (1999).[3]

In 1997 Mark Juergensmeyer wrote his influential article "Terror Mandated by God."[4] This was followed in 1998 by a series of works chronicling the shift: "Catastrophic Terrorism: Tackling the New Danger," by Ashton B. Carter, former CIA director John Deutch, and Philip Zelikow; "Confronting Nuclear, Biological, and Chemical Terrorism," by Richard Falkenrath; "Terror's New Face," by Walter Laquer; and *The Future of Terrorism: Violence in the New Millennium*, edited by Harvey Kushner.[5]

Countering the New Terrorism, by Ian Lesser, Bruce Hoffman, John Arquilla, David Ronfeldt, Michele Zanini, and myself, appeared in 1999, along with *The Ultimate Terrorist*, by Jessica Stern, and *Nuclear Terrorism*, by Gavin Cameron.[6]

The year 2000 saw *Living Terrors: What America Needs to Know about the Coming Bioterrorist Catastrophe*, by Michael Osterholm and John Schwartz; *6 Nightmares: Real Threats in a Dangerous World and How America Can Meet Them*, by former national security adviser Anthony Lake; *Terror in the Mind of God: The Global Rise of Religious Violence*, by Mark Juergensmeyer; and *The New Terrorism: Fanaticism and Arms of Mass Destruction*, by Walter Laquer.[7] *The New Terrorism: Threat and Response*, edited by Gideon Rose and James Hoge, appeared in January 2001.[8]

The titles convey a big part of the story: The word *new* appears eight times; the words *God, holy,* and *religious* appear a total of six times; the terms *nuclear, biological* or *bio-terrorist, chemical,* and *nerve gas* appear six times; end language in the form of *ultimate, catastrophic, end of the world, Apocalyptic,* and *Armageddon* appears six times.

The escalation in terrorist violence was driven not by new weapons or other technology. It was true that over time, terrorists in general improved their bomb-making skills, but none of the bloodiest attacks involved any weapons that had not already been in the terrorist arsenal for many years. The same scale of death could have been achieved in the 1960s. The change was in terrorist thought even more than deed.

Several things seemed to drive the violence. Any long conflict brutalizes combatants. Killing becomes easier. It happens during wars, too. The early debates in terrorist circles about whether it was right to destroy property belonging to workers were replaced by debates about whether murder by terrorists might tarnish their cause. These debates were then replaced by arguments about who is "guilty" and therefore a legitimate target of violence, and who is "innocent," a category that was steadily shrinking. While brutalization can be expected over time among combatants in a single organization, in the case of terrorism, it seemed to transcend organizational and generational boundaries. New terrorist groups coming on the scene did not start over with the old debates and replicate the escalation. They started out at the current level of terrorist violence and escalated from there. Just like tactical innovations that when seen to be successful by other terrorists were emulated, escalation by one terrorist group set the bar for others. All terrorism ramped up.

Terrorism also contained a built-in requirement for escalation. The spread of terrorist tactics made escalation inevitable. In order to attract attention, to cause fear and alarm, terrorism had to remain novel. The first terrorist hijacking was page-one news. By the fiftieth hijacking, it was old hat. In a crowded field, terrorists had to do something new to capture attention. With a limited tactical repertoire, the easiest way to keep everyone's attention was to escalate. If a small pipe bomb in front of a corporate headquarters at midnight no longer made headlines or put people on edge, a larger bomb that killed would, and a bomb that killed ten or one hundred people could not possibly be ignored.

The biggest change, however, seemed to be in the area of motives. In the 1960s and 1970s, political ideologies drove terrorists. They had political programs and at least pretend constituencies. In the 1980s, and especially in the 1990s, armed conflicts were increasingly driven by ethnic hatreds and religious fanaticism. Ethnic hatreds lend themselves to genocidal strategies, massacres, ethnic cleansing, and other atrocities–the kinds of things we have seen in Rwanda, the Balkans, and Sudan. There are no innocents among those defined as the "other." And any constraints imposed by a reluctance to tarnish a political cause or alienate a perceived constituency or by conventional morality simply do not apply to those who believe they act for God, however God is defined. If the victim is heathen, pagan, infidel, or heretic, doomed to burn in hell anyway, constraints do not apply. This is not to say that secular conflicts cannot involve slaughter–witness events in Cambodia in the 1970s, Germany under Hitler, or Russia during its civil war in the 1920s.

With terrorist incidents already rivaling the scale of natural disasters, it was easy to envision potential terrorists pushing into the domain of mass destruction. Conventional explosives could produce fatalities in the hundreds. Turning four hijacked airliners into missiles could kill thousands. But escalation beyond this would require unconventional weapons, specifically, biological attacks that could set off an epidemic–or a nuclear bomb. Terrorist use of nerve gas, anthrax, and ricin, although it did not kill great numbers of people, underscored the unconventional threat.

Although the escalation of terrorism is statistically demonstrable, as we have seen, that does not put terrorists on an inexorable trajectory toward the ultimate weapon of mass destruction. Extrapolation is always a risky form of analysis. A nuclear bomb is not just a great big truck bomb. There are technical, operational, even psychological breakpoints between the two. Truck bombs are low-tech weapons. Fabricating a nuclear weapon is orders of magnitude more difficult than fabricating a truck bomb, even assuming that terrorists had the requisite nuclear material. And while the immense destructive power of a nuclear weapon is theoretically attractive to terrorist groups such as al Qaeda, the use of a nuclear weapon would fundamentally alter the perceptions of both friends and foes in unpredictable ways. It would risk betrayal along the way and organizational suicide if the attack were successful.

Finally, while self-imposed constraints on terrorism have clearly eroded, they have not disappeared altogether. Even jihadists must calibrate their violence or risk isolation. While asserting that they are justified in killing millions, they argue among themselves about the application of violence. The slaughter of civilians has been criticized by some as "unmanly." The terrorist bombings of civilians at hotels in Amman, Jordan, in 2005 prompted street demonstrations against al Qaeda. Worried about a strategy of indiscriminate violence that killed thousands of Muslims and deliberate attacks on Shi'ites in Iraq, including their mosques, al Qaeda's number two man, Ayman al-Zawahiri, wrote a letter to Musab al-Zarqawi, al Qaeda's nominal leader in Iraq, warning that al Qaeda's constituents might not easily understand Muslims killing Muslims.[9]

Asserting his position as commander in the field, Zarqawi dismissed the counsels of constraint from distant headquarters. His brutal tactics in Iraq not only provoked Shi'ites but also eventually encouraged some of al Qaeda's Sunni allies to turn on the organization. Zarqawi would continue his campaign. Ultimately, al

Qaeda was able to force Zarqawi into a council of leaders, of which he was but one. With alternative leadership established, Zarqawi became less crucial. He was subsequently killed, quite probably betrayed by his al Qaeda rivals. But the damage was done.

Al-Zawahiri's admonitions to Zarqawi are evidence of self-imposed constraints and opportunities for deterrence. Eventually, Zarqawi was removed, possibly to save the movement, but too late, since the damage to al Qaeda's cause in Iraq was already done. (We are not entirely certain here whether it was Zarqawi's slaughter of fellow Muslims, Shias and Sunnis, or al Qaeda's fanatical imposition of a cruel sharia that alienated the Sunnis of Anbar Province. Both may have played a role.)

Chapter 11
FROM A BALANCE OF TERROR
TO A WORLD UNHINGED

For more than four decades, two nuclear-armed superpowers stood warhead to warhead. Each possessed an arsenal capable of ending modern civilization. Avoiding nuclear war became the major preoccupation of leaders on both sides. This required military planners to persuade their opponents that neither side could gain sufficient advantage to make starting a nuclear war even thinkable—neither could escape annihilation by launching a preemptive attack.

To achieve this balance, each side had to maintain sufficient nuclear capability to retaliate with equal or greater force and to persuade the other side that it was willing to do so if attacked. It sounds simple, but it required careful calculations, convincing communications, and complex negotiations aimed at preventing either side from gaining a destabilizing advantage. Deterrence was achieved by mutual assured destruction (MAD), a tense standoff aimed at preventing nuclear war. Some described this as a "balance of terror." The term is apt. It implies that although the threat was backed up by capacity to inflict destruction on a scale never before seen in the world, the intended effect was psychological—

terror—rather than any serious notion of actually waging and winning a nuclear war. We now know, however, that Soviet leaders came around to the idea that a nuclear war was unwinnable later than their American counterparts did.

The doctrine of mutual assured destruction did have one significant consequence in the popular mind. It meant that cities, not narrowly circumscribed military targets, would be bombed. Indeed, the collocation of "military" targets and population centers and the magnitude of destruction caused by large nuclear weapons rendered such a distinction, to a large extent, irrelevant. In popular culture, it meant that the entire population of a nation, not its soldiers on some distant front line, would be attacked in a nuclear war. Americans had fewer points of reference than others in this area. We had suffered no blitz as London had; we had experienced no sustained bombing campaigns as the cities of Germany or Japan had—no Hamburgs, no Dresdens, no Tokyos, no Hiroshimas. We had only the specters, the images of the ruined cities, to instruct us. As Richard R. Muller points out in his survey of aerial wartime bombing in the twentieth century, "Fear of city bombing was one of the most striking cultural developments of the modern age."[1] For more than forty years after the end of World War II, the cold war perpetuated that terror.

The sudden disintegration of what had been the principal adversary of the United States for forty years required a reevaluation of America's defense policy and military posture. Who was the enemy now?

Some saw the end of the cold war exclusively in terms of military budget, which could now safely be reduced. In their minds, there was no enemy to replace the Soviet Union, and they viewed growing concerns about terrorism with suspicion, seeing them as a desperate attempt to make up a threat deficit.

For a long time, conventional cold war planners remained unconvinced of the dramatic changes that were taking place in

Russia. They saw Russia's lurch toward democracy and capitalism and its embrace of the West as a temporary aberration. Convinced that Russia would soon become an adversary again, those of the old guard who are still around today feel somewhat vindicated by Russian president Vladimir Putin's more assertive diplomatic and military posture. And there is always China.

A third set of strategic thinkers worried about a confluence of worrisome trends, some of which, paradoxically, were accelerated or even set in motion by the changes in the former Soviet Union. The first trend affected world stability. Within the frontiers of its ideology, communism froze other conflicts, and beyond these frontiers, the cold war imposed constraints on local belligerents. Although the end of the cold war facilitated the resolution of some conflicts, notably the long-running guerrilla wars in Central America, the breakup of the Soviet Union also created new tensions in Central Asia and the Caucasus. Centrifugal forces in the Balkans led to a decade of war. Secular seers warned of global disorder, anarchy, pandemonium.

The collapse of the Soviet Union's authoritarian control also created new space for organized crime, which in Russia and Eastern Europe rapidly expanded beyond its traditional areas of drugs, human trafficking, prostitution, extortion, and black marketeering to seizing control of national economies. This was a new era of gangster capitalism allied with corrupt and criminal regimes. It coincided with the rapid globalization of criminal enterprises, matching the globalization of the economy.

Three other developments in the 1990s worried national security planners. First, with respect to Russia, it was not just that its government authority had rapidly receded, replaced by corruption and organized crime, or that a substantial portion of the economy had become little more than organized looting, but that this was taking place in a country that possessed thousands of nuclear weapons, hundreds of tons of fissile material, entire secret cities building weapons—cities that were now suddenly impoverished.

At the same time, nuclear proliferation continued to be a concern, with the possibility that the number of nuclear weapons states might soon nearly double. In addition to the United States, the Soviet Union, the United Kingdom, France, and China (with India having detonated a "peaceful" nuclear device and Israel believed to have nuclear weapons) were Ukraine and Kazakhstan, which became nuclear powers, albeit briefly. Other countries suspected of nuclear weapons ambitions included North Korea, Pakistan, Iran, Iraq, Libya, and Algeria. Could a nuclear black market be prevented? Arms inspectors dispatched to Iraq after the first Gulf War in 1991 found that the country's nuclear weapons program was further along than intelligence services had realized. North Korea was definitely developing nuclear weapons. In 1998 both India and Pakistan tested nuclear bombs and they nearly went to war in the following year.

Concurrent with these developments, terrorism was escalating. Iraq, Iran, Libya, and North Korea were already on Washington's list of state sponsors of terrorism, and some thought that Pakistan should also be on it.[2]

Inadequately secured nuclear weapons and unemployed nuclear scientists in Russia, clandestine nuclear programs in countries accused of sponsoring terrorism, and terrorists who appeared bent upon mass destruction were, in any assessment, a bad combination. Would Russian material and Russian know-how accelerate proliferation? Would terrorists be able to buy or steal nuclear weapons from Russia? Would sympathetic proliferators provide terrorists with a nuclear capability?

Several US commissions were created in the 1990s to examine the new threats and to review whether the country was adequately prepared to deal with them. The Commission to Assess the Organization of the Federal Government to Combat the Proliferation of Weapons of Mass Destruction, chaired by former CIA director John Deutch, warned of the diversion of weapons of mass destruction from Russia; the development of weapons of mass destruction by hostile states; the clandestine delivery of a nuclear weapon to the United States—an old concern even during the cold war—and the possible terrorist use of such weapons in the United States.[3]

The National Commission on Terrorism, led by former ambassador L. Paul Bremer, echoed the warning that terrorists might carry out large-scale attacks, possibly involving chemical, biological, and radiological weapons in the United States. The Bremer Commission cautiously avoided using the term *weapons of mass destruction,* in part because of the significant difference in difficulty of execution and consequences between chemical weapons, biological weapons, and radiological weapons. The commission also avoided that usage because it recognized that terrorist employment of these weapons, even if mass casualties or destruction did not result, could still cause widespread alarm and panic.[4] These were weapons of mass effect.

The Advisory Panel to Assess Domestic Response for Terrorism Involving Weapons of Mass Destruction, chaired by former Virginia governor James Gilmore, agreed in 1999 that the United States had to prepare for catastrophic attacks.[5] That terrorists would somehow acquire weapons of mass destruction and use them in the United States was the underlying concern of all three commissions. While Pentagon planners continued to prepare for war with other armies, national security was being redefined with the threat of terrorism at its heart. The realms of nuclear strategy, nuclear proliferation, and contemporary terrorism were merged into a single domain. Terrorism went geostrategic.

It is not clear that unfriendly states with clandestine programs to develop nuclear weapons—even if they were, as they are believed to be, state sponsors of terrorism—would turn such weapons over or would facilitate their acquisition by terrorists. Providing terrorists with sanctuary, financial support, training, and technical assistance is one thing. Giving them a nuclear capability is quite another. The donor would have to assume that the terrorists receiving the weapon intended to use it; at the very least, the donor state would lose control of that decision. The donor would also run the risk that the connection would be discovered and that the donor would bear the consequences, especially since countries are easier to attack than terrorists. Even if it were confident that its role could be successfully disguised, the donor could anticipate that a nuclear terrorist attack—the first hostile nuclear explosion since Nagasaki—would focus intense scrutiny on all suspected nuclear programs, including its own, leading to the possible imposition of restrictions, including a requirement to temporarily suspend development. Finally, the donor would have to accept the risk that the victim of the nuclear attack might not care about proof of complicity. The United States, Russia, Israel—three likely targets—might simply decide to eliminate all suspect nuclear programs. Helping terrorists go nuclear would bring a lot of risk and would leave the assisting nation with very little control over what the terrorists would do or what would happen as a result. Therein lies a potential deterrent strategy—directed at unfriendly states, if not at terrorists themselves. We will return to this point.

Chapter 12
AN AGE OF ALARMS

The new terrorism culminated spectacularly in the September 11, 2001, attacks on the World Trade Center and the Pentagon–a multiple-suicide hijacking that killed nearly three thousand people. It could easily have been worse. The terrorists intended to kill more, but thousands successfully evacuated the towers before the buildings collapsed, and passengers in the fourth hijacked airliner fought back, causing the plane to crash before reaching its intended target.

The attack confirmed the nation's worst fears, demonstrating both the determination and the ability of terrorists to carry out attacks of mass destruction. It raised concerns that in their efforts to kill on an even greater scale, terrorists might resort to unconventional weapons: a more effective version of the Tokyo nerve-gas attack; a biological attack; the dispersal of radioactive material; possibly the detonation of a nuclear weapon.

The 9/11 attacks had a profound psychological impact on the country. Like earlier generations of Americans who recalled exactly where they were when news of the attack on Pearl Harbor was announced or when President John F. Kennedy was assassinated, Americans today recall the moment of the attack. Most Americans watched ten to twelve hours of television that day. Six years later, 81 percent of all Americans said they saw the 9/11 attacks "as the most significant historical event of their lifetimes." The figure was 90 percent on the East Coast. Sixty-one percent said they thought of the events at least once a week, 16 percent said "every day."[1]

The 9/11 attacks shattered America's sense of national security and Americans' sense of their own personal security. All Americans were potential targets. The attacks altered the way we assess threats, the way we calculate risk. They made safety a national obsession. Years later, the question most frequently asked by the news media was "Are we safer now?" The attacks on 9/11 propelled the nation into an age of alarms.

In the case of Pearl Harbor, we saw the film well after the event. Americans watched the grainy footage of President Kennedy's motorcade taken at the moment the assassin's bullets struck. But we saw much of 9/11 as it happened. The images of the second plane slicing through the silver skyscraper, the towers collapsing one after the other, panic-stricken people running down the street, fleeing, disappearing into the devouring gray mass of dust and debris, strange human-shaped lumps of ash staggering out of the maelstrom, smoldering ruins that could have been left by a nuclear explosion mesmerized viewers around the world. As theater, it was riveting, but these were not the special effects of some Hollywood disaster film. This was real life—real death.

The intense television coverage of 9/11 created millions of vicarious victims. How often have we watched these scenes—a trailer previewing the end of the world? Most people guess somewhere between fifty and one hundred times.

The vast majority of Americans, including those distant from the attacks, suffered increases in stress-related symptoms—insomnia, depression, restlessness, irritability, anxiety, nightmares–the classic indications of post-traumatic stress disorder. Not surprisingly, according to a survey conducted by the RAND Corporation after the 9/11 attacks, 90 percent of adult Americans experienced at least one stress-related symptom to some degree, while 44 percent reported one or more "substantial" symptom of stress. Children were affected, too–47 percent were worried about their own or their loved ones' safety.[2] In the course of dealing with cascading business crises caused by the terrorist attacks, corporate executives pulled me aside to quietly confess to someone not in the chain of command that they were finding it difficult to concentrate, they couldn't sleep, they had become addicted to twenty-four-hour news channels. While reminding them that I was not a psychologist, I suggested that under the extraordinary circumstances, these were not abnormal reactions. Americans were in combat.

People also typically exaggerated the degree of personal danger posed by terrorist attacks. Doom was in the air. For months, the country lived with foreboding and dread, uncertain whether another attack on the scale of 9/11 was on the way.

It wasn't only 9/11. Within a week of the terrorist attacks, an anonymous killer with a scientist's knowledge of biological weapons began sending letters filled with deadly anthrax to recipients in the government and the news media. The campaign ended, but not before it killed five people, sent seventeen to the hospital, shut down several buildings, including a portion of the Senate office building in Washington, and raised the specter of biological warfare. Initially, it was unclear whether the anthrax letters and the 9/11 attacks might somehow be linked. It seemed too much of a coincidence. Later, authorities decided that the two events were not connected, but no perpetrator of the anthrax attacks was ever identified.

Continuing attacks by al Qaeda affiliates and aspirants around the world kept terrorism in the headlines. In the six years following 9/11, jihadist groups from Southeast Asia to Western Europe carried out thirty-four major terrorist attacks, not counting any of those that were part of the ongoing insurgencies or terrorist campaigns in Afghanistan, Kashmir, Iraq, Israel and the Palestinian territories, or Russia. These attacks were all pre-9/11 scenarios in scale, but more than thirteen hundred people were killed, and thousands were injured.[3]

Revelations of even more-ambitious terrorist plots added to the din. Although the plots were foiled or failed, they kept terrorism in the headlines and people on edge. Interrogations and trials of terrorists who were apprehended revealed that at one point in the planning process, the 9/11 terrorists considered hijacking and crashing ten planes, five on each coast, and that the initial plan called for crashing the planes into nuclear power plants. Richard Reid, an al Qaeda operative, tried to detonate a bomb concealed in his shoe while aboard a trans-Atlantic flight but was spotted by an alert flight attendant and overpowered by passengers—a close call. Singaporean authorities arrested twenty-one terrorists who planned to blow up the US and Israeli embassies, along with the Australian and British High Commissions. A terrorist arrested in Mumbai reported that hijacked planes were to be flown into Big Ben and London's Tower Bridge. British authorities uncovered a plot to fly a hijacked airliner into a passenger terminal at Heathrow Airport. An al Qaeda training manual found in Afghanistan recommended attacking targets such as the Statue of Liberty and the Eiffel Tower, as well as skyscrapers, airports, nuclear power plants, and football stadiums. The arrest of a key terrorist planner in Thailand uncovered a plot to crash a hijacked airliner into Singapore's Changi Airport.

Authorities uncovered a plot to blow up the US embassy in Sarajevo, Bosnia. Italian police uncovered a plot to disperse cyanide from tunnels beneath the US embassy in Rome. French authorities uncovered a plot to attack the Russian embassy in Paris with chemical or biological weapons. American authorities uncovered a plot to release cyanide on New York's subways.

An arrest in 2003 revealed that al Qaeda terrorists were reconnoitering the Brooklyn Bridge. In 2004 authorities uncovered terrorist reconnaissance of the World Bank headquarters in Washington, the New York Stock Exchange, and other financial institutions in New York and New Jersey. New York police arrested a man plotting to set off a bomb in the subway. According to a White House statement in 2005, authorities had foiled terrorist plots to hijack a plane and crash it into the US Bank Tower (the tallest building in Los Angeles), to attack targets on the East Coast, and to bomb apartment buildings elsewhere in the United States.[4]

In 2006 authorities in Britain uncovered a terrorist plot to blow up commercial planes flying over the Atlantic, a campaign that, if successful, would have caused casualties on the scale of 9/11.

A continuing stream of threats and warnings from al Qaeda's top leaders added to the tension. Between September 11, 2001, and December 31, 2007, Osama bin Laden appeared in twenty-eight videotapes or audiotapes, delivering vague warnings of further attacks. These appearances received enormous attention in the news media and invariably provoked comment by top government officials. Ayman al-Zawahiri was even more prolific, starring in almost twice as many video and audio productions.[5]

The message from Washington after 9/11 was one of unrelenting fear. On October 11, 2001, one month after the attacks, President George W. Bush, in a prime-time news conference, confirmed that the Justice Department had issued a blanket alert in recognition of a general terrorist threat.[6] Then, on October 29, the administration warned that intelligence sources had found credible evidence of terrorist plans to attack the nation "in the next week."[7] Nothing happened within the predicted time frame, but on December 12, the newly appointed director for homeland security warned the public that terrorist attacks "could happen within the next few weeks."[8] Later in the month, Richard Reid made his unsuccessful attempt to blow up a passenger airliner with a shoe bomb, underscoring the continuing terrorist threat.

In January 2002, the US attorney general announced that suicide attacks might be expected.[9] In February, he publicly called for Americans to be on the "highest state of alert," while the FBI warned that a terrorist attack might be imminent.[10] In March, the government issued a terror alert to US citizens in Italy.[11] In May, Vice President Dick Cheney warned that it was "not a matter of if, but when" al Qaeda would again attack the United States.[12] In the same week, Secretary of Defense Donald Rumsfeld declared that terrorists would "inevitably obtain weapons of mass destruction."[13] FBI Director Robert Mueller added that suicide bombings were "inevitable."[14]

In June 2002, Attorney General John Ashcroft announced that the FBI had arrested Abdullah al-Mujahir, the jihadist name adopted by José Padilla, a young former Chicago street gang member and ex-convict who had been recruited by al Qaeda. According to the announcement, Padilla was the point man for an al Qaeda plot to detonate a radioactive "dirty bomb" in an American city.[15] (In fact, the arrest had been made a month earlier but was announced only in June.)

In September 2002, one year after 9/11, President Bush announced that the government had raised the national threat level to orange, indicating a "high risk of terrorist attacks" under the new color-coded system.[16] Vice President Cheney moved to a "secure location" to ensure continuity of government if Washington were destroyed and the president killed.

The year 2002 ended with the arrest of a document forger in Canada who told authorities that nineteen Pakistanis were attempting to infiltrate the United States from Canada. FBI and law enforcement officials launched a nationwide manhunt, during which another source told the FBI that terrorists were planning to detonate eight diversionary bombs in New York Harbor on New Year's Eve.[17] This diversion, the source said, would be followed by a larger, genuine attack. (Authorities later learned that the original story from the arrested forger was, like his professional work, a complete fabrication.)

In February 2003, the government raised the national terrorist-alert level to orange for the second time, in response to a threat that was "the most specific we have ever seen," warning that al Qaeda terrorists might use a "radiological dispersal device as well as poisons and chemicals."[18] Citizens were advised to buy duct tape and plastic sheeting to protect themselves at home in case of a radiological, biological, or chemical attack. Authorities later discovered that this source, too, fabricated the information.

In March 2003, the government raised the national alert level to orange for the third time. Authorities feared that the imminent American invasion of Iraq would provoke attacks by "allied or sympathetic terrorist organizations, most notably the al Qaeda network."[19] At the same time, the Arizona National Guard was deployed to the Palo Verde nuclear power plant because an attack by al Qaeda extremists was believed to be "imminent."[20]

In May 2003, the threat level was again raised in response to the possibility of an al Qaeda attack during the Memorial Day holiday. This warning seemed to be based largely on surmise, as Secretary of Homeland Security Tom Ridge stated that there was no credible, specific information about tactics or targets.[21]

In September, the Department of Homeland Security issued an advisory warning that al Qaeda had developed plans to hijack airliners flying over the United States from Canada.[22]

In November 2003, Americans abroad were warned of an increased threat of terrorist attacks on US citizens and facilities in the wake of terrorist attacks in Istanbul. (This warning was renewed in March 2004, following an unsuccessful attempt to kill or capture Ayman al-Zawahiri.)[23]

In December 2003, intelligence reports indicated possible terrorist attacks on public events and on trans-Atlantic flights during the Christmas holidays. Dozens of flights were grounded, and the nation again went to orange.[24] (The scare was renewed in February 2004, when more flights were canceled.)[25]

Following the March 11, 2004, terrorist bombing of commuter trains in Madrid, which killed 191 people, the FBI and the Department of Homeland Security warned of similar attacks on trains and buses in the United States.[26] Then in June 2004, the attorney general announced that authorities had thwarted a plot to blow up a shopping mall in Columbus, Ohio.[27] (In fact, the suspect had been arrested in November 2003.)

In August 2004, the federal government again raised the terrorism-alert level to orange, but only for financial institutions in New York, New Jersey, and Washington.[28] The narrower focus of the alert indicated a shift in policy. Between March 2002, when the color-coded terrorism-alert level system was introduced, and August 2004, the nationwide threat level had been raised to orange and lowered to yellow five times. (During this same period, al Qaeda-inspired terrorists had carried out nineteen attacks worldwide.) In response to complaints that the nationwide alerts were too vague, too broad, too disruptive, and that they imposed heavy financial costs on cash-strapped cities, the federal government tried to limit their scope. There were no more nationwide general alerts.

The next alert came in July 2005, immediately after terrorists carried out suicide bombings on London subways and a London bus, killing fifty-two people. Fearing similar attacks, authorities ordered an orange alert for mass-transit and ferry systems across the United States.[29] The alert was suspended in August, but in October, citing a "credible threat" to its subway system, New York City went on its own alert.[30]

In August 2006, after the uncovering of an ambitious terrorist plot to smuggle liquid explosives aboard trans-Atlantic jets, the US government raised the threat-alert level on flights from the United Kingdom to an unprecedented red.[31] All airports remained at orange, while the rest of the country stayed at yellow.

The following year provided another hot summer, with numerous comments by government officials that some kind of terrorist attack on US targets was believed imminent, but there was nothing specific enough to raise the national threat level.

Part intel-speak, part breathless melodrama, the language of threat announcements had its own peculiar poetry:

"We are very worried . . ."

"We're at war and the war goes on . . ."

"We are going to get hit again . . ."

"Credible reports that extremists are planning additional attacks . . ."

"Actively plotting attacks . . ."

"Imminent credible threat . . ."

"Credible terrorist threat . . ."

"Credible information . . ."

"The information is good . . ."

"Very strong indicators . . ."

"Specific intelligence . . ."

"Specific to time, date and location . . ."

"The most specific we have seen . . ."

"Never before had such specific threat . . ."

"All Americans everywhere to be on the highest alert . . ."

"Targeted for death and destruction . . ."

"One of the most chilling plots imaginable . . ."

"Unfathomable damage, deaths, and destruction . . ."

"Weapons of mass destruction, including those containing chemical, biological, or radiological agents or materials . . ."

"Radiological or biological attack . . ."

"Radiological dispersal device, poisons and chemicals . . ."

"Banks, rail and transit systems, the Statue of Liberty, the Brooklyn Bridge . . ."

"Transportation and energy sectors . . ."

"Financial and transportation sectors . . ."

"Mass transit and ferry systems . . ."

"Buses and trains . . ."

"Subways . . ."

"American hotels and apartment buildings . . ."

"Not a matter of if, but when . . ."

"Might be expected . . ."

"In the coming days . . ."

"Within the next few weeks . . ."

"Within the week . . ."

Although it was understandable that in the shadow of 9/11 authorities already stung once by what was perceived as a failure of intelligence prior to 9/11 would err on the side of caution in sharing new intelligence with the public, people were becoming increasingly skeptical about Washington's constant cry of wolf. More-cynical observers questioned the coincidence of threat alerts with political difficulties at the White House. But it was not that there were too many alerts. It was the melodramatic tone with which they were communicated that created alarm, which later cooled to cynicism.

National alerts grew less frequent after 2005, but not because terrorist activity slowed down worldwide. In part, the decrease in alerts reflected a better understanding of the great volumes of information that surged through intelligence channels. In part, it reflected a deliberate policy decision not to further erode government credibility.

The 9/11 terrorist attacks altered our perceptions. Before 9/11, although projected by analysts and increasingly worried about by government officials, the scenarios of super-terrorism—mass-casualty attacks—remained abstract. This was an arcane area of intelligence and research, slowly entering public and political consciousness, largely through popular culture. That changed in a day. Everything was suddenly plausible. Scenarios that were once regarded as far-fetched became presumptions. Hardly any hypothetical terrorist scheme could be dismissed.

The events of 9/11 altered how we assessed threats in an insidious way, the consequences of which were not realized at the time. Traditionally, threat assessments had been based on analysis of the enemy's intentions and capabilities—what did the enemy want to do and what could he do? In a situation where the tactics and weapons of battle were known and agreed upon, this was a relatively straightforward calculation. During the cold war, it meant calculating Soviet military might and counting its missiles and warheads. Soviet intentions were presumed: the missiles were aimed at us, not Paraguay.

The terrorist threat could not be quantified so easily. Hostility was a given, but where and what would terrorists strike? And if terrorists with box cutters could turn planes into missiles, how could we measure terrorist capabilities? Not by numbers or firepower! Perhaps only by the breadth of their imagination.

The 9/11 Commission investigating the attacks described the government's lack of foresight and preparedness as a "failure of imagination." That made it imperative not just to outgun the terrorists but to out-imagine them.

Uncertainty about terrorists' intentions and capabilities pushed us from threat-based to vulnerability-based analysis. Instead of starting at the front end with terrorist intentions, the analysis now started at the back end by identifying a vulnerability, postulating a hypothetical terrorist foe, and building a scenario—invariably a worst-case scenario with terrible consequences. These invariably begin, "Suppose terrorists were to . . ."

Vulnerability-based analysis provides a reasonable way of assessing consequences and evaluating response capabilities. It is, however, not a substitute for threat assessment. Nonetheless, the hypothetical scenarios are often transformed into threats that are perceived to be real. What begins as a possibility slides into something that is deemed probable and then inevitable–not "if," but "when." Imminent![32]

Terrorists, or we on their behalf, can conjure up attack scenarios faster than we can put into place measures to thwart them, even if we had the resources to do so. Vulnerabilities in an open, highly developed, technology-dependent society are infinite, while resources for security are finite. That sets up a competition among those concerned about whatever vulnerability they consider most important.

This competition manifests itself in threat advocacy, in which champions of a particular vulnerability or attack scenario compete with one another for public attention and a share of the security budget, each making the argument that failure to protect a particular set of targets or to prevent a particular threat will result in catastrophe.[33] We see this in competition among cities for homeland security dollars, with each recipient arguing that it has more vulnerabilities or that it is more likely to be attacked than its rivals for the funds. We see the competition among industrial sectors. Should we spend more on protecting commercial aviation, which already receives a large share of the total homeland security budget in order to prevent another 9/11 or the sabotage of aircraft, or on installing antimissile technology, or on protecting public surface transportation, which terrorists have attacked repeatedly, causing large-scale casualties? Or should we put more resources into protecting nuclear reactors, where the consequences of a successful terrorist attack could be disastrous? Do we invest more in detecting conventional explosives or in preventing nuclear terrorism?

Since it is difficult to estimate the probabilities of an attack, threat advocates make it a contest of consequences. Indeed, most current assessments of the terrorist threat are consequence-driven, especially in their rhetoric. But a detailed discussion of consequences also makes the threat more real. In a democracy, we do all of this in public. Needless to say, it is a spectacle that contributes to fear, a foreboding sense of imminent doom.

A focus on dire consequences also affects political decision making. In the case of catastrophic consequences, as in an attack on the United States involving true weapons of mass destruction, the possibility of tens of thousands or hundreds of thousands of casualties trumps the probability of occurrence. Even a 1 percent chance becomes an unacceptable risk requiring preventive or preemptive action. Suspicion suffices. The United States launched an invasion of Iraq on that basis. Although the intelligence proved wrong, many still argue that the invasion was justified. Similar arguments have been voiced in favor of preemptive military action against Iran if it fails to halt its suspected development of nuclear weapons.

Chapter 13
AMERICA THE ANXIOUS

While nuclear terror is not unique to American society—Japan is, after all, the only nation that has suffered nuclear attacks—American society is uniquely susceptible to nuclear terror. Why is this so?

In the minds of many Americans, we live on the brink of doom, underscored by cold war apprehensions, 9/11 nightmares, and end-time visions. To supplement our fears, America's highly creative popular culture provides a steady stream of nuclear terrorist novels, movies, and television shows that give dramatic, if fictional, expression to national anxieties. Nuclear terror also receives official endorsement. After 9/11, the government relentlessly promoted a message of fear, declaring that next time around, terrorists could be armed with nuclear weapons—perhaps supplied by Iraq's Saddam Hussein, or Iran's President Mahmoud Ahmadinejad. While President Franklin D. Roosevelt told the American people that "the only thing we have to fear is fear itself," President George W. Bush and much of his administration warned us incessantly that we must be afraid, very afraid.

Without setting out to do so, the news media have become

active collaborators in the diffusion of terror. The media report repeated concerns about nuclear nightmares coming true in ever more lurid detail to grab ratings and readers and to fill the insatiable appetites of cable TV news channels and the Internet. News stories and programs show us diameters of destruction, computer animations, and illustrations of cities flattened. They hypothesize about millions of casualties and painful deaths and trot out experts to speculate on all manner of sensational scenarios. As a result, what in truth is remotely possible becomes plausible and soon almost a foregone conclusion in our minds. The question becomes no longer *if* terrorists will hit us with nukes, but *when*. We get the message from our TV screens, computer screens, and newspapers that thinking anything else is naive and hopelessly optimistic.

DECLINE AND DOOM

Beneath America's belief in progress, our coveted material achievements, and our characteristic optimism lies an American obsession with decline and doom. America the most powerful is also America the most anxious. We worry that America will lose its place in the world. We fear that US military superiority will be challenged by new foes–China or a resurgent Russia. We lose sleep wondering if our security and even our lives will be wiped out by foes and tactics against which we have little defense–bloodthirsty terrorists who will readily kill themselves and anyone who gets in the way of their extremist vision. Although we are a nation of immigrants, we fear that our borders no longer protect our territory or our culture. We demand walls to protect us from outside intruders, but we also fear subversion from within. For decades, the supposed threat to America was godless communism. Today, it is terrorist sleeper cells of crazed Muslim fanatics, annihilation from within, or even the Antichrist.

Although America's taste for doom often takes on religious tones, it transcends religious faith. Not all prophets of doom are found in the Bible. Those forecasting the decline and fall of America are part of a long and rich tradition. Exaggerated emphasis on military defeat, imperial stretch, manufacturing decline, rising crime, moral decay, political corruption, unconstrained materialism, unwillingness to sacrifice, government deficits, feckless leaders, and the loss of community, conviction, and courage have all been deployed by domestic declinists and critics abroad as reasons for America's days being numbered.

The Soviet launch of *Sputnik* in 1957, the riots and assassinations of the 1960s, the 1973 Arab oil embargo, the failure in Vietnam, the Iran hostage crisis, the rise of Japan and later China as world economic powers, the frustration over Iraq, the unsupportable fiscal and trade deficits, the falling housing prices, the political divisions, and the failures of our education system have all provoked worries that the end of American prosperity and power is near and inevitable.

Terrorism contributes to these current woes. It has caused a significant diversion of resources to security—a modest incremental increase in the costs of homeland security, but a massive increase if the sum includes the costs of the wars in Iraq and Afghanistan. Beyond the direct costs are the insidious indirect effects of heightened security on the economy and public attitudes. Bright students, technical experts, and business executives from abroad can no longer easily travel to or stay in the United States. Insurance premiums are higher. Factories and stores, fearing disruptions, are keeping larger inventories. Delays, distractions, and diversions are tiny individually, but their cumulative effect is significant.

War and war talk in the Middle East have raised the price of oil to unprecedented heights, contributing further to the imbalance of trade and the outflow of American dollars, although growing world demand for oil is the principal source of upward pressure on price.

Terrorists talk about waging economic warfare. It makes us nervous, even though without a sophisticated and sustained campaign of sabotage the terrorists probably cannot do more than cause fright spikes in oil prices. And unless they ascend very high into the domain of nuclear or biological weapons, terrorists can't significantly affect the diversified economy of a nation as large as the United States. Nor can terrorists bring down financial markets, although they are a continuing source of market anxiety.

Declinist theories rarely envision America being destroyed by nuclear weapons. Instead, the nuclear threat, real or imagined, contributes to a more general sense of uncertainty, anxiety, and gloom. All this creates greater receptivity to secular declinist theories, just as the threat of nuclear terrorism encourages religious end-time thinking. But it also runs the other way. The vague sense of unease created by fears of decline manifests itself in an increased apprehension of terrorism in general and of nuclear terrorism in particular. Free-floating anxiety finds expression in nuclear terror. Just as terror increases gloom, gloom increases terror.

The cold war left behind a legacy of lingering nuclear terror. For more than four decades, Americans lived with the threat of annihilation. American thinkers and decision makers thought about the unthinkable—city-melting multimegaton bombs and planetary suicide with doomsday bombs and nuclear winters, the end of civilization as we know it.

Cold war fears later morphed into post-9/11 fears. Frequent warnings of further terrorist attacks betrayed the jittery atmosphere that prevailed in the United States after September 11, 2001. In fairness, these warnings reflected the reality of the jihadists' continuing global terrorist (not just terror) campaign. In the first five years after the 9/11 attacks, there was intense terrorist activity, with major jihadist terrorist attacks occurring somewhere in the world—Bali, Istanbul, Madrid, London—on an average of one every two months. Many other terrorist plots were discovered and thwarted, and further attempts were expected. Terrorists boasted that the destruction would be greater the next time. American fear grew along with the boasts.

THE BEGINNING OF THE END

America's inherent religiosity, a powerful element in our nation's history, increasingly expresses itself in a fundamentalist faith that proclaims the Bible to be the literal truth, from its account of the Creation to its prophecies of the cataclysmic end of time. This faith has produced a rich corpus of inspirational works, but biblical prophecy has also produced an extraordinarily popular literature of imminent doom.

We have no way to calibrate precisely what someone believes, no device to x-ray the human soul, no thermometer to measure intensity of faith. But by all external measures, America is a deeply religious nation, a country of churchgoers. Many Americans openly express their faith, consider it important, and expect their leaders to believe. American leaders openly call upon God's counsel, kneel to pray, and often express themselves in religious terms. Although the US Constitution expressly denies the state any role in fomenting faith, religion weighs heavily in American elections. Freedom of religion is guaranteed, but any political candidate who admitted to not believing at all would almost certainly be defeated.

Christianity, in its many forms, dominates, and America's Christianity increasingly leans toward fundamentalism. According to various public opinion polls, more than a third of all Americans describe themselves as evangelical born-again Christians.[1] Forty percent of the entire American public believes that the Bible should be taken literally, not as literature or allegory or metaphor, but as gospel truth, from the Garden of Eden to the end of time.[2]

How the world will end—as expressed in the books of Enoch,

Daniel, and Ezekiel, and above all, the book of Revelation–has become an increasingly significant element of contemporary evangelical Christian faith. Although there are numerous interpretations and debates about the sequence of the events, the end-times include a series of signs that the end is near, the appearance of an Antichrist (a false prophet who will beguile the masses and rule the world), the tribulation (a period of great human suffering), the rapture (the summoning to heaven of true Christian believers), the return of the Savior, and Armageddon (a final battle between the forces of good and evil, followed by heavenly peace).

The Apocalypse provides psychologically powerful material for evangelists. It is a harrowing vision that can be deployed to arouse those who are complacent in their substandard zeal. It deals with everyone's anxieties about death. It offers the attractive possibility that, through faith, one can escape suffering and ultimate oblivion. It appeals in particular to those who see life itself as dangerous and precarious and to those who believe that evil is no mere theological abstraction but an active force–that evil has a name. The mysterious language of the Apocalypse attracts intelligent and ingenious analysts to decipher its secret codes in order to attain knowledge of the contemporary world and the enviable power to predict its future.

The vivid language of biblical passages begs interpretation: What are the signs? How close are we to the end? How will it happen? Who is the Antichrist? Has the ordeal of the tribulations already begun?

Many Christian fundamentalists believe that we are getting close and that we will witness the end in our lifetime. Renewed interest in end-time thinking was inspired by the creation of the state of Israel in 1948, which many Christians regarded as a fulfillment of biblical prophecy. President Ronald Reagan, a devout Christian himself, thought that we were close. "The day of Armageddon isn't far off," he said. "Everything is falling into place."[3] There is intense interest in applying biblical language to current events, especially in the Middle East, where many believe the final battle of Armageddon will be fought.

Since biblical language is obscure to a modern reader, it allows considerable leeway and invites ingenuity in interpreting the end signs. The Antichrist may be identified as any contemporary figure seen as malevolent. Or, since evil intent may be disguised behind purportedly noble aims of world peace, almost anyone of great influence (but arousing a quantum of suspicion) may be seen as the Antichrist. Candidates in the past have included obvious villains like Adolf Hitler and Josef Stalin; more recent figures are the Ayatollah Khomeini, Saddam Hussein, and Osama bin Laden.[4] But some believers have suspected Nobel Peace Prize laureates, including former Egyptian president Anwar Sadat (who was assassinated by Muslim fanatics for making peace with Israel), former Soviet premier Mikhail Gorbachev, and former secretary of state Henry Kissinger.[5] Even prominent evangelist Pat Robertson has been accused by some of being the Antichrist.[6]

Satan's host has been variously identified as the Soviet Empire—in President Reagan's words, an "evil empire." The host has also been identified as the states accused of both sponsoring terrorism and secretly building nuclear weapons—in President George W. Bush's words, an "axis of evil" comprising Iraq, Iran, and North Korea. The biblical host may be the terrorists, the "evildoers." In the eyes of some Christian fundamentalists, evil emanates from Islam itself.

The Muslim outsider makes an easy target for the apocalyptic imagination. Early Christian writers described the original advance of Islam as the "eruption of the sons of Ismael."[7] This referred to Arabs from the desert whose military expansion under the banner of Islam in the seventh century was seen as a grave threat to Christianity, just as today, many Christians worry about the resurgence of Arab fundamentalists. The spread of Islam in the seventh century was interpreted by some at the time as God's punishment for the sins of Christians, including homosexuality.[8] It is a theme echoed in contemporary society, with some very prominent evangelists suggesting that the 9/11 terrorist attacks were God's punishment for America's toleration of homosexuality. More ingeniously, some see the Apocalypse's "beast" as revealed in a contemporary map of the Middle East, which, when one fills in certain Muslim countries but leaves Saudi Arabia as negative space, creates a silhouette that vaguely resembles an attacking animal. It is not an image that leaps out at you. We humans are pattern makers, but the creator of this image had to start with a presumption that Islam is the beast of the Apocalypse, then invent the visual confirmation.

The vivid but disturbing apocalyptic words and visions of the end resonate both with the terrifying fictional violence we see at the movies and on television and with the real-life violence we see and read about in daily news reports. The original images of the Apocalypse were meant to inspire terror. They continue to do that today.

Biblical language readily adapts to nuclear terror with its references to a "great red dragon," a "lake of fire," "utterly burned with fire," "a sun . . . black as sackcloth," a "full moon like blood," and "strange and lasting scars." The Apocalypse is populated by strange monsters, by victims who will "long to die" and who will die "horrible deaths." These phrases are interpreted by some as descriptions of nuclear explosions and the effects of radiation. At the same time, contemporary secular accounts of the effects of a terrorist nuclear explosion just as easily slide into a biblical lexicon. The horrific effects of nuclear weapons lend themselves to lurid descriptions, while the awesome destructive power of those weapons propels one into a philosophical and religious contemplation that finds expression in an apocalyptic vocabulary. Biblical literalists and nuclear doomsayers speak the same language.

Endism finds its popular voice in novels of biblical prophecy such as Hal Lindsey's 1970 *The Late Great Planet Earth*, which forecasts persecution of the "true Christians" and growing tension in the Middle East.[9] In the novel, this situation leads to world war and an increase of drug use, crime, and insanity. Lindsey also foretold the rise of what we would now call new age religions, economic decline, moral decay, loss of American military power, and the emergence of a united Europe destined ultimately to be taken over by the Antichrist. In the book, this is followed by the use of nuclear weapons somewhere in the world and increasing natural catastrophes.[10] In some of these prophecies, Lindsey would find company among the declinists. But in Lindsey's view, these harrowing events should not be the cause of despair but rather should be seen as evidence of a grand design to bring about a revival of faith—a ticket out before the world plunges into judgment.

Tim Lahaye's 1972 *The Beginning of the End* turned out to be the beginning of a large-scale multimedia enterprise, which provides suspense-filled accounts of the tribulation.[11] One of the recent volumes, co-authored by Lahaye and Ed Hindson, *Global Warning: Are We on the Brink of World War III?* addresses the "Axis of Evil," the "Islamic Threat," and the "Nuclear Nightmare" from a biblical perspective.[12] Hindson believes that if the jihadists had a nuclear weapon, "they would probably use it."[13]

Another end-time work, John F. Walvoord's *Armageddon, Oil and the Middle East Crisis*, predicted that access to oil and the rise of Islamic terrorism would be at the center of end-time events, leading to a nuclear confrontation between Iran and Israel.[14]

The same themes are taken up by Mark Hitchcock in *Iran, the Coming Crisis: Radical Islam, Oil and the Nuclear Threat*. Hitchcock sees an invasion of Israel by Russia, Iran, and other Muslim nations as confirmation of the prophecies of Ezekiel. An advertisement for the book notes that "President Bush has stated that the greatest threat to America is nuclear terrorism."[15]

Secular works about nuclear terrorism reinforce Christian end-time thinking. John Hagee, the author of *Jerusalem Countdown: A Prelude to War*, quotes President Bush, Vice President Cheney, Senator John Kerry, Professor Graham Allison, and Paul Williams (the author of several books on nuclear terrorism) to make the case that nuclear terrorism on US soil is inevitable and imminent.[16]

End-time authors are extraordinarily prolific. Tim Lahaye, working with co-authors, has written more than fifty books, as well as an additional forty books for young readers. Walvoord has written thirty books. Since 1991, Hitchcock has written fourteen books. And end-time books are frequently on the best seller lists. *The Late Great Planet Earth* sold thirty-five million copies. Lahaye's *Left Behind* series has sold more than fifty million copies. Their popularity reflects an understandable desire to know the future, to turn to the last page to see how things turn out. How will the greatest story ever told end? And to possess what is presented as secret knowledge brings a sense of power to those who may feel powerless. It makes the reader part of a knowing elite, even if it is a large elite of fifty million readers.

But end-time book sales also reflect a deeper insecurity. We live in turbulent times, tossed about by powerful forces seemingly beyond our control—natural disasters, diminishing resources, wars, and madmen, from shopping mall shooters to suicide bombers bent upon death and destruction. In times of uncertainty and danger, people often turn to God. Apocalyptic writings don't promise that things will get better; they tell us that events are not random and that they have meaning. In that alone some find comfort. And for those propelled by apocalyptic terror to embrace Jesus Christ, there is the promise of personal salvation.

Christian fundamentalists are, however, ambiguous about how they should respond to the Apocalypse. Should the fulfillment of the Bible's terrifying prophecies be welcomed as validation of faith and promise that the rapture and eternal peace lie just ahead? Or are the current interpretations a summons to battle the forces of evil? Should one serenely await the end or prepare to fight on God's side against the forces of the Antichrist? While end-of-the-world cults of all religious stripes may pray on hilltops or poison themselves, the recommended response in Christian fundamentalist end-time literature is not passivity or self-destruction but mobilization and preparation, both spiritual and physical.

End-time believers have their own worldview. It is in part a mind-set shared by all true believers, whatever their ideology or faith, but many aspects of it are unique. Like all true believers, end-time believers are uncomfortable with uncertainty and ambiguity. Like all true believers, they see the world in black and white, good versus evil, although end-time believers place greater emphasis on evil and evil men.

End-time believers see the world as hostile and dangerous, life as precarious and fragile. It is what attracts them to end-time beliefs. End-time believers are social conservatives, deeply concerned about protecting the American way of life—physically, culturally, and morally. Like the declinists, they worry about America's porous borders; large-scale immigration, legal and illegal; and the ability of the nation to assimilate large numbers of foreigners without diluting what they regard as American culture.

End-time believers tend to be deeply suspicious of the mainstream news media. Many see the media as too liberal, anti-religious, out of tune with mainstream America, unpatriotic, and biased in their coverage. Instead, the end-timers tend to get their news from the pulpit, from conservative TV and radio talk shows that reinforce their views—and increasingly from favored sites on the Internet that provide what they believe is the "real story."

End-time believers view government with suspicion, frequently suspecting it of concealment—even though they believe that it may behave this way for the common good. They suspect, for example, that authorities do not tell the people all they know about terrorists armed with nuclear weapons, for this could easily lead to national panic. Yet end-time believers see no inconsistency when end-time authors uncover and disseminate what the public is not supposed to find out. "What the government and the media will not tell you" is an irresistible come-on.

End-time believers are prone to believe that there are hidden, often divine explanations for known events. They see knowledge as revealed, rather than acquired through experience and reasoning. They uncritically accept information on faith. They see biblical prophecies as intelligence–communications intercepted directly from the mind of God.[17]

End-time believers tend to see the terrorist violence of al Qaeda not as an aberrant ideology but as an authentic expression of Islam. They view the current conflict not as a war on terrorism but as a global religious conflict. End-time believers see Islamic apocalyptic beliefs as threats to peace. And end-time believers have not forgotten the cold war. They remain deeply suspicious of Russia, frequently seeing it in league with Muslim opponents of Israel in fulfillment of biblical prophecy.

Some attributes of the end-time mind-set mirror the beliefs of Muslim extremists. No less than Osama bin Laden are end-time believers absolutely convinced of the righteousness of their own cause. Like the jihadists, they share the view that America's war on terrorism is, in fact, a defensive religious war–a clash of civilizations. No less than any of al Qaeda's own recruits do some Christian end-time believers believe that religion justifies–sometimes requires–the use of violence and that any compromise in matters of faith is apostasy. Although they are on the opposite side of the issue, they agree with Muslim fanatics that the existence of Israel lies at the heart of the current conflict. End-time believers support Israel's expansion. Islamist extremists want Israel eliminated. Jihadists believe that God will punish America for its sins, for its lack of faith, its lack of morality, and its tolerance–even protection–of homosexuality. End-time believers agree.

TIMELY THRILLERS TORN FROM THE HEADLINES

The same fears that inspire secular doom and religious end-time thinking provide a rich source of raw material for novelists and screenwriters, who have invented an array of arch villains and armed them with nuclear weapons, vaporized American cities, and given us glimpses of the dismal day after.

Washington, New York, London, Paris, Geneva, along with other cities across the globe, have been obliterated by terrorists' nuclear bombs in films and novels. Scores more cities have been threatened with destruction but saved at the last minute from wild-eyed fanatics by the courage and heroic determination of maverick loners, often operating on their own, outside established intelligence services, beyond bureaucratic constraints.

This is the stuff of nuclear terrorism novels like *The Day before Midnight*, *The Doomsday Contract*, *The Fifth Horseman*, *Gadget*, *Goodbye California*, *The Hamlet Warning*, *The King of Bombs*, *The Road to Armageddon*, *The Sum of All Fears*, and *Z Warning*, and of movies and television shows like *Peacemaker* and *24*.[18] If not a reality in reality, nuclear terrorism has long been a reality in popular culture.

Although a few science fiction novels described wars fought with hypothesized nuclear weapons years before the actual atomic bomb, it was the bombing of Hiroshima and Nagasaki that prompted an immediate outpouring of nuclear war fiction. The genre peaked again in the mid-1950s, when cold war tensions reached a new height. It peaked again after the Cuban Missile Crisis in 1962, and again when the intense international debate surrounding the deployment of new nuclear missiles in Europe pushed the production of nuclear war fiction up to unprecedented highs in the 1980s.

Waging nuclear war itself has received little attention in fiction. Because a nuclear war would likely be brief—perhaps only minutes long–it provides few opportunities for battlefield heroism. Therefore, novels and movies explore the before and after–the possibility of a nuclear war being initiated by rogue generals or started accidentally, or the effects of radiation in creating mutant monsters or doomed survivors. Fiction focuses on the societal effects of massive destruction–panic, the breakdown of law and order, the brutish life of survivors–as the real terror.

Science fiction has gone further, depicting post–nuclear war civilizations where godlike scientists engineered utopian societies or where apes ruled and humans lived underground worshipping the bomb. In her review of editor Brian Aldiss's *A Science Fiction Omnibus*, Dinah Birch notes that "it is the business of science fiction to alarm, in the sense of providing the excitement of thrilling dangers, and of scaring readers with the prospect of a future in which human values are threatened. Ruthless invasions, apocalyptic plagues, wars, and famine . . . have been its favourite devices."[19]

The possibility that enemy agents might smuggle nuclear weapons into the United States to launch a sneak attack–a nuclear Pearl Harbor–was a national obsession in the decade following World War II.

In 1946 Edward Condon, a veteran of the Manhattan Project, wrote, "In any room where a file case can be stored, in any district of a great city, near any key building or installation, a determined effort can secrete a bomb capable of killing a hundred thousand people and laying waste every ordinary structure within a mile." Asked in a closed Senate hearing "whether three or four men couldn't smuggle units of an [atomic] bomb into New York and blow up the whole city," nuclear scientist J. Robert Oppenheimer responded, "Of course, it could be done, and people could destroy New York." The scientist was then asked by a senator, "What instrument would you use to detect an atomic bomb hidden somewhere in a city?" Oppenheimer replied, "A screwdriver." He said it would be necessary to open up every crate, every suitcase. Oppenheimer believed that there "was no defense against nuclear terrorism"–and he felt there never would be.[20]

Smuggled nuclear bombs were the subject of Philip Wylie's 1948 novel, *The Smuggled Atom Bomb*.[21] His later best seller *Tomorrow*, written in 1954, describes in lurid detail the physical and societal effects of a sneak Soviet nuclear attack on the United States. In a secular version of Armageddon, the United States responds by detonating a secret doomsday bomb that wipes out the entire Soviet Union, thereby providing the opportunity to rebuild a better world. "Then the bomb would be no catastrophe at all, but pure benefit," the author writes.[22] This was a secular version of end-time vision–massive destruction followed by what some considered heaven on earth. Few other authors shared Wylie's cheerful perception of nuclear destruction as deliverance. Most nuclear war fiction remained rooted in doom.

The clandestine delivery of nuclear weapons continued to be a concern, both in fiction and in real life. Researchers at the RAND Corporation explored possible scenarios involving the smuggling, as opposed to the launching, of nuclear weapons into the United States. How many bombs would the Soviets have to preposition in order to be certain that they had neutralized America's ability to retaliate? How many Soviet agents would it take? How would they maintain the weapons once they were in place? How might the weapons be concealed? Would it be worth the risks if the plan was discovered before it was completed?

A few contemporary authors assert that the Soviets did at least partially execute their plan and that concealed nuclear weapons have been in the United States since the cold war. One version of this story goes on to assert that former Russian officials, who still know where the nuclear weapons are buried, were hired by al Qaeda to help locate them.[23]

Today's renewed clandestine-delivery concerns take us back to the shipborne-bomb scenario of the 1940s, updated to shipping containers. Oppenheimer's screwdriver has been replaced by new cargo documentation procedures, the dispatch of customs agents to ports overseas, and the deployment of radiation detectors and other inspection technology at US ports.

Clandestine fabrication, as opposed to clandestine delivery, of nuclear weapons did not become a feature of the fictional literature until Ted Taylor and others in the early 1970s began to assert that although building a nuclear bomb was not something any bright lunatic could do in his garage, neither did it require the equivalent of the Manhattan Project. In the years since 1945, they said, the secrets of nuclear fission and the principles of nuclear weapons design were widely known. And with the spread of nuclear energy facilities and a growing international traffic in fissionable material, terrorists just might be able to obtain the necessary ingredients. These concerns set the nuclear terrorism novel in motion. News headlines provided prototypes for terrorist villains and inspiration for terrorist plots. And unlike nuclear war literature, nuclear terrorist fiction offered a venue for heroes from Ian Fleming's James Bond to *24*'s Jack Bauer—men of action in a race against time to thwart the diabolical schemes of evil masterminds.

Book titles combined dramatic words like *ultimatum* (the most frequently used word in a title) with *nuclear, Armageddon, doomsday,* and *disaster.* Post-9/11 titles brought in *jihad* and *Allah.* Cover illustrations depicted familiar icons—mushroom clouds over recognizable city skylines, skulls, radiation signs—but some also indicated Islamic foes. The cover of Sheldon Filger's *The King of Bombs* features the fierce visage of Osama bin Laden in a mushroom cloud rising from a city skyline.[24]

Many Muslims justifiably resent the obvious stereotyping that occurs on book covers—and even more in recent movies and television shows with terrorist themes, where the terrorist villains are often depicted as Muslim fanatics. But it is not only the novelists, illustrators, and casting directors who create the stereotype. Their fictional images closely resemble the equally fantastic images created by the jihadists themselves. Jihadist Web sites feature images of Osama bin Laden next to a mushroom cloud or glowering over a city studded with little mushroom clouds. Another image depicts a mushroom cloud emanating from bin Laden's open hand, a trope presaged on the cover of *Hamlet Warning*, written by Leonard Sanders in 1976, which shows a mushroom cloud arising from an open hand.[25]

Some of the fictional works come with messages: Nuclear weapons make war unthinkable. The power to destroy the planet cannot be entrusted to fallible human beings. Nuclear energy is too dangerous. Nuclear weapons demand world government. Nuclear terrorism is inevitable. But most of the works are simply entertaining thrillers, their plot lines bouncing off contemporary concerns: the emergence of terrorism, tensions in the Middle East, the rise of organized crime in the former Soviet Union, the emergence of al Qaeda.

In the nuclear terror fiction of the 1960s and 1970s, the terrorists used nuclear weapons as instruments of coercion, which was how analysts saw the threat at the time. In precise formal English, Ian Fleming's crime syndicate, SPECTRE, warns the world, "If, within 48 hours, . . . willingness to accept our terms is still not communicated, there will ensue the destruction of a major city situated in an undesignated country of the world."[26] Reacting to the shift in terrorism, later novels presented nuclear weapons as instruments of pure destruction. In the novel *Red Mercury*, Max Barclay describes the new terrorism villain: He "will do everything he can to detonate that . . . device." "No stopping him?" "Stop him? Maybe. But only with force." "Does he care about dying?" "Not at all."[27]

The pantheon of fictional villains includes terrorists, international crime syndicates, underworld brotherhoods, megalomaniacal dictators, and embittered nuclear scientists, often operating in combination. Operationally, they would easily rank at the top end of the hypothetical composite adversary created by RAND for the US Department of Energy. They combine dedication, discipline, unlimited financial resources, military skills, technical know-how, and insider assistance. They are modern super-villains, but their motives are classic: greed, revenge, power.

All the nuclear terrorist novels in the world combined will not tell you how to make a nuclear bomb. The novels contain vague descriptions with enough technical jargon to persuade the reader that someone outside of government can make one, but the objective is just plausibility. Pushing for reality, some authors have turned to nuclear scientists as advisers to make the technical language more convincing.

Popular fiction imposes few limits on plausibility. The yields of fictional terrorist bombs have grown from mere Hiroshima-size devices to megaton city busters to multimegaton monsters ten thousand times larger than the actual bomb dropped on Hiroshima—a bomb capable of destroying half a continent. Some novelists have armed their fictional terrorists with cobalt-laced doomsday devices whose fallout could end all life. In exploring doomsday scenarios, novelists are merely mimicking the musings of scientists who in the 1950s pursued the idea of a doomsday bomb or a stockpile of nuclear bombs programmed to detonate automatically if America were attacked, thereby ending all life on the planet.

Imaginative, good at getting inside the minds of their characters, unfettered by institutional constraints, novelists are sometimes able to convincingly describe events that haven't occurred and thereby inspire the thinking of other imaginative people. In his nonfiction book *Doomsday Men,* P. D. Smith tells how Leo Szilard, the scientist behind the idea of a nuclear chain reaction and a participant in the Manhattan Project, was himself inspired by H. G. Wells's novel *The World Set Free.*[28] Written in 1913, *The World Set Free* describes a radiation-emitting "atomic bomb" capable of destroying a city.[29] Szilard later theorized about the creation of a cobalt superbomb, the ultimate doomsday device that would, if detonated, wipe out all life on Earth.

However, apart from one nuclear hoax perpetrated by a not too tightly wrapped author, it is difficult to identify any specific terrorist attack that was inspired by a novelist's scenario. Again, according to P. D. Smith, who has thoroughly explored the popular culture of the nuclear bomb, al Qaeda terrorists revealed under interrogation in 2002 that they had been inspired by watching Hollywood's 1998 remake of the science fiction movie *Godzilla*, a Japanese classic in which a giant flame-breathing monster wreaks havoc in Tokyo. The terrorists hoped to "emulate the monster's destruction of landmark buildings in New York, such as the Brooklyn Bridge."[30]

I don't for a minute doubt that terrorists under interrogation may have said this, but it seems unlikely that the 1998 movie was in fact the inspiration for 9/11 or any other recent terrorist plot. The World Trade Center was already a target of jihadist terrorists in 1993. By that time, terrorists had already taken down buildings, using conventional explosives. And the Brooklyn Bridge and other landmarks were on the target list of a second team of conspirators arrested in New York later in the year. In fact, blowing up landmark buildings–Great Britain's Houses of Parliament, for example–goes back at least to the seventeenth century. *Godzilla* does not get the credit for terrorists targeting the Brooklyn Bridge. On the other hand, Shoko Asahara's inspiration for his cult of believers who would survive nuclear war was the 1959 movie *On the Beach.*

Well-informed fiction slides into official circles in a variety of ways. War-game and simulation planners regularly turn to fictional works to craft the scenarios that probe how government might respond to various contingencies. The Deutch Commission to Assess the Organization of the Federal Government to Combat the Proliferation of Weapons of Mass Destruction crafted its own fictional scenarios to describe how the United States might be affected by terrorists armed with weapons of mass destruction.[31] Former national security adviser Anthony Lake skillfully dramatized new threats to national security in the form of fictional scenarios that were related in his book *6 Nightmares.*[32]

Like the rest of us, presidents also read terrorist thriller novels and may ponder whether such events are feasible in real life. Here's the difference: We may wonder, but even a casual presidential inquiry can trigger a major effort. The answer that comes back may well turn out to be that it is indeed conceivable, which, in turn, can have immediate policy effects.

This is not to say that had it not been for novelists, such terrorist threats would have been ignored. In most cases, the novelists' plots reflect what many government officials are already worried about. The chance reading of a novel may serve merely to spotlight the issue at a high level.

The effect of nuclear terrorist novels and films on the general public is more circular. Publishers bill nuclear terrorist novels as torn from today's headlines. Readers who post their reviews on blogs and booksellers' sites see the novels as tomorrow's headlines. "This may be a fictional story," wrote one, "but it could very easily become reality." That is fiction's major contribution to this issue. Fiction draws upon national anxieties, makes them specific, gives them life, allows readers to live through them vicariously. In the process, fiction and reality become blurred.

The underlying message of the novels is that a nuclear attack could be carried out—more easily than one might imagine. The fictional accounts promise ever-expanding destruction. Terrorists can not only fabricate a nuclear bomb, they can make a nuclear bomb that is big enough to destroy a city. Terrorists can launch a nuclear attack sufficient to wipe out an entire nation. Terrorists can make a doomsday bomb capable of ending the world—the ultimate terror.

PROMOTING A MESSAGE OF FEAR

The dark musings of declinists, end-time writers, and authors of nuclear terrorism fiction would have remained a merely interesting chapter in the psychohistory of America had they not been reinforced after 9/11 by a continuing cannonade of frightening messages from the nation's capital. Citizens were repeatedly warned that further terrorist attacks were imminent.

The warnings from Washington went beyond alerts arising from the continuing jihadist terrorist campaign, which was real. In future attacks, officials said, terrorists would attempt to use nuclear weapons—this was offered as a certainty, not speculation. The campaign against al Qaeda thus became a war against anticipated nuclear terrorism. In the run-up to the invasion of Iraq, Washington argued that preemptive war was necessary to stop hostile states such as Iraq from getting nuclear weapons and giving them to terrorists. But confident claims that Iraq possessed weapons of mass destruction or that Saddam Hussein had an operational relationship with al Qaeda turned out to be just wrong, although even today not everyone accepts this.

The fear that Iran, too, was developing nuclear weapons and, given its track record, might also give them to terrorists prompted warnings from government officials that military action would again be necessary, even while military analysts warned that the consequences of a US attack on Iran were likely to be far worse than those of the invasion of Iraq. Revised US intelligence reporting in 2007 indicated that Iran had halted its nuclear weapons program several years before.[33] Many dismissed this finding as politically motivated or as irrelevant because Iran had not stopped enriching uranium. Iran is still viewed as a threat.

The point here is not to declare who was right in the debates about the intelligence that led up to the war in Iraq or what we currently know about Iran's ambitions, but to note the cumulative effect of these government statements on public attitudes. Warnings ratcheted up national alarm—people were intentionally terrified. There was little attempt to calm fears or even any admission by officials of uncertainty. I cannot recall a single speech by any official of the executive branch counseling the nation against "nameless, unreasoning, unjustified terror."[34] On the contrary, the message was precisely one of fear. We were repeatedly warned of worse to come.

At the same time, as a consequence of the confrontations with Iraq and Iran, the credibility of the US government, which should have been the official voice—the authoritative voice—on the nuclear capabilities of hostile states and terrorist groups, was eroded. As one worried citizen said, "Who knows what to believe?"

Whether the spies got it wrong in Iraq or right in Iran, whether savvy diplomats were deliberately saber-rattling to energize allies or intimidate adversaries, whether cynical politicians were beating the drums of war for narrow electoral advantage or vendetta— these are matters of continuing heated debate. What we do know is that the underlying official themes of terrorism on US soil, nuclear weapons, war in the Middle East, and terrorists with nuclear weapons coincided with the very same topics addressed for decades in end-time thinking and by the writers of nuclear terrorist fiction. Official policy became increasingly blurred with prophecy and fiction. All converged on nuclear doom.

These dark streams of American culture coursed through the dense network of America's media in books, blogs, movies, talk shows, news channels, newspapers, and chat rooms. Warnings of imminent terrorist attack, rumors of war, sensational revelations, wild speculation, news, and news-driven fiction were blended and liquefied in an incandescent swoon.

JOLTS PER MINUTE

The media play an essential role in enabling modern terrorism. Terrorists employ dramatic violence to create an atmosphere of fear and alarm, which in turn causes people to exaggerate the capabilities of the terrorists and the importance of their cause. The news media link the actors, terrorists, and victims with the audience, who become vicarious victims.

Not surprisingly, the rise of contemporary international terrorism coincides with advances in communications technology—radio, television, highly portable television cameras, communications satellites, and uplinks. All this technology enables the media to provide instantaneous live visual coverage of events as they unfold. This technology has provided terrorists with access to an audience of global proportions. It also has made the media targets of government controls based on the assumption that if the link between the terrorists and their intended audiences can be severed, terrorism will cease to be an effective mode of political expression or conflict. Authoritarian nations have resorted to censorship. Open societies have struggled with the issue.

Journalists themselves have debated their unavoidable role in terrorism, attempting to balance what they see as their duty to report the news with the prospect of endangering lives, contributing to public panic, or otherwise inadvertently becoming accomplices of the terrorists. Self-imposed rules of reporting, easily discussed in the abstract, are difficult to adhere to in the context of an actual terrorist attack, where a desire to get the story and competitive pressures take over. Nonetheless, there are numerous examples of terrorist threats where the media have held off reporting to avoid causing needless alarm.

As the terrorists' self-imposed constraints have eroded over the years, so have the media's. This is due, in large measure, to fundamental changes in the business of reporting the news. Televised network news coverage was once confined to ABC, NBC, and CBS and was limited to feature-driven morning shows and half-hour evening news programs. PBS began a half-hour evening news program in 1975 that expanded to an hour in 1983, with fewer viewers than the commercial networks. Local TV newscasts were limited to short cut-ins into the network morning programs, a half hour in early evening, and a half hour at the end of evening prime-time entertainment shows. Newspapers came out once a day–in the morning or the afternoon–and began declining in the 1960s as growing numbers of Americans began relying on television as their primary news source. Radio news was largely confined to short reports at the top of each hour. Millions of Americans turned to the broadcasts and a daily newspaper each day as matter of routine–regardless of what was happening in the news–to get an update on the world, the nation, and their communities.

The creation of CNN in 1980, followed by CNN Headline News, MSNBC, the Fox News Channel, and other twenty-four-hour news networks–along with all-news radio–changed everything. The all-news networks had unlimited time to fill and couldn't rely on profitable entertainment programming to foot the bill for their news-gathering operations. Their goal was to grab and hold the attention of viewers for as many hours as possible each day. To do that, they needed to make the news exciting and dramatic and to frequently update reports to get viewers to keep watching and to tune in multiple times each day for the latest developments. Breaking news–live reports of "this just in"–sent CNN ratings soaring when dramatic developments like the attempted assassination of President Ronald Reagan, the destruction of the space shuttle *Challenger*, and the US bombing of Baghdad at the opening of the first Gulf War received live coverage for hours at a stretch. The other cable news networks copied the "breaking news equals rising ratings" formula, as did news Web sites when they arose on the Internet in the 1990s. Instantaneous coverage of the dramatic—as opposed to more in-depth reporting and thoughtful analysis—was seen as the key to cable and Internet news profitability. This contributed to an even more rapid decline of the printed newspaper—seen by many readers, especially younger ones, as the bearer of old news that couldn't be updated or illustrated by video reports.

The shift from reading to watching news reports on TV and on the Internet has special meaning in the reporting of terrorism. Print journalism can be cooler, more reflective, and contextual. Terrorism is inherently dramatic and visual and thus very well suited to television and Webcasts—inherently "hot media" for presenting visuals in real time. For cable news and, later, Web sites, the status of being first to show the most dramatic pictures became critical. This left little time for explanation and, for live broadcasts, no time for editing. This has encouraged a frenetic, breathless style of reporting, which treats the viewing audience as attention-deficit-disordered channel flickers and Web surfers.

News programs and their expert guests are judged according to "jolts per minute," the number of shocking, attention-grabbing statements made that will, it is presumed, keep audiences from going elsewhere. It is all breaking news, live coverage, fast talk on screens filled with additional news crawls, stock quotes, color-coded threat levels—a visual extravaganza, more sensation than sense, full of sound and fury—often, like Shakespeare's tale of an idiot, signifying nothing.

Tight budgets have persuaded networks to substitute unpaid talking heads—hastily summoned, eager-to-be-heard "experts"—for serious investigative reporting. Debates are encouraged. It is like the bizarre combat of the Roman Colosseum: a seasoned intelligence analyst finds himself matched against the convinced end-timer, the nuclear physicist against the conspiracy theorist. I was once invited to talk on the air about suicide terrorist bombings, but at the last minute, I was told that I would be debating with an individual who had a sympathetic view of the tactic, because the show wanted a "balanced view." I wondered what a "balanced view" of suicide terrorist bombings was but decided to decline the invitation. On another occasion, I appeared on a live TV program that featured call-in questions, including one from a conspiracy theorist who loudly argued that the 9/11 attacks were really carried out by the US government to solidify the power and popularity of the Bush administration.

While the Internet has created undeniable good and put endless amounts of information at our fingertips, the same technology has empowered fanatics and terrorists by giving them direct access to our computer screens. Terrorists regularly use the Web to disseminate videotapes of gruesome beheadings, along with lengthy sermons from their leaders and other propaganda directly to potential recruits, sympathizers, and broader audiences. No longer dependent on the mainstream media to cover their activities and disseminate their message, terrorists–like our own government, businesses, and all types of organizations–can now communicate with us directly to spread their messages.

The Internet is not just a medium by which terrorists can communicate. It is a universe where everyone can offer views on any subject, and in the masked ball of cyberspace, all sources appear equal. Terrorism, nuclear weapons, doomsday devices, and end-time scenarios loom large among the issues of popular concern. These subjects invite inquiry and discussion, but they also attract a peculiar set of participants with whom terror and doom resonate. The most informative entries coexist with weird science and conspiracy theories. We are thus bombarded by more information than ever before, but separating fact from fiction and insight from incitement is a growing challenge.

It is not simply that the volume of news coverage of terrorism has increased dramatically in all media. After 9/11, that was to be expected. The problem is the content and quality of that coverage. It is often sensationalist, with television favoring the alarmists and the doomsayers simply because they are more interesting. In many cases, there is no critical scrutiny. Bad science goes unchallenged. Docudramas reconstruct real events, while screenwriters incorporate real terrorist scenarios into their scripts. Experts on terrorism are invited to discuss the fictional offerings. Facts are lost in the blur.

A detailed analysis of post-9/11 news coverage of terrorist threats concludes that "by over-covering in particular the frequent 'fear messages' by administration officials, the media contributed to what one critic described as 'creating a culture of hysteria.'"[35]

Another analysis of media coverage of weapons of mass destruction after 9/11 concluded that the media have treated weapons of mass destruction as a "single category of threat," without noting the significant differences in operational difficulties and potential consequences of chemical, biological, radiological, and nuclear weapons. The study also noted that the media regularly "associated mass destruction . . . with the phenomenon of terrorism." "That is undoubtedly an accurate reflection of common fears," said the researchers, "but it is not an accurate reflection of established fact."[36]

The Bush administration set the terms of the public discussion of terrorism, which was hardly difficult after 9/11. The pursuit of al Qaeda became an ambitious Global War on Terrorism, but its key component was the prevention of nuclear terrorism. The official line of the administration remained that nuclear terrorism is the greatest threat to the national security of the United States. It conflated al Qaeda with Iraq to fool the public. There has been little corresponding discussion of the likelihood of nuclear terrorism becoming a reality. Our leaders tell us, and many of us accept, the view that a nuclear terrorist attack somewhere in the United States is inevitable.

Terrorists are in the business of terrorizing and terrifying us.

When we accept as fact that they will one day destroy an American city in a horrific nuclear blast, we provide al Qaeda's terrorists with an enormous opportunity. If Americans are anxious, it serves the terrorists' cause to make us even more anxious. Our enemies are not stupid, and they realize that a campaign of terror might even yield what an act of terrorism could not.

Chapter 14
THE FIRST TERRORIST NUCLEAR POWER

Al Qaeda has become the world's first terrorist nuclear power without, insofar as we know, possessing a single nuclear weapon. Yet al Qaeda's weapons do exist, if only in the fevered imaginations of its followers and in the worst fears of its foes. (Those who are certain that al Qaeda *has* acquired nuclear weapons will surely take exception to this observation.) Al Qaeda is certainly the first terrorist group to have a nuclear policy.

Al Qaeda has achieved its unique nuclear status in several ways. It has actively sought to acquire nuclear weapons for more than fifteen years–an effort that has been known to authorities but is also believed to be unsuccessful. Osama bin Laden has publicly asserted al Qaeda's right to acquire nuclear weapons, calling this a religious obligation. Al Qaeda left behind in Afghanistan a trail of reports and training manuals that document its continuing interest and research in nuclear weapons. Its leaders have hinted in interviews that al Qaeda has, in fact, acquired nuclear weapons. And al Qaeda's jihadist chorus has publicly discussed their use, as if it had them.

Coming from any ordinary terrorist group, such assertions

would be dismissed as utter nonsense, but the spectacular success of al Qaeda's September 2001 attacks and its continued interest in nuclear weapons make it difficult, even while doubting the organization's current nuclear capabilities, to ignore its ambitions or its determination to carry out mass destruction. Add to this al Qaeda's impressive resiliency. More than a decade after declaring war on the West, more than six years after 9/11, despite an intensive worldwide manhunt, al Qaeda's top leaders are still at large, presiding over a reconstructed global terrorist network, communicating frequently, ever determined to continue their terrorist campaign.

What is most remarkable is that al Qaeda created the *illusion* of nuclear power even while its concrete operational capabilities were being ground down by counterterrorist operations around the world. Indeed, it is in the context of its diminishing operational capabilities that al Qaeda has sought to ensure its continuing relevance by increasing its communications and thereby "taking credit" for efforts by its so-called "affiliates," al Qaeda "wannabes," and other jihadist groups.

The strategy of terrorism itself is to create a climate of fear and alarm through dramatic attacks as well as threats of violence, which al Qaeda's leaders clearly understand. They have a coordinated communications strategy. However, al Qaeda's "strategy" of creating nuclear terror appears to have evolved from its jihadist network rather than from a central campaign plan. While al Qaeda does have a media arm, its creation of nuclear terror is a group project, formulated and implemented by its participants without central coordination.

The communications strategy that emerges has not been drafted, reviewed, and scrubbed. It is a strategy that has no general staff but rather is a distributed effort. It is formulated by a network of eager, like-minded jihadists, assembling thoughts, ideas, and images; thinking and implementing at the same time; making incremental improvements without doctrine. It is a Wikipedia effort.

The idea of a network of autonomous members acting in concert but without command is an anarchist's dream. Indeed, al Qaeda's modern jihad owes as much to twentieth-century revolutionary theories as it does to religious imperatives, and its implementation depends entirely on recent developments in modern information technology. *This kind of warfare, in which perceptions count more than the destructive power of physical weaponry, is only beginning to be understood in the West and has not yet fully penetrated Western military institutions.*

Terrorism, as a mode of conflict, abolishes front lines; it dissolves distinctions between combatants and bystanders. The terror it creates affects everyone. We are all its actual or its vicarious victims. But al Qaeda's nuclear terror campaign also blurs the distinction between the authors of terror and their intended audience. Members of the audience themselves participate in the propagation of terror, contributing unwittingly to what might be called a nuclear anxiety feedback loop—a vicious psychological cycle of provocation fueling fear, feeding further provocation. It causes a chain reaction analogous to the physical action-reaction processes of a nuclear explosion but dependent on psychology and imagination at its core. In short, it is an accelerating dynamic of agitated messages that could ultimately generate an explosion of terror.

At the most rudimentary level, we ourselves have contributed mightily to bin Laden's reputation by giving him prominent display in our daily news and in the speeches of our policy makers. We pay close attention to his every utterance. We have posted an extraordinary reward for his capture—a reward that has been increased from $5 million to $25 million to $50 million. We credit almost every attack by Islamist terrorists to bin Laden's al Qaeda. We have elevated the campaign against al Qaeda to the level of war. We have built bin Laden's stage. That has made him a celebrity, but that is not the same as being a nuclear power.

Some would challenge the assertion that we have exaggerated al Qaeda's importance, made too much of bin Laden. While agreeing with the general thrust that we pay too much attention to bin Laden the man, the terrorist threat is real. The jihadist enterprise, inspired by al Qaeda's ideology, which is so effectively communicated by bin Laden, represents the principal threat to American national security. Many, if not all, of the major jihadist terrorist attacks since September 11, 2001, have not merely been inspired by al Qaeda but are in some fashion operationally linked to al Qaeda, whose "guiding hand" has both recruited local terrorist volunteers to training camps in Pakistan and delivered assistance locally through itinerant jihadist expediters. The US government did not invent this terrorist bogeyman, as some critics have asserted, to distract citizens from other pressing issues, to fill a threat deficit, to justify huge expenditures on national defense and homeland security, or to impose dictatorial powers–the common criticisms.

At the same time, some in office did help to create and exploit a culture of fear to win elections, expand executive authority at the expense of other branches of government, mobilize support for military action elsewhere in the world, and advance other political agendas. This was not a national conspiracy to elevate al Qaeda or the broader threat of terrorism. What we see is simply the way things can work in a noisy, politically contested, media-rich democracy, perhaps wobbling on its course as a consequence of a massive terrorist blow. Immediately after 9/11, some of this behavior was to be expected. However, the failure to get a grip soon afterward and the sustained campaign of domestic-driven fear are less supportable.

Our own immense communications capability and highly competitive media have done their thing, putting a human face on a complex phenomenon, thereby elevating a villain, cultivating his celebrity, fomenting–in their insatiable appetite for instant, if superficial, commentary—a small industry of terrorism experts who act as threat reflectors, amplifying terrorist threats. Today's politically partisan, commercially competitive, news-as-entertainment networks clearly have contributed to the shallow reporting and sensationalism that encourage dramatic alarms and invite wild claims. At the same time, it has also been perfectly natural for publishers and producers to sense a market for fictional offerings ripped from headlines, drama that would excite fear but provide psychologically satisfying, if only fictional, closures in an otherwise frustrating, unending struggle. After 9/11, these portrayals were virtually guaranteed. But to dramatize the threat of al Qaeda is still not to designate it a nuclear power. Nor have the media, as the conveyors of terror, set out to act as the terrorists' accomplices.

What we are talking about here is a phenomenon that goes beyond terrorist propaganda and network newsrooms. In the propagation of terror, there are no sharp battle lines. Government officials concerned about national security, analysts worried about terrorists acquiring nuclear weapons, journalists hunting for stories, networks looking for ratings, talking heads seeking attention, writers searching for plot lines, attention-deficient audiences looking for jolts, believers seeking confirmation of imminent doom—*all collaborate in creating a fission of fear.*

Osama bin Laden and his lieutenants are not mere props in this play. They skillfully exploited their post-9/11 notoriety to consolidate their position as the vanguard of global jihad. They have verbally intervened in every conflict and exhorted attacks on every front, positioning themselves to then claim credit for whatever might occur, to be seen by all—followers, foes, and multiple audiences in between—as being in command.

THE MEDIA JIHAD

The 9/11 attacks were meant to provoke a Western reaction that al Qaeda hoped would, in turn, galvanize Muslim masses worldwide to rise up and join its ranks. It was a miscalculation. The attacks did provoke a swift Western reaction, but it was tightly focused and disciplined, at least at the beginning. The United States did not bomb Mecca or level Middle Eastern cities in a spasm of retaliation. The reaction was fast and successful. Within a few months, al Qaeda was pushed out of Afghanistan and on the run. Whatever their sympathies, the Muslim masses remained seated.

To keep al Qaeda's cause alive, continued terrorist operations were essential. In the months following 9/11, jihadist attacks directed or inspired by al Qaeda continued at the rate of about one every two months, and every terrorist success was invariably branded al Qaeda, a necessary shorthand that covered a much more complex set of actors and relationships. Every attack ensured al Qaeda's continued relevance, attracted new recruits, brought fresh contributions. But its successes also provoked further crackdowns. Al Qaeda stayed in the headlines, but jihadist operational capabilities were steadily being eroded. Unable in the increasingly hostile operating environment to put together another attack on the scale of 9/11, al Qaeda exhorted its affiliates and recruits to carry out terrorist attacks where they were, providing assistance when it could.

Communications became critical to holding together the dispersed and disconnected jihadist enterprise, maintaining its unanimity of focus, attracting new recruits, and inspiring them to take action, while wearing down its enemies with threats and alarms. Al Qaeda was always about building an army of believers, not winning battles. It has directed or inspired operations to galvanize others; it has carried out attacks hoping to provoke overreactions. It has exploited existing conflicts as a means of spreading its belief, offering assistance to potential allies, drawing them into its own orbit, imposing its own ideology, asserting its overall authority. Al Qaeda's notions of military strategy have always been limited and primitive, but its base-building has been modern and sophisticated.

Osama bin Laden, who had granted journalists few interviews before 9/11, became a regular communicator in the six years after 9/11, appearing in more than twenty videos and audiotapes. As noted earlier, his second in command, Ayman al-Zawahiri, communicated even more frequently, starring in more than forty al Qaeda productions during the same period. Other al Qaeda personalities, including Suleiman Abu Gheith, Abu Yahya al-Libi, and Adam Gaddahn, also regularly appeared in the group's media productions. As the frequency of communications from al Qaeda Central increased, so did production values, reflecting updated technology and enhanced skills. The video productions featured all the attributes of a contemporary news broadcast: stage sets, good lighting, edited insertions, background music, subtitles, and network symbols.

Al Qaeda's central studios were supplemented by local affiliates that combined archival material with local content. Their products were delivered to sympathetic television networks, circulated on the Internet, and more recently even made available for cell phone downloads. Below these top tiers of media impresarios was an army of virtual jihadists who, if they couldn't blow things up, could offer their computer and graphic skills to what became known as the "media jihad."

Al Qaeda Central believes that 90 percent of its fight is in the media jihad. Videos, audiotapes, threats, and commentary circulate via Web sites, bulletin boards, chat rooms, blogs, and file-sharing schemes. On 9/11, there were only a handful of jihadist sites on the Internet. Today, there are thousands—a true network where there is inspiration from the center but deliberately no central control.

This virtual jihad is constantly evolving. It invites mass participation. It encourages local initiative. Acolytes become mission-
aries. Audiences become activists. The army of believers grows.
Its content reflects the grandiose ambitions of al Qaeda's leaders
as well as the fantasies of its online warriors. The online chatter
may also conceal the network's clandestine traffic. At the very
least, the high volume of noise complicates the task of intelligence.

The purpose of the media jihad is both to recruit new members—indoctrinating them and instructing them in the means of
violence—and to keep the enemy in a perpetual state of alarm.
This is consistent with al Qaeda's own operational code. Its
leaders know that they cannot defeat America's superior military
technology in open battle. But throughout history, the Prophet's
warriors have always confronted foes who were superior in man-
power and weapons. Derived from the Koran and the Hadith, al
Qaeda's approach to war rests on guile and deception. It seeks to
wear down its foes, attacking them when they are inattentive,
making their lives untenable. Threats are an integral part of the
tactical repertoire. Al Qaeda's leaders are well aware of our fears—
they listen to us—and how to exploit them, obliging us to live in a
constant state of anxiety, forcing us to divert vast resources to
security, draining our will to persist in the struggle.

This is consistent with the jihadists' belief that their experience
corresponds to what happened to Muhammad and his followers
in the early days of Islam. They started as a minority, were perse-
cuted, had to flee, fought battles against a superior enemy but ultimately prevailed.

Verbal threats are intrinsic to al Qaeda's war. "The Arab
custom of trying to intimidate an adversary is . . . a prevalent feature of the Arab personality," wrote Raphael Patai, in his classic
1973 study *The Arab Mind*.[1] One has to be cautious about citing a
work whose very title can be attacked as Orientalist analysis, but
both Arab and non-Arab observers have noted that verbal threats

are very much a part of Arab culture and do not necessarily carry the same weight that they do in the West. Forever feeling threatened requires forever having to threaten–verbal bellicosity is a form of defense. People do it as a habit, without even realizing that much of it is exaggerated, empty rhetoric.

Oral combat is no less manly than physical combat. In fact, talking may supersede action. An Arab may make "statements which express threats, demands, or intentions . . . which once uttered, give psychological relief and at the same time reduce the pressure to engage in any act aimed at realizing the verbalized goal."[2] As Patai points out, "The intention of doing something, or the plan of doing something, or the initiation of the first step toward doing something–any one of these can serve as a substitute for achievement."[3]

It is not that the speaker consciously intends to avoid action, rather, it is a deliberately emotional and dramatic mode of expression. The more dramatic a speaker is, the more sincere he is considered to be.

This does not mean that bin Laden's threats can be dismissed as mere rhetoric. Indeed, much of his stature in the Arab world derives from his demonstrated commitment and capability to carry out attacks, contrasted with the idle boasts and empty threats of many Arab leaders in the past. He talks the talk and walks the walk. The issue is not his intentions but the distance between intention and accomplishment. Osama bin Laden wants a nuclear weapon and probably would use it if he had one. Thus, when bin Laden or al-Zawahiri say they have nuclear weapons, this can be read as a clear intention to acquire nuclear weapons, not necessarily a reflection of fact.

The "Arabic language itself tends to bring about 'a displacement of the perceptual images by the linguistic ones.'"[4] Al Qaeda's leaders are not fooling themselves with words; they are following well-worn linguistic and cultural paths in communicating to an audience in which such threats are appreciated and applauded, adding to the prestige of their source. The circulation, repetition, and embellishment of threats, a participatory process that the Internet itself facilitates and encourages, creates a group "reality" that is psychologically satisfying to its participants in two ways: It fulfills the obligation to participate in jihad in a way that is considered manly and it visibly alarms the enemy.

It is against this background that we view al Qaeda's strategy of nuclear terror. We have seen that long before 9/11, bin Laden tried unsuccessfully to acquire nuclear weapons. His public comments on the subject affirmed that it was a right and a religious duty of the jihadists to acquire such weapons and that they would be used in retaliation to any American aggression.[5] We also have heard that although some in al Qaeda thought it unlikely that the organization could develop true weapons of mass destruction, the jihadists nonetheless agreed that they would continue to call their arsenal "weapons of mass destruction" because this would give the movement credibility and psychological influence.[6]

Al Qaeda's terror campaign is amplified in the news media. The threat of al Qaeda acquiring a nuclear weapon or carrying out a dirty-bomb attack dazzles the press. Mere mention of the words *al Qaeda* and *nuclear terrorism* in the same article or aired piece contribute to the climate of fear. As of May 2008, a Google search of the terms *nuclear* and *al Qaeda* produced more than a half million hits.

Even immediately after 9/11, as al Qaeda's leaders were being put on the run and its operational planners were being killed or captured, its nuclear "capabilities" were a subject of growing, often lurid speculation. We can get some idea of the rising trajectory of coverage and concern by using a search on the Lexis-Nexis Academic Universe database, which covers hundreds of international news sources. Variants of the term *al Qaeda* appearing within ten words of *nuclear* produced only seven hits in 1999 and eleven hits in 2000. But in 2001, the year of the 9/11 attacks, the total number of *al Qaeda-nuclear* mentions soared to 1,742. With the discoveries of instructional manuals on nuclear weapons in al Qaeda's training camps in Afghanistan, the number in 2002 rose to 2,931. It stayed roughly at this level for the next two years, then declined to 1,475 hits in 2005, 1,655 in 2006, and 1,051 (as of September 7) in 2007. The advancing and retreating "hits" suggest a rough measure of the attacks waged in the campaign of jihadist nuclear terror.

THE NOVEMBER 2001 INTERVIEW

There seems to have been a deliberate shift in al Qaeda's communications strategy after 9/11 with respect to nuclear weapons, although we must tread carefully here, because we have only one source for the comments on nuclear weapons made since 9/11 by al Qaeda's top leaders: Hamid Mir, a Pakistani journalist who has frequently asserted that al Qaeda does, in fact, possess nuclear weapons.

Mir is currently writing a biography of Osama bin Laden—a project that he has pursued for more than ten years. He appears to have superb contacts within al Qaeda and the Taliban. At the same time, some of his claims strain credulity.

Mir had interviewed bin Laden in the 1990s. He interviewed him again in November 2001, the only journalist to have done so after 9/11. It was the third meeting between the two men. Since this interview has been frequently cited by Mir himself in subsequent articles and by others discussing al Qaeda's quest for nuclear weapons, it is worthwhile to devote some attention to it.

According to Mir, the interview took place on the night of November 7, 2001, somewhere near Kabul, Afghanistan. Mir says that he "was taken blindfolded in a jeep . . . to a place where it was extremely cold and one could hear the sound of anti-aircraft guns firing away. After a wait of some time, Osama bin Laden arrived with about a dozen bodyguards and Dr. Ayman al-Zawahiri [*sic*]." With twenty other people in the small room, bin Laden, al-Zawahiri, and Mir sipped tea while bin Laden answered questions.[7]

One has to keep in mind what was going on at that very moment in Afghanistan. In response to the 9/11 terrorist attacks, the United States demanded that the Taliban turn Osama bin Laden over, and when they refused, American planes began an intensive bombing campaign. Initially, the campaign focused on al Qaeda's suspected training camps; it then increasingly turned to the Taliban forces, permitting the Taliban's opponents and America's proxies in Afghanistan to begin a ground offensive. By November, al Qaeda was on the run and the Taliban was in retreat. Kabul itself would fall within a few days of the interview.

There are several versions of exactly what Osama bin Laden said to Hamid Mir. According to the original version published in Urdu, Pakistan's national language, bin Laden told the reporter, "I want to make it clear that if the United States uses chemical or nuclear weapons against us, we will not perish." In other words, we can take whatever the Americans throw at us—a boast.[8]

The full text of the exchange, however, gives us more detail and gives bin Laden's reply a slightly different meaning. Mir asks, "Some Western media claim you are trying to acquire chemical and nuclear weapons. How much truth is there in such reports?" to which bin Laden replied, "I listened to President Bush's speech yesterday. He was trying to frighten the European countries into thinking that Osama bin Laden wanted to attack the whole of Europe with lethal weapons. I want to make it clear that if the United States uses chemical or nuclear weapons against us, we will not perish." Bin Laden then continued, "The United States is indeed using chemical weapons against us, and has decided to use nuclear weapons too, but our war will continue."[9]

Bin Laden was up to date with his information. The speech to which he was referring was delivered by President Bush on November 6, 2001, to the Warsaw Conference on Combating Terrorism. In the speech, Bush warned his European audience that "al Qaeda operates in more than 60 nations, including some in Central and Eastern Europe. These terrorist groups seek to destabilize entire nations and regions. They are seeking chemical, biological, and nuclear weapons."[10]

In this context, bin Laden's statement seems to be an assertion of survival no matter what weapons America uses against al Qaeda, a rejection of President Bush's allegation as a mere scare tactic, and a declaration that al Qaeda will continue its struggle–not a confirmation that al Qaeda has nuclear weapons. However, the English-language newspaper in Pakistan replaced the phrase "We will not perish" with "We might respond with chemical and nuclear weapons. We possess these weapons as a deterrent."[11]

The second version of the interview, which appeared in the Karachi newspaper *Dawn*, says considerably more than the first, and it raises the question of whether the English translation of bin Laden's words was manipulated to increase the apparent terrorist threat. The man who points out this discrepancy is Bruce Lawrence, the editor of *Messages to the World: The Statements of Osama bin Laden*. Lawrence concludes that the interpretation that appears in the English version must be apocryphal.[12] It is possible that the editor altered the phrase to increase its impact, but if so, it was with Mir's participation, for Mir speaks fluent English, and the English version of the interview carries his byline. It is theoretically possible that the Urdu version was intended for an indigenous audience, one more sympathetic to bin Laden, and therefore the emphasis is on survival, while the English version was aimed at a Western audience more likely to be concerned by bin Laden's possession of nuclear weapons, hence the emphasis on threat.

Hamid Mir gave another version of the same interview, in which he quoted Osama bin Laden saying, "We have nuclear deterrence and this is for our defense," a comment that prompted the skeptical Mir to turn to al-Zawahiri and say, "It is difficult to believe that you have a nuclear weapon. How can you purchase those kinds of weapons?" Al-Zawahiri responded that it was not difficult. "If you have thirty million dollars, you can have those kind of suitcase bombs from the black market at Central Asia."[13] This version of the dialogue lends credence to the English version of the interview, which has bin Laden himself actually mentioning nuclear weapons. If he did not mention them at all, why would Mir then ask al-Zawahiri about the difficulty of obtaining them?

The source of this exchange with al-Zawahiri, which was related in Mir's 2004 interview, is again Mir himself.[14] Oddly, al-Zawahiri's comments were not included in Mir's original 2001 account. And then, in the published account of a 2006 interview with Mir, a slightly altered version of al-Zawahiri's words is attributed to Osama bin Laden himself: "Bin Laden announced that he had managed to acquire nuclear weapons for use in the great jihad against the United States. 'It is not difficult [to obtain tactical nukes],' the al-Qaida Chieftain said, 'not if you have contacts in Russia with other militant groups. They are available for $10 million and $20 million.'"[15]

This sounds very much as if bin Laden or al-Zawahiri, whichever one may have made the statement, had read and believed various press accounts of Russian tactical nuclear weapons for sale on the black market. In fact, there was a series of news stories between 1991 and 1993 reporting alleged sales of Russian tactical nuclear weapons to the Palestine Liberation Organization for $10 million each. At the very least, it is not clear whether the quotes from al Qaeda have been exciting the news media or quotes from the news media have been exciting al Qaeda.

Each subsequent iteration of the original interview alters the exchange, adds details not included in previous accounts, and cranks up the dramatic effect. The analyst inevitably becomes skeptical that the malleable story is more drama than documentary.

Neither bin Laden nor al-Zawahiri made any public claims beyond the Mir interview in 2001. But concerns about al Qaeda's nuclear efforts grew nonetheless in the following weeks with the discovery of evidence in the al Qaeda training camps that al Qaeda had an active chemical weapons research program and clearly had continued its interest in acquiring nuclear weapons.

Then in 2002, al Qaeda's avowed nuclear weapons policy seemed to shift from deterrence to "reciprocation," as others beyond bin Laden and al-Zawahiri took up the theme. In a three-part article posted on the Internet, al Qaeda's spokesman Suleiman Abu Gheith asserted that the United States, as "the head of heresy in our modern world," is responsible for the deaths of millions of Muslims in Palestine, Sudan, the Philippines, Bosnia, Chechnya, Iraq, and Afghanistan. "America is the reason for all oppression, injustice, licentiousness, or suppression that is the Muslims' lot. It stands behind all the disasters that were caused and are still being caused to the Muslims; it is immersed in the blood of Muslims." Therefore, in accordance with Islamic law, al Qaeda has the right to punish America to the same degree. Abu Gheith calculated that since at least four million Muslims have died, al Qaeda has "the right to kill four million Americans—two million of them children."[16]

This line of argument was subsequently endorsed by a religious fatwa from a fugitive Saudi cleric. In his "Treatise on the Legal Status of Using Weapons of Mass Destruction against Infidels," Sheikh Nasir bin Hamd al-Fahd wrote, "Anyone who considers America's aggressions against Muslims and their lands during the last decades will conclude that striking her is permissible on the basis of the rule of treating one as one has been treated. No other argument need be mentioned. Some brothers have totaled the number of Muslims killed directly or indirectly by their weapons and come up with a number of nearly ten million. . . . If a bomb that killed ten million of them and burned as much of their land as they have burned Muslim land was dropped on them, it would be permissible with no need to mention any other argument." Al-Fahd concluded with an apparent offer of future legal assistance: "We might need other arguments if we wanted to annihilate more than this number of them."[17] In other words, get back to me if you need to kill more.

Al-Fahd was subsequently arrested by Saudi authorities. While in custody, he testified that he knew that al Qaeda had been negotiating for the purchase of some Russian devices, but he did not know the nature of the devices or whether in fact al Qaeda had obtained them. After six months in jail, al-Fahd appeared on Saudi television to publicly rescind his fatwa and express "regret for the error of his religious interpretation."[18]

The public remarks by al Qaeda's leaders prompted a broader discourse among jihadists about the circumstances and conditions of using nuclear weapons, thereby further reifying their existence. In chat rooms, bin Laden's followers discussed nuclear strategy as if al Qaeda's pretensions were real. Nuclear threats were posted on jihadist Web sites, accompanied by dramatic visuals. Video clips showed a giant fireball covering the city of New York, skyscrapers falling one by one along with the Statue of Liberty, a radioactive cloud spreading over the metropolis. In another video, Washington was shown being consumed in a fireball. Yet another showed bin Laden's visage superimposed on a mushroom cloud. With these vivid special effects, it was easy to forget that there were, in fact, no nuclear weapons. Some of this can be explained as mere artistic license. Some of it is a reflection of the culture that allows words, or in this case, images to create a desired reality, which is then accepted as real.

One of the more striking pieces of nuclear terror art posted on a jihadist Web site shows a seated Osama bin Laden looking over a tabletop layout that appears to be midtown Manhattan. His raised right hand pushes out a glowing ball of fire, which, upon closer examination, turns out to be a tiny nuclear explosion. Twelve more miniature nuclear explosions dot New York City. It is a visual assertion of bin Laden's nuclear capability and his likely target.

The images are symbolic, to be sure, but not easily ignored. In fact, shortly after 9/11, corporations headquartered in Manhattan and insurance companies were filling their own maps of Manhattan with circles depicting the range of total destruction of one-kiloton and ten-kiloton nuclear devices superimposed on landmarks thought likely to be targets in future terrorist attacks. Proximity to too many circles became an argument for dispersing vital functions to maintain business continuity, or for insurance companies to limit coverage. In other words, *possible terrorist threats drove vulnerability assessments, which, in turn, made the terrorist threats seem more credible, a circular analysis that gave al Qaeda a nuclear capability without a nuclear bomb.*

Al Qaeda's propaganda machine propelled this discussion by indicating precisely how many Western infidels Muslims were entitled to kill in retaliation for that many Muslims having been killed by the infidels. Calculating the number of people al Qaeda could justifiably kill took its nuclear discourse into the domain of consequences, which is almost invariably where Western discussions of nuclear terrorism end up. Such discussions begin with anecdotes, terrorist threats, assessments of terrorist capabilities, and move on to descriptions of hypothetical events—the "what if" scenarios. Much of this is pure speculation. Analysts gain more-solid footing only when they move to discussions of consequences. Whether terrorists can obtain or fabricate nuclear weapons and how they might seek to use them are matters of debate. In contrast, the effects of nuclear explosions can be calculated. We don't know, for example, whether terrorists will ever detonate a ten-kiloton nuclear bomb in the Port of Los Angeles, but we can certainly estimate the effects of such a bomb, as a recent study by the RAND Corporation did.[19] It is not the debate about likelihood but the mere discussion of concrete consequences that ultimately shapes our fears and our policies. By changing the topic from chances to consequences, al Qaeda buys further belief in its ability to effectuate them.

THE REFLECTORS

Media reports that al Qaeda had nuclear weapons preceded September 11, 2001. In October 1998, *Al-Hayah*, an Arabic-language newspaper in London, claimed that "bin Laden purchased tactical nuclear weapons from the Islamic Republics in Central Asia."[20] In November of that same year, the Lebanese newspaper *Al-Watan Al-Arabi* reported that Chechens and the Russian mafia had sold nuclear weapons to al Qaeda. According to these accounts, for a price of $30 million in cash plus $70 million in heroin, al Qaeda had acquired more than twenty warheads, which it was storing at a secret base in Afghanistan.[21]

DEBKA-Net-Weekly, an Israeli online news service that reportedly has ties to Israeli intelligence but also publishes rumors, reported that eight to ten Russian atomic demolition munitions were in al Qaeda's hands.[22] This story was repeated in October 1999 by Youssef Bodansky in the *Jerusalem Report*.[23]

A month before Hamid Mir's November 2001 interview with bin Laden and al-Zawahiri, the London *Sunday Times* reported that an al Qaeda operative had offered "a Bulgarian businessman $200,000 to set up a front company to purchase radioactive waste from a nuclear power station in Bulgaria."[24] And in November 2001, the *Frontier Post*, a newspaper in Pakistan, asserted that al Qaeda might already have nuclear weapons in the United States.[25]

"Alarmed by growing hints of al Qaeda's progress toward obtaining a nuclear or radiological weapon," the *Washington Post* reported in March 2002, "the Bush administration has deployed hundreds of sophisticated sensors since late November to US borders, overseas facilities and choke points around Washington. It has placed the Delta Force, the nation's elite commando unit, on a new standby alert to seize control of nuclear materials that the sensors may detect."[26] Some of these actions were in response to concerns raised in the October 2001 intelligence report from Dragonfire claiming that a nuclear weapon had been smuggled into New York, which we now know to be false. The *Washington Post* article went on to say that "the Bush administration's nuclear anxieties have intensified since American-backed forces routed Osama bin Laden's network and its Taliban backers in Afghanistan. 'Clearly . . . the sense of urgency has gone up,' said a senior government policymaker. . . . These heightened US government fears explain Bush's activation, the first since the dawn of the nuclear age, of contingency plans to maintain a cadre of senior federal managers in underground bunkers away from Washington."[27]

In October 2002, *WorldNetDaily*, a popular online news service, recycled the 1998 story of bin Laden's purchase of twenty suitcase nuclear weapons as "detailed in a new book by an FBI consultant on international terrorism."[28] The book was *Al Qaeda: Brotherhood of Terror*, by Paul L. Williams, a popular American author. According to this book, the purchase of twenty nuclear weapons was one of three purchases in the previous decade.[29]

Williams wrote that in 1988 Osama bin Laden had hired a team of five nuclear scientists from Turkmenistan. The scientists had previously worked at Iraq's Osiirak reactor before it was bombed by the Israelis. Their assignment from bin Laden was to build a small nuclear bomb "that could be placed in a package smaller than a backpack." Williams indicated that by 1990, "bin Laden had hired hundreds of atomic scientists from the former

Soviet Union for $2000 a month." They worked at a secret sophisticated laboratory in Kandahar, Afghanistan.[30] Williams also asserted that in 1998, al Qaeda purchased the "20 suitcase nukes from Chechen mafia figures including former KGB agents. The $30 million deal was partly cash and partly heroin with a street value of $700 million." According to Williams, the devices were turned over to Arab nuclear scientists who "were probably trained at American universities."[31]

In December 2003, a jihadist Web site announced that al Qaeda would destroy New York in a nuclear blast on February 2, 2004. Accompanying the claim was the aforementioned video clip showing three scenarios: a giant fireball that engulfs the city; a nuclear storm cloud that topples skyscrapers one by one, along with the Statue of Liberty and the Brooklyn Bridge; and an explosion aboard a chartered aircraft that shrouds the city in a radioactive cloud. The Web site promptly disappeared, but the report was repeated in the Italian newspaper *Il Giornale*.[32]

In 2004, Williams continued what became a series of books exposing the nuclear ambitions and achievements of Osama bin Laden, with the second volume titled *Osama's Revenge: The Next 9/11—What the Media and the Government Haven't Told You.*[33] It was this book that set the tone of Williams's campaign to warn the American public about the likelihood of nuclear terrorism on US soil. Echoing the 1998 stories in *Al-Hayah* and *Al-Watan Al-Arabi,* Williams asserted that in the chaos following the collapse of the Soviet Union, the Chechen mafia got their hands on portable nuclear weapons, which they then sold to bin Laden's representatives. Williams went further, however, saying that these bombs may already be in the possession of al Qaeda cells in a number of American cities.[34]

It was in March 2004, when Hamid Mir, this time in an interview with the Australian Broadcasting Company, elaborated again on his 2001 interview with bin Laden and al-Zawahiri, adding that al-Zawahiri told him that disgruntled Soviet scientists "have contacted us, we sent our people to Moscow, to Tashkent, to other Central Asian states and they negotiated, and we purchased some suitcase bombs."[35]

In August 2004, an individual calling himself "EOM" posted a threat on the Internet, claiming that "nuclear detonations will occur in New York City, Washington, D.C., Baltimore, and Miami on August 5."[36] Most analysts dismissed EOM as an al Qaeda wannabe determined to spread alarm. However, in April 2005, new CIA director Porter Goss testified before the Senate Intelligence Committee that "it may only be a matter of time before al Qaeda or another group attempts to use chemical, biological, radiological and nuclear weapons."[37]

In the histrionically titled *Countdown to Terror: The Top Secret Information That Could Prevent the Next Terrorist Attack on America . . . and How the CIA Has Ignored It,* Congressman Curt Weldon argued that the next 9/11 would be nuclear. Weldon claimed to have learned from a secret Iranian source about a terrorist plot to hijack a Canadian airliner and crash it into the Seabrook nuclear reactor near Boston, a scheme that, he said, would kill hundreds of thousands of Americans by radiation poisoning.[38]

Weldon described writing his book as an act of desperation, because he could not get the American intelligence community to act on his information. One reason for the intelligence community's skepticism was that Weldon's principal source was the same notorious Iranian exile who had helped set up the arms-for-hostages deal that led to the 1986 Iran-Contra scandal and who had since come to be judged by most Western services to be a serial fabricator.[39] That did not appear in most reviews, which instead referred to feckless bureaucrats unwilling to prevent imminent doom.

Paul Williams sounded the alarm again in 2005 in his third book, *The al Qaeda Connection: International Terrorism, Organized*

Crime, and the Coming Apocalypse, in which he wrote that "U.S., Saudi, Pakistani, Russian, Israeli, and British intelligence sources have confirmed that al Qaeda possesses a small arsenal of tactical nuclear weapons—weapons that are being prepared for the 'American Hiroshima.'"[40] Williams goes on to say that "the consensus of global intelligence about the nuclear capacity of al Qaeda can be summarized as follows:

- There are fully assembled nuclear weapons in bin Laden's arsenal. The only disagreement comes with the number. The Russians say twelve to fifteen; the Saudis claim forty to seventy.
- Bin Laden obtained these weapons through his connections with the Chechen rebels and the Russian Mafia.
- The Chechen rebels helped to recruit Soviet scientists and SPETZNAZ technicians so that the weapons could be properly assembled and maintained.
- The location of the weapons remains unknown . . .
- Several nuclear weapons, including suitcase bombs, mines, rucksacks, and crude tactical nuclear warheads, have been forward-deployed to the United States . . .
- The next attack is planned to occur simultaneously at various sites across the country. Certain targets include Boston, New York, Washington, D.C., Las Vegas, Miami, Chicago, and Los Angeles."[41]

My purpose here is to describe the amplification of nuclear terror, not to prove or disprove the content of reports. But I must admit that I was dubious about these claims, and I would not agree that there was a consensus among intelligence services supporting them.

To put to rest any lingering doubts about al Qaeda's nuclear weapons, Williams quoted Michael Scheuer, the CIA agent in charge of the bin Laden section of the agency: "On November 14,

2004, Scheuer appeared on *60 Minutes* . . . alerting the American people that a nuclear attack by al Qaeda 'is pretty close to being inevitable.'"[42]

Williams is correct. Scheuer did indeed say that detonating a weapon of mass destruction on American soil was "pretty close to being inevitable." When asked what type of weapon al Qaeda could detonate, Scheuer responded that it would be a "nuclear weapon of some dimension, whether it's actually a nuclear weapon or a dirty bomb, or some kind of radiological device . . . [the detonation is] probably a near thing." However, Scheuer went on to explain that the reason he thought such an attack was close to inevitable was that bin Laden had told us, "We are going to acquire a weapon of mass destruction, and *if* we acquire it, we will use it."[43] The "if" makes Scheuer's comment an observation about al Qaeda's *intentions*, not a confirmation that al Qaeda already had tactical nuclear weapons inside the United States. And once again, for Scheuer, it is bin Laden's rhetoric that drives the assessment—we know bin Laden will attack us with nuclear weapons because he told us—not evidence of acquisition.

In 2006 Hamid Mir again returned to the nuclear front. In a May interview, he stated that he was convinced al Qaeda has nuclear weapons. "I came up with this conclusion after eight years of investigation and research in the remote mountains of Afghanistan and Pakistan," he said. "I traveled to Iraq, Iran, Sudan, Syria, Uzbekistan and Russia. . . . I interviewed not only Al-Qaeda operatives but met scientists and top U.S. officials. . . . At least two Al-Qaeda operatives claimed that the organization smuggled suitcase nukes inside America. But I have no details on who did it. But I do have details about who smuggled uranium inside America and how." Mir promised in the interview that the details of his investigations would be published in his forthcoming biography of bin Laden, in which he would "disclose his [bin Laden's] future plans and details of his nuclear designs."[44]

Asked how many nuclear weapons al Qaeda possessed, Mir answered, "As far as I know, they smuggled three suitcase nukes from Russia to Europe. They smuggled many kilos of enriched uranium inside America for their dirty bomb projects. . . . They have planned an attack bigger than 9/11, even before 9/11 happened."[45] Mir said that bin Laden had initially trained forty-two fighters to destroy the American economy; nineteen were used on 9/11, leaving twenty-three "still sleeping" inside America "waiting for a wake-up call from bin Laden."[46]

Asked why, if al Qaeda had tactical suitcase nukes, not just dirty bombs, the terrorists had deployed them to Europe instead of the United States, Mir responded, "Actually, I lost track of the three suitcase nukes after they were smuggled into Italy. . . . I only received one tip that Chechen members of Al-Qaeda wanted to smuggle one bomb to London, one into Paris, and one into California, but some dispute developed with the Italian underworld over the method of payment." Mir, however, went on to say that his sources told him that weapons were smuggled to the United States through Mexico.[47]

And why hadn't al Qaeda used the nuclear weapons it possessed? Mir answered, "They are waiting for the proper time. They want the U.S. to be involved in a mass killing of Muslims, so that they will have some justification." Mir then said that "an American Hiroshima" would occur as soon as the United States launches an attack on Iran's nuclear facilities, claiming that Iran and al Qaeda have a long relationship. Mir added, "Iran will organize some attacks inside America and you will accuse Al-Qaeda."[48]

Concerns about a nuclear terrorist attack peaked in the fall of 2006. The scare began with Mir claiming in early September that bin Laden was planning to carry out new, more-destructive attacks inside the United States.[49]

In October 2006, "through a previously tested channel" that was not further described, the *Sunday Times* received a videotape showing bin Laden addressing an audience of about one hundred al Qaeda operatives somewhere in Afghanistan.[50] What makes the tape particularly interesting, however, is the appearance of Mohammed Atta and Ziad Jarrah, two of the 9/11 hijackers, together. One after another, in front of the camera, the two men read their last testaments. What they said could not be heard, for the tape has no sound.

The tape was recorded in January 2000. It was unedited and not delivered through al Qaeda's usual channels, so it is not clear how to interpret its timing. Analysts doubted that it came from al Qaeda, but Hamid Mir immediately portrayed it as a signal to al Qaeda operatives to go ahead with the planned nuclear attack on the United States. According to Mir, bin Laden had now completed the cycle of warnings required by Islamic custom before launching an attack. He said that the participants and pieces of the plot were already in place.[51] Playing Mohammed Atta's role as in-country coordinator in 2006 would be Adnan al-Shukrijumah, who, according to Paul Williams, had received training in nuclear technology. Mir said that he was nicknamed "al Qaeda's nuclear whiz."[52]

Al-Shukrijumah was born in Saudi Arabia but moved with his family to the United States when he was a boy. Sometime in the late 1990s, he was swept into the jihadist orbit that circled around the Al Farouq Mosque in New York City. He may have attended an al Qaeda training camp in Afghanistan before 9/11 and possibly returned to the United States around 1999 or 2000 to attend flight training. In 2003, captured al Qaeda planner Khaled Sheikh Mohammed identified al-Shukrijumah, who became the subject of a worldwide manhunt, with a $5 million reward offered for information leading to his arrest. In 2004 the US attorney general identified al-Shukrijumah as one of seven al Qaeda operatives believed to be planning terrorist operations in the United States.[53] He has been named as a suspect in several terrorist plots since.

Hamid Mir said that al-Shukrijumah had smuggled nuclear

material into the United States via Mexico. According to Mir, al Qaeda's nuclear attack was planned to occur during the Islamic observance of Ramadan, from September 24 to October 23, 2006.[54]

Stories circulating on the Internet stated that Abu Dawood, the new al Qaeda commander in Afghanistan, had confirmed that final preparations for the "American Hiroshima" had been completed; the attackers were already in place awaiting final orders from their commander, Adnan al-Shukrijumah; and that Muslims living in the United States should leave without further warning.[55]

Analysis of intelligence requires constant revision as new information becomes available. Old hypotheses are discarded, replaced by new frameworks that better encompass what is known. However, it is not clear why Hamid Mir's stories from 2001 to 2006 shifted. Their presentation as hard fact and Mir's apparently great confidence that these things will happen arouses skepticism among those raised on caveats.

Ramadan passed without a nuclear detonation in the United States, but in November 2006, British intelligence officials warned that al Qaeda was determined to attack the United Kingdom with a nuclear weapon. The officials said that they had detected "an awful lot of chatter" on jihadist Web sites expressing the desire to acquire chemical, biological, radiological, and nuclear weapons, which was certainly true. Asked whether there was any doubt that al Qaeda was trying to gain the technology to attack the West, including the United Kingdom, with a nuclear weapon, "a senior Foreign Office counterterrorism official said, 'No doubt at all.' The official explained: 'We know the aspiration is there, we know the attempt to get the material is there, we know the attempt to get technology is there.'"[56]

There is, of course, a critical difference in language between British intelligence officials talking about aspirations and attempts and others talking about weapons already deployed for imminent attacks. But to a frightened public, this transition from certain ambition to certain achievement is hardly noticed.

Yet another scare occurred in the spring of 2007, when George Tenet's memoir was published. For eight years, Tenet had been director of the CIA, serving two presidents from 1997 to 2004. While many rushed to read the book for its possible revelations about the faulty intelligence that supported the invasion of Iraq, Tenet provided a more thorough and authentic account than anything that had previously appeared in an open publication about al Qaeda's continuing quest to obtain nuclear weapons.[57]

The by-now-familiar mile markers were there—Osama bin Laden's early attempt to obtain nuclear material while he was in Sudan, his discussions with sympathetic Pakistani scientists just one month before 9/11, Suleiman Abu Gheith's statement in 2002 asserting al Qaeda's right to kill four million Americans, the continuing reports that al Qaeda's representatives were trying to purchase nuclear weapons in Russia, small quantities of fissile material being smuggled out of Russia, unsubstantiated rumors of some sort of nuclear device being smuggled into the United States—but Tenet added numerous new and disturbing details.

We would never know whether bin Laden had acquired nuclear material while in Sudan. Tenet described American efforts to find out. He noted that two American-educated Muslim scientists, both of whom had attended the University of Arizona, had become radicalized jihadists. They joined bin Laden when he was in Sudan and helped run his businesses. They were still there in 2002, but the United States did not have enough evidence on the two to request extradition. Tenet related in his book how a CIA emissary was sent to Sudan, with the cooperation of the Sudanese government, in an effort to persuade the two scientists to willingly cooperate. The mission ended in failure. "There would be no reconciliation, no common ground or shared sense of decency and humanity with the two al-Qa'ida associates," Tenet wrote. "On the contrary, they articulated the hatred, the need for revenge, that they shared."[58]

Tenet was convinced that the United States and Pakistan had interrupted a dangerous dialogue between al Qaeda and sympathetic Pakistani scientists, and he was satisfied with the vigorous action Saudi authorities took to break up al Qaeda's network in that country, but he worried about the lack of more than nominal cooperation by Russian authorities and the absence of dialogue with the Iranians.[59] What comes through as well is Tenet's continuing frustration at the fragmentary nature of the intelligence; the unreliability of the al Qaeda operatives who had much to say, then promptly recanted; and the inability to determine the outcomes of reported negotiations for nuclear weapons or whether reported transactions were ever completed. Tenet's book did not confirm that al Qaeda had nuclear weapons, but neither did it inspire much confidence that we would know if it did.

Tenet's worries were echoed in the April 2007 CBS broadcast of *Face the Nation*. Vice President Dick Cheney said that "the threat to the United States now of . . . a nuclear weapon in the middle of one of our own cities is the greatest threat we face. . . . It's something we have to worry about and defeat every single day."[60]

In July 2007, new videotapes from Ayman al-Zawahiri and Adam Gaddahn materialized, followed by one in September from Osama bin Laden himself after a three-year absence from the screen (apart from archival footage), demonstrating that al Qaeda's top leaders were alive and well and determined to continue their campaign.[61] The tapes were, of course, part of al Qaeda's propaganda offensive. Al-Zawahiri's July tape was the fifty-ninth audio or video statement released in 2007 by the as-Sahab Institute, al Qaeda's media arm, in comparison with a total of fifty-eight public statements released during all of 2006. By mid-September 2007, as-Sahab was up to seventy-five videos—an average of one every three days. It released three tapes, including the one featuring bin Laden, on the sixth anniversary of the 9/11 attacks. The quantity of releases and the short lag times between current events and the speakers' mention of them suggested al Qaeda's heightened confidence in its security; comments by its leaders could be recorded and disseminated with little concern that authorities could exploit the production and delivery processes to locate and go after them.[62]

The quality of the productions has continued to improve. Bin Laden's September video "was made available in five different versions, ranging from high-definition to a special format called 3G that can be downloaded to mobile devices," according to IntelCenter, a US firm that tracks and analyzes al Qaeda's productions.[63] The versions were downloadable at more than twenty different places on the Web, and most messages were also released on a CD-ROM as well.

Another video, posted by as-Sahab in August 2007, showed an altered photograph of President Bush and Pakistani president Pervez Musharraf standing in front of a burning White House. The ad bore the headline "Wait for the Big Surprise" and ended with the words "Soon–God willing." This image recalled a similar animated sequence that began appearing on the Internet in May 2007 showing the Capitol enveloped by a fireball.[64]

The increase in communications corresponded with a decrease in terrorist operations worldwide, confirming that al Qaeda's media campaign did not reflect its operational capability. If anything, the divergence confirmed that the two functions– terror and terrorism–were separate missions, with al Qaeda placing the greatest emphasis on terror.

In contrast to al Qaeda's sharpened high-tech communications campaign, there were quality-control problems on the operational front. The Internet could be used to inspire jihadists to take action–the main theme of almost all of al Qaeda's communications–but it could not guarantee their competence. Botched terrorist attacks in London and Glasgow in June 2007 provided evidence that determination alone does not produce successful operations. The London and Glasgow attacks were nonetheless frightening. They underscored the fact that despite increased intelligence efforts, jihadist recruits could still operate.

Al Qaeda's leaders had reason to be confident. According to the US National Intelligence Estimate (NIE)–a report reflecting the consensus of the entire intelligence community–al Qaeda itself, despite nearly six years of intense efforts by the United States and its allies to destroy the enterprise, had recovered much of its pre-9/11 strength.[65]

The NIE, which was released in July 2007, only days after al-Zawahiri's latest barrage of threats, concluded that al Qaeda remained the "most serious terrorist threat to the homeland, as its central leadership continues to plan high-impact plots." It went on to say that "the group has protected or regenerated key elements of its homeland attack capability, including: a safe haven in . . . Pakistan, operational lieutenants, and its top leadership."[66]

More than five years earlier, in 2002, I delivered a briefing to defense and intelligence officials in Washington in which I said that under increasing pressure, "to survive as the center of jihad, al Qaeda must reconfigure itself and find a new way of operating; protect its surviving leadership, find a secure base, develop a functioning command and control able to operate in total clandestinity . . . , [and] communicate with leaders, operatives, recruiters, potential volunteers, and constituents." The NIE indicated that five years later, al Qaeda appeared to have succeeded in doing all of these things.

A separate, classified assessment of al Qaeda's capabilities, prepared by the US National Counterterrorism Center and released in July 2007, echoed the NIE. Titled *Al-Qaeda Better Positioned to Strike the West*, the assessment noted that al Qaeda had "regrouped to an extent not seen since 2001" and had "greater ability to plan attacks in Europe and the United States."[67]

The NIE indicated that al Qaeda's "plotting is likely to focus on prominent political, economic, and infrastructure targets with the goal of producing mass casualties, visually dramatic destruction, significant economic aftershocks, and/or fear among the U.S. population." The intelligence analysts concluded that to achieve this goal, al Qaeda "will continue to try to acquire and employ chemical, biological, radiological, or nuclear material in attacks and would not hesitate to use them if it develops what it deems is sufficient capability."[68] These were grim assessments. For al Qaeda supporters, it was great news.

Hamid Mir continued his running commentary, now claiming that bin Laden's September 2007 message contained a phrase that official transcripts of the videotape had left out, one that was possibly erased by government sources. The omitted phrase, according to Mir, was, "We must sacrifice our lives to attack the enemy." Mir said this was a call for suicide attacks to take place throughout the United States. He indicated that these suicide attacks might involve the use of radiological devices or tactical nuclear weapons. He said that leaders of the Taliban in Afghanistan informed him that "al Qaeda's long-planned American Hiroshima—a nuclear attack on seven to ten U.S. cities—will occur in 2008 but could come sooner."[69]

The statements from al Qaeda's leaders inevitably set off a chorus of chatter on jihadist Web sites. As noted earlier, some of the jihadists were irritated by the failure of Americans to take seriously the video message of Adam Gaddahn released at the beginning of August. "They will soon realize their mistake when American cities are hit by quality operations," said one message.[70] Another said that attacks would be carried out by "trucks loaded with radioactive material against America's biggest city and financial nerve center"—a clear reference to New York.[71] A third message identified New York, Los Angeles, and Miami as targets.[72] As a precaution, the New York police department increased its radiological monitoring and established checkpoints to examine vehicles in Lower Manhattan and at other locations around the city.

While much of the Internet chatter could be dismissed, the prospect of an al Qaeda attack still worried officials throughout the summer of 2007. Al Qaeda had regained strength; its leaders were making threatening noises, evidently more comfortable about raising expectations. Recent attacks had occurred in the United Kingdom, and summertime seemed to be the preferred time for jihadist terrorist attacks.

All this caused Homeland Security Secretary Michael Chertoff to say in a meeting with the editorial board of the *Chicago Tribune* on July 10 that, while there was "no credible, specific intelligence to suggest an imminent threat to the homeland at this time"–the stock phrase–he nonetheless had a "gut feeling" that the nation faced a heightened chance of an attack.[73] The secretary's comments provoked both anxiety and anger.

With America's massive buildup in intelligence capabilities, critics charged, why didn't the government know more, and why were warnings based on the secretary's gut feeling? In fact, as I noted earlier and as any analyst knows, in assessing the continuing deluge of intelligence reports, threats, and warnings, gut feelings derived from long experience and good instincts are not to be discounted.

In September during testimony before Congress, Chertoff noted that "while the [Homeland Security] department's goal is to keep nuclear weapons from entering the country, . . . it also is focusing on how it would respond should a nuclear device get through and explode–particularly how to identify and track the nuclear materials."[74] It is a perfectly sensible thing to do, but it was an alarming revelation.

While avoiding any mention of their own digestive systems, other officials sounded similarly concerned. Vice Admiral John Scott Redd, director of the National Counterterrorism Center, said in an interview that "we are going to get hit again." "We've got this intelligence threat," Vice Admiral Redd continued, "we're pretty certain we know what's going on. We don't have all the tactical details about it." He went on to say, "We have very strong indicators that al Qaeda is planning to attack the West and is likely [to try] to attack, and we are pretty sure about that."[75]

In a public speech, CIA Director Michael Hayden followed with the observation that "our analysts assess with high confidence that al Qaeda's central leadership is planning high impact plots against the American homeland." The terrorist organization was, Hayden said, "focusing on targets that would produce mass casualties, dramatic destruction and significant economic aftershocks."[76]

These warnings from American officials were reinforced by comments from abroad. Rolf Ekeus, the former top UN weapons inspector, told reporters at a press conference in Luxembourg that al Qaeda was "searching for nuclear technology. . . . They are looking for simple weapons for mass destruction." Ekeus added that "the threat of a nuclear attack on a European city was tangible."[77]

At the same meeting in Luxembourg, former US defense secretary William Perry declared that it was "not alarmist to assume that there was over a 50 percent chance of a nuclear terrorist attack taking place in a European city."[78]

These expressions of public concern, amplified in the news media, excited and emboldened the Internet jihadists still further. With mere words, they could observe the tangible effects of creating fear. The chatter increased, creating, in the words of one seasoned intelligence analyst, a jihadist "feeding frenzy that migrates even to the suspected al Qaeda affiliates and supporters" who were being electronically monitored by the intelligence services, further worrying the authorities. The effect is circular.

Deconstructing al Qaeda's campaign of nuclear terror reveals a small number of confirmed events: al Qaeda's efforts in the early 1990s to acquire nuclear weapons in Sudan; bin Laden's recruitment of two American-educated Arab scientists; his discussions with sympathetic Pakistani scientists before 9/11; documents discovered in Afghanistan indicating interest in nuclear weapons; bin Laden's or al-Zawahiri's cryptic claim in the 2001 interview with Hamid Mir; continuing vague reports and rumors of efforts to acquire nuclear weapons or material in the former Soviet Union; claims that al Qaeda was entitled to kill millions.

This small core of narrative material was recycled and blended with the tips, boasts, threats, embellishments, fabrications, and other debris of undetermined credibility that flow toward any investigative reporter inquiring about such matters and that clog intelligence channels, making it hard to distinguish fact from fable. Stories of nuclear terrorism also have a way of combining with other issues of intense national concern, such as porous borders, illegal immigration, organized crime, proliferation, and Russian perfidy.

The resulting remix was presented as "newly uncovered," "terrifying contentions," "explosive information" about al Qaeda's plan for an imminent American Hiroshima. Although the actual facts of these reported contacts, deals, and deliveries were shrouded in mystery, the "shocking revelations" were often shorn of uncertainty and offered as "empirical proof," presented as fact and accepted on faith.

The primary work of sounding the alarm was carried on by a handful of determined, prolific, and convinced reporters. They communicated through a fairly narrow window of media outlets—books, news interviews, but mainly on the Internet. Although these were not mainstream media, they nonetheless reached large audiences, reflecting the general trend toward Internet and talk shows, radio, and television as the primary sources of news. Indeed, the very fact that these reports did not often appear in mainstream media, already mistrusted by many in the audience, only heightened their appeal and resonated with those seeking revealed truth rather than tempered explanations—secrets, not news. When stories of imminent terrorist nuclear attack occasionally did reach the news networks, the tyranny of time gave court advantage to shock and fear. There is no time for caveats in a sound bite. Talking heads warning of imminent doom–"in not more than 90 days"–have the advantage over "but wait a minute, we can't be certain" wonks.

This media activity has unwittingly fanned the flames of nuclear terror. Statements from al Qaeda Central initiated a chain reaction of commentary through the ranks of eager jihadists for whom the media jihad offered an opportunity to participate without blowing themselves up.

Like al Qaeda's global terrorist campaign, the media jihad was an uncoordinated group effort, yet it nonetheless qualifies as a campaign, even if many within the group are well meaning, believing we are on the cusp of imminent doom. Since 9/11, the jihadists gradually grasped the importance of this new front. The al Qaeda video marking the sixth anniversary of the 9/11 attacks calls on its followers to create a "climate of fear."[79] Terrorist attacks are preferable–real bombs and real blood–but absent attacks, threats, and alarms also serve. There is, of course, a danger to al Qaeda that its campaign might go completely virtual–a vast jihad video game. For a while, it can draw on its 9/11 capital, but in the long run, real operations are required.

Government officials, meanwhile, have contributed to the terror. While they did not say that al Qaeda was about to launch an attack with tactical nuclear weapons already deployed inside the United States, they warned repeatedly of further terrorist attacks, "not if, but when," of "dirty bombs." They spoke of al Qaeda's nuclear ambitions, of the "very real threat" of a nuclear terrorist attack inside the United States. They spoke of "carnage" and "catastrophe." They did irresponsible things, such as demonstrating how easy it was to smuggle radioactive material across the Canadian border. They placed a high probability on the likelihood of a terrorist nuclear attack. They prepared for the consequences of a terrorist nuclear attack–a reasonable step–but then advertised it to the public, and so the preparation signaled anticipation.

The sum effect has been nuclear terror.

Chapter 15
IS DETERRENCE DEAD?

"How do you deter or dissuade someone whose reward is in the 'afterlife?'" The irony of this question is that it was posed by Admiral Richard Mies, a former commander in chief of the US Strategic Command.[1] Here is a man who once commanded the most awesome nuclear arsenal in the world–who could have, with the president's permission, destroyed the planet–admitting that we don't know how to deter terrorists. Is our mighty arsenal even relevant?

Put the admiral's question in the context of the nuclear weapons designers who assert that if terrorists somehow get the necessary fissile material, they will, without a doubt, be able to fabricate at least a crude nuclear bomb. Recall the grim descriptions of the consequences of detonating even a crude nuclear device in a densely populated city–tens, perhaps hundreds of thousands dead, massive devastation followed by years of severe economic depression. Add the comments of the analysts who assert that the probability of such a terrible event is fifty-fifty, or the repeated funereal refrain of the political leaders who remind us, "It's not a matter of 'if,' but 'when.'" And we can't do a damn thing about it! It is a recipe for terror.

Nuclear terror is driven by the notion that terrorists cannot be deterred–that if they get their hands on a nuclear weapon, they will use it without hesitation. And there is no realistic way the United States, or any other country that the terrorists might choose to attack, can retaliate. In her 2008 book, *Memo to the President Elect*, former US secretary of state Madeleine Albright said it this way: It would be "doubly dangerous" if terrorists were able to buy or steal nuclear weapons, because "some terrorists claim to welcome death and are therefore impossible to deter and because many lack an address against which retaliatory or preemptive action might be taken."[2]

Undeterrable, undetectable, unstoppable–it would seem that terrorists have gained what cold war strategists once called "escalation dominance"–they can escalate with impunity. This is not because of terrorists' superior military power but because of their fanatical commitment–they might say it is because of their moral superiority or their superior faith in God. And terrorists are difficult to retaliate against because they have no military formations, installations, or territory to protect. They lack the very things against which military power can be used.

This has enormous consequences. The acquisition of nuclear weapons by terrorists, when the world has no apparent means of deterring them from using those weapons, would represent a fundamental shift in power and potentially a threat to civilization itself. Military history records such shifts, in which hordes of inspired irregular combatants, using what were at the time unconventional tactics, obviated the mighty armies that protected the political order and commerce. The end of the Bronze Age and the fall of the Roman Empire come to mind as examples. Often the results were collapses that ushered in lengthy "dark ages" of disorder and turbulence.

When we contemplate nuclear terrorism, the actual death and destruction that would result from a nuclear explosion is only part of what we fear. Instant death is easy. We fear the consequences of fear itself. Terror arises from fears of the immediate social disruption—the nightmare of panic, hysteria, predatory mobs, looting, rape, and murder—the continuing shadow of insecurity, economic decline, and disorder or dictatorship, all of which have been vividly depicted in literature and film.

Would democracy itself survive? According to Tommy Franks, the four-star general who commanded American forces in the Middle East, perhaps not. The first high-ranking official to openly speculate that the Constitution could be scrapped in favor of a military government, Franks said that if terrorists were to use a weapon of mass destruction that inflicts heavy casualties, it would cause "our population to question our own Constitution and to begin to militarize our country in order to avoid a repeat of another mass, casualty-producing event."[3]

This possibility has bothered me for decades. In 1974 I worried that power, defined in its crudest sense as the capacity to kill, destroy, disrupt, alarm, and oblige us to expend vast resources for security, was descending to smaller and smaller groups—gangs whose grievances, real or imaginary, could not always be satisfied. Or to put it another way, the bands of irreconcilables, fanatics, and lunatics that have existed throughout history were becoming an increasingly potent force. How we, as a democracy, would meet this threat and remain a democracy was, in my view, one of the major challenges of our age.[4]

But is deterrence really dead? A strategy of deterrence rests in large measure upon an assumption of rational behavior. The adversaries must have goals and must understand the risks and consequences of their decisions and behave in a manner that is neither self-destructive nor counterproductive in achieving those goals. States are generally presumed to be rational actors, which does not always seem to be the case. For all sorts of reasons, national leaders with public approval may pursue courses of action that appear to be irrational to all others. They may be messianic, poor judges of risk, or deliberately crazy to intimidate their foes. And terrorists are frequently presumed to be irrational actors, which also is a mistake. Our views of terrorists' irrationality are heavily influenced by suicide attacks, which represent not only an effective tactic but an even more effective form of psychological warfare. They turn a willingness to die into a weapon of terror.

Many view suicide attacks as evidence of the inherent, irrational, self-destructive behavior of all terrorists. It is true that suicide attacks are increasing. Indeed, suicide terrorists have become a commodity. It has been demonstrated hundreds of times that young men and women can be persuaded to strap explosives onto their bodies and become human bombs, to willingly take the wheel of a truck loaded with explosives and drive into a crowded marketplace, or to seize the controls of an aircraft and hurtle themselves into the sides of skyscrapers. And as we saw on September 11, 2001, it is possible to persuade at least nineteen persons to do this together. How can such fanaticism be deterred?

Strictly from the standpoint of individual behavior, a suicide attack cannot be considered a rational act, unless the attacker truly believes that he or she will be rewarded in the hereafter, a notion that our own secular society rejects. We can see suicide attacks as rational only if the individual sacrifice is seen to benefit a greater cause, as when a soldier throws himself on a grenade or charges a machine gun nest to save his comrades. We accept this when it is done in the heat of battle as an act of "extreme heroism," but we do not see this as being the same as a deliberate suicide attack, nor does it change our view that suicide attackers are irrational. But we are on slippery ground here. In the twentieth century, perfectly rational people were persuaded that it was necessary to kill and die by the millions for ideological abstractions, emperor, fuehrer, or party chairman. Were their out-of-this-physical-world expectations more rational than the anticipated afterlife rewards of the suicide bombers? How many degrees of madness separate the mass slaughter of World War I's trenches from the individual martyrdom of the suicide bomber?

Having suffered the horrific consequences of the two world wars, most Europeans today, and most Japanese, too, regard such sacrifice as stupid and consider its contemporary proponents worthy of institutionalization. Convincing them that war is necessary would be a lot more difficult. America suffered terrible casualties, too, but these were modest compared to those of Europe or Japan. Americans, therefore, may be more willing to reach for a rifle for God and country but as a nation of pragmatists quickly turn against what looks like a bad investment in blood and treasure. Americans, too, regard suicide attacks as insane.

Yet even enthusiastic martyrs take steps to conceal their plans until the last moment, stick to well-established tactics, and seek soft targets. They may care nothing for their lives, but they want to succeed in their mission. For some, success is evidence of God's approval. Conversely, failure may be interpreted as God's disapproval—a dangerous outcome if the martyr's only reward is to be reaped in the hereafter. And suicide attackers get only one shot.

Al Qaeda's martyrs are celebrated as exemplars of commitment and courage, but the same leaders who applaud the martyrs take great pains to protect their own security. Suicide attacks are a weapon, not an organizational goal.

Terrorist *groups*, in contrast to individual terrorists, tend to behave more rationally, in our sense of the term. This is not to say that they think as we do or that they necessarily share our calculus of values. It is simply to say that terrorists operate in ways that, in their view, best serve their own goals.

Despite the rhetoric of mass destruction, terrorist leaders must assess its utility. Large-scale violence must be weighed against how it contributes to the image and message of the group, how it will be perceived by constituents and sympathizers. Martyrdom should not be seen as meaningless sacrifice. Killing ought not to appear as irrelevant slaughter. In other words, even the most fanatical terrorist leaders must make rational decisions. This provokes debates between the more politically minded and the more thuggish operators. We see this in al Qaeda.

By its spectacular terrorist attacks, al Qaeda clearly has gained publicity, established its credentials, spread its message, and attracted new followers, but its terrorist operations thus far have prompted no global uprising. Osama bin Laden has achieved notoriety, but there is no groundswell of favorable opinion toward al Qaeda's bloody interpretation of religion. There is even evidence of rejection. In Jordan, al Qaeda's terrorist attacks brought thousands of demonstrators into the streets to denounce the organization.

In Iraq, al Qaeda's campaign of indiscriminate large-scale violence, which has killed far more Muslims than infidel invaders and has alarmed al Qaeda's central leadership, has backfired. It succeeded in exacerbating tensions between Sunni insurgents and Iraq's Shia majority, but it also provoked a backlash even among Sunni allies who have taken up arms against it. This, in turn, prompted al Qaeda to launch a wave of assassinations of chieftains who opposed it, which in the Middle East will lead to further acts of revenge. Al Qaeda's contribution to the insurgency against the infidel occupier seems to have degenerated into a vendetta.

The desire for tactical and strategic success, the lessons learned in Iraq, the debate within jihadist circles, and criticism of the jihadists from within the Muslim community all create opportunities for deterrence.

To think creatively about how deterrence might apply to terrorists, one has to disaggregate the terrorists and broaden the concept of deterrence. We are, at the moment, understandably focused on al Qaeda and the jihadist enterprise, but not all terrorist groups behave like al Qaeda.

Not all terrorists welcome death. Jihadists currently pose the greatest threat, but many other contemporary groups that use terrorist tactics do not share al Qaeda's lust for slaughter and martyrdom. And not all terrorists lack a return address. Hamas, Hezbollah, and Sri Lanka's Tamil Tigers all have populations to protect, territory to defend.

Even al Qaeda, with its exultation of martyrdom and pronouncement of fatwas that permit it to kill millions of infidels, including women and children, is not a monolithic entity but rather a complex galaxy of leaders, supporters, sympathizers, contributors, and confederates. Leaders inside and outside al Qaeda debate strategy, tactics, Koranic constraints, what is legitimate in warfare, and what is manly behavior for warriors.

Deterrence and self-imposed constraints are linked. An effective deterrent can reinforce existing self-imposed constraints by suggesting that any terrorist attack involving nuclear weapons will not only provoke retaliation but will leave the terrorist group isolated from its constituents, its hosts—those upon whom it depends for sanctuary and support.

Of course, not all within the terrorist galaxy will agree. Convinced that only greater ruthlessness will bring greater success, some will discount the potential loss of constituents, world condemnation, and the threat of retaliation. Others will foresee it as a disaster and take extreme measures to forestall it. In terrorist organizations, such disputes are often lethal. The prospect of provoking serious and potentially bloody internal divisions that imperil the leaders themselves as well as the unity of the organization becomes a constraint, which can be fashioned into a deterrent.

Moreover, deterrence is not confined to the threat of retaliation. It was never that simple even during the cold war. Deterrence may be achieved by affecting the terrorists' calculations of success. It may be achieved by reducing the perceived consequences of their attacks, denying them what they hope to achieve. If the terrorists' assessment of potential damage is reduced while perceptions of internal and external risks are increased, the effect is deterrence.

Sympathizers and supporters may be repelled by the violence itself, as many were in Iraq and Jordan, and they are likely to be more vulnerable to and therefore fearful of retaliation than hard-core terrorist leaders with little to lose. Retaliation may be carried out not in the form of a single strike but as a relentless pursuit—the kind of pressure al Qaeda has been subjected to for years. That has a deterrent effect. If we were somehow able to poll terrorist leaders worldwide, how many would want to change places with al Qaeda?

A society's demonstrable resiliency contributes to deterrence. While authorities worry about the chaos that could result if terrorists were to use nuclear weapons, the evidence we have from the few large-scale terrorist attacks that have occurred thus far does not support a thesis of social breakdown. With some ugly exceptions, people behave with remarkable stoicism, courage, and resiliency. And with education and improved preparedness, the threat of panic and social disorder can be further reduced.

Terrorists will never have enough nuclear weapons of sufficient destructive power to destroy an entire country. More likely, their arsenal will be limited to one or two low-yield devices. The losses would still be tragic, but the republics will survive—wounded, angry, determined, and very dangerous.

In 1918 America lost an estimated half-million people to the Spanish flu epidemic, a figure that today would be the equivalent of a million and a half fatalities. There was no social collapse, and America went on to the prosperity of the 1920s.

Nearly 300,000 able-bodied Americans were killed in World War II and another 672,000 were wounded—a total that at the time represented roughly 0.7 percent of the entire population. It would be the equivalent of more than two million casualties today. But the country quickly recovered after the war.

Europe and Japan, of course, suffered much greater death and destruction than America did. By 1945 millions of their citizens had died, their economies were smashed, their cities lay in ruins, and refugees numbered in the millions. Yet by the early 1960s, recovery was nearly complete.

The German bombing of England in 1940 was intended to create terror and disorder. Despite the intensity of the campaign, which killed nearly thirty thousand persons, mostly civilians, in the first eight months of bombing, there was no evidence of widespread panic. People were frightened–terrified even–but remarkably, they went on with their lives.[5] The same was true of New York in the harrowing hours immediately after the attacks on September 11, 2001.

This raises a fundamental question about the utility of terror. Those most concerned about the possibility of serious nuclear terrorism believe that a quantum of terror is a prerequisite to action. Only by terrifying people can the nation be persuaded to exert pressure on national leaders to pay attention to the threat and devote the necessary resources to its prevention. Others worry that by exaggerating the likelihood and likely consequences of nuclear terrorism, we may weaken public will. Instead of action, constant threats produce only useless anxiety and risk overreaction if something happens.

There is little discussion of deterring nuclear terrorism in official policy circles. The Global War on Terror calls for the eradication of terrorists, a goal incompatible with deterrence. The idea of deterrence is similarly banished from discussions of nuclear weapons aspirants like North Korea and presumably Iran, out of fear that deterrence implies a surrender to proliferation and therefore undercuts current efforts aimed at the total elimination of their nuclear weapons capabilities.

Still, a handful of analysts have addressed the question of how nuclear terrorism might be deterred. Each of these takes a different approach to the issue. All agree that we have to broaden the concept of deterrence beyond the threat of military retaliation. In a speech to the National War College, Admiral Mies talked about adding dissuasion (political warfare), defense, and denial to a policy of deterrence.[6]

Amitai Etzioni, a senior adviser to the White House during the Carter administration, argues that deterrence can work for rogue states but will not work for failing states, or for terrorists. In his view, fissile material must be put beyond the reach of terrorists. Etzioni advances the idea of preemption through "deproliferation," a concept that envisages removing fissile material from failing states and dissuading new states from developing nuclear weapons capabilities. At the same time, however, the existing nuclear weapons states must seriously pursue disarmament.[7]

One must concede an inherent contradiction between demanding that other nations abandon their nuclear ambitions while nuclear weapons states refine their nuclear arsenals. Yet, the perception that the more recent aspirants to the nuclear weapons club are also more likely to use them (or hand them over to terrorists) makes it harder to make a case for disarmament. That brings us to retaliation.

Two other essays endorse retaliation. Writing in the *Washington Quarterly*, Caitlin Talmadge, a doctoral candidate at the Massachusetts Institute of Technology, agrees that terrorists cannot be deterred but argues that they cannot manufacture fissile material on their own or make nuclear weapons without a state's being involved at some stage. Therefore, the way to deter a terrorist nuclear attack is to threaten any state that transfers nuclear material or weapons to the terrorists. This, however, requires good nuclear forensics—the ability to correctly attribute the origins of nuclear material used in any attack through science and intelligence and thereby credibly threaten retaliation. In Talmadge's view, the United States does not currently possess this capability.[8]

Anders Corr, a doctoral candidate at Harvard, introduces the idea of "a negligence doctrine" as the basis for retaliation. Like Talmadge, he argues that it would not be just the terrorists who should be held to account in the case of a terrorist nuclear attack but also those who provided the fissile material or who failed to secure it adequately. He also agrees with Talmadge that implementing such a doctrine would require improving our ability to identify the origins of fissile material used in a terrorist bomb, but he goes further. He proposes that lack of evidence should not prevent retaliation: "Retaliation in the case of no-evidence ought to be specified in advance, . . . and ought to list targets, such as states that are rogue nuclear proliferators or that do not abide by international standards of fissile material storage."[9] Guilty or not, someone is going to get it.

Such specificity may, however, reduce the deterrent effect of uncertainty. Rather than specifying what the United States will do if it is ever attacked with a nuclear weapon, the government may instead wish to convey the message that in such extraordinary circumstances, no one in office or seeking office can be sure what he or she would do. Nothing is ruled out.

"The idea that religiously oriented terrorists cannot be deterred from . . . using WMD . . . is a relatively unexplored assumption, based on anecdotal evidence," writes David Auerswald, a professor of strategy at the National War College. "Nonetheless, this assumption is consistently made by most academicians and the U.S. Government." He concedes that "deterring terrorists by threatening punishment is extremely difficult . . . and may even be self-defeating." Instead, he argues, a strategy of deterrence should focus on the arms traffickers and organized crime groups, which are the terrorists' most likely source of weapons of mass destruction or WMD material and who are susceptible to deterrence.[10]

Thomas Schelling, who received the Nobel Prize for his

research on deterrence theory during the cold war, recognizes that terrorists pose a unique challenge to the concept of deterrence: "We don't know what they value that we might threaten, or who or where it is." Yet he remains hopeful that deterrence may still apply. "Any organization that gets enough fissile material to make a bomb will require highly qualified scientists, technologists, machinists, working in seclusion . . . for months with nothing much to talk about except what their A-bomb might be good for, for whom. They are likely to feel justified, by their contribution, to have some claim on participating in any decisions on the use of the device."[11]

Schelling's view of terrorist technicians who think does not match the popular perception of the unthinking, amoral automatons who unquestioningly follow the orders of fictional master villains such as Fu Manchu or run the huge clandestine laboratories of evil found in James Bond novels. Real terrorists are much more complicated and quarrelsome beings. Schelling is correct in pointing out that the construction of a nuclear bomb is no kitchen table project. Unless someone hands some terrorist commander a nuclear weapon with instructions for use, building a nuclear weapon is likely to be a long-term, large-scale enterprise.

Schelling believes that terrorist weapons builders "will conclude—I hope they will conclude—over weeks of arguing that the most effective use of the bomb, from a terrorist perspective, will be for influence. Possessing a nuclear weapon, if they can demonstrate possession . . . will give them something of the status of a nation."[12] This would seem to be consistent with the original motives for bin Laden's early attempts to acquire a nuclear weapon—envy, status, influence in the world.

"Keeping [the weapon] intact, . . ." Schelling concludes, "may appeal to them more than expending it in a purely destructive act. Even terrorists may consider destroying large numbers of people as less satisfying than keeping a major nation at bay."[13] Palestinian leaders seemed to have arrived at a similar conclusion forty years before. They asserted that if Israel developed nuclear weapons, the Palestinian organizations would be able to get their own nuclear weapons. Palestinian leaders also expressed the view that the ensuing balance of terror between Israel and the Palestinian groups would favor the latter as the less predictable, more "irresponsible" party.[14]

It is, as Schelling admits, a hopeful view of deterrence. This brings us halfway around the circle from what we thought terrorists might do thirty years earlier. In the 1970s, analysts thought that terrorists were most likely to use a nuclear weapon, if they got one, as an instrument of coercion to extract concessions. In simulations, it seldom worked. As terrorism escalated in the real world, it seemed more likely that terrorists would use a nuclear weapon as an instrument of destruction.

But Schelling's view takes us to a different place. He envisions terrorists reaching the same conclusion that the two superpowers did decades earlier. In other words, terrorists will find that nuclear weapons don't work very well as instruments of coercion, and their actual use is likely to be suicidal. Terrorists, of course, might decide to use nuclear weapons to deter us, but from what? From attacking them with nuclear weapons? From attacking their sanctuaries? From attacking them at all? I am dubious.

It is true that Osama bin Laden's comments just after 9/11 suggest that by then, he, too, viewed possession of a nuclear weapon as a deterrent. Still, it is hard to imagine how the United States or any other nation could accommodate to a permanent terrorist nuclear power. Schelling has the advantage of long historical perspective. The notion of deterrence did not descend as revelation with the Soviet Union's detonation of an atomic bomb. In the late 1940s, it was probably equally difficult to imagine how the two nuclear powers would accommodate to one another. Arguments for blowing the enemy off the face of the planet remained prevalent on both sides for some time. Deterrence had to be worked out.

But Schelling's comments raise another interesting point: If terrorists were to actually start building a nuclear weapon, they would be forced to think about how they would use it. As long as terrorist acquisition of a nuclear weapon remains theoretical, a detonation without warning—a nuclear 9/11—is a default decision. Since terrorists don't have a nuclear weapon, it benefits them to declare that they will use it without hesitation. As a threat, it enables them to create nuclear terror even without possessing a nuclear weapon. It suffices to keep us guessing.

In 2002 Paul Davis—a principal researcher at RAND—and I tackled the issue of deterring terrorists in a monograph titled *Deterrence and Influence in Counterterrorism: A Component in the War on al Qaeda.*[15] We conceded the difficulties of applying deterrent strategies to terrorists, including their very strong motivations, their passionate hatred, and their presumptions of divine mandates. We recognized that a strategy aimed at eradication might be inconsistent with a strategy aimed at deterrence. What more can you threaten when you are actively engaged in a campaign of annihilation? Still, eradication of one group might usefully deter future terrorist groups.

However, rather than accept the conventional wisdom that deterrence won't work on terrorists, we explored the circumstances under which and against whom it might work. As the title of the monograph implies, we broadened the concept of deterrence to encompass a range of measures from co-opting terrorists to assured destruction. And we broke up al Qaeda into classes of actors: top leaders, lieutenants, foot soldiers, supportive populations, external suppliers and facilitators, supportive states or elements within states, sources of moral and religious support. A strategy of deterrence might address each set of actors differently.

For example, there might be some way to deter Osama bin Laden, but killing or capturing him offers more promise. We identified some things his terrorist followers might hold dear—the lives of their families, for example–but recognized our limitations in threatening these things. On the other hand, others in the jihadist universe might be deterred. His wealthy financiers, those engaged in profitable criminal enterprises like drug trafficking, the tribes that provide him with sanctuary, obviously have something to lose. Those who provide political or moral support might withdraw it under certain circumstances. The very things that caused terrorists to worry about the consequences of their own behavior, to even consider constraints on their violence, could be exploited to create deterrents. Davis and I concluded that "terrorists" could be influenced or deterred in the broadest sense by using a wide array of strategies ranging from political warfare, an area where the United States is deficient, to assured destruction.

As part of any deterrent strategy, the United States would have to demonstrate that terrorist attacks will not bring the nation down or cause it to close itself down "but that it will be resilient . . . and will hit back very hard." Pursuit of transgressors would be relentless. There would be no respite, no forgetting, no quarter. We added that terrorists and their supporters must be helped to understand that in responding to a major terrorist attack, the United States is likely to "lower the standards of evidence, presume guilt, violate sovereignty, attack preemptively," if necessary. Ruthless pursuit does not, however, mean indiscriminate violence or other actions inconsistent with core American values.[16]

Chapter 16
A SELF-SUSTAINING
FISSION OF FEAR

"Ithink we have to live with the expectation that once every four to five years a nuclear explosion will take place and kill a lot of people." That chilling forecast was related to John McPhee, who included it in his 1973 book, *The Curve of Binding Energy.*[1] If it had proven correct, the world would by now have suffered seven or eight nuclear explosions and many thousands of casualties.

Will terrorists ever get–and use–the bomb? Many Americans think it is likely that they will. When a 2006 Gallup Poll asked people whether they thought it likely that terrorists in the next five years would "set off a bomb that contains nuclear or biological material," 47 percent considered it likely, while 49 percent considered it unlikely.[2] The results of the survey are skewed by conflating nuclear and biological material, but according to a Harris Poll conducted in 2007, when asked to rate the likelihood of "a nuclear bomb exploding in a city" in the next five years, 42 percent thought it likely, 14 percent deemed it "very likely," and 28 percent considered it "somewhat likely."[3]

When one thinks about it for a moment, that seems to be an

extraordinary result: Just imagine, four out of ten Americans go through life expecting that terrorists will set off a nuclear bomb in an American city in the next five years. And we are counting down.

QUANTIFYING TERROR

Henry Sokolski, executive director of the Nonproliferation Policy Education Center and former deputy for Nonproliferation in the Pentagon, disagrees. He puts the odds of a terrorist nuclear bomb being detonated in the next ten years at "one in a million, up from one in ten million before 9/11."[4] Nuclear weapons designer Richard Garwin estimated a "20 percent per year probability of a nuclear explosion in either an American or European city."[5] Harvard professor Matthew Bunn estimates the probability of a nuclear terrorist attack over a ten-year period at precisely 29 percent.[6] This estimate was identical to the median estimate from a poll of international security experts commissioned by Senator Richard Lugar in 2005.[7] Graham Allison, the author of *Nuclear Terrorism: The Ultimate Preventable Catastrophe*, believes that there is a better than 50 percent chance that terrorists will detonate a nuclear bomb in the United States within the next ten years–he actually wrote this in 2004.[8] Former US secretary of defense William Perry thinks this is too optimistic. America's savviest investor, Warren Buffett, considers a nuclear attack "virtually a certainty."[9] Many argue that it is only a matter of time–not "if," but "when."

In the course of writing this book, I conducted my own informal survey. I was looking for "expert" opinions. Those invited to participate included intelligence officials, senior military officers, government officials with national or homeland security responsibilities, nuclear scientists, and members of the security research community.[10] Approximately one hundred and eighty respondents were asked to estimate the probability that terrorists will successfully detonate a nuclear bomb, not just a dirty bomb, somewhere in the world in the next ten years. And since the concern that terrorists might go nuclear has been around for decades, the survey asked why it has not happened. Survey respondents were asked what they believe to be the principal reason for terrorists not having carried out a nuclear attack.

There is, of course, no right answer to these questions, and none of the answers has any predictive value. How can you underestimate or overestimate the probability of something that has never occurred? The responses, however, do reflect perceptions. In a way, they are a measure of anxiety.

The range of the responses reveals great uncertainty. Respondents are deeply divided. Their answers ranged from zero probability to absolute certainty. Even if we omit the responses at the two ends, the remaining estimates still ranged between "one in a million" and "98 percent certainty" that such an attack would occur. The median among the respondents was a 10 percent probability of a nuclear attack, which seems to be lower than the popular view of nuclear terrorism.

The numbers, however, don't fully reflect the perceptions. Some described their 10 percent estimates as a high probability. Others considered their 20 percent estimate to be fairly low. Some indicated that they had hedged their guess, increasing the probability because of a lack of confidence in the ability of our intelligence services to know what terrorists actually may be up to.

The responses also showed a significant difference between Americans and Europeans on the issue, with Americans inclined to view a terrorist nuclear attack as far more likely than their European counterparts. Europeans estimated the probabilities as somewhere between zero and 50 percent. No European estimated it higher than 50 percent, and the median was 1 percent, while the median for the Americans alone was 20 percent—twenty times greater. Europeans see this disparity as evidence of American alarmism. Americans see the lower European estimates as remarkable insouciance.

Although not asked to do so, many of the respondents volunteered reasons for their belief that a terrorist nuclear attack was likely. "Al Qaeda has clearly indicated its intent," wrote one, "and there is no reason not to take it at its word." While some respondents thought that terrorists would not want to provoke the kind of extreme reaction a nuclear bomb would cause, others remarked on the jihadists' lack of constraints.

Those who doubted that terrorists could build a nuclear bomb by themselves still worried that they might get one from Russia, where security was viewed as poor. Others worried that political turbulence in Pakistan might provide terrorists with an opportunity to get to one of that country's nuclear weapons.

A number of respondents indicated that they thought the probability of nuclear terrorism was increasing. They cited "growing alienation and radicalization in the Muslim world," mounting anger against what not only the terrorists but also others perceive to be "imperialism and Western arrogance," and the emergence of new nuclear weapons states.

Respondents reflected great concern about Iran's possible acquisition of nuclear weapons. While some thought it unlikely that any government would be crazy enough to arm terrorists with a nuclear weapon, several echoed the concern that "Iran may do something stupid." Iran's acquisition of nuclear weapons, wrote one respondent, would increase his estimate of the probability of nuclear terrorism from 2 percent to 40 percent.

Many participants in the survey offered more than one reason for the fact that terrorists had not yet detonated a nuclear bomb. Most of these reflected the lack of capabilities: Terrorists had not been able to obtain a nuclear weapon or fissile material to make one, they lacked the technical knowledge to fabricate a nuclear weapon, or they were unable to deliver one. While some respondents thought that states might arm terrorists with nuclear weapons, others thought that states would not do so. "No one who has nuclear weapons to date . . . would leave it to the hands of terrorists," wrote one. Added another, "Even the nastier ones are paranoid enough not to hand them over to the players outside of their immediate control."

In all, lack of capabilities accounted for about 60 percent of the total reasons given. Although the inability of terrorists to obtain a weapon or material would seem to imply good security, less than 3 percent of the reasons specifically said that security had prevented terrorist acquisition, and the idea that intelligence efforts had successfully prevented terrorist acquisition was mentioned only twice. A few respondents did think that lack of a safe sanctuary in which to build a weapon was an impediment. This view is an endorsement of a policy aimed at keeping terrorists on the run.

Lack of terrorist intent accounted for about 27 percent of the reasons offered for terrorists not going nuclear. Respondents thought that terrorists simply lacked the interest, the will, the resolve to acquire nuclear weapons, that it was simply not a priority, or that it was not clear how going nuclear would contribute to their objectives. Some respondents thought that the risks of failure were simply too high, while some went further and suggested that terrorists worried that going nuclear would be counterproductive, dangerous to their cause. "It doesn't contribute to achieving strategic objectives, and actually might be counter to those objectives or otherwise be too risky and expensive to those objectives to justify," one respondent wrote. A few thought that a decision to go nuclear would be divisive and cause dissension within the terrorist ranks. A "taboo" against using nuclear weapons was mentioned twice. Despite the escalation in terrorism over the decades, analysts still perceive self-imposed limitations on terrorist violence. Their view is endorsed by events in Iraq, where jihadists bent upon slaughter clearly overplayed their hand

and provoked a popular backlash, which is just what jihadist leaders outside Iraq had warned against.

Nine percent of the reasons posited a different set of terrorist calculations. Other weapons were more accessible or other tactics were easier than attempting to acquire and use nuclear weapons. "Terrorists have readily available other, more conventional methods of pursuing their objectives," wrote one respondent. "When you live and act in a dangerous environment, you stick to well-known techniques and methods," observed another. Several respondents thought that generating nuclear terror—the anticipation that terrorists would go nuclear—was more effective than nuclear terrorism, given the high risks of failure. Several, however, thought that terrorists were merely waiting for the right moment, and one speculated that terrorists would want more than one nuclear weapon before launching an attack. Several respondents suspected that terrorists were working on it right now. Two credited the absence of a terrorist nuclear attack to pure luck.

Again, American and European perceptions differed. While Americans saw lack of capability as three times more likely to be the principal constraint than lack of intent, European responses credited lack of capabilities and lack of intent equally. The Americans generally viewed terrorists as bent upon maximum violence, checked only by technical limitations. The Europeans tended to see terrorists as more subtle decision makers.

The diversity and complexity of the reasons offered for terrorists not having detonated a nuclear device indicates that many respondents, both American and European, viewed going nuclear as a complicated decision process that involves both capabilities and intentions. It is not simply a matter of know-how. Although capabilities were considered most important, terrorists were perceived as having to make decisions about the risks of failure compared with those associated with other weapons and tactics, needing to weigh obvious benefits against possibly creating internal divisions, alienating constituents, and provoking a fierce global backlash. As one respondent summed it up, "Terrorists aren't smart enough to build a nuclear bomb, and if they were smart enough to build a nuclear bomb, they would be smart enough not to."

Thomas Schelling, although not a participant in the survey, expressed it differently. The fabrication of a nuclear weapon is not a trivial task, he pointed out. It would require a large group effort of highly intelligent people working together for a long time to make a nuclear bomb, time enough to contemplate the terrible consequences of what they were doing. Some probably–hopefully–would have second thoughts.

A terrorist Manhattan Project would be technically far more demanding than 9/11. While murderous fanatics with a detailed knowledge of physics, engineering, and explosives rarely come in groups, it is difficult to say whether scale and technical complexity would guarantee conscience and exposure. I am not sure. There were doubts, crises of conscience among the members of the team that produced the first atomic bomb. Some were opposed to its use, but all went along–no one walked away from the project. They were, of course, in the middle of a bloody war, but that is also the mind-set of our terrorist adversaries.

Complexity would certainly affect terrorist calculations of success. Terrorists would have to acquire nuclear weapons or nuclear material. They would then have to be able to bypass protective measures to gain the ability to use a purchased or stolen nuclear weapon or fabricate a device themselves, which would take time and resources and require a safe base, and they would then have to be able to successfully deliver the infernal device to a target–at least three difficult tasks. All three would have to be completed for terrorists to succeed. This, in turn, would affect their own, as well as our, estimates of the probability of success. A 50 percent chance of success at each step would give terrorists only a 12.5 percent chance of success overall, or an 87.5 percent chance of failure—a lot of risk. Looking at it in reverse, a 50 percent chance of success overall would require a demanding 80 percent probability of success at each step of the operation. Most of the survey respondents who followed this line of analysis arrived at low estimates.

Of course, we don't know exactly what terrorists consider to be an acceptable level of risk. Suicide attacks should not mislead us to infer that terrorists are oblivious to risk. Although some individuals may be willing to sacrifice their lives, even suicidal terrorists are loath to fail in their operations. Although they are at times audacious, notably in low-tech attacks that depend more on human will than on technology, terrorist planners prefer easy successes. They abhor uncertainty. The greater the investment, the greater the demand for success of the operation, particularly when the risks of discovery or of ultimate failure would not merely involve the lives of a few easily replaced operatives but might fundamentally change world attitudes and lead to the widespread denunciation and destruction of the group.

Estimates of the likelihood that terrorists will go nuclear are related to our own tolerance for risk. Graham Allison argues that even if terrorists had only a 10 percent chance of success, that is an intolerable risk given the consequences of a terrorist nuclear bomb.[11] Estimates of consequences always override estimates of probabilities.

Vice President Cheney has argued that considering what is at risk, even a 1 percent chance cannot be accepted.[12] Therefore, "if there was even a one percent chance of terrorists getting a weapon of mass destruction . . . the United States must now act as if it were a certainty." The doctrine has significant consequences, which Cheney is quoted as pointing out himself. It's not about "our analysis," it's about "our response." This "effectively sidelines the traditional policymaking process of analysis and debate, making suspicion, not evidence, the new threshold for action."[13]

A DOMAIN OF APPREHENSION AND DREAD

In psychological parlance, *reify* means to treat an abstract concept as something concrete, giving corporeal reality to a sensation, or treating an unsupported assertion as established fact and acting upon it as if it were true. The reification of hypothetical terrorist scenarios into imminent threats would fall into this category. Our terrorist foes do this all the time, boasting of their intentions as if they were actual achievements. We, too, reify hypothetical scenarios into imminent threats. The product is terror.

Nuclear terrorism and nuclear terror are separate but overlapping domains. Nuclear terrorism comprises just about any criminal action involving nuclear facilities or material: minor acts of sabotage; reports of smuggling and nuclear black markets; dirty-bomb plots; an assassination with polonium; alarming nuclear hoaxes. All of these contribute to nuclear terror, the fear that terrorists will do something far more serious: sabotage a reactor to create a terrorist Chernobyl; contaminate a city with radioactive material, making it uninhabitable for centuries; acquire or fabricate and detonate a nuclear bomb to kill tens or hundreds of thousands of people.

We are right to worry about nuclear terrorism. What could be of greater consequence to society than the detonation of a nuclear bomb in a densely populated city? Fear is a powerful motivator. It encourages us to take concrete steps to prevent what we fear. Even without any history of nuclear terrorism, the fear of nuclear action by terrorists has led to measures to improve safeguards and security at nuclear sites. Fear of loose nukes and unemployed weapons designers prompted US efforts to assist a tottering Russia in shoring up security around its nuclear weapons and in finding useful alternative employment for scientists working in its weapons programs. Fear made sense, and it may well have prevented dangerous developments during a chaotic period in Russia.

No one, therefore, suggests that we should not fear nuclear terrorism. We must, however, understand that nuclear terror operates according to different rules. Nuclear terror is an abstract concept. It is founded not on a history of terrorist incidents but rather on an accumulation of fears and perceptions, some of which even precede the nuclear age. Nuclear terror floats freely above the ground of proven fact and demonstrable reality. It is a domain of apprehension and dread, shaped by perception and imagination, related to but separate from the chronology of actual—and thus far, fortunately, minor—nuclear terrorist events. It is a domain governed as much by fiction as by science, by terrorist threats as much as by assessments of terrorist capabilities. Nuclear terror is a hypothesis.

Yet nuclear terror shapes the views of policy makers as much as it does those of the general public, perhaps more so, since officials want to see themselves as guardians of the future as well as the present. It was a tangled thought, but my audience understood perfectly when, in the course of a briefing on nuclear security, I once mused, "If the world ends tomorrow, future generations will hold us accountable."

As we have seen, nuclear terror does not derive solely from what terrorists say or do. Nuclear terror is the product of a collective endeavor involving not only terrorists but a broad spectrum of contributors who function as critical communicators. They are connected, they interact, they reinforce one another, each according to his own ends, but in a discordant concert to create terror, either as a prerequisite to achieving their goals or as a principal by-product of achieving them. Some are convinced our very survival is immediately at stake; others, not so. The result is that actors and audience are both producers and consumers of nuclear terror.

CRITICAL COMMUNICATORS

In the language of nuclear weapons, we might say that terrorists are the trigger for nuclear terror, but by themselves they would have limited effect if the audience were merely a passive absorber. Instead, key components of the audience reflect and amplify the threat, not as the terrorists' accomplices but according to their own predetermined beliefs and positions.

Within this audience are those who are convinced that governments are not doing enough to protect nuclear weapons or prevent nuclear terrorism. They view any manifestation of the threat as both confirmation and ammunition for their cause. In order to concentrate the minds of a frightened but distracted public and government, those who are most worried about nuclear terrorism must work to deliberately reify–the word is appropriate here–the threat, converting free-floating anxiety into concrete measures aimed at prevention and preparedness. These communicators publicize terrorist incidents, extrapolate potential terrorist actions, craft worst-case scenarios to arouse supine officials and to wrest resources from tight-fisted politicians. Public alarm is both an objective and a by-product of their campaign.

Then there are those with political agendas who see the threat of nuclear terrorism as a means of gaining or maintaining political power, as a way of mobilizing support for absolutist agendas at home or military expeditions abroad. It is easy to categorize them as cynical manipulators of fear; some are. But their ranks also include those who sincerely believe that the consequences of nuclear terrorism are so horrendous that they must fundamentally change how we pursue homeland and national security.

Within this audience are those who oppose nuclear weapons or nuclear energy on any account. They view the terrorist threat as merely one more dimension of danger, confirmation of their fears but useful in enlisting support for their cause.

There are also those who view nuclear terrorism as confirmation of biblical prophecy, a sign of the Apocalypse, the Second Coming, to be embraced and broadcast as validation of their faith, a call to repent because the end is near, a summons to fight the Antichrist.

Survivalists, yet another contingent of America's anxious, see the prospect of nuclear terrorism as they saw the possibility of nuclear war with the Soviet Union. The threat of nuclear terrorism fulfills their dark fantasies and justifies their preparations for the world that will come after.

Then there are the individuals whom 9/11 vaulted to celebrity as "talking heads" on myriad radio and television shows. In a crowded field, continued celebrity requires escalation, though some in this field undoubtedly believe the threat is imminent. Still, the threat of nuclear terrorism guarantees people's attention. Sensationalist news media provide the forum.

Finally, there are those who find in nuclear terrorism the inspiration for novels and scripts; suspense-filled dramas that raise the specter of shadowy villains with the power to destroy cities. Creative thinkers, the writers embellish what they take from headlines, give terrorism a face, make it real, and feed it back to the public and public officials.

These communicators help sustain the chain reaction.

AMPLIFYING THE THREAT

As outlined above, *assessments of the terrorist nuclear threat are almost never communicated without an underlying objective.* Almost all writing about nuclear terrorism is tendentious case-building. The threat is imminent—urgent action is required. To support this contention, communicators assemble all indicators. They document contemporary terrorists' thirst for large-scale violence, their quest for weapons of mass destruction (WMD), their fascination with and forays into the nuclear arena. The chronologies include the relatively few actual nuclear incidents augmented by threats, by reports that cannot be confirmed but remain plausible, and by surmise and reasonable speculation about what terrorists can or might do. All merit inclusion, provided they are appropriately labeled, but crucial distinctions between confirmed fact and surmise are often blurred. Stacked in a pile, they give the impression that a great deal is going on. The whole seems greater than the sum of its parts.

These communicators extrapolate this history into the future, which in my experience has always proved to be a dangerous form of analysis. Still, one does have to keep in mind that well-informed warnings have often preceded actual events, not always in a specific predictive fashion, but in a general way. As we have seen, the first warnings about nuclear terrorism preceded the rise of contemporary international terrorism. As another example, the scenario that terrorists might hijack an airliner and deliberately crash it into a building was considered a possibility almost two decades before 9/11. Nonetheless, extrapolation can easily suggest inexorability, which is wrong. It is not a straight-line march from a terrorist truck bomb to a terrorist nuclear bomb, but with the worst incidents of terrorism measured by fatalities increasing by an order of magnitude every ten to fifteen years, it is easy to project incidents with fatalities in the tens of thousands in the next decade or so. It then becomes a tautology. To achieve fatalities in the tens of thousands would require a nuclear weapon (or a very successful biological attack), making it therefore seem that because terrorist violence is escalating, nuclear terrorism is likely.

High estimates of probability further amplify the threat. The survey discussed at the beginning of this chapter showed a significant spread in estimates of the likelihood of nuclear terrorism. Those advocating action tended to come in on the high end of the estimates—estimating a 50 percent or greater probability of a nuclear attack, although it is noteworthy that many of those who estimate that probability to be much lower also advocate increasing security and other preventive measures. An estimate of 1 percent or less does not indicate complacency.

Estimates of probability, however, are often distorted by imprecise language. Asked if terrorists are likely to use nuclear weapons, the response can easily be, "Terrorist use of WMD is very likely." However, terrorist use of nuclear weapons and terrorist use of WMD are very different categories. *Weapons of mass destruction* is a term that is used often but is seldom precisely defined. It is not clear what the word *mass* designates in terms of the number of fatalities or the extent of destruction. If it means terrorist incidents with deaths in the hundreds, there have been very few. And there has been only one terrorist incident with the number of deaths in the thousands. Should these be considered incidents of *mass* destruction?

The alternative acronym CBRN, for chemical, biological, radiological, and nuclear weapons, specifies the instruments but no criterion for scale. In fact, there have already been a number of incidents in which terrorists have employed or have attempted to employ chemical weapons. These range from chlorine-enhanced truck bombs in Baghdad to the nerve-gas attack in Tokyo, which sent fifty-five hundred people to the hospital but resulted in only twelve deaths. There also have been terrorist incidents involving ricin and anthrax, again with very few fatalities. CBRN weapons are not necessarily WMD.

Imprecise language also lumps dirty bombs together with nuclear bombs, although the two differ greatly in complexity and consequences. Terrorists have thought about dirty bombs (radiological weapons), and they are much easier to construct than nuclear weapons, but apart from individual murders, there have been no incidents of radiological warfare.

These elisions allow the most serious but least probable nuclear event to acquire the perceived probability of the easiest chemical attack, stretching the range of potential death and destruction upward without breaking the connection with the greater likelihood of events far down the scale.

Worst-case scenarios provide further amplification. Instead of likely nuclear fizzles, partial yields, or low yields (in the tenths-of-a-kiloton range), a ten-kiloton nuclear device is adopted in many assessments as the standard yield of a terrorist nuclear bomb. Some speak of fifteen-kiloton devices—more powerful than the bomb dropped on Hiroshima. Some communicators even speak of megaton devices—the dreadnoughts of the cold war and far beyond the reach of any terrorist organization. Likewise, scenarios involving dirty bombs postulate significant quantities of radioactive material.

In sum, we stack the threats, extrapolate from there, estimate high probabilities of occurrence, and credit terrorists with great capabilities. The final means of persuasion focus on consequences—not whether something will happen, but what its consequences will be if it does.

These free neutrons of self-amplifying fear crash into one another in a media-drenched society where the news—especially the hot medium of televised news—favors the sensational over the contemplative, fear over calm. Avid consumers of doom, predisposed to believe the end is near, burdened with free-floating anxieties, hard-wired to fear since 9/11, *the audiences themselves become the fuel feeding a self-sustaining fission of fear.*

THE PUNISHMENT OF PROMETHEUS

Some measure of fear is rational. There are terrorists who want to acquire and would use nuclear weapons, and because there is no agreement on the probability of nuclear terrorism, no one can say that as a society the American people are dangerously complacent or needlessly overreacting. How afraid should Americans be? There is no answer.

Yet Americans seem particularly prone to nuclear terror. There are many reasons for this. In the minds of many Americans, we are guilty. Americans were the first to unlock atomic power, and the United States was the first and thus far the only country to employ it as a weapon in war. Robert Oppenheimer, the man who directed the effort to build the first atomic bomb, remarked that physicists knew sin in creating the bomb. Like Prometheus, we stole fire from the gods and gave it to mortal men. We now must pay the price. In Greek mythology, Zeus punished Prometheus by sentencing him to eternal torment. Prometheus was chained to a rock, and each day a huge eagle would tear out his liver, but each night, it would grow back, enabling the predator to tear it out again. It seems that Americans have likewise sentenced themselves to eternal terror.

Though not all Americans think of Greek mythology, many remember and are haunted by Hiroshima. However justified in the context of Japan's aggression or of twentieth-century total war or of the necessity of shocking the Japanese leadership into surrender, the decision to use atomic weapons nevertheless remains controversial. For many, it is a source of guilt, raising vague expectations of some eventual punishment in kind. Terrorists are shrewd to warn of an "American Hiroshima," thereby increasing their own legitimacy while playing on Americans' guilt-borne fears.

America's characteristic optimism is matched by a national obsession with decline and doom. The nation's hedonistic materialism is countered by the anticipation of loss. Imminent catastrophe, financial meltdown, pandemic—doom sells. Aware of their own hubris, Americans instinctively fear its nemesis: humiliation. It is as if the country's vast military power invites annihilation—not on the battlefield, where America's superior military technology can crush opposing armies, but from those against whom conventional military power is largely irrelevant. What if these foes acquired nuclear weapons? Would it spell the end of civilization? A terrifying thought indeed.

The legacy of the long cold war still affects American attitudes as well. For decades, generations of Americans grew up knowing that just as thousands of American nuclear weapons were pointed at the Soviet Union, thousands of Soviet nuclear weapons were pointed at American cities. We could not see them, but we could see the nuclear weapons tests in the South Pacific and the Nevada desert, awesome reminders that we lived on the edge of destruction. I remember, as a young boy, climbing up into a tower with my older cousin to watch for enemy aircraft—a volunteer duty performed by thousands of young people in the 1950s. Those of my generation recall the civil defense bomb shelter signs that were everywhere, the duck-and-cover exercises at school that regularly put millions of children under their school desks in preparation for nuclear attack.

Air-raid sirens were tested weekly, do-it-yourself magazines featured backyard bomb shelters, movies about mutants produced by radiation scared us on Saturday mornings, interspersed with tests of the emergency broadcast system. More mature films such as *On the Beach* (1959) and *The Day After* (1983) portrayed the horror of what the world might be like after a nuclear war. We watched in worried anticipation the unfolding of the Cuban Missile Crisis. Presidential candidates debated missile gaps and windows of vulnerability. It is easy now to dismiss all this as prolonged national hysteria, but the Soviet threat was real, and at times the two nuclear adversaries came very close to war. It was a continuous source of anxiety, and it had its effect. It conditioned a nation to think often and think hard about its own annihilation. The fear outlived the Soviet foe as new terrorist adversaries easily slid into the role.

We don't know whether ordinary citizens of the Soviet Union were equally affected by nuclear terror, especially given their actual experience with the massive destruction of Soviet cities in World War II. The fundamental difference is that Soviet media were far more controlled than American media. Americans were freer to publicly discuss nuclear war, to give free rein to their imaginations, to express their anxieties, to invent and broadcast scenarios of the end—the day after nuclear war. Some people in the Soviet Union who were schoolchildren during the cold war recall being bombarded with the message that the Americans were coming to kill them all. *If nuclear terror is more a function of communications and perceptions than of concrete facts, then a society characterized by constant, unfettered communication is fertile ground for the propagation of fear.*

Another factor feeding nuclear terror is 9/11. Americans still live in the shadow of that attack, an event without precedent in the annals of terrorism. Since then, citizens have been reminded repeatedly of 9/11 and of the continuing threat. They have been hard-wired for fear, according to Martha Stout, author of *The Paranoia Switch*. She argues that the trauma of 9/11 overwhelmed our brains' ability to process information, leaving "incoherent memory traces and sensations, constituting a . . . paranoia switch" that can reside in peoples' brains for the rest of their lives. These memory shards can provoke "fearful behavior later on." What she describes is a kind of continuing subconscious state of anxiety and terror, a persistent post-traumatic stress disorder easily activated by even the mention of certain related words.[14] It is easy to see, then, how words and images suggesting even greater destruction than the obliteration of the World Trade Center—the threat of nuclear terrorism—can easily trigger an extremely fearful response. As Joseph Cirincione, the author of the book *Bomb Scare: The History and Future of Nuclear Weapons*, observed, "As terrible as another 9/11 attack would be, a nuclear 9/11 would destroy an entire city, kill hundreds of thousands, wreck the economy, and change the political life of the nation, perhaps permanently."[15] It is precisely this fear that al Qaeda's threats and images exploit. Stout goes on to argue that these feelings of fear are "contagious" as we sense and adapt to each others' emotions.[16]

Social psychologists have taken a different investigative path to arrive at similar conclusions. Through a series of fascinating experiments, they have demonstrated that reminders of one's own mortality can trigger a range of emotions leading to increased patriotism and religiosity, reinforcement of traditional values, a preference for strong protective leaders, and heightened suspicion and hostility toward others who are readily portrayed as evil. The 9/11 attacks were a massive reminder of our individual mortality. These findings are hardly counterintuitive, but they may help to explain why, as we saw in our small survey, Americans tend to estimate the probability of nuclear terrorism as being much higher than Europeans do, perceiving terrorists as inherently evil rather than as cautious decision makers. *Cold war memories and 9/11 trauma, along with its constant reminders, it would seem, have left the country uniquely susceptible to nuclear terror.*

The September 11 attacks also fundamentally altered perceptions of plausibility. Considered a remote possibility before 9/11, the idea of terrorists armed with nuclear weapons or nuclear dispersal devices can no longer be easily dismissed. We have also seen that the way in which the United States allocates resources to security in essence leads to a form of threat advocacy. Officials with differing views of where the greatest terrorist danger lies compete for budget funding by arguing that theirs is the most dire threat. This, in turn, encourages worst-case scenarios and campaigns calculated to heighten public awareness.

It also seems that terrorism is a condenser of other anxieties that beset Americans–loss of economic supremacy, rising trade deficits, porous borders, uncontrolled immigration, violent crime, violations of personal space, fear of the alien "other." Scenarios of nuclear terrorism are often linked to these worrisome issues. In one scenario, nuclear weapons are concealed among the millions of cargo containers that flow into American ports; in another, the weapons are smuggled across the Mexican border; in another, radioactive material is obtained in Canada and brought across the northern border of the United States. How can the United States keep out terrorists if it cannot keep out millions of illegal aliens? Nuclear terror reveals the anxieties of contemporary society as much as it reflects the strategy of terrorists.

EMOTIONAL BIASES IN MEASURING RISK

People ordinarily don't think like statisticians. We are driven by survival instincts and complex emotions. We don't get up in the morning worrying about whether we will safely complete our commute to work, but we may worry about walking home alone at night, even though, statistically, the former journey may be more perilous. Our perceptions of risk and, hence, fear, are based not upon mathematical calculations but upon intuitive, emotional, often irrational processes that create identifiable biases. Terrorism and how it is covered by the news media generate quite a few of these biases.

Psychologists James Breckenridge and Philip Zimbardo describe a number of these biases in their groundbreaking chapter "The Strategy of Terrorism and the Psychology of Mass-Mediated Fear." They note that fear itself stimulates a pessimistic assessment of risk—we overestimate the likelihood of the things we fear.[17] This is especially true when the things we fear are the products of malevolent intent. Therefore, terrorism has a more powerful impact on us than natural disasters have. Moreover, survivors of a natural disaster tend to think in terms of returning to normality, not of another disaster, while a terrorist attack creates a "new normality" in which perception of the threat continues.

People also tend to worry more about extraordinary events than they do about everyday events, and therefore they assign to them a probability that exceeds any statistical assessment of the risk. We overestimate the risk of another 9/11, while we underestimate common dangers, such as morning commutes.

Large-scale events, although statistically rare, have greater psychological impact on people than more-frequent small-scale events. One hundred automobile accidents with one fatality each are viewed as a series of ones, while an airplane crash with one hundred fatalities, some psychologists say, has a psychological impact of one hundred squared, or ten thousand fatalities. The reality is that the average American has about a one in eight thousand chance of dying in an automobile accident, while the chances of dying in a terrorist attack are one in hundreds of thousands.

People have a higher perceived probability of vivid, easily imagined events. At the same time, unfamiliar events outweigh familiar events. Aimed at the people watching, terrorism produces events that are both unusual and vivid, visual, and easily imagined. Except for those who reside in places such as Baghdad, people don't deal with terrorist events on a daily basis, but the images of death and destruction, of torn bodies and grieving survivors, are readily recognized and easy to imagine in one's own hometown.

This bias can easily be transferred to the domain of nuclear terror. A nuclear explosion would clearly be a highly unusual event, but the mushroom cloud has become a familiar icon, and the effects of nuclear weapons have been described and replayed enough times in newsreels and fictional offerings to make them readily recognized and easily imagined.

The very randomness of terrorism also makes it more frightening, as does the innocence of its victims. Suicide attacks give the impression of an implacable, unstoppable enemy, contributing to greater fear, even though in the context of a terrorist nuclear attack, they are operationally irrelevant.

MELTING METAL AND CHARRED FLESH

While the possible scenarios of a terrorist nuclear explosion are hypothetical, the consequences of one are concrete and calculable. The calculations of scientists have provided us with tables and charts that describe the effects of nuclear blasts on structures of concrete, steel, and wood. From the survivors of Hiroshima and Nagasaki, we have eyewitness accounts of the human carnage.

To make nuclear terrorism real, to make people feel concerned, communicators move beyond debate about whether terrorists could fabricate, deliver, and successfully detonate a nuclear device to a discussion of the consequences if they were to succeed. It is the reality of melting metal and charred flesh that enthralls the terrorized mind and trumps any debate about probability. Potential consequences drive perceptions of the threat and estimates of risk.

Canny terrorists instinctively know this. Osama bin Laden's messages are most graphic in describing the torn limbs of his infidel foes. In the nuclear domain, as we have seen, al Qaeda has exploited the phenomenon by shrewdly moving its discourse from overtly threatening to use nuclear weapons, which would invite discussions of its capabilities, to religious rulings that it interprets as justifying the slaughter of millions. Assertions of capabilities can be challenged. But an assertion of the right, and therefore the intention, to kill millions cannot easily be contested on a factual plane. Moving from capabilities to consequences makes nuclear terror real.

We see this in the writings of Western authors. "It's a bright and busy spring afternoon in a major U.S. city," writes Irwin

Redlener in *Americans at Risk.* "Working people are returning to their offices from lunch and meetings, parents and childcare providers are waiting outside school yards to pick up students, delivery people are loading and unloading goods in and out of trucks. The day is entirely ordinary."[18]

This paragraph is a classic setup. Its author is obviously a caring man, perhaps a medical or public health professional ("childcare providers" is the clue) and probably a parent. He deliberately depicts a pleasant day, framed by the familiar routines of a community—working people, parents, children—those we care most about. There is no foreboding sense of doom, no foreshadowing clouds; you may think you are safe and secure, but then he continues.

> Without warning, the light and heat blinds people staring at the blast from as far as ten miles. Everything goes dark. . . . Virtually every building within a half-mile radius is destroyed. . . . Occupants of these buildings and individuals outdoors are dead. Massive burn casualties occur within a 2.5-mile radius. . . . Within the 2.5-mile radius, thermal energy from the nuclear blast has created a horrific blazing inferno, creating treacherous conditions for people who survive the initial blast and radiation effects. Up to nine miles away . . . as many as 50 percent of the exposed people will die of acute radiation poisoning. Even at fourteen miles, at least half of the unprotected citizens will likely be radiation casualties.

The cause of the carnage in this scenario is a ten-kiloton nuclear device. If detonated in Chicago, the author estimates, such a blast would cause three hundred thousand deaths and severe injuries.[19]

Irwin Redlener is not a novelist. He is the director of the National Center for Disaster Preparedness at Columbia University's School of Public Health and the president of the Children's Health Fund. His purpose in describing this scenario is not to sensationalize nuclear terrorism or sell fear but to preach basic preparedness; rapid safe evacuation; quick, effective self-decontamination; a national campaign to educate citizens—knowledge that can save lives and reduce alarm. But to reinforce his message, he must resort to graphic, sobering, perhaps unbearable speech about the consequences of a nuclear explosion. In effectively doing so, for good cause, he unavoidably gives reality to a hypothetical event.

Calculating nuclear blast effects, once the exclusive domain of cold war targeteers, has become a popular genre of journalism. Concerned about nuclear terrorism, reporters and columnists depict in lurid detail the effects of a hypothetical nuclear explosion in their hometown.

Describing the effects of a ten-kiloton nuclear weapon detonated in Times Square, Nicholas D. Kristof wrote in the *New York Times* that "the fireball would reach tens of millions of degrees Fahrenheit. . . . It would vaporize or destroy the theater district, Madison Square Garden, the Empire State Building, Grand Central Terminal and Carnegie Hall (along with me and my building). The blast would partly destroy a much larger area, including the United Nations. On a weekday some 500,000 people would be killed."[20]

On a popular Web site, Roland Watson describes the effects of a one-kiloton blast—the yield of a suitcase or backpack nuclear bomb: "On that fateful morning, the citizens close to ground zero will note the unremarkable drone of a light aircraft flying above their buildings." Again the setup. All seems normal, but, the writer continues,

> It is the last thing they will ever hear. Whether the blinding, split second flash of a hundred suns registers with them is unlikely because the intense heat that kills them also travels at the speed of light. As the fireball expands rapidly to its maximum diameter of 460 feet, its centre rages at a temperature of 10,000,000° C. . . . Metallic objects up to 450 feet from ground zero . . . will vaporize . . . [those] up to 670 feet away will melt. It is needless

to guess what happens to people caught out in the open at these ranges—they cease to exist in any meaningful sense of the word and join the raw material for the later fallout. At 1400 feet from ground zero, rubbers and plastics will melt whilst wood will char and burn. For victims out in the open, 3rd degree burns are inflicted up to 0.4 miles away, 2nd degree burns up to half a mile away, and 1st degree burns up to nearly a mile away.

Watson persists: "Those buildings which survived the melting effects of heat radiation will be finished off by the high winds . . . as winds approaching 670 mph will level or badly damage even steel concrete structures within 740 feet of the blast . . . survivors of the heat pulse will suffer potentially fatal lung injuries." Watson concludes that such a blast in an urban area would kill twenty thousand and injure another twenty thousand.[21]

In less vivid language, researchers at the RAND Corporation describe the estimated consequences of a ten-kiloton explosion at the Port of Los Angeles:

> The infrastructure and ships in the Port of Long Beach and the adjoining Port of Los Angeles are completely destroyed by the blast and fires. Sixty thousand people die or will die soon because of direct blast effects and radiation poisoning. The radioactive fallout of water and sediment from the port exposes 150,000 people to hazardous radiation levels, requiring prompt medical attention. . . . Six million people will try to evacuate the Los Angeles region to avoid the radioactive fallout. . . . Radioactive fallout contaminates a 500-km region, prohibiting residence for 10–20 years. Two to three million residents will require relocation facilities.[22]

The RAND report lacks the harrowing quality of the Kristof and Watson descriptions and the inherent humanity of the Redlener account, but it lends the weight of the respected institution to the reality of nuclear terror.

Kristof places ground zero in Manhattan, by far the favored target of most scenarios. Watson muses about the ideal location but specifies no city. In conjunction with the publication of Graham Allison's book *Nuclear Terrorism: The Ultimate Preventable Catastrophe*, a do-it-yourself Web site was created that allows users to enter a zip code and observe the effects of a ten-kiloton nuclear explosion on their communities.[23] The vivid graphics do not adjust for topography or the shielding effects of large buildings. The point is not an accurate projection of death or destruction but popular participation. It does add to an atmosphere of fear, but many see this as a prerequisite for doing more than we are doing now to prevent such a detonation from ever occurring. Those worried about dirty bombs do the same thing on Web sites, depicting plumes of fallout spreading over selected cities. To my knowledge, there is not yet a publicly accessible Web site offering radioactive plumes by zip code.

For the ordinary citizen, looking at diameters of destruction— whether you will be incinerated if a nuclear bomb goes off near your neighborhood—may be a mere matter of morbid curiosity, but these same grim calculations are used by insurance under-writers and corporate officials concerned about business conti-nuity. After 9/11, corporations in New York drew one-kiloton and ten-kiloton circles centered on the city's key landmarks to calcu-late the possible effects on their corporate headquarters. A corpo-rate presence within too many circles even became an argument for relocation or dispersal. Commercial property development in New Jersey and Connecticut benefited from this mind-set. Fearing an exodus, New York City fought back to remain the world's financial center, and by mid-decade the outward trend reversed.

Bringing the story home further amplifies the threat. When-ever a major terrorist event occurs anywhere in the world, local television stations quickly translate it into a local story, increasing the psychological impact by underscoring the mortal danger to all. Planting themselves in front of a similar venue–the local air-port, the train station, a shopping mall–local reporters invariably ask, "Could it happen here?" Invariably, the answer, provided by the local police chief or available talking head, is, "Potentially, it could." The scenario remains hypothetical, but the setting is real. The result is alarm.

TERROR'S TRAJECTORY

Nuclear terror began before the bomb was dropped on Hiroshima, as writers crafted the words that President Truman would use to tell the Japanese that this was no ordinary ammunition but something far more terrifying.[24] Nuclear terror escalated sharply in 1949, when the Soviet Union demonstrated that it, too, had nuclear weapons. Nuclear terror persisted through the cold war as the nuclear arsenals of the United States and the Soviet Union increased to thousands of warheads on each side, including multimegaton bombs that could vaporize entire cities–and end civilization as we know it.

Détente made no dent in nuclear terror. Instead, nuclear terror expanded with the acquisition of nuclear weapons by a growing number of countries. The actual and anticipated growth of nuclear power for civilian purposes added to concerns about nuclear pro-liferation and the possibility of terrorist attack. While nuclear terror might have lessened with the end of the cold war, in fact, it increased, with heightened concerns about the security of nuclear material and weapons in Russia, especially in a global environ-ment of escalating terrorism.

The 9/11 terrorist attacks made nuclear terrorism seem more plausible, while evidence of al Qaeda's efforts to acquire nuclear weapons turned it into a perceived imminent threat, ratcheting up nuclear terror another notch. Al Qaeda's deliberate campaign of nuclear terror–and the communications industry it created–have kept anxieties high.

Add to this the predictable biases in measuring risk; the many causes and agendas served by promoting awareness of the nuclear terrorist threat; an audience that is already highly susceptible because of historical, cultural, and religious reasons–and a media-saturated environment–and the result is nuclear terror, fear of imminent doom, worry that on one "entirely ordinary" day, a brilliant yellow light will fill the sky.

PART IV
A CHOICE OF REACTIONS

Chapter 17
A BRILLIANT YELLOW LIGHT

8:15 a.m.–News media are reporting a huge explosion in Manhattan. Witnesses describe a burst of brilliant yellow light, bright as the sun, followed by a wave of heat, then what sounded like thunder.[1]

During a meeting with foreign dignitaries in the Oval Office, you are handed this note. You pause to ponder what it may mean. For an instant you recall where you were on the morning of 9/11. You contemplate sharing the contents of the note with your visitors but decide not to. One of the foreign officials says something, but you have no idea what he just said. You nod and he continues. Your thoughts are elsewhere.

As president, you reflect on the decisions you may have to face. What if it is a terrorist attack? The beginning of another 9/11? Not again. What did the latest intelligence reports say? Assistance will have to be mobilized quickly. Have to reassure the country. Prevent panic. Got to get ahead of the situation. Demonstrate strength. God help us. All these ideas flow through your head within a few minutes.

Then another note:

8:20 a.m.–Media reports indicate that the explosion in New York was far bigger than any conceivable truck bomb. Television cameras in Brooklyn are showing what appears to be a mushroom cloud over Manhattan. It could be a nuclear explosion.

The meeting quickly ends. Handshakes. A photo op with the press is canceled in favor of a few quick shots by the White House photographer. Unaware of events, the beaming dignitaries leave. You walk at a measured pace to the White House Situation Room. So many grim faces. Some of the staff are unable to hold back tears. You are handed another message.

8:25 a.m.–New York authorities are reporting massive damage. It appears that several high-rise buildings have simply vanished. Fires are raging for blocks around the blast site. Clouds of smoke are pouring out of the city.

Your national security adviser speaks first. "We have just received reports that the radiation detectors carried by the fire crews are indicating significant radioactivity. It's nuclear. No doubt about it. Given the apparent magnitude of destruction, it seems almost certain that it is a nuclear explosion. What we have feared for years has happened . . ."

His voice rises and quavers. He pauses, takes a deep breath, and continues deliberately, calmly. "The casualties are likely to be in the thousands, probably tens of thousands. People are evacuating the island."

Should you leave Washington?

". . . we must anticipate that more nuclear devices will be detonated. Remember that 9/11 involved multiple attacks. As president, your first task is to ensure the continuity of government.

"The vice president and key members of the government are already relocating to a protected location. You, too, must leave

Washington. You can address the nation from a safe location. We have plans in place for this."

"Those plans made sense when our adversary was the Soviet Union, and a nuclear attack meant almost certainly that Washington would head the target list, but if the public sees the president leaving the White House, getting out of the city, everyone else in Washington will run for his life. It will create a panic. Government will shut down. Issuing instructions will be of no use if there is no one to implement them.

"Shouldn't the people see their president staying in the capital of the nation? Didn't the king and queen stay in London during the Blitz? So did prime minister Winston Churchill. It sustained morale during Britain's darkest hour."

"No, that's wrong! With all due respect, look at the television. People are already evacuating Washington. You were elected to run the country, not to prove your personal courage.

"Yes, the king and queen were great for morale, but they didn't run the government. And Churchill lived in a deep underground bunker, where he was reasonably safe from the bombs. This isn't the Blitz. We are talking about *nuclear* bombs here. We prepared for this contingency during the cold war. You need to move now! As president, you don't have a choice."

But you do have a choice. Sure, the Secret Service may push you to the ground if a shot is fired. When there is imminent danger, they may physically lift you off your feet and carry you out of a room. But you are the president. Whether you stay in the White House in a rapidly emptying city or go to some bunker where you can communicate with government officials and the people is ultimately your choice. What do you decide?

10:15 a.m.—The situation in New York is grave. The explosion has vaporized an entire city block. Fires are burning out of control. The death toll will easily be in the tens of thousands. A procession of people is streaming out of the

city. Spontaneous evacuations are occurring in other cities.

Should you try to halt spontaneous evacuations elsewhere in the country?

Your national security adviser again speaks first. "New York City probably should be evacuated, but we have to try to prevent evacuations elsewhere. We've gamed this type of thing before, and the general evacuations are disastrous.

"The news channels are showing mass evacuations in East Coast and Midwest cities. People fear another nuclear bomb. They are running for their lives. In some places, the situation is getting ugly. We already have reports of massive traffic jams, fist-fights, shootings."

Another voice disagrees. "This is not the president's job. The media always exaggerate these things. Evacuations are a local problem. Let the governors handle it. Anyway, what can the federal government do? Block the roads?"

"It is the president's job to keep the country working. If people leave the cities, how will they get fed? Do food prices go sky-high? When will they come back? What will happen to the financial centers?"

"But don't we want people to get to safety? Aren't we evacuating a good portion of the federal government from Washington? Is our message, 'We'll leave, but you stay?' If there is another bomb somewhere, leaving will save lives."

"Yes, but there is a difference between an orderly evacuation and a national panic in which thousands could die. Shouldn't the president go on the air and call for national calm?"

"The president can call for national calm, but he can't tell people not to evacuate. First, right now, those heading for the hills won't listen. They have lost faith in the ability of their government to protect them. Second, the president can't tell people not to evacuate when the very next minute, either because of radioactive fallout from this bomb or the discovery of another device, local authorities may order evacuations. Or worse, what if the president tells everybody to stay put and another nuclear bomb goes off somewhere, which we probably all expect to happen? That will destroy whatever credibility we have, and we will never be able to recover it. We have to be straight with the people, not pretend that we have the situation under control."

"Well, the president sure as hell can't go on national television and say we're expecting another nuclear bomb but I want everyone to remain calm!"

"Of course, but neither can the president go on television and tell the nation that what happened in New York was awful, but we're through it. We don't know that."

"The president is going to have to say something to the nation and say it soon. And it can't be, 'As your president and commander in chief, I'll be damned if I know what's going on.'

"The president can tell people what has happened, that it is terrible—our country's worst disaster—that he will offer no false reassurances that we will not face further attacks, and therefore the situation calls for extraordinary courage on the part of every American. The president can tell the public that each person must make his own decision but that the fate of the nation lies in the collective decisions we make. We can flee in fear or resolve to stand together and confront the danger everyone in the country faces at this moment with the moral strength and sense of community that enabled our forefathers to survive the dangers they faced in the past.

"I know from experience that there is something calming in being told 'It's bad, and it may get worse before it gets better'; we must remain calm, think, take care of what we can, and call on our deepest strengths to do what is right. This is no time for panic, running, or selfishness."

"That's a pretty good speech, I admit, but it's not enough. The president has to tell the people that we're doing something to prevent another attack, not just waiting to get hit again. The president has to be seen taking action."

What would you suggest?

10:30 a.m.–The explosion in New York has ignited a firestorm that is swirling around the center of the fire.

Should you mobilize the Reserves and National Guard and declare martial law?

"You can order the immediate arrest of all terrorist suspects–anyone in the United States thought to be an Islamic extremist, anyone currently being watched.

"We should mobilize the armed forces and declare martial law. We are at war, not just in Afghanistan and Iraq, but here at home. We have to anticipate the possibility of another attack and do everything we can to prevent it. The country is on the edge of panic. Law and order could break down entirely, making it easy for terrorists to take another shot. Even if al Qaeda isn't our immediate threat, the crazies are coming out. We have to take charge, do something dramatic and visible to reassure people that the government is functioning.

"Therefore, I respectfully suggest that you call all Ready Reserve and National Guard units to active duty under federal control and declare martial law. At least that will give us 2.8 million men and women to deploy in the cities to show strength and maintain public order. They can help track these terrorists down. You have the authority. You must use it."

"No. The president should not do that. There is no question that the situation is grave, but I would disagree with my colleague in recommending that you declare martial law. Sure, people are frightened, and there is some spontaneous evacuation, but there is no evidence of national panic. Mayors will mobilize additional police as they need to. The governors will deploy their National Guard units if necessary."

New video footage streams in from New York. All eyes turn to the screen.

12:15 p.m.–Fires continue to burn out of control in a sixteen-square-block area of Manhattan. Fire and rescue crews are being hampered by intense radiation readings. Several violent electrical storms have passed over the city. The mayor has prohibited fire and rescue crews from going within a half-mile radius of the explosion unless they have protective equipment. Those inside, if still alive, have been stranded.

"It looks very bad for New York, but mobilizing the guard in Kansas will reassure no one. Instead, people will think we know something they don't, or worse, they'll think that they are about to be attacked. Putting soldiers on the streets will look desperate. It will only add to the apprehension. This is not the moment to project a message of fear. We must have faith in the courage and common sense of our own citizens.

"As for declaring martial law, it's a bad idea. The Constitution imposes limits on any suspension of guaranteed rights. I'm not a historian, but as I recall, there have been only a handful of times when the federal government imposed martial law. Andrew Jackson imposed martial law in New Orleans after the Battle of New Orleans in 1812. Abraham Lincoln imposed martial law on a limited basis during the Civil War. The territory of Hawaii was placed under martial law after Pearl Harbor. But the entire United States has never been placed under martial law.

"In fact, until 2006, the law explicitly prohibited using federal forces in any law enforcement function without explicit congressional approval. That law was changed in 2006. Now, technically, the president does have the authority to declare a state of emergency and take over all National Guard units, even if the governors of the states object, but this new law, we all know, is very controversial and has never been tried. And there is nothing in the law that gives the president any greater authority to declare martial law and suspend the rights of citizens—not while the courts are still open and in business.

"Besides, troops on every street corner would be entirely useless in preventing another terrorist attack. Remember when National Guard soldiers were deployed at the airports right after 9/11? They were about as useful as parsley, a green garnish that adds nothing to the meal. Soldiers have no experience in this type of mission."

"That's not true! They have gained a lot of experience dealing with terrorists in Iraq—just the kind of situation we face now."

"With all due respect, sir, the very last thing we want is to turn Boston into Baghdad! We soon may find ourselves obliged to undertake dangerous and costly missions. We don't want to do anything to provoke a constitutional crisis and divide the nation at this critical moment. We can't squander legitimacy. And we certainly don't want to look like tyrants. The people are with us, not against us."

"Of course the people are with us, but they want us to be tough. The lives of millions are in peril. I know some think he is an extremist, but Congressman Tancredo was applauded when he said that if the United States were ever threatened by terrorists with nuclear weapons, we should adopt the tactics of Jack Bauer on *24*. Well, we've been hit by a nuclear weapon. This is no time for philosophical or legal debates. I remind you again that we are at war and we have just lost Manhattan. The civil libertarians aren't going to save the country. In the middle of a war, people look to their commander in chief. It's the president's job to be that commander in chief."

Eyes again shift to the screen. A homeland security official is speaking.

> **12:45 p.m.**–The winds in New York are blowing from the west. That is good news, since they will carry much of the radioactive fallout out over the Atlantic Ocean. However, the radioactive plume is drifting over a part of Long Island, with Nassau County receiving the greatest effect. Given the wind speed, FEMA and local authorities decided that it would have been dangerous to evacuate people just as the plume was passing over. Instead, they are telling people that it is safer to remain indoors for 24 to 48 hours. Most people are obeying the order.

Meanwhile, you are informed that several heads of allied governments are waiting to speak to you on the telephone. Before you step out of the meeting, you think about your friends in Manhattan, knowing that all eyes will be on you, you steel yourself, and you ask your advisers to prepare a list of options–how should the United States respond to the attack?

What are your options?

The meeting reconvenes at 2:10. There is a new bulletin.

> **2:10 p.m.**–On the basis of aerial photography of the blast site and seismic measurements, scientists at Los Alamos believe that the blast was a fizzle–a partial fission, meaning that only a small portion of the nuclear material in the device was converted to explosive energy. It could have resulted from a faulty design or premature fission. The yield of the device in New York is estimated to be in the tenths of a kiloton–that is, equivalent to several hundred tons of TNT. Radiation effects, however, will be greater as the fissioned material is blown into the atmosphere by the explosion. Initial radiation analysis indicates that the device contained enriched uranium rather than pluto-

nium. It indicates a crude device, and that is good news. Radioactivity from uranium is far less deadly and persistent than that from plutonium. Nonetheless, portions of the city will be uninhabitable for years.

Again, your national security adviser leads off:

"In response to your request for a range of options, we have drawn up a list of ten actions."

1. Mass arrest of suspected Islamic extremists within the United States. Authorize severe interrogation if necessary where there is reason to believe they have information.
2. Initiate a massive and continuing air campaign against suspected Taliban and al Qaeda sites in Afghanistan and Pakistan. This could include bombing, using conventional bombs, of any areas where Osama bin Laden might be hiding, any suspected al Qaeda or Taliban headquarters, and any other possible targets. It might not accomplish much more than we're already doing now, but it would advertise a new no-holds-barred policy, not carpet bombing cities, but nothing out of bounds.
3. Warn Pyongyang that it must dismantle its nuclear weapons and shut down all facilities related to its nuclear weapons program without delay, or, alternatively . . .
4. Destroy North Korea's nuclear facilities, warning that any aggression by North Korea will result in the total destruction of Pyongyang.
5. Impose a naval blockade on Iran, or . . .
6. Give Iran a nonnegotiable ultimatum to immediately end its nuclear program, permit international inspectors to confirm its shutdown and supervise its destruction, or face unspecified consequences, or . . .
7. Bomb selected targets in Iran, beginning with Iran's air defenses and the Iranian Air Force, then move on to Rev-

olutionary Guard camps, naval vessels, missile sites, and all known and suspected nuclear facilities, or . . . bomb selected government buildings in Tehran with precision munitions as we did in Serbia in 1999, making clear that our actions are directed exclusively against Iran's leaders, not its people, or . . .

8. Destroy the main mosque in Qom.
9. Destroy one major mosque near Mecca. This event can be labeled as an error in targeting but should be read as a warning that Mecca itself could be the next target, or . . .
10. Destroy the Holy Temple in Mecca with a tactical nuclear weapon.

"The consensus favors a combination of actions, including an intensified bombing campaign against al Qaeda and the Taliban in Afghanistan and Pakistan; bombing selected targets in Iran, including its air force, nuclear facilities, and Revolutionary Guard installations; and indicating some physical threat to Mecca. I should mention that Congressman Tancredo has already gone on the air suggesting that we should bomb Mecca."[2]

"Bomb Mecca? Are you crazy? Talk about a clash of civilizations —bombing Mecca would ignite a religious war lasting centuries!"

"But haven't we been engaged in a religious war lasting centuries? Osama bin Laden says this conflict began centuries ago and will end on Judgment Day or when all infidels have converted to Islam, whichever comes first. And bombing Mecca may not be so crazy. What do Muslims revere most? If nuclear terrorism provoked the destruction of Mecca, Muslims wouldn't be so enthusiastic about it."

"That means *threatening* to bomb Mecca, not actually bombing it. The president can't announce, 'We've been bombed in New York, so we've just bombed Mecca.'"

"What if we bomb Medina instead? That will let them know

Mecca is on the list. We have to make sure our terrorists, their supporters, their sympathizers, those who continue to spew hatred of non-Muslims, who secretly celebrate terrorist attacks while pretending to be on our side, those who tolerate them—all of them—understand that nuclear terrorism profoundly changes the world. The old rules don't apply. Going nuclear opens Pandora's box. Nothing is off the table. Now we, not our enemies, will decide what targets we will strike, where the firebreaks are."

"Bombing Mecca, or Medina, is strategically senseless, and it is morally reprehensible. Saudi Arabia didn't attack us. And we don't deliberately bomb religious targets. Al Qaeda does that, not the United States. It is completely contrary to American values. Even in the most brutal days of World War II, we chose not to bomb Kyoto, which was the closest thing the Japanese had to a national religious shrine. It had no military value. It would have been an act of pure vandalism."

"True, we chose not to bomb Kyoto, but meanwhile we were busy leveling other Japanese cities instead. I recall that immediately after 9/11, some of my most liberal friends were suggesting that we level one or two Arab cities as an object lesson to deter further attacks on the United States. We operated within moral constraints then. Now we have lost New York."

Can we determine who did this?

"The president asked for a range of options. The options you listed are ten ways to start wars without a shred of proof that they are in any way related to what happened in New York.

"I have no argument against ruthlessness. We knew the Japanese attacked us at Pearl Harbor. We knew that al Qaeda attacked us on 9/11. We don't yet know who did this. If we can establish culpability, then I'm for massive retaliation."

"I agree that it would be nice if we could be certain who did it, but this is not some episode of *CSI* where incredible science will solve the mystery. The reality is, we may never know.

"The perpetrators were vaporized along with any physical evidence. The crime scene will be a radioactive crater—nothing. We have made strides in nuclear forensics. Nuclear material does have fingerprints, but we have no complete database to check them against. The labs may be able to estimate the strength of the device, how effective it was in using up all of its fissile material or whether it was a partial fizzle. They can tell us whether it was made of plutonium or highly enriched uranium, and that, in turn, tells us something about the design of the device. They may even be able to get a handle on the origins of the material, although that could take a lot of time.

"Remember that it took three years after the sabotage of Pan Am Flight 103 in 1988 to put together the evidence that Libya was behind the bombing. More than ten years after the 1996 bombing of the Khobar Towers in Saudi Arabia, we still haven't figured out for sure whether it was carried out by Hezbollah operatives acting on their own, what role al Qaeda played, and whether Iran had a hand in it. And it took Argentine authorities thirteen years to get enough evidence to be persuaded to finally go after the Iranian operatives who planned the 1994 terrorist bombing in Buenos Aires and to ask Interpol for an international arrest warrant, which Iran blocked. Are we going to wait thirteen years to respond to this attack?"

"Why would Iran bomb something in Argentina?"

"I remember that case. One of the allegations was that Argentina suspended a contract for the transfer of nuclear technology to Iran. The bombing was retaliation. More likely it was related to something in the Middle East. The investigation was thwarted every step of the way."

"Even if we knew absolutely everything about the contents and design of the bomb, what would that tell us? We know it was probably a crude design within the capacity of any number of weapons designers in any of a dozen countries, or that some smart terrorists and rogue scientists got lucky with a partial yield. As for the contents, maybe they were stolen from Russia ten years ago. Maybe they came from Pakistan two months ago. Perhaps the bomb makers accumulated material from several sources. And we have to be careful that the terrorists or their state sponsors didn't deliberately plant some false clues calculated to make a positive identification impossible or lead us down a false path. Maybe the device was constructed by the most sophisticated designers who made it look like a crude home-built bomb.

"The same may be true of our intelligence inquiries. Inevitably there will be claims of responsibility by every lunatic and terrorist wannabe. There will be false claims and false clues to deliberately lead us astray. Our allies may assist in the investigation, but many of those who cooperate with us will be worried about what we may do with the information they pass on. They may not want us to do anything at all. They will be guided by their own agendas. We will not be able to trust anything we get. Even if we knew everything, we could still be certain of nothing. If persuasive proof of culpability is a prerequisite to action, we can take no action.

"We can only build a high lead wall around the contaminated portion of Manhattan, mourn our dead, and move on. So launch the investigation. But meanwhile we have to take action . . ."

2:30 p.m.–Based upon estimates of population density and the magnitude of the blast, immediate fatalities are likely to run into the tens of thousands. We have no information on the number of those injured by flying glass or other debris, or on the number killed in subsequent fires. Near-term deaths–in one to two weeks–from exposure to radiation are more difficult to estimate. Fortunately, the still-standing buildings themselves provide a great deal of shielding.

"Look at this report. This is not the time to warn what we might do if we are attacked again. Terrorists here attacked the

United States with a nuclear weapon. An American city has been devastated. Hundreds of thousands of Americans may die, maybe the ultimate death toll will go to a million—more people than we lost during all of World War II. There is likely to be panic all over the world. This is an unprecedented catastrophe. It is meaningless to threaten what we might do if we ever figure out who carried out this attack. We may never know who is responsible. And while we do nothing, they can prepare another nuclear attack. By doing nothing, we invite further attacks."

"But if you don't know who was behind this attack, who should we go after? We have no idea who is responsible."

"Given our objective, that may not be important. You know the Israelis have regularly retaliated in response to terrorist attacks in Israel. They always hit back. They had their targets preselected. They didn't always wait for evidence of whether it was this group or that group. It didn't make any difference which of the dozen terrorist groups they hit—all were bad guys. You couldn't go wrong. If one group carried out the terrorist attack, but another one got hit back, its turn would come eventually. It was on the list. The more important point was to demonstrate that Israel would always hit back, and hit hard. And the reason for this was not simply to use the opportunity to punish the terrorist organizations—to knock out some terrorist capability that the Israelis wanted to knock out anyway—but also to reassure Israeli citizens that they were not simply going to be victims. The Israeli government retaliated to give the Israeli public satisfaction, to offer them hope, to maintain its own authority as the sole source of reprisal.

"We have to think like that. We have to hit back hard, ten times as hard as we have been hit, in order to demonstrate that America is not simply going to take terrorist punches. More important, we have to prevent the American people from feeling helpless, which will only breed a corrosive fear that will cause greater danger to the republic than anything the terrorists can throw at us. When the president announces action, that's when the public panic stops. The important thing right now is not who did this, but what do we want to do to reduce the danger in the long run? What will best suit our purpose to eliminate the threat of nuclear terrorism? What hostile nuclear capabilities do we want to take out? What can we do to reduce our enemies' capabilities? Their attack is intended to demoralize us. What can we do to demoralize them? It will be a long, hard campaign."

Where do we start?

2:40 p.m.–Hamas has launched a barrage of rockets from Gaza into Israel. There are casualties.

"There aren't that many suspects. Let's start with capability. Who has nuclear weapons or knows how to make them? The British have nuclear weapons–they didn't do this to us. The French didn't do this. The Chinese didn't. And not the Indians either. Who does that leave?"

"The Russians? Why would they do this? They are *not* behind the attack, although they may have some indirect responsibility as a result of negligence. We do know some of their bombs were stolen and could have been sold on the black market."

"Actually, we don't know that at all. There were a lot of stories about loose Russian nukes in the 1990s, but none of them were ever confirmed."

"But we can't confirm that Russian weapons *weren't* sold either. George Tenet himself said that the Russians haven't been that cooperative on nuclear security issues. And it's gotten worse under Putin."

"Actually, thanks to Nunn-Lugar, even with increasing strains in US–Russia relations, we have made important progress in securing nuclear weapons, but there are still some dangerous gaps–"

"Dangerous gaps, I'll say! Didn't the Russians fire the general in charge of security at Russia's closed nuclear cities last year—for organizing smuggling in and out of those cities? There may be a Russian renegade in this event, but I'll concede that Moscow has a weak motive."

"And the North Koreans? Maybe. They have nuclear weapons. They're under pressure from us to dismantle their nuclear arsenal. They may have tried to stash some in another country. Maybe they decided to sell a couple of weapons. They're definitely on the list of suspects."

"Bin Laden has motive, and we know he has been trying to acquire nuclear weapons for the past fifteen years. Al Qaeda has money. It may have access to Russian or Pakistani scientists. Al Qaeda may be getting help from the Iranians. Bin Laden could have been planning this for years. But we're already going after al Qaeda."

2:57 p.m.—Tens of thousands of people continue to stream out of New York. The edge of the East River is covered with the dead and the wounded. Subway service into Manhattan has been halted, and evacuees are being guided through the subway tunnels, which are serving as safe evacuation routes. Some commuter trains, however, are still operating, carrying people out of the city and bringing emergency crews in. Right now, that is the city's lifeline. The total evacuation will exceed a million people. People inside buildings in Manhattan and the surrounding boroughs are being encouraged to remain indoors to avoid radiation. Decontamination centers have been set up in upper Harlem, the downtown financial district, Brooklyn, Queens, and New Jersey.

Your national security adviser continues:
"The government of Pakistan has no reason to do this and a lot to lose because of it."

"Haven't we been assisting the Pakistanis in securing their own nuclear weapons? Aren't we on top of this?"

"We have been working with them, and we're pretty sure we know where their nuclear weapons are, but we can't be sure about renegade elements."

"Pakistan's intelligence service, its army, and its scientific community are bastions of jihadist sympathies. Certainly no one can believe that A. Q. Khan and his cronies were able to bring in millions of dollars in cash, or buy real estate, and invest huge amounts in local businesses by selling their nuclear know-how without arousing some suspicions in the government. Where did the authorities think all this money was coming from?"

"Khan and other Pakistanis were traveling all over the world while scientists from Iran, Libya, Saudi Arabia, and North Korea were visiting Pakistan's nuclear facilities. And no one in the government of Pakistan asked why? Sensitive materials were being sent in special aircraft to Libya, Iran, and North Korea, and yet no one in the Pakistan government asked what was going on? Can you really believe that all of this went on for years, secretly coordinated just by Khan and a couple of bad guys without anyone else in the government knowing anything about it until our own intelligence figured it out? Only then did Musharraf and the boys in Islamabad wake up? If we were asleep, they had to be determinedly comatose. This terrible attack could easily have been a joint al Qaeda–Pakistani operation. Pakistan can't be taken off the list."

"Iran has to be at the top of the list."

"But you are not suggesting that we attack everyone on your list, are you?"

"Absolutely not. We make a choice. Remember in the 1980s, when we were confronted with the growing threat of state-sponsored terrorism? Iraq, Iran, Syria, Libya, North Korea, all were state sponsors of terrorism. The violence increased while we debated whether it was legitimate to use military force in response to terrorism. I remember Secretary of State Shultz's frustration at the time. He said we can't be the Hamlet of nations. Finally, we bombed Libya in 1986. Qadaffi wasn't the only culprit at the time, but he was the noisiest. The bombing was a lesson to Libya and a demonstration to the others."

"But as I recall, it didn't stop Libya's involvement in terrorism. Didn't you yourself just say that the Libyans were responsible for bringing down Pan Am 103 in 1988?"

"They were, although the Iranians also may have had a hand in it. And of course, our bombing didn't end state-sponsored terrorism, but Qadaffi got a lot quieter. And the others became more circumspect. And keep in mind the terrorist attacks at that time were not even close to 9/11 or the catastrophe we now have in New York."

"But when we bombed Libya in 1986, we also had proof of Libya's involvement in terrorism, in terrorist attacks against us. We have no proof of Iran's involvement now. Or anyone else's for that matter . . ."

"True, but we are not likely to have proof of anything other than the fact of a nuclear explosion in the middle of Manhattan. Don't you see that it doesn't make a damn bit of difference? Who we should attack is not based on evidence. It is based on logic. Our goal is *not* retaliation. Retaliation focuses on the past. What we have to look at is the future. Nuclear terrorism is now a reality. That changes everything. Either we hunker down with our fingers in our ears and wait for the next nuclear attack or we eliminate the threat to us, to all nations, to civilization as we know it. In a post-nuclear terrorist world, no nation with a clandestine nuclear program can be tolerated. We need no further provocation. This is preemptive retaliation."

"But what if, as you indicate, al Qaeda got the material and assistance from Pakistani scientists?"

"We don't stop investigating. Pakistan has to be in our sights, too. A. Q. Khan is living comfortably under house arrest. These Pakistani scientists who spoke with bin Laden got mild jail sentences. They and their Pakistani colleagues are now all targets. It must be demonstrated that nuclear terrorism brings terrible consequences. There are no bystanders. Either we remove these threats now or the world waits for the next nuclear attack. Iran is the most hostile. Iran is the most dangerous."

Should we attack Iran?

"Do we have any evidence of Iran's involvement?"

"Iran is telling everybody they are not behind this, which may or may not be true. Who believes them? Anyway, it doesn't make any difference."

"Iran has motive, means, and opportunity. The country is run by a bunch of fanatics. They have not abandoned their efforts to develop nuclear weapons. They have refused to cooperate with international inspections. They have provided sophisticated weapons to the terrorists who are killing US soldiers in Iraq. They have said that Israel should be wiped off the map. They might be worried that eventually international pressure will force them to delay their nuclear efforts, so why not hit America with a crude nuclear device, confident that we will blame al Qaeda? It is their M.O. to work through proxies."

"How do we claim Iran is responsible for a nuclear attack on America when our own intelligence says that Iran halted its nuclear weapons program years ago?"

"They may have temporarily suspended the nuclear weapons development we knew about, or maybe they just successfully fooled our intelligence. They never stopped their enrichment program. But this attack would not necessarily come out of Iran's formal nuclear establishment. This is the kind of evil enterprise that mad mullahs and Revolutionary Guard diehards work on outside the formal channels of government."

"But don't they perceive the danger that we will come after them?"

"They might calculate that we won't be able to figure it out. Or they might figure that we won't attack them without positive proof. They might think that we will be reluctant to attack. Iran is a big country filled with mountains. They know we won't invade Iran while we're tied down in Iraq and Afghanistan. They might reckon that even if we attack with air power alone, they can survive a bombing. So what if they lose one million or ten million people— they readily sacrificed their own during the Gulf War in the 1980s. The country is filled with fanatics who exult in death, even their own. Remember what the Ayatollah himself said, something like, 'Let this land go up in smoke, provided Islam triumphs.'"

3:05 p.m.–Police in Houston, Texas, have identified and surrounded a suspicious truck. Details are not clear, but three people have been shot. A bomb-detection unit is on the scene. The episode is causing some panic and evacuation of the city.

"You want the president to go on the air to say that he is going to bomb Iran?"

"The president should go on the air saying he *has* bombed Iran as one part of a campaign to eliminate the threat of nuclear terrorism. Let others worry about who will be next."

"You make it sound too easy. Don't forget Iraq."

"This is not going to be a ground invasion. We have the military capability for the necessary air strikes—one carrier in the Gulf, another at the east end of the Mediterranean, planes on Diego Garcia, other assets in the region. We can fly bombers from the States. In addition to cruise missiles, we have ICBMs."

"Are you suggesting that we use nuclear weapons in an attack on Iran?"

"For most targets it won't be necessary, but we know that some of their nuclear facilities are deeply buried in underground bunkers. Assuring their destruction may require tactical nuclear weapons. If we make the political decision to employ one nuclear weapon, employing others is simply a matter of following military logic. We would have to hit them all."

"To prevent nuclear terrorism, you are suggesting that the United States drop more nuclear weapons on Iran than we did on Japan."

"Remember our cold war strategy of mutual assured destruction, which essentially was, if you launch a nuclear attack on the United States, your world ends?"

"Yes, but that was a deterrent posture. Each side had enough nuclear weapons to destroy the other, to destroy the entire planet."

"Correct, and right now, Iran doesn't have a nuclear arsenal to wage a nuclear war. That gives us the opportunity to put their nuclear program out of business before they build a nuclear arsenal. How many more American cities—after losing one of our most important cities—are we prepared to sacrifice before we say this stops now and demonstrate that we mean it?"

"Shouldn't we first give Iran the opportunity to cooperate with the investigation, at least give Tehran an ultimatum?"

"Demanding what? That Iran publicly admit its participation in the nuclear attack and apologize? If they admit it, then we have to bomb them."

"I just don't think that the American people will support military action against another country without proof of their complicity. Let's be frank. This government blew its credibility alleging weapons of mass destruction in Iraq."

"Save it for the courtroom. A majority of Americans already supported military action against Iran even before this terrible event. Right now, the American people are in a state of shock, seeing what happened to New York City. They are also anticipating another attack. They are outraged and expect action. Doing nothing will only increase their anxiety. Their anger will turn on us. The government could lose all control. And the republic could collapse. We either lead events or we will be swept along by them. The American people will support a campaign to remove the threat of nuclear terror anywhere. Action will rally the nation, shake it out of its stupor. We will make history or we will be history!"

Should we go it alone or involve our allies?

3:40 p.m.–Police in Houston have announced an all-clear. Suspects are in custody. No explosives were found. The possibility of another nuclear incident was merely media speculation.

In the past few hours, the president has received expressions of massive international support. Except for the usual crowd that celebrates every American calamity, the world is overwhelmingly on our side, as it was just after 9/11. The British prime minister has expressed his condolences and his support for action. The president of France has even called for joint action. As it did after 9/11, NATO almost certainly will again invoke Article 5, declaring this attack on the United States as an attack upon all NATO members.

"We have suffered terrible harm. It provides us with an opportunity to bring about fundamental changes that will reduce the danger of this kind of tragedy ever happening again, anywhere. Whatever we do must be done in a way that preserves this support. When we find out who is behind this horrendous attack, our actions must be taken not in retaliation, but on behalf of the entire world.

"We should seize this moment to lead an international effort to reinforce the taboo on all weapons of mass destruction, halt further nuclear proliferation, internationalize nuclear fuel production, ensure adequate security at all nuclear facilities, significantly reduce existing nuclear arsenals, increase international programs aimed at inspection–"

"You can't be serious! A nuclear bomb has just destroyed New

York, and you are going to invite the world to a disarmament conference?"

"I certainly agree that we have suffered grievous harm. And I also agree that it provides us with an opportunity to make fundamental changes, but I am far less optimistic about getting much international support."

"This is an opportunity to start taking out the nuclear weapons programs we have not been able to eliminate with internationally supported diplomacy or internationally supported sanctions. This is an opportunity to demonstrate that a clandestine nuclear weapons program is not a way to extort concessions, that it is not a strategic asset but a strategic liability."

"This is an opportunity to remove a very dangerous regime that is a threat now and that will be an even greater threat if it gets away with making reckless threats, defying international sanctions, supporting terrorism. This is an opportunity to show terrorists and the tin-pot dictators who support them that going nuclear provokes unimagined responses."

"Our allies have no stomach for that kind of action. Their condolences are no doubt sincere—they are scared too. But their expressions of support are hollow."

"Although some measure of international support would be desirable, the United States can carry out all of these actions unilaterally. Indeed, despite expressions of sympathy, we do not consider international support to be likely. We believe that the Europeans will dither by calling for an international investigation; NATO will delay action and contribute nothing anyway; and the Russians and Chinese will block and subvert any international move against Iran or North Korea.

"Sure, the British prime minister told you that the United Kingdom, as always, will stand with us. But he added that, as traditional allies, we will naturally be consulting about what to do. What he really means is that British support depends on prior consultation and approval. It is conditional and contingent. And if approval means enough proof to satisfy the readers of the *Guardian*, we are not likely to get it.

"True, France's president has called for joint action. That is a breathtaking change from the previous backstabbing and sabotage that characterized French policy. But 'joint action' is a clever French way of inserting French decision making into our own strategic decisions. And NATO still can't muster enough troops to support a UN-mandated military operation in Afghanistan. What we need to do now will be even tougher. If we bog this down in endless meetings in Brussels while committees review proof and debate options, we'll be lucky to get one Dutch frigate delivering a strongly worded rebuke.

"We need to act. We need to take action now—within the first forty-eight hours. Allied support will only hinder, not facilitate, America's response. And it will blow the secrecy necessary for our military success. After that, we can publicize their previous expressions of support. Publicly, our allies may squirm and hiss. Privately, they will be relieved that the Americans have once again done what everyone knew had to be done."

"I disagree. This is precisely what is wrong with my colleague's thinking. His model for what to do in the United States is a TV show, *24*. His strategic horizon for what we should do abroad is forty-eight hours. Suppose we stiff our allies again, as we did in Afghanistan in 2001. Suppose we take unilateral action. Suppose we bomb a thousand targets in Iran. Then what? In the long run, America cannot sustain this campaign alone."

"A unilateral, unjustified military attack on the Iranians will have terrible consequences. It will only strengthen the hold of the mullahs who now run Iran. Even the Iranians who now oppose them will rally to defend their country. Internationally, they will become the victims, not us. An attack on Iran will unleash the Shia militias in Iraq, where we still have tens of thousands of American troops and civilian contractors. Iraq will explode in violence. Every American in the Middle East will be a target for terrorism—for decades. Every American embassy will be under siege."

"Iran could launch whatever missiles it has into Iraq or Israel, not nuclear, but armed with chemical or biological weapons. Iran can destroy the oil terminals on the Persian Gulf and launch suicide attacks against tankers. One-third of the world's oil supply would be affected. We would see a breathtaking increase in the price of oil. Think of the consequences of oil at several hundred dollars a barrel—a severe worldwide recession. With its oil and gas, Russia would gain new power as the savior of Europe."

"It would isolate us diplomatically for a generation or more. It would make us the pariah of nations."

"We face a global threat. We need international cooperation, not because it is nice to have allies, but because it is what has prevented many terrorist attacks thus far. It is about doing what will contribute to our long-term national security."

"Before we start singing 'Kumbaya,' let me remind my timid colleague that Iran sneered at our international diplomacy and that international cooperation did not prevent this attack. Nor will it prevent future attacks. Thank the allies for their condolences, then let's do what we have to do."

"You argue against military action. You describe it as unimaginable given what we know. But it is mind-boggling to me for this country to have suffered losses that may be greater than all of the losses we suffered during World War II, to have been struck with this devastating diabolical attack on one of the most important cities in the world, and to announce that our national response is going to be that we will dedicate increased resources for enhanced security at nuclear facilities worldwide, that we will urge more international cooperation against nuclear proliferation, that we are willing to discuss disarmament. That is not prudent policy. That is capitulation to evil. Our foes will spit on us. Our allies will tremble at the implications of our supine cowardice for their own safety. It will be the autumn of America."

Should you ask the Israelis not to launch any attack?

"Intelligence is reporting that the Israelis have gone on a full military alert. They may be preparing to launch an air attack. Our sources in Tel Aviv indicate they may be arming their aircraft with nuclear weapons."

"What they are doing makes perfect sense. The Israelis are realists. They have to get ready for all contingencies. They also could be signaling their foes that any hint of hostile action will bring a devastating response. But they just might go after Iran themselves. They have already demonstrated their capacity to fly through what were supposed to be impenetrable Russian-built air defenses in Syria. But we also have to be cautious in how we interpret this, especially since our sources seem to have found out about these top-secret preparations so easily. The Israelis may be engaged in some showmanship here in order to exert pressure on us to attack—we move or they move."

"Why wouldn't we want the Israelis to bomb Iran and save us the trouble?"

"A conventional Israeli attack on Iran won't be enough to take out its nuclear facilities, and it will provoke another war in the Middle East. We will share the consequences. Most important, it means that we will lose control of the situation. What if the Russians also know about this and think they can threaten Israel if we're not seen to be with them? Then we slide into a confrontation with Russia."

"Didn't that fellow Cordesman write something about this?"

"He gave a briefing on the consequences of a hypothetical future nuclear war between Israel and Iran. As I recall, he said Israel could hit just about anything they wanted to in Iran. In an all-out nuclear attack, they could wipe out Iran's major cities killing sixteen to twenty-eight million people. Iran would not survive as a country.[3]

"Should the president call the Israeli prime minister and tell him not to do anything precipitous?"

"The Israelis aren't fools. The prime minister is likely to say that Israel must protect its own existence. And what does the president say if the prime minister asks, 'What do you intend to do?' What do we say then?"

What should you do about Pakistan?

Look at this new bulletin:

Pakistan has declared a state of emergency. US intelligence sources in both Islamabad and Delhi are reporting that the Pakistanis have gone on full military alert. Our sources indicate intense activity around sites where Pakistan's nuclear weapons may be stored.

"Obviously, something is up. The Pakistani government may be worried about a coup attempt or a terrorist attack. Elements inside Pakistan may try to seize control of its nuclear weapons. But the Pakistanis also may be worried that India, which we know has also gone on full alert, may launch a preemptive strike to destroy Pakistan's nuclear arsenal. Or maybe the Pakistanis are worried that we might decide to disarm Pakistan, and they are moving their nuclear weapons to more-secure locations."

How likely is it that India might attack Pakistan?

"Can't be ruled out. The two countries have fought four wars since partition in 1947, and they came close to war on several occasions even after both had nuclear weapons. If Pakistan makes any threatening move right now, India conceivably might read it as a possible nuclear attack and launch a preemptive strike; and if Pakistan sees its arch foe India ramping up, it could just as easily take actions that India will interpret as imminent attack. Things have improved since the last war scare, but neither side has much confidence in the other or much experience with nuclear brinkmanship. Miscalculation is a real danger here."

Should the United States try to intervene?

"Both Pakistan and India see us as friends, but our leverage here is very limited. Pakistan is a closer ally, but an unstable one. If Pakistan is going to descend deeper into sectarian anarchy, it might not be a bad idea if India takes out its nuclear arsenal. Saves us the trouble."

"I should point out that we are not the only ones making decisions at this moment. Israel may be about to launch an attack, possibly nuclear, on Iran. India and Pakistan may be on the edge of war. The situation could easily slip beyond our control."

Should we risk a confrontation with the Russians?

Where are the Russians in all this?

Shortly after Putin's earlier call to the president to express his shock and condolences, the Russian prime minister made a public statement:

> **Prime Minister Putin has expressed his shock and sorrow at the terrible tragedy in New York, noting that we live in a dangerous world. He said that the Russian people must understand that Russia itself was also a potential target of terrorists, but that Russian authorities were prepared to deal with any threats. (He did not make any public reference to putting Russia's military and internal security forces on full alert, which we know from intelligence sources he ordered shortly after the detonation in New York.)**

> **Prime Minister Putin said that the response to this event should be an international one based upon a full understanding of the facts. Russia will cooperate closely with others in arriving at an appropriate solution. However, he went on to warn that while he fully understood America's anger, "hastily conceived unilateral military action would only make an already dangerous situation even more dangerous."**

The Russian prime minister said that it was premature to speculate on who was responsible, but he repeated the comments he made last year, when he said, "We have no information that Iran is striving to produce nuclear weapons. . . . We don't believe they are." But the Iranians, Mr. Putin said, should remove any suspicions by being fully transparent about all aspects of their nuclear program. He repeated that an American military attack on Iran would be a grave mistake, one that would provoke reverberations among Iran's neighbors and throughout the region.

"Is that a threat? If it is, Putin's bluffing. Surely, Russia won't go to war to defend Iran."

"I don't think it is a threat, just because we don't think Russia will go to war to defend Iran. They wouldn't want us to attack Iran, making the Russians look impotent when they do nothing. Remember, Putin has tried to pull the Caspian Sea nations together into an alignment under Russian leadership. He would also like to frighten off any European allies we might enlist by portraying the US leadership as reckless hotheads who will drag the Europeans into a wider war. Besides, this kind of belligerency goes down well in Russia."

"So we can ignore it."

"No, we shouldn't ignore it. A US attack on Iran, as Putin points out, will have repercussions throughout the region. The Russians won't retaliate militarily, but an attack would put us back into the cold war, where we will lose the last shreds of cooperation."

"In other words, given the current state of Russian noncooperation, we can ignore it."

"I would suggest that the president not ignore Putin but publicly engage him. Putin knows that Russia could easily be a target for the next terrorist nuclear attack, and that's good. Putin wants the respect due a great power. If at all possible, we want him inside the tent."

"The president has to address the nation. We have to start preparing his address. We have been outlining the front end of his speech during our discussion, but we need decisions on the critical issues . . ."

Now what?

The Department of Defense is reporting that Israeli military aircraft are on the runway.

What the hell are they doing?

We are receiving reports of intense fighting at Pakistan's main nuclear weapons sites.

Indian military aircraft are in the air.

We may have little time . . .

Chapter 18
REFLECTIONS ON THE SHADOWS OF DOOM

Having just been thrust into the role of decision maker, the reader may understandably protest. This was an extraordinary event far beyond anyone's experience. It demanded life-and-death decisions. Events moved too fast. The information was not adequate. The options were unappealing. They offered little between war without proof and diplomacy without hope. But these are the standard ingredients of international crisis, as any high-ranking official can attest.

A president may have a few more hours or a few more days to decide upon a course of action, but the pressure of time is felt no less. The information available is never adequate and it may be wrong. Decision makers often complain about the paucity of options. Discomfort comes with the situation.

The scenario was calculated to illustrate the multiple and complex decisions a president would face if terrorists detonated a nuclear weapon in the United States. In real life, things would be even more complicated.

"Everything seems to slow down," recalls Victor Gilinsky. In 1979 he was the senior commissioner of the Nuclear Regulatory

Commission and in charge during the first hours of the nuclear accident at Three Mile Island. The incident led to the release of a small amount of radioactive steam into the atmosphere and did not compare to the detonation of a terrorist nuclear bomb, but it was a major national event at the time and the pressure was intense. "Your body feels heavy because information is uncertain and no one really knows what is going on or what to do, but you know the consequences of anything you do are tremendous. You get useless advice from all directions that is intended to make the advisor look like he is doing his job or establish a record that will absolve him. You realize the bureaucracy is ready to walk you off the cliff. You wish you had spent more time understanding the possibility beforehand but now it's too late." Gilinsky, who happens to be a nuclear physicist, continues, "Everyone expects you to know things you don't begin to understand."[1]

No hypothetical scenario is ever exactly duplicated in real life. However, we can assume that many of the issues raised in this scenario would also arise if a nuclear device were ever detonated in an American city. The country would be momentarily dazed, in a state of shock. There would be widespread alarm. A grief-stricken nation would huddle together, pray, wonder how to assist those directly affected by the attack.

It is likely that we would assume that there may be more nuclear devices, already deployed or on the way. There might be some spontaneous evacuations of urban areas. Government officials would warn of the consequences if there were further attacks, but that would not suffice. Grief would quickly congeal to outrage. Many would think, this is not a natural disaster. Someone is responsible. Someone must be made to pay. Perhaps even more than immediately after 9/11, the national mood might not flinch at destroying entire cities in retaliation if we know who was responsible.

Two levels of amplification were operative in the scenario, as they probably would be in a real-life event. The president's source of immediate information would be televised news. To the extent that television could even cover a nuclear explosion, we can expect visual and verbal drama. Comparisons with Hiroshima would be sure to be mentioned. Fires would be reported as firestorms, although these would be unlikely in a small nuclear explosion. The human toll would not simply be unknown, it would be unimaginable.

The second level of amplification came from the president's advisers who wanted immediate action. As the debate sharpened, their claims of the likely number of fatalities rose from the estimated tens of thousands to greater than those of World War II to a million, which would be highly unlikely.

Among those who reviewed this chapter before publication, views about the likelihood of panic and spontaneous evacuation broke both ways. Some thought that the scenario underestimated the panic. Cities would empty before the president could do anything about it. Others thought that, outside of New York and Washington, people would stay put, glued to their television sets, perhaps holding hands. The next day they would go back to work.

There would be great anger at the authorities for failing in their primary mission of protecting society. After 9/11, surprise no longer suffices as an excuse. This is what government has been warning us about. The government would find itself faced with the choice of yielding to the clamor for war or being the victim of the people's wrath.

Anger often provokes loose talk and stupid ideas, although were I president in such circumstances, I personally would kick out of the room anyone who proposed bombing Mecca or any other holy sites, unless, perhaps, there was solid evidence that the masterminds of the attack were headquartered there, preparing another attack. It would achieve nothing, but it could set off a worldwide financial collapse and certainly ignite a real global holy war against us. Yet the detonation of a second nuclear bomb would increase domestic public pressure for dramatic revenge and might erode any constraints. Nothing could be ruled out.

Nuclear terrorism could easily initiate what Paul Schulte aptly refers to as "the uncontrollable action/reaction cycle of revenge—'the politics of the last atrocity' in Northern Ireland terminology." Schulte prefers the French term *engrenage*, literally the engaging of gears. In the bloody Algerian struggle for independence—and in the later Algerian Civil War, both of which featured the employment of indiscriminate violence to provoke terror—*engrenage* meant a reciprocal process of violence and retaliation, a chain of events that once initiated becomes "involuntary and mechanistic," overwhelming any individual ability to reflect or restrain the next action.[2]

What made the nuclear attack scenario above particularly frustrating was the fact that the perpetrators of the nuclear attack were unknown. That would only increase anxiety and anger. *None of the simulations of nuclear terrorism I know about have addressed an attack of unknown origin, nor is there any firm policy for dealing with such an event.*

In such a circumstance, some will argue that we may never know and should not wait to know. Instead, they will say, the United States should seize the opportunity to dismantle or destroy all suspected nuclear efforts without waiting for concrete proof of a connection, doing so on the grounds that in a postnuclear terrorist world, the United States could not afford to tolerate any nuclear program that is not under strict international controls. Iran, North Korea, Pakistan could be on the short list of likely targets. With American forces on full alert, any attempt to move weapons or other activity would likely be regarded as suspicious and might precipitate a preemptive strike.

The only way for suspect nations to escape this preemptive retaliation would be to immediately invite inspection, offer cooperation. Otherwise, target nations might calculate that they will be attacked regardless of what they do, and therefore that they would have only days, perhaps hours, to protect or use whatever weapons they might possess against their principal foes. North Korea might threaten to attack South Korea. Pakistan might ponder action against India. Iran, if still without nuclear weapons, could attack Israel or US forces in the Middle East with chemical, biological, or conventional weapons, or by sponsoring terrorist attacks.

In this particular scenario, the president's advisers advocated two diametrically opposed courses of action. Sometimes this can lead to a compromise, something in the middle, but in the circumstances described here, a little bit of war and a little bit of international diplomacy—a barrage of cruise missiles and a call for international cooperation—might be even less desirable. Sometimes one of the extremes is a better choice.

There is no obvious course of action. When variations of this scenario were tried out on various audiences, the participants were deeply divided. Some advocated extreme measures. Others counseled constraint. The debate was heated.

The argument among the president's advisers raises a fundamental issue. Should the United States respond to the terrible terrorist attack that has occurred in the scenario or to the terror of a future world populated by a growing number of hostile states and stateless actors with nuclear capability? Is it the scary reality we know or the hypothetical—imagined—world of tomorrow we fear that determines our collective attitude and dictates our national response? That is what this book is about.

The trajectory of America's domestic response to terrorist threats since 9/11 has been to move away from a traditional law enforcement investigation approach toward preventive intervention. That may be a necessary route that, within strict limits, is compatible with justice. In dealing with threats to its national security from abroad, the United States has moved from a defensive posture to one that embraces preemptive war. Preemptive military action to intercept an immediate threat when there is no other effective recourse can be justified. War by choice demands a careful calculation of the risks. America is, at heart, a good and just nation as well as a mighty military power. Nonetheless, the power to destroy does not endow us with the wisdom or the prerogatives of divinity.

Terror alone, fear itself, cannot dictate decisions. That would take us out of the realm of reality and into the realm of imagined threats and imagined outcomes, a slippery foundation for the hard realities of war. When we fight, as sometimes we must, let it be against definable enemies, not demons of the dark.

The last scenario was intended to make the point that the United States would not be the only government making decisions. A nuclear terrorist attack, were one to occur, would cause a number of nations to recalculate their assumptions and consider their actions. Guns would be drawn. One twitch could set off a chain reaction of events that would propel the world toward wider war. The historical model is August 1914, when the assassination of a Hapsburg archduke in Sarajevo initiated a sequence of events that led to World War I, the bloodiest conflict in human history up to that time. In the first hours after a nuclear terrorist attack, the world would be a very dangerous place.

It is that unavoidable uncertainty about what the other side will do, or in this case, what a number of sides might do, that Nobel laureate Thomas Schelling has talked about in the context of nuclear deterrence.[3] Uncertainty might provide a useful deterrent to nuclear terrorism, at least to nuclear terrorism by actors who hoped to gain something beyond collective martyrdom. The explosion of a nuclear bomb, outside of the more predictable parameters of war, would create an entirely new paradigm. No one knows what others might do. Indeed, even having participated in this simulation, can you say with any confidence what you would do as president in the actual circumstances of a nuclear terrorist attack?

Nor, in my view, should the United States attempt to reduce this uncertainty. In fact, the government may want to signal in advance that, if ever confronted with the reality of nuclear terrorism, the United States will *not* respond according to any predictable norms—everything will be on the table, nothing will be excluded.

These questions have come up before. In 1979 the CIA convened a meeting to examine the consequences of nuclear proliferation. The discussions were based on the assumption that by the 1990s, "at least 50 countries will have the capability to develop nuclear weapons" and "that more than a dozen of them of varying motivations and capabilities will have developed or otherwise acquired a nuclear weapons capability . . . [while] many others will be able to do so in a brief period." It was assumed that the new nuclear weapons states might include some of those regarded as dangerous because of their political instability, unstable or reckless leaders, involvement in continuing international crises, revanchist ambitions, or records of military adventures. In other words, the participants in the meeting predicted that we would live in a very dangerous, proliferated world.[4]

Fortunately, this assumption proved to be just a bit pessimistic. By 1999 there were only eight known or suspected nuclear weapons states, including Israel. North Korea hadn't tested a nuclear weapon yet. Even now, nearly thirty years after the meeting, there are still only nine nuclear weapons states—a remarkable situation given that the same period of time saw the breakup of the Soviet Union.

At the CIA meeting, I was, as usual, asked to specifically address the terrorism question. For my response, I made one more assumption, which was that in addition to assuming that terrorists somewhere had acquired a nuclear weapon, I also assumed the scenario that they had used it—not threatened to use it in some coercive event but detonated a nuclear device. Then what? Although the reactions to such an event would very much depend on the specific situation, I outlined what I thought would be the salient issues and the general thrust of any response.[5]

I reckoned that even if the nuclear yield of the device was modest and the casualties were in the thousands, not in tens of thousands, a threshold would clearly have been crossed. Subsequent actions would be shaped by a number of presumptions, one of which would be that it would happen again and would be worse the next time. At all costs, a subsequent attack had to be prevented. We would envision other real or hypothetical future terrorists waiting to see what would happen. If they perceived the event to be a success—causing death, destruction, and distress without the complete annihilation of those responsible—nuclear terrorism would become a more attractive course of action for others who had the wherewithal. Therefore, future prevention or deterrence would be more important than retaliation. We would, I thought, tend to doubt that terrorists could have done such a thing by themselves. We would invariably suspect that a state was somehow behind it.

At a minimum, I thought, a nuclear terrorist event would increase demands for greater international cooperation to prevent another occurrence. The security of nuclear programs would no longer be seen as a concern of each country, but rather as an international imperative.[6]

In reality, although there had been no nuclear attack, increased concern about the threat of nuclear terrorism as a consequence of crumbling security in the former Soviet Union led to the Nunn-Lugar Act, which provided assistance to Russia for dismantling its nuclear weapons and maintaining adequate security at Russian nuclear facilities. At the same time, the United Nations International Atomic Energy Agency began and continues to be steadily increasing its role in nuclear security, with international support.

International concerns about nuclear security, however,

inevitably bump into assertions of national sovereignty. Protecting nuclear weapons is tightly bound with national security, a jealously guarded prerogative of the state. The world might be concerned about the security of nuclear weapons in a turbulent country like Pakistan, but Pakistan is not likely to allow any outside interference in how it protects its nuclear weapons and fissile material. One way to deal with such circumstances would be to adopt a policy of retaliation for actions caused by negligence–that is, if a country's nuclear weapons or material is stolen and subsequently used by terrorists, that country would bear responsibility for the consequences.[7] In reality, however, delivering on such a threat would be difficult, as there will always be some countervailing consideration.

If terrorists were to detonate a nuclear bomb, I suggested, some governments would go further and argue for international control of all nuclear facilities, or at least of the key components of civilian nuclear energy programs such as nuclear enrichment and fuel fabrication.[8] That, however, would run into even more resistance, although such international schemes have been proposed, for example, as a means of dealing with concerns about Iran's nuclear efforts.

Beyond international calls for increasing security, it is likely that we would see increased international efforts to prevent or respond to any future terrorist nuclear threat. These would range from intelligence-sharing arrangements to the creation of international mechanisms for specific actions in the case of an imminent threat. There are, in fact, already some proposals in this area, and international cooperation has improved overall, but no specific mechanisms have been implemented.

Contrary to intuition, I thought in 1979 that an incident of nuclear terrorism would increase the demand for a nuclear black market. In response to efforts to increase the control of nuclear technology or material, states that continued to harbor nuclear weapons ambitions or that simply sought nuclear energy programs independent of control by a handful of supplier nations, which they might suspect would be inclined to impose sanctions or cut off supplies as a means of exerting political pressure, would want to develop alternative and clandestine paths of acquisition.[9]

For example, whatever one concludes about Iran's ambition to acquire nuclear weapons, proposals that would offer internationally controlled fuel supplies as a substitute for indigenous enrichment would be met with suspicion by Tehran's rulers. They would view dependence on any international supply mechanism as a potential limitation on Iran's right to behave in a way that is contrary to the wishes of those who would control the supply. Where we read "international," Iran tends to see a cabal of hostile Western nations. It may be that Iran's desire to develop nuclear weapons is less important than its determination and, in its view, sovereign right, to be able to behave in a way that the rest of the world doesn't like, without its opponents having a stranglehold on its energy supply.

Pakistan's A. Q. Khan found ready customers for his guide to enrichment, precisely because concerns about proliferation made enrichment know-how hard to come by. This is not an argument against international controls, merely an observation that tight controls on any commodity almost always encourage black markets.

"In sum," I wrote in the 1979 paper, "while nuclear terrorism may be universally perceived as a common threat, this will not translate into a consensus on the necessity and nature of greater international cooperation and control." Even after a terrorist nuclear explosion.[10]

"In the absence of effective international action," I argued, "the most threatened nations might warn that they would take unilateral preemptive military action if necessary to prevent another occurrence of nuclear terrorism." I also thought that threatened nations might "warn others that they would hold responsible for the consequences of nuclear terrorism any nation that had assisted the terrorists or had failed to take adequate measures to prevent terrorists from carrying out a plan to fabricate, use, or transport a nuclear device."[11]

I also thought that "governments everywhere were likely to become more repressive in an age of nuclear terrorism. Known terrorist groups and political dissidents would be the target of crackdowns." In some cases, the crackdowns would be motivated by genuine fear. In other cases, the act of nuclear terrorism might be an excuse for declaring war on antigovernment dissidents.

"Since society could not afford to await the commission of [another] nuclear crime," I thought that efforts would "be made to move back the moment of crime further into the conspiracy stage. . . . Intelligence activities would increase. . . . Apprehension about further acts of nuclear terrorism might also lead to durable changes in police procedures." I thought that

> faced with a threat of nuclear terrorism, police might be permitted to detain persons for an indefinite period without having to bring charges against them, might conduct areawide searches without warrants, and use otherwise prohibited interrogation techniques. . . . Specific legislation might be introduced authorizing the imposition of martial law and the use of military forces to assist in searches. . . . Inevitably, the contemplation of such measures . . . would provoke civil rights arguments. Nonetheless, a badly frightened public might permit, even demand, such measures to preserve their sense of security.[12]

It is noteworthy how far we have gone down this path in response to the 9/11 terrorist attacks, which were not nuclear but did cross a threshold in terms of their scale.

Reviewing the 1979 paper years later, I am struck by its innocence. Although I did think that there would be a "built-in tendency to see government collusion in an act of nuclear terrorism whatever the evidence," to think that the response to a nuclear attack by terrorists would be limited to calls for better security, tighter control of all nuclear trafficking, and threats of military action, but would not lead to war, at least to the brink of war, seems now naive. The detonation of a nuclear device by terrorists today would almost certainly guarantee a military response somewhere. And while I thought in 1979 that the fact of nuclear terrorism would provoke a crackdown on dissidents, a change in rules, a broadening of police powers, and previously prohibited interrogation techniques, what I had in mind then was "lie detector tests without permission of the subject."[13] I did not contemplate water boarding. That future good-guy American heroes would torture bad-guy terrorists and be cheered by television audiences was unimaginable then. What would we be capable of if the nuclear terrorism of today's fictional television drama became tomorrow's dramatic news headline?

Fortunately, nuclear terrorism remains a frightening hypothetical—still "if," not "when"—while nuclear terror, as we have seen, is an imagined reality with a long and rich history and enormous power to shape our perceptions and our behavior. While we cannot do more than guess at the probability of terrorists detonating a nuclear bomb or causing a significant radioactive release, nuclear terror, the anticipation of that event, has a brilliant black future.

Current circumstances support the contention. We are now engaged in what many see as a war without end. This has been accepted as "normal." In another paper written in the mid-1980s, I suggested that

> terrorists will escalate their violence, their attacks will become more indiscriminate. . . . Terrorism will become institutionalized, as a mode of armed conflict for some, no less legitimate than other modes of conflict. The media will increase its ability to cover terrorist incidents; we will *see* even more terrorism. The extraordinary security measures taken against terrorism will

have become a permanent part of the landscape, of our life style. They will not attract comment. That may be the most insidious and perhaps the most worrisome development in the coming years. Terrorism will become an accepted fact of contemporary life—commonplace, ordinary, banal, and therefore somehow "tolerable."

Sadly, this has happened. Even in the absence of terrorism, we live in terror. And no change is in sight.

Neither the death of Osama bin Laden nor the destruction of the jihadist enterprise—a campaign that could take decades—nor the withdrawal of US forces from Iraq, nor the pacification of Afghanistan will resolve the broader regional and global conflicts we confront. They certainly will not end terrorism as a mode of conflict. They will not end the dreams of some terrorists to acquire the ultimate instrument of destruction. They will not quell our fears that terrorists may someday do so. Any minor terrorist action in the nuclear domain will be interpreted as confirmation of worse to come.

The very real prospect that Iran, despite whatever agreement may be reached, will continue to edge toward developing a nuclear weapon or will eventually become, like Israel, an undeclared nuclear power may, in turn, trigger a clandestine race by others to develop nuclear weapons. Nuclear proliferation has not occurred as fast as some expected thirty years ago, but it is by no means under control.

The fall of the Soviet Union was comparatively peaceful, although it left in its wake some nasty conflicts in the Balkans, the Caucasus, and Central Asia. The potential collapse of Pakistan could be a bloodier affair, causing even greater concerns about who might eventually gain control of that country's nuclear arsenal. What might be the result of an implosion in North Korea?

Finally, concerns about the soaring price of oil and global warming have thawed the frozen option of nuclear power. In the

United States alone, power companies are expected to apply to build up to twenty new reactors in the near future, although they also want huge subsidies to cover spiraling costs. Resistance to nuclear power on environmental, safety, and security grounds, as well as by local residents who simply don't want nuclear power plants in their backyards, will inevitably reignite public debate about the terrorist threat, which will further fuel our fears.

Nuclear terrorism is a real threat, but whether or not nuclear terrorism, in any form, occurs in the next decade or beyond, nuclear terror will hold a prominent spot in our minds.

Chapter 19
COUNTERING OUR OWN FEAR

"**Y**ou have to make the risks credible," nuclear weapons designer Ted Taylor once observed, "or people will find a way not to believe you."[1] That meant conjuring up scenarios that would grab people's attention, make them listen. In the early 1970s, when Taylor launched his campaign to warn that terrorists could make nuclear bombs, persuading an uninformed public, a deeply skeptical government, and a nuclear industry with a lot of economic momentum behind it was an uphill battle.

One of Taylor's favorite scenarios was a terrorist nuclear attack on the Capitol Building in Washington. "A one-kiloton bomb exploded just outside the exclusion area during the State of the Union Message would kill everyone inside the Capitol . . . the heads of all branches of the United States government—all Supreme Court justices, the entire Cabinet, all legislators, . . . the Joint Chiefs of Staff . . . it would kill the line of succession to the Presidency—all the way to the bottom of the list."[2]

At the time, the idea of terrorists with one-kiloton bombs seemed far-fetched to many, too much like something out of H. G. Wells's *War of the Worlds*. Now it is an accepted scenario.

The State of the Union address is currently classified as a national security event. The exclusion area has been expanded. No planes fly over the District of Columbia when the president speaks. Vehicles stop at a distance. Heavy security is in effect throughout the city.

In the late 1970s, Robert Jungk sketched an Orwellian view of a future society in which fear of nuclear terrorism was pervasive. It was a society ruled by background investigations, constant identity checks, and frequent searches. People would be under constant surveillance by informants and undercover police. Government eavesdropping would become widespread. Behavior would be monitored. Authorities would acquire the power of preventive detention.[3] At the time, Jungk's grim prognosis also seemed far-fetched.

Taylor's scenario of nuclear terrorism fortunately remains hypothetical. Jungk's vision, unfortunately, is not far from the reality of a post-9/11 world. Frequent government warnings of worse terrorist attacks to come coupled with admonitions to keep shopping have succeeded in disconnecting belief from behavior. Even as we grow increasingly complacent about security, according to public opinion polls, we live in anticipation of nuclear terror.

As we have seen, nuclear terror does not derive from an assessment of the threat. It rests instead upon a set of widely held beliefs that have become the basic tenets of nuclear terror.

What scientists argued that terrorists theoretically could do, others subsequently asserted terrorists would in fact do. Theory became threat. The possibility of nuclear terrorism became the reality of nuclear terror.

It has come to be widely believed, for example, that nuclear weapons are not very hard to make, that if terrorists somehow get their hands on the necessary fissile material, it is virtually certain that they will be able to fabricate a nuclear bomb.

It is widely believed that terrorists armed with a nuclear weapon—stolen, secretly fabricated, or simply turned over to them by a state sponsor—will use it without hesitation. Unlike countries, terrorists have no interest in mere possession for the sake of defense or deterrence. It is believed that terrorists will give no advance warning, make no prior demands, offer no negotiations. We will know about it when it explodes.

It is widely believed that terrorists cannot be deterred, that they give no thought to consequences, that there are no self-imposed constraints. They hold nothing dear that we can threaten. There is no meaningful threat of retaliation.

It is widely believed that once they embark upon their plan, terrorists are unstoppable, individually and collectively ready to commit suicide.

It is widely believed that our intelligence services will not be able to detect and thwart an act of nuclear terrorism. Intelligence failed to detect nuclear tests in India and Pakistan. The intelligence on Iraq's weapons of mass destruction proved wrong. Intelligence failed to prevent 9/11.

It is widely believed that we have no defenses, that we are vulnerable, wide open to attack. Terrorists will get through our borders, past our security perimeters, undetected.

It is widely believed that a terrorist nuclear explosion will achieve a significant yield, destroy a large portion of a major city. Immediate casualties will run to the hundreds of thousands. Many thousands more will die of radiation.

It is widely believed that a terrorist nuclear attack will threaten the nation's survival. At the very least, it will produce widespread panic, the threat of social anarchy, the response to which will be the destruction of democracy itself.

All of this is widely believed to be inevitable—a matter not of "if," but "when." And it is believed that this will happen soon. Within five years, ten at the most.

Each of these assertions, of course, can be challenged. It is true that college students and novice physicists have designed nuclear bombs without access to classified information, but getting the necessary nuclear material and assembling the necessary skills to build one are complicated matters. Kitchen table nuclear bombs are myths. Dropping one block of uranium on another block of uranium from a stepladder will not create a nuclear explosion. Every national program to build a nuclear weapon has required significant resources and has taken years. While the possibility that some talented team of terrorists conceivably might someday design and build a crude nuclear device cannot be entirely dismissed, no terrorist group, not even those with potential access to poorly guarded nuclear sites like Russia's Chechens or those with hundreds of millions of dollars to spend like al Qaeda has come close.

Terrorists, assuming they have a nuclear weapon, may be more likely to use it than nations are, but this may only make state sponsors less likely to provide them with one. It is also noteworthy that the event closest to a serious terrorist nuclear attack was the planting of a radioactive device by the Chechens in Moscow's Ismailovsky Park. And in that case, the terrorists chose to warn the authorities rather than detonate their device.

Al Qaeda appears to have figured out that fomenting nuclear terror does not require possession of nuclear weapons at all. This puts us in the realm of threats, warnings, boasts, perceptions, calculations of leverage, internal debates—a more complicated universe than that of unthinking detonation.

Although terrorists cannot be deterred in the same way that the use of nuclear weapons was deterred during the cold war, there are national governments that may provide support to terrorists, terrorist constituencies, and terrorist sympathizers, and all of those are vulnerable to the direct or retaliatory consequences of a terrorist nuclear attack. Even within an organization like al Qaeda, demonstrably dedicated to large-scale violence, terrorist leaders debate the utility of indiscriminate carnage. Deterrence as a concept need not be abandoned.

If there is an immediate lesson, it is that al Qaeda must be utterly destroyed, to prevent it from ever acquiring any weapons of mass destruction and as an object lesson to all other groups that would ever dream of using nuclear weapons.

The spreading tactic of suicide terrorist bombings has had a significant psychological effect. But recruiting volunteers for suicide missions is not the same as committing organizational suicide. The suicide mission is an effective terrorist tactic, not a group death wish. Terrorists do consider consequences. They are stoppable.

Not every terrorist plot will be discovered. At the same time, the unprecedented unanimity of focus and cooperation among the intelligence services and law enforcement organizations of the world has succeeded in degrading terrorist capabilities and improving the international record in uncovering and thwarting terrorist plots.

We have too easily slid from the scientists' first estimates of terrorist nuclear devices with yields likely to be in the tenths of a kiloton range to a now-assumed standard of a ten-kiloton terrorist bomb. The worst case has become the baseline assessment. A nuclear explosion in the tenths of a kiloton range would still be a catastrophic attack, capable of killing thousands–tens of thousands if detonated among skyscrapers filled with people–but there is a huge difference between destroying a major building and obliterating an entire zip code. With proper preparation and training, thousands could be saved. The nation will survive.

Undoubtedly, a terrorist nuclear explosion of any size would have a huge psychological impact on the nation, but whether it would lead to social anarchy would depend heavily on the prior attitudes of the nation's citizens and the behavior and communications of its leadership. We may not be able to prevent an act of nuclear terrorism, but if we destroy our democracy as a consequence of nuclear terrorism, it will be our own act of suicide.

Finally, there is nothing inevitable about nuclear terror. Far too often, nuclear terror serves as the stock and trade of frightened leaders or of leaders whose purpose is to make us very afraid, who declaim that nuclear terrorism is "not 'if,' but 'when.'" It is a mere assertion that can only be accepted on faith alone. It is not the perception of most authorities, including those most worried about nuclear terrorism.

Nonetheless, these beliefs have become deeply embedded in society and therefore are very difficult to dislodge. As articles of faith rather than conclusions of analysis, they are not easily deconstructed and challenged. They are interwoven with and reinforced by other deeply held fears, by religious faith, and by political agendas.

Even those who may not subscribe to all of the above may still see nuclear terror as a worthwhile prerequisite to mobilizing concern and resources to prevent nuclear terrorism. Public persuasion, they may believe, requires frightening scenarios. To raise questions about nuclear terrorism is deemed dangerous heresy—at the very least, inadequate zeal in supporting perfectly sensible efforts to prevent nuclear terrorism. If you are not sufficiently alarmed, you are an unbeliever—or worse, an opponent of nuclear safeguards and security.

However, this posture builds bias into the continuing debate over nuclear terrorism. Those who would dare to argue that the threat has been exaggerated must first assure everyone that they, too, are worried; that they support current efforts to slow nuclear proliferation, improve controls, tighten security. Orthodox assumptions must be attacked obliquely. On the other side of the argument, the advocates of action repeat things we now know to be untrue—the bogus reports of nuclear weapons about to be detonated—if only to warn us that such things could happen. And they rarely raise their voices against the absurd assertions of the sensationalists.

WHAT CAN BE DONE?

The nature of war has changed. Terrorism, while not new in concept, has become a component of armed conflict. It has blurred the distinction between combatant and noncombatant, between battlefield and home front, between military operations and law enforcement. Providing for the common defense now must include homeland security. This has brought about visible changes in the landscape, invisible changes in the national mindset. Inevitably, heightened homeland threats have generated fear and, for some, terror–the dread and anticipation of horrors to come. The extreme form of this terror is nuclear terror–the anticipation of annihilation.

What is to be done? It makes sense for governments to maintain a powerful taboo against the offensive use of nuclear weapons, to reduce the size of existing nuclear arsenals, to ensure the protection of those that remain, and to attempt to dissuade others from developing nuclear weapons.

We should maintain the deterrent principle that states will be held accountable for the actions of terrorists when there is evidence of collaboration, and that when all else fails, preemptive action will not be ruled out. It should also quietly be pointed out that, in the hours following a terrorist nuclear attack, the pressures for action will be enormous, the standards of evidence may be lowered, governments with secret nuclear programs may have little time to prove their innocence, many nations will similarly be making snap decisions, and in that uncertainty there is great danger to all.

Highly enriched uranium should be removed from research reactors, many of which often have inadequate security. Stockpiles of plutonium and highly enriched uranium should be rendered safe. Nuclear safeguards and security should be enhanced. International institutions to monitor and enforce safeguards and security should be strengthened.

International cooperation in general should be enlisted and strengthened. The issue is not simply the defense of the United States but the avoidance of catastrophic terrorist events that could affect any nation and could potentially lead to world war.

It makes sense overall to focus on intelligence, to improve counterterrorist capabilities, to identify and destroy any group suspected of moving toward nuclear weapons. If the United States and the United Kingdom are going to play a persuasive international role, they will need to restore the credibility of their intelligence and how it is used to support policy, both of which were so badly damaged by our reasons for invading Iraq.

Finally, it makes sense not only to prepare for nuclear and other large-scale attacks at national and local government levels but also to educate and enlist the public into behaving in ways that will save lives. This can be accomplished without generating terror. In fact, the very act of involving the public in its own defense will help to defuse terror.

We have to take the long-shot possibility of nuclear terrorism seriously, but we must not allow ourselves to be terrorized by it. The United States must always be "the land of the free and the home of the brave." Fear is not free.

Frightened populations are intolerant. Frightened people worry incessantly about subversion from within. They worry about substandard zeal. Frightened people look for visible displays to confirm unity of belief—lapel-pin patriotism, a superficial substitute for the real thing. Fear creates its own orthodoxy. It demands unquestioning obeisance to a determined order of apprehension. In that order, it does not suffice merely to agree that nuclear terrorism is a cause for concern. Nuclear terrorism demands exclusivity. To focus on lesser, more likely threats is apostasy. Nuclear terrorism is the end of the world.

It is not the end of the world, of course. During the cold war, an all-out nuclear exchange would have meant planetary suicide.

Today, we face one tyrant with a handful of nuclear weapons, another enthralled by first-use fantasies, and a terrorist with an effective propaganda machine—dangerous, vexing, but not the end of the world, not the end of the nation, not the end of a single city. The country will survive a nuclear incident generated by such individuals. Yet no political leader dares utter such heresy.

Fear can distort the way we address the threat of nuclear terrorism itself. In the shadow of nuclear terror, it is difficult to rationally assess the obvious risks versus the overall benefits of nuclear power as a possible solution to the world's energy and global-warming problems. If nuclear terrorism is assumed to be Armageddon, then we operate in an artificial environment of absolutes, not the real world of relative risks. We ignore lesser, more likely threats in order to strive for impossible goals—perfect systems that will account for every gram of fissile material. We readily assume scenarios that merit debate, scenarios in which tin-pot tyrants will arm terrorists with nuclear weapons. Nuclear terror perversely prohibits us from even thinking about what we might do to save lives.

Fear warps our judgment. Fear of another 9/11 quickly morphed into fear of worse—a nuclear 9/11, a tenfold, hundredfold inflation of the terrorist threat, with no discount for probability. Fear of that magnitude paved the way for circumventing legislatively established procedures for the collection of intelligence, for attempts to operate outside the courts, for the justification of torture. Distinguished scholars discuss the durability of the US Constitution in the face of nuclear terrorism. That we now question a document that has survived invasion, civil war, world wars, decades of confrontation with a Soviet superpower armed with tens of thousands of nuclear weapons, suggests that the price of nuclear terror is too high.

Security is necessary. But security is not an antidote to terror. Reducing needless fear will require a different kind of public communications, replacing the corrosive message of fear with the inspirational language of courage, substituting podium pounding and swaggering rhetoric devoid of content with serious discussion. The media may never be weaned off their addiction to sensationalism, but leadership still sets the agenda and tone of public discourse. In that sphere, Americans continue to be disappointed. We have gone from calls to courage to calculated hype.

Ultimately, however, whether or not we as citizens yield to nuclear terror is our decision. We can behave like frightened sheep, content to fill our stomachs while we are herded about by terrorists and cynical politicians who would chip away at our liberty. Or we can behave as citizens whose first mission is to defeat the tyranny of terror. If we value our democracy, our choice is clear.

ENDNOTES

CHAPTER 1. A SHIVER OF TERROR

1. "Super Sunday to Super Tuesday: Saga Foundation Supports Bipartisan Issue Ad Campaign on Nuclear Terror," Saga Foundation Press Release, February 1, 2008.

2. "Suicide Bomber Strikes Near Nuclear Site in Israel," Associated Press, February 5, 2008.

3. "Terrorism: Al-Qaeda 'Eyeing Nuclear Weapons,'" adnkronos-international, February 4, 2008, http://www.adnkronos.com/AKI/English/Security/?id=1.0.1843140498.

4. "Threat of N-Weapons Falling into Terror Hands Real, Say Pranab," rediff.com, February 5, 2008, http://www.rediff.com///news/2008/feb/05nuke.htm.

5. Dipesh Gadher, "Al-Qaeda 'Planning Big British Attack,'" *Sunday Times*, April 22, 2007.

CHAPTER 2. THE FIRST IMAGININGS

1. Mary Ann Thomas and Ramesh Santanam, "Government Agencies Investigated Missing Uranium, NUMEC," *Pittsburgh Tribune Review*, August 25, 2002.

2. Ad Hoc Advisory Panel on Safeguarding Special Nuclear Material, *Report of the Advisory Panel on Safeguarding Special Nuclear Material* (Washington, DC: Atomic Energy Commission, March 10, 1967).

3. Telephone conversation with Ralph Lumb, 1974.

4. Dan Stober, "No Experience Necessary," *Bulletin of the Atomic Scientists* (March/April 2003): 60. The original two members of the team were Dave Dobson and David Pipkorn. Pipkorn dropped out of the project in 1965 and was replaced by Robert Seldon.

5. Ibid., p. 61.

6. Theodore B. Taylor, "Nuclear Power and Nuclear Weapons," July 1996, p. 2, http://www.wagingpeace.org/articles/1996/07/00 _taylor_nuclear-power.htm.

7. Theodore B. Taylor, "Reactor Safety Considerations Related to Sabotage and Wartime Bombardment of Nuclear Power Plants," unpublished manuscript, 1968.

8. T. B. Taylor, "International Safeguards of Nonmilitary Nuclear Technology. 1. The Rapid Growth of Nuclear Technology: Implications for Nuclear Safeguards," *Nuclear Journal* 1, no. 1 (January 1969): 1–51.

9. John McPhee, *The Curve of Binding Energy* (New York: Farrar, Straus and Giroux, 1973).

10. Ibid., p. 124.

11. Theodore Taylor and Mason Willrich, *Nuclear Theft: Risks and Safeguards* (Cambridge, MA: J. B. Lippincott Company, 1974).

12. Ibid., pp. 20–21.

13. Ibid.

14. J. Carson Mark, "Nuclear Weapons Technology," in *Impact of New Technologies on the Arms Race*, ed. Barnard T. Feld et al. (Cambridge, MA: MIT Press, 1971), pp. 131–39.

15. David B. Hall, "The Adaptability of Fissile Materials to Nuclear Explosives," in *Preventing Nuclear Theft: Guidelines for Industry and Gov-*

ernment, ed. Robert B. Leachman and Phillip Altoff (New York: Praeger, 1972), pp. 275–83.

16. Ibid.

17. Discussion with Victor Gilinsky, January 2008.

18. Robert W. Seldon, *Reactor Plutonium and Nuclear Explosives* (Livermore, CA: Lawrence Livermore Laboratory, 1976).

19. Personal communication from Victor Gilinsky, May 4, 2008; see also Egbert Kankeleit, Christian Kuppers, Ulrich Imkeller, *The Usability of Reactor Plutonium in Weapons* (Darmstadt, Germany: Technical College Darmstadt, 1989), p. 13.

20. Stober, "No Experience Necessary," p. 59.

21. International Panel on Fissile Materials, "Fissile Materials & Nuclear Weapons," http://www.fissilematerials.org/ipfm/page5_US _en/fissile/fissile/fissile.php.

22. Ibid.

23. "Enola Gay–An Air Force Association Special Page," Air Force Association, http://afa.org/new_root/enolagay/AB.asa#top.

24. Ivan Waddoups, *Malevolent Uses of Less Than Strategic Quantities of Special Nuclear Material* (Albuquerque, NM: Sandia Laboratories, SAND75-0534, 1974).

25. Brian Michael Jenkins, *Will Terrorists Go Nuclear?* (Los Angeles: Crescent Publications, 1975).

26. Robert Jungk, *The New Tyranny: How Nuclear Power Enslaves Us* (New York: Grosset & Dunlop, 1979).

27. Ibid.

28. Ibid., p. 131.

29. Ibid., pp. 127–30.

30. Ibid., p. 136 (Jungk refers to me as "Bruce Jenkins").

31. Ibid., pp. 152–70.

32. Ibid. The quote is from a blurb on the cover of Jungk's book *The New Tyranny,* by Benjamin Spock, a pediatrician, author, and vocal critic of the Vietnam War and nuclear power.

33. This position is taken in an addendum to the *Report of the International Task Force on Prevention of Nuclear Terrorism* written by task force member Inga Thorsson, former Swedish undersecretary of state for disarmament.

34. Conversation with a senior official at Sandia Laboratories, 2007.

35. Augustus R. Norton and Martin H. Greenberg, *Studies in Nuclear Terrorism* (Boston: G. K. Hall & Co., 1979).

36. Spurgeon M. Keeny Jr., "Plutonium Reprocessing: Twenty Years Experience (1977–1997)," *Frontline,* http://www_c.pbs.org/wgbh/pages/frontline/shows/reaction/readings/keeny.html. In fact, President Ford had already declared on October 28, 1976, that "the reprocessing and recycling of plutonium should not proceed unless there is sound reason to conclude that the world community can effectively overcome the associated risks of proliferation." Anthony Andrews, *Nuclear Fuel Reprocessing: US Policy Development* (Washington, DC: CRS Report for Congress, November 29, 2006).

37. Nuclear Energy Policy Study Group, "Nuclear Terrorism," in Norton and Greenberg, *Studies in Nuclear Terrorism,* pp. 294–95.

38. R. W. Mengel, "Terrorism and New Technologies of Destruction: An Overview of Potential Risk," in Norton and Greenberg, *Studies in Nuclear Terrorism,* pp. 189–245.

39. Norton and Greenberg, *Studies in Nuclear Terrorism,* pp. 295–97.

40. Office of Technology Assessment of the US Congress, "The Non-State Adversary," in Norton and Greenberg, *Studies in Nuclear Terrorism,* pp. 306–36.

41. Carson Mark et al., *Can Terrorists Build Nuclear Weapons?* (Washington, DC: Nuclear Control Institute, 1987).

42. *Report of the International Task Force on Prevention of Nuclear Terrorism* (Washington, DC: Nuclear Control Institute, June 25, 1986). See also Paul Leventhal and Yonah Alexander, eds., *Preventing Nuclear Terrorism* (Lexington, MA: Lexington Books, 1987).

43. *Task Force Report,* p. 1.

44. Ibid., p. 3.

45. See, for example, Carl Behrens and Mark Holt, *Nuclear Power Plants: Vulnerability to Terrorist Attack* (Washington, DC: Congressional Research Service, February 4, 2005).

46. The "Cooperative Threat Reduction Program" was initiated in 1991 by legislation introduced by Senators Sam Nunn and Richard Lugar. Details of the continuing work of the CTR are described at the Web site of the Nuclear Threat Initiative, http://www.nti.org.

47. John Mueller, *Overblown: How Politicians and the Terrorism Industry*

Inflate National Security Threats and Why We Believe Them (New York: Free Press, 2006).

48. McPhee, *Curve of Binding Energy*, p. 226. See also "Amateur A-Bomb?" *Time Magazine*, May 13, 1974.

CHAPTER 3. MOTIVES

1. Brian Jenkins, *Will Terrorists Go Nuclear?* (Los Angeles: Crescent Publications, 1975).

2. This discussion appears in Fuad Jabber, *Israel's Nuclear Option and U.S. Arms Control Policies*, California Seminar on Arms Control and Foreign Policy, Research Paper No. 9, February 1972, and William Quandt, Fuad Jabber, and Ann Lesch, *The Politics of Palestinian Nationalism* (Berkeley: University of California Press, 1973).

3. Mark Holt and Anthony Andrews, *Nuclear Power Plants: Vulnerability to Terrorist Attack* (Washington, DC: Congressional Research Service, 2007), p. 5, citing interview on al-Jazeera claiming that al Qaeda terrorists had "initially planned to include a nuclear plant in its 2001 attack sites."

4. William Pierce, *The Turner Diaries* (Hillsboro, WV: National Vanguard Books, 1978).

5. Ibid.

6. Sabrina P. P. Ramet, *Balkan Babel: The Disintegration of Yugoslavia from the Death of Tito to the Fall of Milosevic* (Boulder, CO: Westview Press, 2002), p. 213.

7. Robert Jay Lifton, *Destroying the World to Save It: Aum Shinrikyo, Apocalyptic Violence, and the New Global Terrorism* (New York: Henry Holt & Company, 1999), pp. 194–97.

8. Ibid., pp. 194–95.

9. David Kaplan and Andrew Marshall, *The Cult at the End of the World: The Incredible Story of Aum* (London: Arrow Books, 1996), p. 31. For additional discussion of Aum's belief system, see D. W. Brackett, *Holy Terror: Armageddon in Tokyo* (New York: Weatherhill, 1996). Haruki Murakami, *Underground: The Tokyo Gas Attack and the Japanese Psyche* (New

York: Vintage Books, 2001). Ian Reader, *A Poisonous Cocktail: Aum Shinrikyo's Path to Violence* (Copenhagen: NIAS Publishing, 1996).

10. H. G. Wells, *The World Set Free* (London: Macmillan and Co., 1914).

11. Author's personal correspondence with David Kaplan, co-author of *The Cult at the End of the World,* July 15, 2007.

12. Lifton, *Destroying the World to Save It,* p. 196.

13. Ibid., p. 194.

14. Sara Daly, John Parachini, and William Rosenau, *Aum Shinrikyo, Al Qaeda, and the Kinshasa Reactor: Implications for Combating Nuclear Terrorism* (Santa Monica, CA: RAND Corporation, 2005), pp. 16–17.

15. D. W. Brackett and Theodore Liolios, *Holy Terror: Armageddon in Tokyo* (New York: Weatherhill, 1996), p. 92.

16. Daly, et al., *Aum Shinrikyo, Al Qaeda, and the Kinshasa Reactor,* p. 14.

17. Ibid., pp. 19–20.

18. Simon Saradzhyan, *Russia: Grasping the Reality of Nuclear Terror* (Cambridge, MA: US-Russian Nonproliferation Working Group, Belfer Center for Science and International Affairs, John F. Kennedy School of Government, Harvard University, 2003), pp. 26–27.

19. There are numerous descriptions of Besayev's device: Simon Saradzhyan (ibid.) described it simply as "a lead container with radioactive cesium-137." He mentions no explosive charge. In his detailed history of the Chechen War, Anatol Lieven (*Chechnya: Tombstone of Russian Power* [New Haven, CT: Yale University Press, 1998], p. 137) describes it as "a package of low-level radioactive cesium." In his initial report on the incident, *New York Times* reporter Michael Specter ("Russians Assert Radioactive Box Found in Park Posed No Danger," *New York Times,* November 25, 1995) referred to it as a "radioactive box." In later accounts, it becomes a "dirty bomb."

20. Paul L. Williams, *The Al Qaeda Connection: International Terrorism, Organized Crime, and the Coming Apocalypse* (Amherst, NY: Prometheus Books, 2005), p. 86.

21. "Sources of Information on Cesium-137," National Library of Medicine Hazardous Substance Databank, http://toxnet.nlm.nih.gov/cgi-bin/sis/search/r?dbs+hsdb:@term+@na+@reltcesium,+radio

active; see also Andy Oppenheimer, "Lessons Learnt: Gioania," *NBC International,* Autumn 2007, pp. 34–36.

22. Lieven, *Chechnya: Tombstone of Russian Power,* p. 33.

23. See Daly et al., *Aum Shinrikyo, Al Qaeda, and the Kinshasa Reactor,* p. 30; Rohan Gunaratna, *Inside Al Qaeda: Global Network of Terror* (New York: Columbia University Press, 2002), p. 48; and Anonymous (Michael Scheuer), *Through Our Enemies' Eyes: Osama bin Laden, Radical Islam, and the Future of America* (Washington, DC: Brassey's, 2002), p. 186.

24. Stefan Leader, "Middle East, Osama bin Laden and the Terrorist Search for WMD," *Jane's Intelligence Review* 11, no. 6 (June 1999).

25. Kimberly McCloud and Matthew Osborne, "WMD Terrorism and Usama bin Laden," in *CNS Reports* (Monterey, CA: James Martin Center for Nonproliferation Studies, 2001), including full text of Jamal Ahmad al-Fadl in the United States District Court, Southern District of New York, *United States v. Usama bin Laden et al.,* February 6, 7, and 13, 2001.

26. Combating Terrorism Center, *Harmony and Disharmony: Exploiting al-Qa'ida's Organizational Vulnerabilities* (West Point, NY: Combating Terrorism Center, Department of Social Sciences, United States Military Academy), p. 76, citing a captured letter from Hassan al-Takji, "The Fifth Letter to the Africa Corps," 1994.

27. Matthew Bunn, *Reducing the Threat of Nuclear Theft and Sabotage* (Cambridge, MA: Belfer Center for Science and International Affairs, John F. Kennedy School of Government, Harvard University, October 29, 2001).

28. The most thorough published account of the encounter between bin Laden and the Pakistani scientists can be found in Holly Higgins, "A Bomb for the Ummah," *Bulletin of Atomic Scientists* 59, no. 2 (March–April 2003): 49–56.

29. Ibid., pp. 50–51.

30. David Albright, "Al Qaeda's Nuclear Program: Through the Window of Seized Documents," *Policy Forum Online,* Nautilus Institute, Special Forum No. 47, November 6, 2002.

31. Nick Fielding, "Bin Laden's Dirty Bomb Quest Exposed," *Sunday Times,* October 19, 2004.

32. Albright, "Al Qaeda's Nuclear Program," p. 1.

33. The Dragonfire incident is described in Graham Allison, *Nuclear*

Terrorism: The Ultimate Preventable Catastrophe (New York: Henry Holt and Company, 2004), pp. 1–4.

34. Peter Bergen, *The Osama bin Laden I Know: An Oral History of al Qaeda's Leader* (New York: Simon and Schuster), p. 339, citing Osama bin Laden's statement of May 14, 1998, following the Indian government's nuclear tests.

35. Ibid., pp. 341–42, citing Abu Walid al Misri, editor of *Al Imara*, the Arabic-language newspaper of the Taliban.

36. "Exclusive Interview: Conversation with Terror," Osama bin Laden interview with Rahimullah Yusufzai, *Time*, January 11, 1999.

37. Bruce Lawrence, *Messages to the World: The Statements of Osama bin Laden* (London: Verso, 2005), p. 72, citing Osama bin Laden interview with al-Jazeera, December 1998.

CHAPTER 4. SELF-IMPOSED CONSTRAINTS

1. Brian Jenkins, *Will Terrorists Go Nuclear?* (Los Angeles: Crescent Publications, 1975), p. 13.

2. John Kerry King, ed., *International Political Effects of the Spread of Nuclear Weapons* (Washington, DC: US Government Printing Office, 1979).

3. Jenkins, *Will Terrorists Go Nuclear?* p. 22.

CHAPTER 5. NUCLEAR COERCION: JUST HOAXES?

1. Baumann gave the interview in secret to a French reporter while he was still a fugitive. *Liberation*, October 7–8, 1978.

2. *Public Papers of the Presidents of the United States: Richard Nixon, Containing the Public Messages, Speeches, and Statements of the President, 1973* (Washington, DC: US Government Printing Office, 1975), p. 157.

3. Robert Kupperman and Jeff Kamen, *Final Warning: Averting Disaster in the New Age of Terrorism* (New York: Doubleday), 1989.

4. Baumann interview.

5. Private discussions with US intelligence official, November 2007.

6. US NIE on terrorism in July 2007.

7. "Chertoff Bares 'Gut Feeling' of Mounting Terror," *Chicago Tribune*, July 10, 2007.

8. "Guest: Fmr White House Official Richard Clarke," *Meet the Press*, March 28, 2004, http://www.msnbc.com/id/4608698/.

9. "Tease for New al Qaeda Video Threatens 'Big Surprise,'" Associated Press, August 2, 2007.

10. "U.S. Terror Attack—'Ninety Days at Most,'" FoxNews.com, July 16, 2007, http://www.foxnews.com/story/0,2933,161962,00.html.

11. "American Al Qaeda Leader Says U.S. Embassies a Prime Target," ABC News, August 5, 2007.

12. *DEBKAfile*, August 8, 2007.

13. Ibid.

14. Ibid.

CHAPTER 6. DESIGNING THE THREAT

1. Peter de Leon, Brian Jenkins, Konrad Kellen, and Joseph Krofcheck, *Attributes of Potential Adversaries of U.S. Nuclear Programs* (Santa Monica, CA: RAND Corporation), 1978.

2. Gail Bass et al., *Motivations and Possible Actions of Potential Criminal Adversaries of U.S. Nuclear Programs* (Santa Monica, CA: RAND Corporation, 1980). This research was updated in Bruce Hoffman et al., *A Reassessment of Potential Adversaries to U.S. Nuclear Programs* (Santa Monica, CA: RAND Corporation, 1986).

CHAPTER 7. BLACK MARKETS

1. For overall descriptions of nuclear black markets, see Matthew Bunn, Anthony Wier, and José Friedman, *The Demand for Black Market Fissile Material* (Cambridge, MA: NTI, 2005), http://www.nti.orgle _research/cnwm/threat/demand.asp; Center for Nonproliferation

Studies, *NIS Nuclear Trafficking*, a database of incidents that can be accessed at the Web page of the Nuclear Threat Initiative, http:// www.nti.org; Myles Collins and Tracey De Francesco, "Nuclear Black Markets: A Proliferated World," unpublished paper, Santa Monica, CA: RAND Corporation, 2005; CSIS Task Force, *The Nuclear Black Market* (Washington, DC: Center for Strategic and International Studies, 1996); William Langewiesche, *The Atomic Bazaar: The Rise of the Nuclear Poor* (New York: Farrar, Straus and Giroux, 2007); Rensselaer W. Lee III, *Smuggling Armageddon: The Nuclear Black Market in the Former Soviet Union and Europe* (New York: St. Martin's Griffin, 1998); Vladimir Orlov, *Addressing the Challenge of Illicit Nuclear Trafficking* (Moscow: Center for Policy Studies in Russia, n.d).

2. Some of the difficulties a thief would have in penetrating a Russian nuclear weapons fabrication facility and getting away with nuclear material are discussed by Langewiesche, *The Atomic Bazaar*.

3. Fred Charles Iklé, Gerald J. Aronson, and Albert Madansky, *On the Risk of an Accidental or Unauthorized Detonation* (Santa Monica, CA: RAND Corporation, 1958).

4. The story appears in numerous places, for example, in Richard Wolfson, *Nuclear Choices: A Citizen's Guide to Nuclear Technology* (Cambridge, MA: MIT Press, 1993), p. 437. It also appears in articles on the Internet, for example, "France's Nuclear Weapons: Origin of the Force de Frappe," 2001, http://nuclearweaponarchive.org/France/France Origin.htm/.

5. Author's discussions with former French intelligence officials, January and February 2008.

6. Fred Charles Iklé, *Annihilation from Within: The Ultimate Threat to Nations* (New York: Columbia University Press, 2006).

7. There have been a number of accounts of A. Q. Khan's black market activities. See Douglas Frantz and Catherine Collins, *The Nuclear Jihadist: The True Story of the Man Who Sold the World's Most Dangerous Secrets . . . and How We Could Have Stopped Him* (New York: Twelve, 2007); International Institute for Strategic Studies, *Nuclear Black Markets: Pakistan, A. Q. Khan and the Rise of Proliferation Networks—A Net Assessment* (London: IISS, 2007); "Special Report: The Khan Network—Kenley Butler, Sammy Salama and Leonard S., Where Is the Justice?" and

Mark Hibbs, "The Unmaking of a Nuclear Smuggler," *Bulletin of the Atomic Scientists* 62, no. 6 (November/December 2006): 25–41, 62–63; Rajeesh Kumar Mishra, "Nuclear Scientific Community of Pakistan: Clear and Present Danger to Nonproliferation," South Asia Analysis Group, http://www.saay.org/papers7/paper601.html; B. Raman, "Pakistan & Dangers of Nuclear Jihad," South Asia Analysis Group, http://www.saag.org/papers10/paper904.html; A. J. Venter, *Allah's Bomb: The Islamic Quest for Nuclear Weapons* (Guilford, CT: Lyons Press, 2007).

8. Lee, *Smuggling Armageddon*, pp. 139–41.

9. Ibid.

CHAPTER 8. A SMALL CUP OF ITALIAN COFFEE

1. Andy Zipser, "A Hard Look at the Mysterious Red Mercury," *Barron's*, February 15, 1993, p. 15. A detailed account of the Kidger murder investigation can be found in Peter Hounam and Steve McQuillan, *The Mini-Nuke Conspiracy: Mandela's Nuclear Nightmare* (London: Faber and Faber, 1995).

2. Hansin Zi, "The Red Mercury Murders," *Esquire*, November 1995, pp. 41–48.

3. Personal conversation with a former Bulgarian intelligence official, December 2007.

4. Zipser, "A Hard Look at the Mysterious Red Mercury," p. 15.

5. Ibid.

6. Sam Cohen, *Shame: Confessions of the Father of the Neutron Bomb* (self-published through Xlibris, 2000), p. 450.

7. Former KGB official in personal conversation with the author.

8. Frank Barnaby, "Red Mercury: Is There a Pure Fusion Bomb for Sale?" *Jane's International Defense Review* 27, no. 6 (June 1994): 79–81.

9. Charles Richards and Harvey Morris, "The Hunt for Red Mercury," *Independent*, April 13, 1992.

10. Ibid.

11. Cohen, *Shame: Confessions of the Father of the Neutron Bomb*, p. 450.

12. Barnaby, "Red Mercury: Is There a Pure Fusion Bomb for Sale?"

13. Richard Miller, "Special Report: DDP 95," 1995, http://saturniancosmology.org/files/cata/ddp95.txt.

14. Ibid.

15. Barnaby, "Red Mercury: Is There a Pure Fusion Bomb for Sale?" p. 79.

16. Personal conversation with a former Bulgarian intelligence official, December 2007.

17. "Red Mercury Seen as a 'Fiction Used in Money Laundering Scam,'" *Pravda*, July 1, 1993.

18. Vladimir Orlov, "Black Holes of Red Mercury," *Moscow News*, August 11, 1993.

19. Alexei Tarasov, "Strategic Metals Take Illicit Routes Abroad: Reports of 'Red Mercury' Smuggling Appear Bogus, but Criminal Interest in Acquiring Other Radioactive Substances Is Very Real," *Izvestia*, February 2, 1993.

20. Zipser, "A Hard Look at the Mysterious Red Mercury."

21. Tarasov, "Strategic Metals Take Illicit Routes Abroad."

22. Rob Edwards, "Cherry Red and Very Dangerous," *New Scientist*, April 29, 1995, http://sci-tech-archive.net/archive/sci-chem/ 2006-08/msg00033.html.

23. Ibid.

24. Christopher Ruddy, "Bomb Inventor Says U.S. Defenses Suffer Because of Politics: Interview with Neutron Bomb Investor," *Tribune-Review*, June 15, 1997.

25. Teller is quoted in Cohen, *Shame: Confessions of the Father of the Neutron Bomb*, pp. 446–47.

26. Ibid., p. 447.

CHAPTER 9. LEBED'S LOST LUGGAGE

1. Cary Sublette, "Alexander Lebed and Suitcase Nukes," http://nuclearweaponsarchive.org/News/Lebedbomb.html (last changed May 18, 2002).

2. Ibid.

3. Ibid.

4. Ibid.

5. Ibid. See also Craig Cerniello, "Russian Officials Deny Claims of Missing Nuclear Weapons," Arms Control Association, http://www.armscontrol.org/act/1997_09/Lebedsept.asp.

6. Robert Windrem, "Did Soviets Build Mini A-Bombs? A Look at What Happened to Miniature Atomic Bombs," NBC News, September 1997, http://www.msnbc.com/news/113675.asp.

7. "'Suitcase Nukes:' Permanently Lost Luggage," n.d., http://exodus2006.com/nukes.htm (accessed September 25, 2007), citing Viktor Myasnikov, "Eto Byl He Hash 'Chemodanchik' (This Wasn't Our Suitcase)," *Nezavisimaya Gazata*, February 11, 2004.

8. Curt Weldon, "Opening Comments by Representative Curt Weldon before the House Military Research and Development Sub-Committee Hearing," US Congress, January 24, 2000.

9. Kai Bird and Martin J. Sherwin, *American Prometheus: The Triumph and Tragedy of J. Robert Oppenheimer* (New York: Random House, 2005), p. 349.

10. The story is related in Gregg Herken, *Brotherhood of the Bomb: The Tangled Lives of Robert Oppenheimer, Ernest Lawrence, and Edward Teller*, chap. 18, n. 92 (New York: Henry Holt and Company, 2002). This version of the footnote, however, appears only in the online version of the book.

11. James Martin Center for Nonproliferation Studies, "'Suitcase Nukes:' A Reassessment," *CNS*, September 23, 2002, pp. 3–13, http://cns.miis.edu/pubs/week/020923.htm.

12. Ibid. Also, author's conversations with US intelligence officials, January 2007.

13. Andrew Cockburn and Leslie Cockburn, *One Point Safe* (New York: Doubleday, 1997).

14. Bruce G. Blair, "Loose Cannon," *National Interest* (Summer 1998), posted on the Brookings Institution Web site, http://brookings.edu/articles/1998/summer_defense_blair.aspx?p=1.

15. Stanislav Lunev, *Through the Eyes of the Enemy: The Autobiography of Stanislav Lunev* (Washington, DC: Regnery Publishing, 1998).

16. Lunev testified before the House Military Research and Development Subcommittee on August 4, 1998, and again before the House Government Reform Committee on January 24, 2000.

17. Sublette, "Alexander Lebed and Suitcase Nukes," pp. 3–5. See also Curt Weldon, *Countdown to Terror: The Top Secret Information That Could Prevent the Next Terrorist Attack . . . and How the CIA Has Ignored It* (Washington, DC: Regnery Publishing, 2005).

18. Christopher Ruddy, "Col. Lunev's Advise [*sic*] Heeded–President Bush Draws Up Nuclear Plans," citing September 24, 2001, column by Stanislav Lunev, http://www.autentico.org/oa09612.php.

19. Ibid., citing October 16, 2001, column by Lunev.

20. "Sources Claim Bin-Laden Has Acquired Nukes from FSU," *Al-Hayah* (London), October 6, 1998, FBIS document no. FTS 19981006000679.

21. "Report Links Bin-Ladin, Nuclear Weapons," *Al-Watan Al-'Arabi*, November 13, 1998, FBIS document no. FTS 1998113001081.

22. "DEBKA: Secret Services Think Key to Bin Ladin's Nuclear Capability Lies in Spain," Jerusalem DEBKA-Net-Weekly, October 12, 2001, FBIS document no. GMP 20010102000065.

23. Youssef Bodansky, *Chechen Jihad: Al Qaeda's Training Ground and the Next Wave of Terror* (New York: HarperCollins, 2007), pp. 102–103.

CHAPTER 10. THE "NEW TERRORISM"

1. Paul Wilkinson, *Terrorist Targets and Tactics: New Risks to World Order* (London: Research Institute for the Study of Conflict and Terrorism, 1990).

2. Bruce Hoffman, *Holy Terror: The Implications of Terrorism Motivated by a Religious Imperative* (Santa Monica, CA: RAND Corporation, 1993).

3. David Kaplan and Andrew Marshall, *The Cult at the End of the World: The Incredible Story of Aum* (London: Arrow Books, 1996); D. W. Brackett, *Holy Terror: Armageddon in Tokyo* (New York: Weatherhill, 1996); and Robert Jay Lifton, *Destroying the World to Save It: Aum Shinrikyo, Apocalyptic Violence, and the New Global Terrorism* (New York: Henry Holt & Company, 1999).

4. Mark Juergensmeyer, "Terror Mandated by God," *Terrorism and Political Violence* 9, no. 2 (Summer 1997): 16–23.

5. Ashton B. Carter, John Deutch and Philip Zelikow, "Cata-

strophic Terrorism: Tackling the New Danger," *Foreign Affairs* 77, no. 6 (November/December 1998); Richard Falkenrath, "Confronting Nuclear, Biological, and Chemical Terrorism," *Survival* 40, no. 3 (November 1998): 43–65; Walter Laquer, "Terror's New Face," *Harvard International Review* 20, no. 4 (September 1998): 48–51; and Harvey Kushner, ed., *The Future of Terrorism: Violence in the New Millennium* (Thousand Oaks, CA: Sage Publications, 1998).

6. Ian Lesser et al., *Confronting the New Terrorism* (Santa Monica, CA: RAND Corporation, 1999); Jessica Stern, *The Ultimate Terrorist* (Cambridge, MA: Harvard University Press, 1999); and Gavin Cameron, *Nuclear Terrorism: A Threat Assessment for the 21st Century* (New York: St. Martin's Press), 1999.

7. Michael Osterholm and John Schwartz, *Living Terrors: What America Needs to Know about the Coming Bioterrorist Catastrophe* (New York: Delacorte Press, 2000); Anthony Lake, *6 Nightmares: Real Threats in a Dangerous World and How America Can Meet Them* (Boston: Little, Brown, 2000); Mark Juergensmeyer, *Terror in the Mind of God: The Global Rise of Religious Violence* (Berkeley: University of California Press, 2008); and Walter Laquer, *The New Terrorism: Fanaticism and Arms of Mass Destruction* (Oxford: Oxford University Press, 2000).

8. Gideon Rose and James Hoge, eds., *The New Terrorism: Threat and Response* (New York: Foreign Affairs Books, 2001).

9. An excellent analysis of al-Zawahiri's letter to Zarqawi is Michael Scheuer's "The Zawahiri-Zarqawi Letter: Al-Qaeda's Tactical and Theater-of-War Concerns," Washington, DC: Jamestown Foundation, November 14, 2005. Zawahiri's letter was sent to Zarqawi in July 2005. In September, Zarqawi declared "total war" on Shi'ites. See "Leader of Al-Qaeda in Iraq Al-Zarqawi Declares 'Total War' on Shi'ites," Middle East Media Research Institute, Special Dispatch Series, no. 987.

CHAPTER 11. FROM A BALANCE OF TERROR TO A WORLD UNHINGED

1. Richard R. Muller, "The Origins of MAD: A Short History of City-Busting," in *Getting MAD: Nuclear Mutual Assured Destruction, Its Ori-*

gins and Practice, ed. Henry D. Sokolski (Carlisle, PA: Strategic Studies Institute, US Army War College, November 2004), p. 46.

2. National Commission on Terrorism, also known as the Bremer Commission, *Countering the Changing Threat of International Terrorism*, Report of the National Commission on Terrorism Pursuant to Public Law 277, 105th Congress, Washington, DC, 2000.

3. Commission to Assess the Organization of the Federal Government to Combat the Proliferation of Weapons of Mass Destruction, also known as the Deutch Commission, *Combating Proliferation of Weapons of Mass Destruction*, Report Pursuant to Public Law 293, 104th Congress, Washington, DC, 1998.

4. National Commission on Terrorism.

5. Advisory Panel to Assess Domestic Response Capabilities for Terrorism Involving Weapons of Mass Destruction, also known as the Gilmore Panel, *Annual Reports to the President and the Congress*, Washington, DC, 1999–2004.

CHAPTER 12. AN AGE OF ALARMS

1. "Zogby Poll: Six Years Later, 81% Still See 9/11 Terrorist Attacks as Most Significant Event of Their Lives," results of a telephone poll conducted between September 6 and 9, 2007, Zogby International, http://www.zogby.com/news/readnews.dbm?ID=1355.

2. Mark A. Schuster et al., "A National Survey of Stress Reactors after the September 11, 2001 Terrorist Attacks," *New England Journal of Medicine* 345, no. 20 (November 15, 2001): 1507–12.

3. A chronology of the post-9/11 jihadist attacks can be found in Brian Michael Jenkins, *Unconquerable Nation: Knowing Our Enemy, Strengthening Ourselves* (Santa Monica, CA: RAND Corporation, 2006).

4. A separate chronology of the jihadists' post-9/11 plots can be found in Jenkins, *Unconquerable Nation*.

5. A chronology of Osama bin Laden's messages through September 7, 2002, can be found in "Chronology–Bin Laden Messages since September 11, 2001," *Reuters*, September 7, 2007. There were four more messages from bin Laden in 2007.

6. President Bush Press Conference, CNN News, October 11, 2001. An excellent, thorough chronology of the warnings and alerts following 9/11 can be found at "Complete 911 Timeline," compiled by the Center for Cooperative Research, http://cooperativeresearch.org/timeline.jsp ?timeline=complete_911_timelinecomplete911_timeline_war_on_terror ism_outside_iraq=complete_911_timeline_terror-alerts. A chronology of the alerts can also be found at "Homeland Security Advisory System," http://en.wikipedia.org/wiki/homeland_security_advisory_system.

7. "Ashcroft: New Terror Attack Possible," CNN News, October 29, 2001.

8. "Ridge Says Terrorist Attacks 'Could Happen within the Next Few Weeks,'" *Mother Jones*, December 3, 2001, cited in "Complete 911 Timeline."

9. NBC News, January 17, 2002, cited in "Complete 911 Timeline."

10. CNN News, February 12, 2002, cited in "Complete 911 Timeline."

11. Richard Boucher, US Department of State, March 27, 2002, cited in "Complete 911 Timeline."

12. CNN News, May 20, 2002, cited in "Complete 911 Timeline."

13. "Complete 911 Timeline."

14. Ibid.

15. Ibid.

16. *Washington Post*, September 10, 2002, cited in "Complete 911 Timeline."

17. ABC News, January 6, 2003; CBC News, January 2, 2003, and other stories, all cited in "Complete 911 Timeline."

18. CNN News, February 7, 2003, cited in "Complete 911 Time-line."

19. "Complete 911 Timeline."

20. Ibid.

21. CNN News, May 20, 2003, cited in "Complete 911 Timeline."

22. Department of Homeland Security Advisory, September 5, 2003, cited in "Complete 911 Timeline."

23. CBS News, November 21, 2003, cited in "Complete 911 Timeline."

24. "British Airways Cancels Flight from London to D.C.," CNN .com, January 1, 2004, http://www.cnn.com/2004/us/01/01/plane .screened/index.html; "Another British Airways Flight Cancelled," *Jihad*

Watch, January 1, 2004, http://www.jihadwatch.org/archives/000540 .php; Ray Suarez, "Security Alert," PBS News, January 2, 2004, http:// www.pbs.org/newshour/bb/terrorism/jan-jun04/flights_01-02.html.

25. Eric Lichtblau, "Airlines Ground 7 Flights to U.S. over Concerns About Terrorism," *New York Times*, February 1, 2004.

26. "U.S. Warns of Terror Threat to Buses, Rail Lines," PBS News, April 2, 2004.

27. CBS News, June 14, 2004, cited in "Complete 911 Timeline."

28. "Financial Sector Is Put on High Alert," *Washington Post*, August 8, 2004.

29. Robert Block, "U.S. Heightens Mass-Transit Alert," *Wall Street Journal*, July 8, 2005.

30. Josh Getlin, "New York Steps Up Subway Security," *Los Angeles Times*, October 7, 2005.

31. "Airlines' Terror Plot Disrupted," BBC News, August 10, 2006, http://news.bbc.co.uk/2/hi/uk_news/4778575.stm.

32. The implications of the shift from threat-based to vulnerability-based analysis is discussed in Jenkins, *Unconquerable Nation*.

33. Threat advocacy is discussed in Brian Michael Jenkins, *Unconquerable Nation: Knowing Our Enemy, Strengthening Ourselves* (Santa Monica, CA: RAND Corporation, 2006).

CHAPTER 13. AMERICA THE ANXIOUS

1. Gary Langer, "Poll: Most Americans Say They're Christian," ABC News, July 18, 2001, http://abcnews.go.com/sections/us/daily news/beliefnet_pol_010718.htm. According to a 2002 Gallup Poll, 46 percent of all Americans declared themselves to be evangelical or born-again Christians, cited in Jonathan Kirsch, *A History of the End of the World: How the Most Controversial Book in the Bible Changed the Course of Western Civilization* (New York: HarperCollins, 2008).

2. Charles B. Strozier, *Apocalypse: On the Psychology of Fundamentalism in America* (Boston: Beacon Press, 1994), p. 5.

3. Kirsch, *A History of the End of the World*, p. 226.

4. Strozier, *Apocalypse*, p. 149.

5. Bernard McGinn, *Antichrist: Two Thousand Years of the Human Fascination with Evil* (New York: HarperCollins, 1994), pp. 260–61.

6. Ibid.

7. Ibid., p. 91.

8. Ibid.

9. Hal Lindsey, *The Late Great Planet Earth* (Grand Rapids, MI: Zondervan, 1970).

10. Ibid., p. 185.

11. Tim Lahaye, *The Beginning of the End* (Carol Stream, IL: Tyndale House Publishers, 1972).

12. Tim Lahaye and Ed Hindson, *Global Warming: Are We on the Brink of World War III?* (Eugene, OR: Harvest House Publishers, 2007).

13. Earl Shorris, *The Politics of Heaven: America in Fearful Times* (New York: W. W. Norton & Company, 2007), p. 120.

14. John F. Walvoord, *Armageddon, Oil and the Middle East Crisis* (Grand Rapids, MI: Zondervan, 1990).

15. Mark Hitchcock, *Iran, the Coming Crisis: Radical Islam, Oil and the Nuclear Threat* (Colorado Springs: Waterbrook Press, 2006).

16. John Hagee, *Jerusalem Countdown: A Prelude to War* (Lake Mary, FL: Frontline, 2006), p. 63.

17. Nicholas Guyatt, *Have a Nice Doomsday: Why Millions of Americans Are Looking Forward to the End of the World* (New York: HarperCollins, 2007), p. 251; see also Richard Abanes, *End-Time Visions: The Road to Armageddon* (New York: Four Walls Eight Windows, 1998).

18. Stephen Hunter, *The Day before Midnight* (New York: Bantam Books, 1989); Tony Williamson, *The Doomsday Contract* (New York: Simon and Schuster, 1978); Dominique Lapierre and Larry Collins, *The Fifth Horseman* (New York: Simon and Schuster, 1987); Nicholas Freeling, *Gadget* (New York: Coward, McCann & Geoghegan, 1977); Alistair Maclean, *Goodbye California* (New York: Fawcett Books, 1981); Leonard Sanders, *The Hamlet Warning* (New York: Warner Books, 1976); Sheldon Filger, *The King of Bombs: A Novel about Nuclear Terrorism* (Bloomington, IN: AuthorHouse, 2006); Larry Collins, *The Road to Armageddon* (Beverly Hills, CA: New Millennium Entertainment, 2003); Tom Clancy, *The Sum of All Fears* (New York: Putnam, 1991); Dan Oran and Lonn Hoklin, *Z Warning* (New York: Ballantine Books, 1979).

19. Dinah Birch, "A Brief History of the Future," *Times Literary Supplement*, no. 5470, February 1, 2008, pp. 19–20.

20. Kai Bird and Martin J. Sherwin, *American Prometheus: The Triumph and Tragedy of J. Robert Oppenheimer* (New York: Random House, 2005), p. 349.

21. Philip Wylie, *The Smuggled Atom Bomb* (New York: Avon, 1951).

22. Philip Wylie, *Tomorrow* (New York: Rinehart, 1954).

23. Jamie Glazov, "An American Hiroshima?–Interview with Douglas Farah," *FrontPageMagazine.com*, August 2, 2005, http://www.frontpagemag.com/Artciles/Printable.aspx?GUID={E15638F6-CD54-4AFA-8C19-DDEB25E23AEB}.

24. Filger, *The King of Bombs.*

25. Sanders, *The Hamlet Warning.*

26. Ian Fleming, *Thunderball* (New York: Viking Press, 1961).

27. Max Barclay, *Red Mercury* (West Hollywood, CA: Dove Books, 1996).

28. P. D. Smith, *Doomsday Men: The Real Dr. Strangelove and the Dream of the Superweapon* (London: Penguin Books, 2007), pp. 197–204.

29. H. G. Wells, *The World Set Free* (London: Macmillan and Co., 1914)

30. Smith, *Doomsday Men*, p. 77.

31. Commission to Assess the Organization of the Federal Government to Combat the Proliferation of Weapons of Mass Destruction, also known as the Deutch Commission, *Combating Proliferation of Weapons of Mass Destruction*, Report Pursuant to Public Law 293, 104th Congress, Washington, DC, 1998.

32. Anthony Lake, *6 Nightmares: Real Threats in a Dangerous World and How America Can Meet Them* (Boston: Little, Brown, 2000).

33. Director of National Intelligence, *Iran: Nuclear Intentions and Capabilities* (Washington, DC: November 2007).

34. The quote is from the 1933 inaugural address of President Franklin Delano Roosevelt in which Roosevelt famously remarked "that the only thing we have to fear is fear itself–nameless, unreasoning, unjustified terror, which paralyzes needed efforts to convert retreat into advance."

35. Brigitte L. Nacos, Yaeli Bloch-Elkon, and Robert Y. Shapiro, "Post-9/11 Terrorism Threats, News Coverage, and Public Perceptions

in the United States," *International Journal of Conflict and Violence* 1, no. 2: 105–26.

36. Susan D. Moeller, *Media Coverage of Weapons of Mass Destruction: May 5–26, 1998; October 11–31, 2002; May 1–21, 2003* (College Park, MD: Center for International and Security Studies at Maryland, University of Maryland, 2004), p. iii.

CHAPTER 14. THE FIRST TERRORIST NUCLEAR POWER

1. Raphael Patai, *The Arab Mind* (New York: HatherLeigh Press, 1973; rev. ed., 2002), p. 63.

2. Ibid., p. 64.

3. Ibid., p. 67.

4. Ibid., p. 68.

5. Interview with Osama bin Laden, al-Jazeera, December 1998.

6. Peter Bergen, *The Osama bin Laden I Know: An Oral History of al Qaeda's Leader* (New York: Simon and Schuster), citing Abu Walid al Misri, editor of *Al Imava*, the Arabic-language magazine of the Taliban, pp. 341–42.

7. Hamid Mir, "Osama Claims He Has Nukes: If US Uses N-Arms It Will Get Same Response," *Dawn*, November 10, 2001, Internet ed., http://www/dawn.com/2001/11/10/top1.htm.

8. Bruce Lawrence, ed., *Messages to the World: The Statements of Osama bin Laden* (London: Verso, 2005), p. 42.

9. Ibid.

10. George W. Bush, "No Nation Can Be Neutral in This Conflict," remarks by the president to the Warsaw Conference on Combating Terrorism, Washington, DC, the White House, November 6, 2001.

11. Mir, "Osama Claims He Has Nukes," p. 3.

12. Lawrence, *Messages to the World*, p. 142.

13. Mir's interview was aired on Australian Television on March 22, 2004. A partial transcript of the interview was released and broadcast on Fox News and other outlets on March 21. "Report: Al Qaeda Has Nukes," http://www.foxnews.com/story/0,2933,114760,00.html.

14. Ibid.

15. Mir provided this account in an interview with author Paul L. Williams and David Dastych. This version appeared, "Osama Alive, Well, Armed with Nukes," *WorldNetDaily*, April 21, 2006, http://www.worldministries.org/prophecynewsarticles/america/060421_osama_alive_well_armed_w_nukes.htm.

16. Suleiman Abu Gheith, "'Why We Fight America': Al-Qa'ida Spokesman Explains September 11 and Declares Intentions to Kill 4 Million Americans with Weapons of Mass Destruction," *In the Shadow of Lances*, posted online at the Center for Islamic Research and Studies, www.alneda.com; excerpts posted by *MEMRI*, June 12, 2002, no. 388, http://www.memri/org/bin/opener.cgi?page=archives&ID=sp38802.

17. Nasir bin Hamd al-Fahd, "A Treatise on the Legal Status of Using Weapons of Mass Destruction against Infidels," May 2003, http://www.carnegieendowment.org/static/npp/fatwa.pdf.

18. George Tenet, *At the Center of the Storm: My Years at the CIA* (New York: HarperCollins, 2007), p. 274.

19. Charles Meade and Roger C. Molander, *Considering the Effects of a Catastrophic Terrorist Attack* (Santa Monica, CA: RAND Corporation, 2006).

20. "Sources Claim Bin-Laden Has Acquired Nukes from FSU," *Al-Hayah*.

21. "Report Links Bin-Ladin, Nuclear Weapons," *Al-Watan Al-Arabi*.

22. DEBKA-file, "Secret Services Think Key to Bin Laden's Nuclear Capability Lies in Spain," *DebkaNetWeekly*, October 12, 2001.

23. David Smigielski, *A Review of the Suitcase Nuclear Bomb Controversy* (Washington, DC: Partnership for Global Security, 2003), p. 9, citing Youssef Bodansky, "Bin Laden Has Several Nuclear Suitcases," October 25, 1999.

24. Sara Daly, John Parachini, and William Rosenau, *Aum Shinrikyo, Al Qaeda, and the Kinshasa Reactor: Implications for Combating Nuclear Terrorism* (Santa Monica, CA: RAND Corporation, 2005), p. 40, citing Adam Nathan and David Leppard, "Al Qaeda's Men Held Secret Meeting to Build Dirty Bomb–Bin Laden's Nuclear Plot–War on Terrorism," *Sunday Times* (London), October 14, 2001.

25. Daly et al., *Aum Shinrikyo, Al Qaeda, and the Kinshasa Reactor*, citing *The Frontier Post* (Peshawar), November 20, 2001.

26. Barton Gellmon, "Fears Prompt U.S. to Beef Up Nuclear Terror

Detection Sensors Deployed Near D.C., Borders; Delta Force on Standby," *Washington Post*, March 3, 2002.

27. Ibid.

28. "Does al Qaeda Have 20 Suitcase Nukes?–Author Claims bin Laden Purchased Them in '98 from Ex-KGB Agents for $30 Million," *WorldNetDaily*, posted October 2, 2002, reposted at http://www.ki4u .com/loose_nukes.htm.

29. Paul L. Williams, *Al Qaeda: Brotherhood of Terror* (Indianapolis: Alpha Books, 2002).

30. Ibid.

31. "Does al Qaeda Have 20 Suitcase Nukes?"

32. DEBKA-file, "Italian *Il Giornale*: Al Qaeda Threatens to Nuke New York on February 2," December 31, 2003, http://www.debka .com/article_print.php?aid=757.

33. Paul L. Williams, *Osama's Revenge: The Next 9/11–What the Media and the Government Haven't Told You* (Amherst, NY: Prometheus Books, 2004).

34. Ibid.

35. "Report: Al Qaeda Has Nukes."

36. "'EOM' Threatens Nuclear Destruction of New York, Washington, Baltimore, and Miami on August 5th," http://www.spiritoftruth .org/nuclearterrorism.htm.

37. Douglas Jehl, "U.S. Aides Cite Worry on Qaeda Infiltration from Mexico," *New York Times*, February 17, 2005.

38. Curt Weldon, *Countdown to Terror: The Top Secret Information That Could Prevent the Next Terrorist Attack . . . and How the CIA Has Ignored It* (Washington, DC: Regnery Publishing, 2005).

39. Jay Solomon and Andrew Higgins, "Intelligence Factor: Exiled Iranian Has Another Run as U.S. Informant; Mr. Ghorbanifar Resurfaces with Material on Tehran after His Iran-Contra Role; Concern He's a New Chalabi," *Wall Street Journal*, July 13, 2006.

40. Paul L. Williams, *The Al Qaeda Connection: International Terrorism, Organized Crime, and the Coming Apocalypse* (Amherst, NY: Prometheus Books, 2005), p. 192.

41. Ibid., pp. 193–94.

42. Ibid., p. 194.

43. "Bin Laden Expert Steps Forward," *60 Minutes*, CBS News, November 14, 2002.

44. Ryan Mauro, "Al-Qaeda's Hidden Arsenal and Sponsors: Interview with Hamid Mir," *World Threats.com*, May 2006, p. 2, http://www.worldthreats.com/general_information/aqarsenal.htm.

45. Ibid.

46. Ibid.

47. Ibid., p. 3.

48. Ibid., p. 4.

49. "Hamid Mir Says Atta Tape Is Al-Qaeda's Signal to Strike!" *Gateway Pundit*, October 1, 2006, http://gatewaypundit.blogspot.com/2006/10/hamid_mir_says_attatape_is_al_qaedas.html.

50. "Video of 9/11 Ringleader Muhammed Atta Posted by British News Site," *USA Today*, October 1, 2006.

51. "Hamid Mir Says Atta Tape Is al Qaeda's Signal to Strike!"

52. "Al-Qaeda's Mr. Nuclear to Head Fresh Attack on U.S.," September 12, 2006, http://www.freerepublic.com/focus/f-news/1700319/posts.

53. "Prepared Testimony of Attorney General John Ashcroft: The Department of Justice's Efforts to Combat Terrorism," Senate Judiciary Committee, Washington, DC, June 8, 2004.

54. "Wanted: Adnan Jumaa for Suspected Nuclear Attack on US," *Gateway Pundit*, September 12, 2006, http://gatewaypundit.blogspot.com/2006/09/wanted-adnan-jumaa-for-suspected.html.

55. Kerry Fox, "Next Attack Imminent: Muslims Ordered to Leave US," *Kerry Fox Live*, September 16, 2006, http://kerryfoxlive.com/worldpress/?p=3412.

56. Vikram Dodd, "Al-Qaida Plotting Nuclear Attack on UK, Officials Warn," *Guardian*, November 14, 2006.

57. Tenet, *At the Center of the Storm.*

58. Ibid., pp. 270–71.

59. Ibid., p. 276.

60. "Interview with Vice President Dick Cheney," *Face the Nation*, CBS News, April 15, 2007.

61. Lin Noueihed, "Qaeda's Zawahiri Threatens More Attacks in UK," *Reuters*, July 11, 2007.

62. IntelCenter, *al-Qaeda Messaging Statistics (QMS) v3.3* (Alexandria, VA: IntelCenter, September 9, 2007).

63. Ibid.

64. James Gordon Week, "Qaeda Vid of Burning Capitol Stirs Terror Fears," *New York Daily News*, June 14, 2007.

65. Director of National Intelligence, *National Intelligence Estimate: The Terrorist Threat to the U.S. Homeland* (Washington, DC: July 2007).

66. Ibid.

67. "US Concern at al-Qaeda Strength," BBC News, July 7, 2007, http://news/bbc/co/uk/gp/pr/fr/-2/hi/americas/6294526.stm.

68. Ibid.

69. Paul Williams, "Bin Laden Biographer: American Media Altered bin Laden's Latest Message," *New Media Journal*, September 12, 2007, http://www.freerepublic.com/focus/f-news/1895171/posts.

70. DEBKA-file, "Exclusive: New Al Qaeda Threat of Radioactive Truck Attack on New York, Los Angeles, Miami," August 10, 2007.

71. Ibid.

72. Ibid.

73. Katherine Shrader, "Officials Worry of Summer Terror Attack," Associated Press, July 10, 2007; see also "Chertoff's Gut, Chicago Tribune," *In Case You Missed It*, DHS Public Liaison Office, July 12, 2007.

74. "Chertoff: We're Preparing for Nuclear Attack," Newsmax.com, September 10, 2007, http://www.newsmax.com/newsfront/chertoff _nuclear/2007/09/10/31560.html.

75. Mark Hosenball and Jeffrey Bartholet, "We Are Going to Get Hit Again: The Head of the National Counterterrorism Center Speaks Out on Al Qaeda's Plans, America's Readiness—and the Nature of the War on Terror," *Newsweek*, August 27, 2007.

76. Michael Hayden, "Remarks before the Council on Foreign Relations," September 7, 2007.

77. Yaakov Lappin, "Al-Qaeda Trying to Go Nuclear," *Israel News*, May 25, 2007, http://www.ynetnews.com/articles/0,7340,L-3404467 ,00.html.

78. Ibid.

79. "Third Al Qaeda Video Calls for 'Climate of Fear,'" ABC News, September 17, 2007.

CHAPTER 15. IS DETERRENCE DEAD?

1. David M. Kunsman and Douglas B. Lawson, *A Primer on U.S. Strategic Nuclear Policy* (Albuquerque, NM: Sandia National Laboratories, 2001), p. 73, citing Richard W. Mies, "Deterrence in the 21st Century," Army War College Symposium, December 8, 1999.

2. Madeleine Albright, *Memo to the President Elect: How We Can Restore America's Reputation and Leadership* (New York: HarperCollins, 2008), p. 145.

3. John O. Edwards, "Gen. Franks Doubts Constitution Will Survive WMD Attack," Newsmax.com, November 21, 2003, http://archive.newsmax.com/archives/articles/2003/11/20/185048.shtml.

4. Brian Michael Jenkins, *International Terrorism: A New Mode of Conflict* (Los Angeles: Crescent Publications, 1974).

5. For a fascinating inquiry into British reactions to the intended terror of the Blitz, see Peter Stansky, *The First Day of the Blitz: September 7, 1940* (New Haven, CT: Yale University Press, 2007).

6. Kunsman and Lawson, *A Primer on U.S. Strategic Nuclear Policy.*

7. Amitai Etzioni, *Pre-empting Nuclear Terrorism in a New Global Order* (London: Foreign Policy Centre, 2004).

8. Caitlin Talmadge, "Deterring a Nuclear 9/11," *Washington Quarterly* 30, no. 2 (Spring 2007): 21–32.

9. Anders Corr, *Retaliation against Nuclear Terror: A Negligence Doctrine* (Cambridge, MA: Harvard University Press, 2004).

10. David P. Auerswald, "Deterring Nonstate WMD Attacks," *Political Science Quarterly* 121, no. 4 (2006): 544–45.

11. Thomas C. Schelling, "An Astonishing Sixty Years: The Legacy of Hiroshima," Nobel Prize lecture, December 8, 2005.

12. Ibid.

13. Ibid.

14. William Quandt, Fuad Jabber, and Ann Lesch, *The Politics of Palestinian Nationalism* (Berkeley: University of California Press, 1973).

15. Paul K. Davis and Brian Michael Jenkins, *Deterrence and Influence in Counterterrorism: A Component in the War on al Qaeda* (Santa Monica, CA: RAND Corporation, 2002).

16. Ibid.

CHAPTER 16. A SELF-SUSTAINING FISSION OF FEAR

1. John McPhee, *The Curve of Binding Energy* (New York: Farrar, Straus and Giroux, 1973), p. 2.
2. Lydia Saad, "Most Americans Say Lives Not 'Permanently Changed' by 9/11," Gallup News Service, September 11, 2006.
3. Harris Poll, "The War on Terror: What Is It? Who Are Our Enemies and How Likely Are Different Types of Terrorist Attacks in the United States?" Harris Interactive, June 22, 2007, http://www.harris interactive.com/harris_poll/index.asp?PID=776.
4. Personal communication from Henry D. Sokolski to the author, November 16, 2007.
5. Graham Allison, "The Three 'No' Knows," *National Interest Online*, November 11, 2007, http://www.nationalinterest.org/article .aspx?id=16004.
6. Ibid.
7. Ibid.
8. Graham Allison, *Nuclear Terrorism: The Ultimate Preventable Catastrophe* (New York: Henry Holt and Company, 2004) and personal communications with the author. Although Allison adopts an urgent tone of advocacy, this remains one of the volumes on nuclear terrorism.
9. "Buffett Predicts Nuclear Attack," Associated Press, May 7, 2002.
10. The survey was conducted by the author via e-mail and in person at various meetings of government officials, analysts, and scholars dealing with terrorism in Santa Monica, Washington, Orlando, London, and Copenhagen during the late summer and early fall of 2007. Respondents were asked to write brief answers to the two questions: 1. What is the probability of a successful terrorist nuclear explosion (not a "dirty bomb") in the next ten years? 2. Why, in your view, hasn't it yet occurred?
11. Michael A. Levi and Graham T. Allison, "How Likely Is a Nuclear Terrorist Attack on the United States?" *Council on Foreign Relations*, April 20, 2007, at http://www.cfr.org/publication/13097/how _likely_is_a_nuclear_terrorist_attack_on_the_United_States.html.
12. The origins and consequences of the "one percent doctrine" are

examined in detail in Ron Suskind, *The One Percent Doctrine: Deep inside America's Pursuit of Its Enemies since 9/11* (New York: Simon and Schuster, 2006).

13. The latter quote comes from a review of Suskind's book by Michiko Kakutani, "Personality, Ideology and Bush's Terror Wars," *New York Times,* June 20, 2006.

14. Martha Stout, *The Paranoia Switch: How Terror Rewires Our Brains and Reshapes Our Behavior—and How We Can Reclaim Our Courage* (New York: Farrar, Straus and Giroux, 2007), pp. 51–57.

15. Joseph Cirincione, *Bomb Scare: The History and Future of Nuclear Weapons* (New York: Columbia University Press, 2007).

16. Stout, *The Paranoia Switch,* pp. 77–83.

17. James Breckenridge and Philip Zimbardo, "The Strategy of Terrorism and the Psychology of Mass-Mediated Fear" in *Psychology of Terrorism* (Oxford: Oxford University Press, 2007), pp. 116–33.

18. Irwin Redlener, *Americans at Risk: Why We Are Not Prepared for Megadisasters and What We Can Do Now* (New York: Alfred A. Knopf, 2006), pp. 72–73.

19. Ibid., p. 73.

20. Nicholas D. Kristof, "An American Hiroshima," *New York Times,* August 11, 2004.

21. Roland Watson, "The Destructive Effects of a Nuclear Suitcase Bomb," Lew Rockwell.com, 2002, http://www.lewrockwell.com/watson/watson27.html.

22. Charles Meade and Roger C. Molander, *Considering the Effects of a Catastrophic Terrorist Attack* (Santa Monica, CA: RAND Corporation, 2006).

23. Graham Allison invites readers of his book and others to visualize the consequences of a nuclear explosion "in the city of their choice" at www.nuclearterror.org, "where concentric circles of destruction are mapped for a portfolio of plausible nuclear terrorist attacks."

24. Michael D. Gordin, *Five Days in August: How World War II Became a Nuclear War* (Princeton, NJ: Princeton University Press, 2007), pp. 85–87.

CHAPTER 17. A BRILLIANT YELLOW LIGHT

1. This description of the explosion has been taken from an eyewitness account of the atomic bombing of Hiroshima. See Father Johannes Siemes, "The Atomic Bombing of Hiroshima," *War Times Journal,* http://www.wtj.com/archives/hiroshima.htm.

2. In 2006, Colorado congressman Tom Tancredo said that "the U.S. could take out Islamic holy sites if Muslim fundamentalist terrorists attacked the country with nuclear weapons." See "Tancredo: If They Nuke Us, Bomb Mecca," Associated Press, July 18, 2005.

3. Anthony Cordesman has prepared a briefing examining a possible nuclear exchange between Israel and Iran. See Anthony H. Cordesman, *Iran, Israel and Nuclear War: An Illustrative Scenario Analysis* (Washington, DC: Center for Strategic and International Studies, November 19, 2007).

CHAPTER 18. REFLECTIONS ON THE SHADOWS OF DOOM

1. Personal communication to the author from Victor Gilinsky, February 7, 2008.

2. Paul Schulte, *State Sponsored Catastrophic Terrorism (SSCT): A Probabilistic Analysis of an Untried but Conceivable Strategy,* December 11, 2002; also private discussions and correspondence with the author, November 2007.

3. Thomas C. Schelling, *The Strategy of Conflict* (Cambridge, MA: Harvard University Press, 1960).

4. John Kerry King, ed., *International Political Effects of the Spread of Nuclear Weapons* (Washington, DC: US Government Printing Office, 1979).

5. Brian Michael Jenkins, "The Consequences of Nuclear Terrorism," in King, *International Political Effects of the Spread of Nuclear Weapons,* also as P-6373 (Santa Monica, CA: RAND Corporation, 1979). Pages cited are from the RAND paper.

6. Jenkins, "The Consequences of Nuclear Terrorism," pp. 23–26.

7. Ibid., p. 30.
8. Ibid., p. 24.
9. Ibid., p. 25.
10. Ibid., p. 26.
11. Ibid., p. 30.
12. Ibid., pp. 21–22.
13. Ibid., p. 22.

CHAPTER 19. COUNTERING OUR OWN FEAR

1. John McPhee, *The Curve of Binding Energy* (New York: Farrar, Straus and Giroux, 1973), p. 126.

2. Ibid., p. 222.

3. Robert Jungk, *The New Tyranny: How Nuclear Power Enslaves Us* (New York: Grosset & Dunlop, 1979), pp. 152–60.

BIBLIOGRAPHY

Abanes, Richard. *End-Time Visions: The Road to Armageddon?* New York: Four Walls Eight Windows, 1998.

Ad Hoc Advisory Panel on Safeguarding Special Nuclear Materials. *Report of the Advisory Panel on Safeguarding Special Nuclear Material.* Washington, DC: US Government Printing Office, 1967.

Advisory Panel to Assess Domestic Response Capabilities for Terrorism Involving Weapons of Mass Destruction, also known as the Gilmore Panel. *Annual Reports to the President and the Congress,* Washington, DC, 1999–2004.

Albright, David. "Al Qaeda's Nuclear Program: Through the Window of Seized Documents," *Policy Forum Online,* Nautilus Institute, Special Forum, No. 47, November 6, 2002.

Albright, David, Katheryn Buehler, and Holly Higgins. "Bin laden and the Bomb." *Bulletin of the Atomic Scientists* (January/February 2002): 23–24.

Alexander, Yonah, and Milton M. Hoenig. *The New Iranian Leadership: Ahmadinejad, Terrorism, Nuclear Ambition, and the Middle East.* Westport, CT: Praeger Security International, 2008.

———. *Super Terrorism: Biological, Chemical, and Nuclear.* Ardsley, NY: Transnational Publishers, 2001.

Allison, Graham. "Confronting the Specter of Nuclear Terrorism."

Annals of the American Academy of Political and Social Science 607, no. 1 (September 2006).

———. "A Nuclear Terrorism Report Card." *National Interest*, no. 83 (Spring 2006).

———. *Nuclear Terrorism: The Risks and Consequences of the Ultimate Disaster.* London: Constable, 2006.

———. *Nuclear Terrorism: The Ultimate Preventable Catastrophe.* New York: Henry Holt and Company, 2004.

———. "The Ongoing Failure of Imagination." *Bulletin of the Atomic Scientists* (September/October 2006): 35–45.

———. "The Three 'No' Knows." *National Interest Online*, November 11, 2007. http://www.nationalinterest.org/article.aspx?id=16004.

Allison, Graham, et al. *Avoiding Nuclear Anarchy: Containing the Threat of Loose Russian Nuclear Weapons and Fissile Material.* Cambridge, MA: MIT Press, 1996.

Apikyan, Samuel, and David Diamond, eds. *Countering Nuclear and Radiological Terrorism. Proceedings of the NATO Advanced Research Workshop on Countering Nuclear and Radiological Terrorism, Yerevan, Armenia, 2–6 October 2005.* Dordrecht: Springer. Published in cooperation with NATO Public Diplomacy Division, 2006.

Auer, Catherine, Linda Rothstein, and Jonas Siegel. "Rethinking Doomsday." *Bulletin of the Atomic Scientists* (November/December 2004): 36–41, 44–47, 73.

Auerswald, David P. "Deterring Nonstate WMD Attacks." *Political Science Quarterly* 121, no. 4 (2006): 543–68.

Baker, David. *Biological, Nuclear, and Chemical Weapons.* Vero Beach, FL: Rourke Publishers, 2006.

Barnaby, Frank. *How to Build a Nuclear Bomb: And Other Weapons of Mass Destruction.* New York: Nation Books, 2004.

———. "Red Mercury: Is There a Pure Fusion Bomb for Sale?" *Jane's International Defense Review* 27, no. 6 (June 1994): 79–81.

Barnard, Paul D. "Super Terrorism: Biological, Chemical, and Nuclear." Book review. *Security Management* 46, no. 8 (August 2002): 122.

Bass-Golod, Gail V., and Brian Michael Jenkins. *A Review of Recent Trends in International Terrorism and Nuclear Incidents Abroad.* Santa Monica, CA: RAND, N-1979-SL, 1983.

Bass-Golod, Gail V., et al. *Motivations and Possible Actions of Potential Criminal Adversaries of U.S. Nuclear Programs.* Santa Monica, CA: RAND Corporation, 1980.

Beckman, Peter R. *Nuclear Weapons, Nuclear States, and Terrorism.* 4th ed. Cornwall-on-Hudson, NY: Sloan, 2006.

Behrens, Carl, and Mark Holt. *Nuclear Power Plants: Vulnerability to Terrorist Attack.* Washington, DC: Congressional Research Service, February 4, 2005.

Benjamin, Daniel, and Steven Simon. *The Next Attack: The Failure of the War on Terror and a Strategy for Getting It Right.* New York: Henry Holt and Company, 2005.

Beres, Louis Rene. *Terrorism and Global Security: The Nuclear Threat.* Boulder, CO: Westview Press, 1979.

Bergen, Peter. *The Osama bin Laden I Know: An Oral History of al Qaeda's Leader.* New York: Simon and Schuster, 2006.

Bhatia, Shyam, and Daniel McGrovy. *Brighter Than the Baghdad Sun: Saddam Hussein's Nuclear Threat to the United States.* Washington, DC: Regnery Publishing, 2000.

Bongar, Bruce, et al., eds. *Psychology of Terrorism.* Oxford: Oxford University Press, 2007.

Boyer, Paul. *By the Bomb's Early Light: American Thought and Culture at the Dawn of the Atomic Age.* New York: Pantheon Books, 1986.

Brackett, D. W. *Holy Terror: Armageddon in Tokyo.* New York: Weatherhill, 1996.

Breckenridge, James, and Philip Zimbardo. "The Strategy of Terrorism and the Psychology of Mass-Mediated Fear." In *Psychology of Terrorism,* edited by Bruce Bongar et al., 116–33. Oxford: Oxford University Press, 2007.

Brewer, Garry D. "The Terrorist Threat to World Nuclear Programs." *Journal of Conflict Resolution* 31, no. 3 (September 1977): 379–403.

Brians, Paul. *Nuclear Holocausts: Atomic War in Fiction, 1895–1984.* Kent, OH: Kent State University Press, 1987. http://www.wsu.edu/~brians/nuclear.htm.

Broderick, Mick. *Nuclear Movies.* Jefferson, NC: McFarland & Co., 1991.

Bunn, George, Christopher F. Chyba, and William James Perry. *U.S. Nuclear Weapons Policy: Confronting Today's Threats.* Stanford, CA:

Center for International Security and Cooperation, Freeman Spogli Institute for International Studies; Washington, DC: Brookings Institution Press, 2006.

Bunn, Matthew, Anthony Wier, and José Friedman. *The Demand for Black Market Fissile Material.* Cambridge, MA: NTI, 2005. http://www.nti.orgle_research/cnwm/threat/demand.asp.

Butler, Kenley, and Akaki Dvali. "Nuclear Trafficking Hoaxes: A Short History of Scams Involving Red Mercury and Osmium-187." Nuclear Threat Initiative. http://www.nti.org.

Butler, Kenley, Sammy Salama, and Leonard S. "Where Is the Justice?" *Bulletin of the Atomic Scientists* 62, no. 6 (November/December 2006): 25–41, 62–63.

Byman, Daniel. "Do Counterproliferation and Counterterrorism Go Together?" *Political Science Quarterly* 122, no. 1 (Spring 2007): 25–46.

Cameron, Gavin. *Nuclear Terrorism: A Threat Assessment for the 21st Century.* New York: St. Martin's Press, 1999.

Caravelli, Jack. *Nuclear Insecurity: Understanding the Threat from Rogue Nations and Terrorists.* Westport, CT: Praeger Security International, 2008.

Carter, Aston B., John Deutch, and Richard Zelikow. "Catastrophic Terrorism: Tackling the New Danger." *Foreign Affairs* 77, no. 6 (November/December 1998).

Case, David, and Kevin Whitehouse. "Dirty Bombs: A Matter of Time." *NBC International* (Summer 2007): 44–77.

Centre of International Studies, University of Cambridge. *Catastrophic Terrorism: Report of the Meeting Organised by the Centre of International Studies, University of Cambridge, November 18–19, 2002.* Cambridge: University of Cambridge, 2002. http://www.cambridgesecurity.net/pdf/catastrophic_terrorism.pdf.

Cilluffo, Frank J., Sharon L. Cardash, and Gordon Nathaniel Lederman. *Combating Chemical, Biological, Radiological, and Nuclear Terrorism: A Comprehensive Strategy: A Report of the CSIS Homeland Defense Project.* Washington, DC: Center for Strategic and International Studies, 2001.

Cirincione, Joseph. *Bomb Scare: The History and Future of Nuclear Weapons.* New York: Columbia University Press, 2007.

Cirincione, Joseph, Jon B. Wolfsthal, and Miriam Rajkumar. *Deadly Arsenals: Nuclear, Biological and Chemical Threats.* 2nd ed. Washington, DC: Carnegie Endowment for International Peace, 2005.

——. "Cassandra's Conundrum." *National Interest* (November/December 2007): 15–17.

Cohen, Sam. *Shame: Confessions of the Father of the Neutron Bomb.* Philadelphia: Xlibris Corporation, 2000.

"Collective Terror: The Nuclear Movie." *All in the Mind,* ABC Radio International, June 8, 2003. http://www.abc.net.au/rn/allinthemind .stories/2003/872045.htm.

Collins, Myles, and Tracey De Francesco. "Nuclear Black Markets: A Proliferated World." Unpublished paper. Santa Monica, CA: RAND Corporation, 2005.

Commission to Assess the Organization of the Federal Government to Combat the Proliferation of Weapons of Mass Destruction. *Combating Proliferation of Weapons of Mass Destruction.* Washington, DC: US Government Printing Office, July 1999. http://www.fas.org/ spp/starwars/program/deutch/11910book.pdf.

Corcoran, Edward A. *Strategic Approaches to Nuclear Terrorism.* A paper presented at the Round Table on Islamistic Terrorism and Means of Mass Destruction, Wildbad Kreuth, Germany: Hans Seidel Stiftung, January 24–26, 2006. (Paper dated March 12, 2006). http://www .corcorans.org/stuff/nucterror.htm.

Cordesman, Anthony H. *Terrorism, Asymmetric Warfare, and Weapons of Mass Destruction: Defending the U.S. Homeland.* Washington, DC: Center for Strategic and International Studies, 2001.

Corr, Anders. *Retaliation against Nuclear Terror: A Negligence Doctrine.* Cambridge, MA: Harvard University Press, 2004.

CSIS Task Force. *The Nuclear Black Market.* Washington, DC: Center for Strategic and International Studies, 1996.

Daly, Sara, John Parachini, and William Rosenau. *Aum Shinrikyo, Al Qaeda, and the Kinshasa Reactor: Implications of Three Case Studies for Combating Nuclear Terrorism.* Santa Monica, CA: RAND Corporation, 2005. http://www.rand.org/pubs/documented_briefings/ 2005/RAND_DB458.pdf.

Davis, Paul K., and Brian Michael Jenkins. *Deterrence and Influence in*

Counterterrorism: A Component in the War on al Qaeda. Santa Monica, CA: RAND Corporation, 2002.

De Groot, Gerard J. *The Bomb: A Life.* Cambridge, MA: Harvard University Press, 2004.

deLeon, Peter, Brian Jenkins, Konrad Kellen, and Joseph Krofcheck. *Attributes of Potential Adversaries of U.S. Nuclear Programs.* Santa Monica, CA: RAND Corporation, 1978.

Donneley, Thomas. *Bad Options: Or, How I Stopped Worrying and Learned to Live with Loose Nukes.* Nonproliferation Policy Education Center, May 28, 2006. http://www.npec-web.org/Essays/20060528 -Donnelly.pdf.

Drell, Sidney D., and James E. Goodby. *The Gravest Danger: Nuclear Weapons.* Stanford, CA: Hoover Institution Press, 2003.

Ervin, Clark Kent. *Open Target: Where America Is Vulnerable to Attack.* New York: Palgrave Macmillan, 2006.

Estabrooks, Sarah. "Nuclear Terrorism: While the Reality of a Nuclear Terrorist Threat Is Much Clearer in the Wake of September 11, Much Can Be Done to Prevent Terrorists." *Ploughshares Monitor,* December 1, 2001. http://www.thefreelibrary.com/Nuclear +Terrorism%3a+While+the+reality+of+a+nuclear+terrorist +threat+is...-a081220118.

Etzioni, Amitai. *Pre-Empting Nuclear Terrorism in a New Global Order.* London: Foreign Policy Centre, 2004. http://www.gwu.edu/~ccps/ PreemptNucTerr.pdf.

Fahd, Nasir bin Hamd al-. *A Treatise on the Legal Status of Using Weapons of Mass Destruction against Infidels.* May 2003. http://www.carnegie endowment.org/static/npp/fatwa.pdf.

Falkenrath, Richard A. "Confronting Nuclear, Biological, and Chemical Terrorism." *Survival* 40, no. 3 (November 1998): 43–65.

Falkenrath, Richard A., Robert D. Newman, and Bradley A. Thayer. *America's Achilles' Heel: Nuclear, Biological, and Chemical Terrorism and Covert Attack.* BCSIA Studies in International Security. Cambridge, MA: MIT Press, 1998.

Faludi, Susan. *The Terror Dream: Fear and Fantasy in Post-9/11 America.* New York: Metropolitan Books, 2007.

Ferguson, Charles D. *Preventing Catastrophic Nuclear Terrorism.* CSR No. 11. New York: Council on Foreign Relations, March 2006.

Ferguson, Charles D., William C. Potter, and Amy Sands. *The Four Faces of Nuclear Terrorism.* Monterey, CA: Center for Nonproliferation Studies, Monterey Institute of International Studies, 2004.

Fielding, Nick. "Bin Laden's Dirty Bomb Quest Exposed." *Sunday Times,* October 19, 2004.

Filreis, Alan. *Cultural Aspects of Atomic Anxiety.* Philadelphia: University of Pennsylvania, 1999. http://www.writing.upenn.edu/~afilreis/ 50s/atomic-anxieties.html.

Flynn, Stephen. *America the Vulnerable: How the Government Is Failing to Protect Us from Terrorism.* New York: HarperCollins, 2004.

Frantz, Douglas, and Catherine Collins. *The Nuclear Jihadist: The True Story of the Man Who Sold the World's Most Dangerous Secrets . . . and How We Could Have Stopped Him.* New York: Twelve, 2007.

Frost, Robin M. *Nuclear Terrorism after 9/11.* Abingdon, NY: Routledge for the International Institute for Strategic Studies, Adelphi Paper no. 378, 2005.

——. "Terrorist Psychology, Motivation and Strategy." Adelphi Paper no. 378, pp. 41–62.

Gheith, Suleiman Abu. "'Why We Fight America': Al-Qa'ida Spokesman Explains September 11 and Declares Intentions to Kill 4 Million Americans with Weapons of Mass Destruction." *In the Shadow of Lances.* www.alneda.com, June 12, 2002, no. 388. http://www .memri/org/bin/opener.cgi?page=archives&ID=sp38802.

Glassner, Barry. *The Culture of Fear: Why Americans Are Afraid of the Wrong Things.* New York: Perseus Books, 1999.

Gurr, Nadine, and Benjamin Cole. *The New Face of Terrorism: Threats from Weapons of Mass Destruction.* London: I. B. Tauris, 2000.

Guyatt, Nicholas. *Have a Nice Doomsday: Why Millions of Americans Are Looking for the End of the World.* New York: HarperCollins, 2007.

Herron, Kerry G., and Hank C. Jenkins-Smith. *Critical Masses and Critical Choices: Evolving Public Opinion on Nuclear Weapons, Terrorism, and Security.* Pittsburgh: University of Pittsburgh Press, 2006.

Hibbs, Mark. "The Unmaking of a Nuclear Smuggler." *Bulletin of the Atomic Scientists* 62, no. 6 (November/December 2006): 25–41, 62–63.

Higgins, Holly. "A Bomb for the Ummah." *Bulletin of Atomic Scientists* 59, no. 2 (March/April 2003): 49–56.

Hoffman, Bruce. "CBRN Terrorism Post-9/11." In *Terrorism and Weapons of Mass Destruction*, edited by Russel D. Howard and James J. F. Forest. New York: McGraw-Hill, 2007.

——. *Holy Terror: The Implications of Terrorism Motivated by a Religious Imperative*. Santa Monica, CA: RAND Corporation, 1993.

——. *Terrorism in the U.S. and the Potential Threat to Nuclear Facilities*. Santa Monica, CA: RAND Corporation, P-7194, 1986.

Hounam, Peter, and Steve McQuillan. *The Mini-Nuke Conspiracy: Mandela's Nuclear Nightmare*. London: Faber and Faber, 1995.

Howard, Russel D., and James J. F. Forest, eds. *Terrorism and Weapons of Mass Destruction*. New York: McGraw-Hill, 2007.

Ignatius, David. "Portents of a Nuclear Al-Qaeda." *Washington Post*, October 18, 2007. http://www.washingtonpost.com/wp-dyn/content/article/2007/10/71/ar2007101702114_pf.html.

Iklé, Fred Charles. *Annihilation from Within: The Ultimate Threat to Nations*. New York: Columbia University Press, 2006.

Ingram, Timothy H. "Nuclear Hijacking: Now within the Grasp of Any Bright Lunatic." *Washington Monthly*, January 1973.

International Atomic Energy Agency. *Combating Illicit Trafficking in Nuclear and Other Radioactive Material: Reference Manual*. Vienna, Austria: International Atomic Energy Agency, 2007.

International Conference on Illicit Nuclear Trafficking: Collective Experience and the Way Forward. President's Findings. Edinburgh, November 19–20, 2007.

International Institute for Strategic Studies. *Nuclear Black Markets: Pakistan, A. Q. Khan and the Rise of Proliferation Networks—A Net Assessment*. London: IISS, 2007.

Jenkins, Brian Michael. "The Consequences of Nuclear Terrorism." In *International Political Effects of the Spread of Nuclear Weapons*, edited by John Kerry King. Washington, DC: US Government Printing Office, 1979.

——. *International Terrorism: A New Mode of Conflict*, Los Angeles: Crescent Publications, 1974.

——. *The Likelihood of Nuclear Terrorism*. Santa Monica, CA: RAND Corporation, 1985.

———. *Terrorism and the Nuclear Safeguards Issue.* Santa Monica, CA: RAND Corporation, P-5611, March 1979.

———. *Unconquerable Nation: Knowing Our Enemy, Strengthening Ourselves.* Santa Monica, CA: RAND Corporation, 2006.

———. *Will Terrorists Go Nuclear?* Los Angeles: Crescent Publications, 1975.

Juergensmeyer, Mark. *Terror in the Mind of God: The Global Rise of Religious Violence.* Berkeley: University of California Press, 2008.

———. "Terror Mandated by God." *Terrorism and Political Violence* 9, no. 2 (Summer 1997): 16–23.

Jungk, Robert. *The New Tyranny: How Nuclear Power Enslaves Us.* New York: Grosset & Dunlop, 1979.

Kamp, Karl-Heinz. "An Overrated Nightmare: There Are a Lot of Dangers Out There but Terrorists Wielding Nuclear Bombs Probably Isn't One of Them." *Bulletin of the Atomic Scientists* 52, no. 4 (July/August 1996): 30–34.

Kaplan, David E., and Andrew Marshall. *The Cult at the End of the World: The Incredible Story of Aum.* London: Arrow Books, 1996.

Katona, Peter, Michael D. Intriligator, and John P. Sullivan. *Countering Terrorism and WMD: Creating a Global Counter-Terrorism Network.* London: Routledge, 2006.

King, Gilbert. *Dirty Bomb: Weapon of Mass Disruption.* New York: Penguin Group, 2004.

King, John Kerry, ed. *International Political Effects of the Spread of Nuclear Weapons.* Washington, DC: US Government Printing Office, 1979.

Kirby, Alex. "The Kitchen Table Atom Bomb." BBC News Online, June 11, 2002. http://newsbbc.co.uk/2/low/science/nature/2038447.stm.

Kirsch, Jonathan. *A History of the End of the World: How the Most Controversial Book in the Bible Changed the Course of Western Civilization.* New York: HarperCollins, 2006.

Krugler, David F. *This Is Only a Test: How Washington DC Prepared for Nuclear War.* New York: Palgrave Macmillan, 2006.

Kunsman, David M., and Douglas B. Lawson. *A Primer on U.S. Strategic Nuclear Policy.* Albuquerque, NM: Sandia National Laboratories, 2001.

Kupperman, Robert, and Jeff Kamen. *Final Warning: Averting Disaster in the New Age of Terrorism.* New York: Doubleday, 1989.

Kushner, Harvey W., ed. *The Future of Terrorism: Violence in the New Millennium.* Thousand Oaks, CA: Sage Publications, 1998.

Lake, Anthony. *6 Nightmares: Real Threats in a Dangerous World and How America Can Meet Them.* Boston: Little, Brown, 2000.

Lakos, Amos. *The Nuclear Terrorism Threat: A Bibliography.* Monticello, IL: Vance Bibliographies, P-1779, 1985.

Langewiesche, William. *The Atomic Bazaar: The Rise of the Nuclear Poor.* New York: Farrar, Straus and Giroux, 2007.

Laquer, Walter. *The New Terrorism: Fanaticism and the Arms of Mass Destruction.* New York: Oxford University Press, 1999.

Leachman, Robert B., and Phillip Altoff, eds. *Preventing Nuclear Theft: Guidelines for Industry and Government.* New York: Praeger Publishers, 1972.

Leader, Stefan. "Middle East, Osama bin Laden and the Terrorist Search for WMD." *Jane's Intelligence Review* 11, no. 6 (June 1999).

Lee, Rensselaer W., III. *Smuggling Armageddon: The Nuclear Black Market in the Former Soviet Union and Europe.* New York: St. Martin's Griffin, 1998.

Leventhal, Paul L., Sharon Tanzer, and Steven Dolley. *Nuclear Power and the Spread of Nuclear Weapons: Can We Have One without the Other?* London: Brassey's, 2002.

Leventhal, Paul, and Yonah Alexander. *Nuclear Terrorism: Defining the Threat.* Washington, DC: Pergamon-Brassey's, 1986.

——. *Preventing Nuclear Terrorism: The Report and Papers of the International Task Force on Prevention of Nuclear Terrorism.* Lexington, MA: Lexington Books, 1987.

Levi, Michael. *On Nuclear Terrorism.* Cambridge, MA: Harvard University Press, 2007.

——. "Stopping Nuclear Terrorism: The Dangerous Allure of a Perfect Defense." *Foreign Affairs* 87, no. 1 (January/February 2008): 131–40.

Levy, Adrian, and Catherine Scott-Clark. *Deception: Pakistan, the United States, and the Secret Trade in Nuclear Weapons.* New York: Walker & Company, 2007.

Lifton, Robert Jay. *Destroying the World to Save It: Aum Shinrikyo, Apocalyptic Violence, and the New Global Terrorism.* New York: Henry Holt and Company, 1999.

Liolios, Theodore, E. *The Effects of Nuclear Terrorism: Fizzles. Europsis*, November 30, 2002. http://arx.org/abs/physics/0212002.

Loory, Stuart. "Is There an A-Bomb in Your Backyard?" *True*, December 1969.

Marrs, Robert W. *Nuclear Terrorism: Rethinking the Unthinkable*. Honolulu: University Press of the Pacific, 1994–2004.

McCloud, Kimberly, and Matthew Osborne. "WMD Terrorism and Usama bin Laden." *CNS Reports*. Monterey, CA: James Martin Center for Nonproliferation Studies, 2001, including full text of Jamal Ahmad al-Fadl in the United States District Court, Southern District of New York, *United States v. Usama bin Laden et al.*, February 6, 7, and 13, 2001.

McFee, Robin B., and Jerrold B. Leikin. *Toxico-Terrorism: Emergency Response and Clinical Approach to Chemical, Biological, and Radiological Agents*. New York: McGraw-Hill, Health Professions Division, 2008.

McGinn, Bernard. *Antichrist: Two Thousand Years of the Human Fascination with Evil*. New York: HarperCollins, 1994.

McPhee, John. *The Curve of Binding Energy*. New York: Farrar, Straus and Giroux, 1974.

McWilliams, Carey. *Moonlight's Meridian: Nuclear Terrorism and the Undead*. Pittsburgh: Red Lead Press, 2005.

Meade, Charles, and Roger C. Molander. *Considering the Effects of a Catastrophic Terrorist Attack*. Santa Monica, CA: RAND Corporation, 2006.

Medalia, Jonathan E., Richard Baker, and Rensselaer W. Lee. *Nuclear Terrorism*. Washington, DC: Congressional Research Service, Library of Congress, 2004.

Mishra, Rajeesh Kumar. "Nuclear Scientific Community of Pakistan: Clear and Present Danger to Nonproliferation." South Asia Analysis Group. http://www.saay.org/papers7/paper601.html.

Mockaitis, Thomas R. *The "New" Terrorism: Myths and Reality*. Westport, CT: Praeger Security International, 2007.

Moeller, Susan D. *Media Coverage of Weapons of Mass Destruction: May 5–26, 1998; October 11–31, 2002; May 1–21, 2003*. College Park, MD: Center for International and Security Studies at Maryland, University of Maryland, 2004.

Mueller, John. "Apocalypse Later." *National Interest* (November/December 2007): 19–20.

——. "Fearing Fear Itself." *Bulletin of the Atomic Scientists* (November/December 2007): 55–56.

——. *Overblown: How Politicians and the Terrorism Industry Inflate National Security Threats and Why We Believe Them.* New York: Free Press, 2006.

——. "Radioactive Hype." *National Interest* (September/October 2007): 59–61.

——. "Reactions and Overreactions to Terrorism: The Atomic Obsession." Paper delivered at the annual meeting of the American Political Science Association, Chicago, IL, August 31 to September 3, 2007.

Muller, Ronald R. "The Origins of MAD: A Short History of City-Busting." In *Getting MAD: Nuclear Mutual Assured Destruction, Its Origins and Practice,* edited by Henry Sokolski, 46. Carlisle, PA: Strategic Studies Institute, November 2004.

Murakami, Haruki. *Underground: The Tokyo Gas Attack and the Japanese Psyche.* New York: Vintage Books, 2001.

Nacos, Brigitte L., Yaeli Bloch-Elkon, and Robert Y. Shapiro. "Post-9/11 Terrorism Threats, News Coverage, and Public Perceptions in the United States." *International Journal of Conflict and Violence* 1, no. 2: 105–26.

National Commission on Terrorism, also known as the Bremer Commission. *Countering the Changing Threat of International Terrorism.* Report of the National Commission on Terrorism Pursuant to Public Law 277, 105th Congress, Washington, DC, 2000.

National Research Council (US). Committee on Opportunities for U.S.-Russian Collaboration in Combating Radiological Terrorism; National Academies Press (US). *U.S.-Russian Collaboration in Combating Radiological Terrorism.* Washington, DC: National Academies Press, 2007.

Newkey-Burden, Chas. *Nuclear Paranoia.* London: Pocket Essentials, 1988.

Norton, Augustus R., and Martin H. Greenberg. *Studies in Nuclear Terrorism.* Boston: G. K. Hall & Co., 1979.

Nuclear Threat Initiative. "Nuclear Terrorism FAQ." *Washington Post,* September 26, 2007. http://www/washingtonpost.com/wp-dyn/content/article/2007/09/24/ar2007092401154.html.

O'Neill, Kevin. *The Nuclear Terrorist Threat.* Institute for Science and International Security, August 1997.

Orlov, Vladimir. *Addressing the Challenge of Illicit Nuclear Trafficking.* Moscow: Center for Policy Studies in Russia, n.d.

Paul, Anthony. "Detecting the Smokescreen around Chances of Nuclear Terrorism." *Canberra Times,* November 11, 2006.

Pells, Richard. "Not with a Whimper: Visions of Mass Destruction in Fiction and Film." *eJournalUSA.* http://usinfo.state/gov.journals/itps/0305/ijpe/pells.htm.

Ponte, Lowell. "Nuclear Exports from the Former Soviet Union: What's New, What's True." *Arms Control Today* (January/February 1993): 3–10.

——. "This Is an Atom Bomb and We're Not Fooling." *Penthouse,* February 1972.

Potter, William C. "Non-Proliferation Parody." *National Interest* (November/December 2007): 17–19.

Primakov, Yergeny M. *A World Challenged: Fighting Terrorism in the Twenty-First Century.* Washington, DC: Brookings Institution Press, 2004.

Pyszczynski, Tom, Sheldon Solomon, and Jeff Greenberg. *In the Wake of 9/11: The Psychology of Terror.* Washington, DC: American Psychological Association, 2003.

Quayle, Steve. "Can Osama bin Laden Go Nuclear?" Steve Quayle News Alerts, October 10, 2001. http://www.stevequayle.com/news.alert/03_nukes/011010.can.ubl.go.nuclear.html.

Raman, B. "Pakistan & Dangers of Nuclear Jihad." South Asia Analysis Group. http://www.saag.org/papers10/paper904.html.

Reader, Ian. *A Poisonous Cocktail? Aum Shinrikyo's Path to Violence.* Copenhagen, Denmark: NIAS Books, 1996.

Redlener, Irwin. *Americans at Risk: Why We Are Not Prepared for Megadisasters and What We Can Do Now.* New York: Alfred A. Knopf, 2006.

Rees, Martin J. *Our Final Century: Will the Human Race Survive the Twenty-First Century?* New York: Basic Books, 2003.

Rensselaer, W. Lee, III. *Smuggling Armageddon: The Nuclear Black Market in the Former Soviet Union and Europe.* New York: St. Martin's Griffin, 1998.

Richelson, Jeffrey. "Defusing Nuclear Terror." *Bulletin of the Atomic Scientists* (March/April 2002): 38–43.

——. "Nuclear Terror." *Bulletin of the Atomic Scientists* (March/April 2002): 38–43.

Robin, Corey. *Fear: The History of a Political Idea.* Oxford: Oxford University Press, 2004.

Rodionov, Stanislav. "Could Terrorists Produce Low-Yield Nuclear Weapons?" *High-Impact Terrorism: Proceedings of a Russian-American Workshop* (2002). Washington, DC: National Academy of Science, 2002.

Rose, Gideon, and James Hoge, eds. *The New Terrorism: Threat and Response.* New York: Foreign Affairs Books, 2001.

Sandler, Todd, and Kevin Siqueira. "Global Terrorism: Deterrence versus Pre-Emption." *Canadian Journal of Economics* 39, no. 4 (November 2006): 1370–87.

Saradzhyan, Simon. "Russia: Grasping Reality of Nuclear Terror." *BCSIA Discussion Paper 2003-02.* Cambridge, MA: Harvard University, Kennedy School of Government, March 2003.

Schell, Jonathan. *The Seventh Decade: The New Shape of Nuclear Danger.* New York: Metropolitan Books, 2007.

Schelling, Thomas C. "An Astonishing Sixty Years: The Legacy of Hiroshima," Nobel Prize lecture, December 8, 2005.

——. *The Strategy of Conflict.* Cambridge, MA: Harvard University Press, 1960.

Scheuer, Michael. *Through Our Enemies' Eyes: Osama bin Laden, Radical Islam, and the Future of America.* Washington, DC: Brassey's, 2002.

Schram, Martin. *Avoiding Armageddon: Our Future, Our Choice: Companion to the PBS Series from Ted Turner Documentaries.* New York: Basic Books, 2003.

Schulte, Paul. *State Sponsored Catastrophic Terrorism (SSCT): A Probabilistic Analysis of an Untried but Conceivable Strategy.* December 11, 2002.

Schweitzer, Glenn E., with Carole C. Dorsch. *Super-Terrorism: Assassins, Mobsters, and Weapons of Mass Destruction.* New York: Plenum Trade, 1998.

Schwellenbach, Nick. "But Don't Be Afraid of the Dark." *Bulletin of the Atomic Scientists* (September/October 2006): 50–57.

Shaheen, Jack G. *Nuclear War Films.* Carbondale: Southern Illinois University Press, 1978.

Sheppard, Ben, et al. "Terrorism and Dispelling the Myth of a Panic Prone Public." *Journal of Public Health Policy* 27 (2006): 219–45.

Shorris, Earl. *The Politics of Heaven: America in Fearful Times.* New York: W. W. Norton & Company, 2007.

Smigielski, David. *A Review of the Suitcase Nuclear Bomb Controversy.* Washington, DC: Partnership for Global Security, 2003.

Smith, Peter D. *Doomsday Men: The Real Dr. Strangelove and the Dream of the Superweapon.* London: Allen Lane, 2007.

——. "Rethinking Nuclear Terrorism." Paper presented at the Round Table on Islamistic Terrorism and Means of Mass Destruction, Bad/Kreuth, Germany: Hans Seidel Stiftung, January 24–25, 2006.

——. "Too Speculative? Getting Serious about Nuclear Terrorism." *New Atlantis*, no. 14 (Fall 2006): 119–24.

Spyer, Jonathan. "The Al-Qa'ida Network and Weapons of Mass Destruction." *Middle East Review of International Affairs* 8, no. 3 (September 2004): 29–45.

Stanton, John J. "Is the U.S. Prepared for Nuclear Terrorism?" *Security Management* 46, no. 3 (March 2002): 156–58.

Stern, Jessica. *The Ultimate Terrorist.* Cambridge, MA: Harvard University Press, 1999.

Stober, Dan. "No Experience Necessary: The Nth Country Experiment Showed that Three Post-Docs with No Nuclear Knowledge Could Design a Working Atom Bomb." *Bulletin of the Atomic Scientists* (March/April 2003): 57–63.

Stout, Martha. *The Paranoia Switch: How Terror Rewires Our Brains and Reshapes Our Behavior—and How We Can Reclaim Our Courage.* New York: Farrar, Straus and Giroux, 2007.

Strozier, Charles B. *Apocalypse: On the Psychology of Fundamentalism in America.* Boston: Beacon Press, 1994.

Suskind, Ron. *The One Percent Doctrine: Deep Inside America's Pursuit of Its Enemies since 9/11.* New York: Simon and Schuster, 2006.

Talmadge, Caitlin. "Deterring a Nuclear 9/11." *Washington Quarterly* 30, no. 2 (Spring 2007): 21–32.

Tanter, Raymond. *Rogue Regimes: Terrorism and Proliferation.* New York: St. Martin's Griffin, 1999.

Taylor, Theodore B. "Nuclear Power and Nuclear Weapons," July 1996, p. 2. http://www.wagingpeace.org/articles/1996/07/00_taylor_nuclear -power.htm.

Taylor, Theodore B., and Mason Willrich. *Nuclear Theft: Risks and Safeguards.* Cambridge, MA: J. B. Lippincott Company, 1974.

Tenet, George. *At the Center of the Storm: My Years at the CIA.* New York: HarperCollins, 2007.

Tuman, Joseph S. *Communicating Terror: The Rhetorical Dimensions of Terrorism.* Thousand Oaks, CA: Sage Publications, 2003.

Upfal, Mark J. *Terrorism: Biological, Chemical, and Nuclear.* Clinics in Occupational and Environmental Medicine, vol. 2, no. 2. Philadelphia: Saunders, 2003.

US Commission of National Security/21st Century (also known as the Hart-Rudman Commission). *New World Coming: American Security in the 21st Century—Major Themes and Implications.* Washington, DC: September 15, 1999. http://www.nssg.gov.

——. *Road Map for National Security: Imperative for Change.* Washington, DC: February 15, 2001. http://www.nssg.gov.

——. *Seeking a National Strategy: A Concert for Preserving Security and Promoting Freedom.* Washington, DC: April 15, 2000. http://www .nssg.gov.

Venter, Al J. *Allah's Bomb: The Islamic Quest for Nuclear Weapons.* Guilford, CT: Lyons Press, 2007.

Walker, Samuel J. "Regulating against Nuclear Terrorism: The Domestic Safeguards Issue, 1920–79." *Technology and Culture* 42, no. 1 (January 2001): 107–32.

Webster, William H., and Arnaud de Borchgrave. *Wild Atom: Nuclear Terrorism: CSIS Global Organized Crime Report.* Washington, DC: Center for Strategic and International Studies, 1998.

Weldon, Curt. *Countdown to Terror: The Top Secret Information That Could Prevent the Next Terrorist Attack . . . and How the CIA Has Ignored It.* Washington, DC: Regnery Publishing, 2005.

Wesley, Robert. "Al-Qaeda's WMD Strategy after the U.S. Intervention in Afghanistan." *Terrorism Monitor* 3, no. 20 (October 21, 2005).

——. "Al-Qaeda's WMD Strategy prior to the U.S. Intervention in Afghanistan." *Terrorism Monitor* 3, no. 19 (October 7, 2005).

Williams, Paul L. *Al Qaeda: Brotherhood of Terror.* Indianapolis: Alpha Books, 2002.

——. *The al Qaeda Connection: International Terrorism, Organized Crime and the Coming Apocalypse.* Amherst, NY: Prometheus Books, 2005.

——. *The Day of Islam: The Annihilation of America and the Western World.* Amherst, NY: Prometheus Books, 2007.

——. *The Dunces of Doomsday.* Nashville, TN: Cumberland House Publishing, 2006.

——. *Osama's Revenge: The Next 9/11 – What the Media Haven't Told You.* Amherst, NY: Prometheus Books, 2004.

Zipser, Andy. "A Hard Look at the Mysterious Red Mercury." *Barron's,* February 15, 1993, p. 15.

INDEX